THE DIVINE PROGRAMMER II

How Humans Create Reality

Aly McDonald
Ed Rychkun

www.edrychkun.com

ISBN: 978-1-927066-11-9

There is no copyright to this book. If it helps you to understand life and choose the better one by allowing you to create miracles of health and wealth, go ahead and copy whatever you need. Please pass it on and credit the website below or credit the dedicated researchers mentioned in this book

www.edrychkun.com.

CONTENTS

		PAGE
	INTRODUCTION	6
	Who REALLY Has The Power?	7
	These Are Not Special Cases	10
1	**THE POWER OF CREATION**	14
	Let's Create A Mind Movie	14
	Now Let Us Play A Computer Game	20
	Is The Computer Game Like Your Game Of Life?	22
	Consciousness Belief Boxes	25
2	**THE ALTERED STATE**	27
	The Common Denominators Of Healing Miracles	27
	The Subconscious And The Altered State	29
	The Fly In The Ointment	30
	The Importance Of Brainwaves	31
	The Importance Of The Altered State	32
	The Hypnotic State	39
	The Biological Process Of Belief	41
	Why A State Of Well-Being?	43
3	**THE ROLE OF THE BRAIN**	48
	Recap About The Brain	48
	Mind And Matter Are Not Separate	49
	The Brain Process Of Programming	50
	The Science Of Neuroplasticity And The Frontal Lobe	52
	Implicit And Explicit Memory	54
	The Power Of Meditation	55
4	**THE ROLE OF THE HEART**	57
	The Heart Energetic System	57
	The Double Torus And Energy Vortexes	58
	The Heart Brain And Emotions	62
	Heart Rate Variability And Coherence	65

	Get Into Alpha Permanently!	68
	Being In The Heart Brain	69
	The Love Center	70

5	**THE HYPNOSIS PORTAL TO SUBCONSCIOUS**	**76**
	Hypnosis As The Subconscious Mind Doorway	76
	Does Hypnosis Work? How?	79
	Process Of Self-hypnosis	81
	How To Set Your Self-hypnosis Goals	83
	Hypnotic Suggestions And Their Rules	84
	Imagery In Hypnosis	85
	A Self-hypnosis Script	86
	Post-Hypnotic Suggestions	87
	Recording The Script	88

6	**THE NEAR DEATH EXPERIENCE**	**90**
	Consciousness Is A Separate Intelligent Energy	92
	The Stages Of Dying - Nearly	93
	What Are We Being Told Here?	95
	NDE's And Miracles	100

7	**THE IMMERSION MOVIE OF LIFE**	**102**
	Did We Really Create A Movie?	102
	Under Free Will We Created Our Plan	104
	The Life Review Process	105
	Your Soul Contract And Life Plan	107
	Creating The Life Plan Movie	110
	Memories Of Afterlife	114

8	**ASTRAL PROJECTION**	**118**
	The Energy Bodies	119
	Astral Projection And Psychic Empowerment	123
	Opening Your Optimum Potential	124
	Crucial Discoveries Of Astral Travel	127
	Astral Projection Processes	129
	The Altered State Hierarchy	132

9	**PAST LIFE REGRESSION**	**136**
	Past Life Regression Therapy	137

     How Regression Healing Works   **139**

10 FUTURE LIFE PROGRESSION   **146**
     What Is Future Life Progression?   **146**
     The Self Hypnotic Trance   **149**
     The Future Is Yours To Review   **150**
     Future Life Progression Processes   **155**
     Your Soul Purpose Review   **156**

11 THE PLACEBO MIND OVER MATTER   **158**
     You Are The Placebo Or Nocebo: You Choose   **159**
     The Process Of Thinking And Feeling   **161**
     The Placebo And Brain In Action   **163**
     The Role Of DNA Or Deoxyribonucleic Acid   **165**
     Changing The Way Of Being   **166**
     Reasons Why The Placebo Works   **168**
     Life Transformation Process   **168**
     The Relation To Quantum   **173**

12 THE QUANTUM REALITY   **176**
     Is Reality Really Real?   **176**
     Our Holographic Universe   **181**
     What Are Quantum Physicists Saying?   **184**
     Nonlocality Of The Human Brain   **189**
     The Human Energy Bodies   **190**
     The Brain Is A Holographic Processor   **192**
     The World And The Universe Are Flat!   **194**
     Is The Universe A Hologram?   **195**
     In Summary Of Science   **200**

13 FREE WILL... REALLY?   **204**
     The Brain Is Not Really In Charge Of Free Will   **204**
     We Are Part Of An Immersion Movie Of Life   **207**
     The Movie You Collapsed Into Reality   **210**
     Control Over Destiny?   **210**

14 WILL THE REAL DIVINE PROGRAMMER STAND UP   **215**
     Ask And It Shall Be Given; Really?   **215**
     Karma, Cause & Effect And The Law Of Attraction   **218**

	And So What Is Reality?	221
	The Second Life Virtual Game	225
	The Real Divine Programmer Is The Real You	228
15	**UNLOCKING SUPER CONSCIOSNESS**	**230**
	Unlocking DNA	231
	Unlocking Superconsciousness	238
	DNA And Superconsciousness	246
16	**THE MYSTERY OF THE MIDBRAIN**	**247**
	The Science Behind Miracles	248
	Sounds Control Consciousness And Matter	252
	The Dr. Pillai Miracle Method	254
	The Dr. Pillai Money Mantra	257
	The Issue Of Karma	259
	The Functions Of The Midbrain	261
	Dr. And Master Sha Miracles	264
	Sha Healing Miracle Process	266
	The Importance Of Sound Waves	269
	In The Beginning Was The Word	271
	The God Code	272
	The Bible Code	274
	The Word And Reality	277
17	**HOW DOES IT ALL WORK?**	**279**
	The Stages Of Human Evolution For The Soul	280
	How Does It All Work?	284
	Creating Miracles Recap	292
	Recap Of Above To Below Process	294
	The Keys: Belief, Acceptance And Surrender	296
	The Key Findings	297
	The New Process of Changing Reality	302
	Testing Your Mind Power	311
18	**SO WHAT IS GOD, REALLY**	**317**

INTRODUCTION

"Is it the pill that makes the brain create the chemical and physiological changes to heal the body or is it the mind? We believe it is the mind outside the belief box that does."

Aly McDonald   Ed Rychkun

> **Is it so that the power of my will
> Can heal my body without a pill?**

Our thesis in this book is simple.

We are all creators and can create our own physical reality.

You have heard that before, but it really never worked, right?

Fact is you already do it. You just haven't figured out exactly how you do it. That's why you have to work for a living and listen to what Doctors tell you about your health. That is the norm you accept to be true. Of course it is true - it is what the group or global consciousness says is true. It is that which the majority believes and that forms the box of rules that create your beliefs. The majority believes these, accepts them and surrenders to them because they are put in place by some higher authority. And you don't mess with a higher authority. So anything that falls outside of this belief box like a healing miracle simply is not true. It does not get registered in the group subconsciousness.

In our previous book we looked at how many are stepping outside of the norm of the group belief boxes to truly be creators of reality, namely health and wealth miracles. Of course we noted that even though some try to step out of the box it does not always work. So the quest in our book **The Divine Programmer Creating Miracles** became one of determining why and how many cases did work. Then we determined the best possible way to make it work.

In this quest, we now continue the story of creating outside the belief box of the group consciousness. We present what we have found so as to freely share without copyright our research and findings so that you and others may bring the new possibility of being proactive creators into your awareness and assist in determining how it can best work for all.

Who REALLY Has The Power?

You go to visit the Doc because you accept the idea you have some medical issue. He checks you out and because he is the authority you believe him when he writes the prescription. As you pick up the pills from the pharmacy, you surrender to the fate that he has prescribed. When you take the pills without question or analysis, dah, dah, magically the body chemicals and physiology suddenly make it better. In every walk of life, this process of believing, accepting and surrendering to someone who is believed to have more knowledge or power over you is common.

Of course we never question it because the Doc is the expert; the higher authority. But in the end, was it the Doc, the Pills, the Body or the Mind that actually made the body better – or worse? Is it possible that the mind actually made the body better? By the time you get through this book, you will understand how the mind can overpower matter and that it may be the mind alone that really can do it. It was only your faith and trust in the Doc and his credibility that convinced your subconscious, your brain, and your cells to do it. On the other hand, if he told you that there was no cure for your ailments, then guess what your mind does? Will it then believe, accept and surrender to that fate?

The belief boxes dictate much of these fates and behaviors. Here is a strange example. You take a shovel and start digging a hole because you're just a silly dude who wants to get to the other side to Australia. After months of digging, you emerge on the other side. Do you come to Australia feet first or head first? What does your most sophisticated scientist say about that? It's not possible so it's a stupid question. By the time you get through this book you will understand that the answer to this has not yet become an actual possibility in our reality awareness and perhaps the world is actually a flat holographic plate, not round at all. The belief box sets the limits to what is possible and what is not.

You have an issue that bugs you and you need some answers. So you start thinking about it constantly. Suddenly, from nowhere comes something that answers the question. Where did it come from? By the time you get through this book, you will understand that you attracted it from your own mind in a world of infinite possibilities.

In our first book, **The Divine Programmer: Creating Miracles** we brought forward the well documented story of a fellow named Wright who had been hospitalized with advanced lymph node cancer. This case, like thousands of others, does not fit within the belief boxes of the group consciousness; so it has no credibility. Yet is exists so we want to bring it forward into your consciousness again. Wright was bedridden needing an oxygen mask to survive. Diagnosed with a few days left to live, this man was filled with tumors of the lymph nodes the size of oranges. All hope of *any* recovery was exhausted. But Wright did not want to die. He heard about Krebiozen, a new drug that was available for trial. Of course this was a waste of time to the doctor but with Wright's persistence, he finally gave in and the drug was administered to Wright on a Friday.

On Monday, when the Doc came in, he found Wright out of bed walking around. Inspections indicated his tumors had melted like snowballs on a hot stove. Ten days later, Wright left the hospital cancer free.

Wright was active for about two months until he read some articles stating that Krebiozen actually had no affect on cancer of the lymph nodes. Being very logical and scientific, Wright suffered a relapse and was readmitted to the hospital. The tumors were back, as were lung issues that required oxygen; it was all the same again.

Quite perplexed about this strange and dramatic shifting, the Doc decided to try something like a placebo. In this experiment he told Wright Krebiozen was actually effective and that the problem was some of the initial supplies had deteriorated during shipping. He said he had a new concentrated version and did Wright want to try it. The Doc had a plan to inject Wright with a plain water placebo with the usual ceremony.

Again within days, the tumors melted, the chest fluid vanished and Wright was back on his feet feeling great. This went on for two months. Then Wright found out the American Medical Association announced that the nationwide study of Krebiozen had found the drug useless in treating cancer. Wright's cancer instantly blossomed and he died two days later.

On one hand, Wright refused to accept a fate which doomed him. He accepted, believed and surrendered to a different outcome and got super excited about it. So his mind and body got their shit together and got rid of the tumors. On the other hand, Wright suddenly accepted a new fate and believed that fate, then surrendered to a different fate. His body and mind lost their power and succumbed to the old reality to bring it all back.

What's happening here? Just consider the number of chemicals and physiological processes of healing and non-healing that are going on here with no "real" cure. What was it that instigated the cure and return of the disease? Who and what instigated these dramatic changes in physical reality?

Makes you think doesn't it? First, what does any pill really do? This is called the Placebo Effect. It is not isolated as it is reported that 30% of medical treatments are due to placebo. And then there is the Placebo's evil brother called the Nocebo created in the mind by the power (or unfettered authority) of your doctor's statements that tell you negative news. What power does your mind actually have that you are not aware of? Is there any reason why anybody can't create an endless supply of placebo pills?

A Baylor school of medicine published in 2002, in the **New England Journal of Medicine** an article which evaluated surgery for a patient with severe deliberating knee pain. Dr. Bruce Moseley knew that knee surgery helped his patients as he stated "*good surgeons know there is no placebo effect in surgery*". To figure out what part of the surgery was responsible for most of the pain, he set up three groups.

He shaved the damaged cartilage in one group. He flushed out the knee joint removing inflammatory material in the second group and the third group got fake surgery. With the fake group the patient was sedated, got 3 incisions and he talked and acted like in a real surgery. He even splashed salt water to simulate the sound of knee washing. After 40 minutes he sewed up the incisions as if it was real surgery. All three groups got the same postoperative care.

The surprise came when the groups who received surgery improved but the placebo group improved equally. A TV provided for viewing graphically illustrated the results. They all got better functionality even though the placebo group did not find out for two years.

Scientific evidence on the placebo effect shows that people are healed through thought alone. The belief that they were taking real medication when actually taking a placebo caused changes in their brain to the degree that it looked like they were taking the real drug.

A 2001 study showed the powerful effects of placebo medication in treating Parkinson's disease. The placebo was induced into the brain to produce more dopamine, a known treatment for Parkinson's. The effect was similar to that of real medication.

Consider a randomized trial of women with **polycystic ovarian syndrome;** a condition that upsets the reproductive system and makes it more difficult to become pregnant. They found that 15% got pregnant while taking a placebo compared to 22% who actually received the drug.

A woman suffering severe nausea was offered a potent new drug and promised it would cure her nausea. Within a few minutes her nausea vanished and stomach contractions settled back to normal. Only what the doctors gave her was a strong substance known to induce vomiting.

In another study, nearly half of asthmatic patients received symptom relief from a fake inhaler or sham acupuncture.

Almost 40% of people with headaches and more than half of patients with ulcer pain received relief with placebo treatment.

When compared to morphine, placebos given to patients in place of morphine were almost equally effective at treating pain.

The Institute of Noetic Sciences (IONS) compiled a database from the Spontaneous Remissions project, with **3500 case studies** of miraculous healings with the placebo effect, showing *seemingly incurable conditions, being cured*. Diseases ranging from patients with stage 4 cancer who were cured spontaneously, HIV positive patient that became HIV negative, thyroid disease that healed without treatment, aneurysms, cardiovascular disease, autoimmune conditions and many more starkly illustrate the power of the mind alone.

In a fascinating study performed by Harvard professor of Medicine, Ted Kaptchuk, he conducted a placebo study whereby the patients were actually told they were receiving an inert substance, a placebo. **They still got better!** He concluded that the nurturing care and support of the healthcare practitioner was actually facilitating the self-healing process in placebo studies, not just the ritual of taking medication.

In the USA, 50% of doctors admit to using placebo in clinical practice, and 97% of doctors in the UK have also prescribed placebo medication.

These Are Not Special Cases

Why do we present these cases? There are actually millions of these unexplained cases, some even more dramatic. We bring these forward into your awareness because sometimes it is the trigger that shifts belief out of the belief box. Why is this important? Well it is the belief box that dictates the type of neurological conditioning and programming in your subconscious and as you will find out in this book, it has the power of placebo and nocebo. Did you believe any of it, or did you look immediately for reasons that it could be a fake? If you look for fakes, it is because you are stuck in the consciousness belief box. Most likely your conscious mind woke up to believe it temporarily, but your subconscious programming from the years of box programming niggled you to look for reasons why it was a fake. And sometimes this subconscious training can be so well in place that you simply said: *"what crap"* and walked away. Well, dear Reader that is how the subconscious mind can sabotage what you *"think"* you believe.

These dramatic cases are documented, observed facts that give you a glimpse into what could manifest as a possibility that you may have never even considered. If you start looking and opening your awareness, the staggering truth of it is that these many cases are not isolated; there are thousands more. No one can be explained but they nevertheless exist. You have simply been conditioned to believe they are some sort of anomaly that is interesting and perhaps entertaining but of no relevance in your life. And your body and mind respond to what you have allowed to be programmed into you. It was probably your Doctor that told you these were crap. Right? Did you believe him? Of course, you accept, believe and surrender to his greater expertise on the matter. It's what everybody does. And that is precisely why it **won't work** for you if you hold that belief in your subconscious. The programs in your consciousness belief box may be so strong you wouldn't even dare ask your doctor!

The first very important thing to understand here is that these physical anomalies like miracles and materialization of reality do exist. Simply because they cannot be explained does not discredit them from existence. It is the limits of the belief box that do. Secondly, how can you ever assume that you yourself cannot benefit from such an experience, or even do it yourself? Moreover, what makes you think that it can't happen again, and again, and to you? Yes, to you? Yes, let go of the beliefs that create the limits. After all, when you purchase a lotto ticket with incredible odds against you, it is your mind that suggests you could be the one... bugger the odds!

In a publication called **New Insights From Clinical and Neuroimaging Studies,** authors and researchers **Nico J. Diederich, MD** and **Christopher G. Goetz, MD, FAAN** published the following:

Placebo (PL) treatment is a method utilized as a control condition in clinical trials. A positive placebo response is seen in up to 50% of patients with Parkinson disease (PD), pain syndromes, and depression. The response is more pronounced with invasive procedures or advanced disease. Physiologic and biochemical changes have been studied in an effort to understand the mechanisms underlying placebo-related clinical improvement."

We detailed many healers and changers of reality in our first book in an attempt to come up with clarity on why these things do happen. But we left with some outstanding questions because this thing called a placebo appears to heal by mind alone without a Facilitator or Divine Intervention. The mind instigates control over matter and makes in many cases a radical change chemically, physically and physiologically.

In this book, we are going to take you on a continued journey into the fringe world of non-science outside the box. Can we make sense out of this placebo "nonsense"? It is our intention to look at this in a different simple way by simply providing a lot of evidence created by cases and out of the box people that are researchers and facilitators actually doing miraculous things. Let's face it, quantum physics, morphic fields, energy bodies, chakras, heart fields, torroids, trinary computers, cell biology and all those topics we introduced in **The Divine Programmer: Creating Miracles** are not so simple to understand. Additionally, they are not really "established" as any proof regarding how controlling reality can be done. So we are going to back up a bit and delve into these main topics.

- **The way the quantum mind works**
- **In-between Life Regression: Your Life Plan movie**
- **The Altered State of consciousness**
- **Near Death and Out Of Body Experiences**
- **Past Life Regression and Future Life Progression**
- **Astral Projection**
- **Head and Heart Brain science**
- **Placebos and the Mind**
- **The way quantum reality works**
- **Who is the real Divine Programmer**

In this process of awareness, we are going to relate the reality of what we live in as our physical reality to the working of the mind – consciousness – that thing of energy that no science can explain. In our first book **The Divine Programmer: Creating Miracles**, we clearly saw that the wave of quantum physics as related to consciousness is evolving exponentially as a "scientific" explanation on how things that have not been explained by traditional Newtonian science can be explained. This includes all so called "esoteric" fringe areas of psychic phenomenon (PSI). In this book, we saw how the energetic, subtle fields of our being behaved in a quantum manner.

We will begin by looking at our minds at what we call imagination, namely thoughts and images, words and feelings that we can construct in our imagination to create an imaginary movie. We are all familiar with this ability to use imagination. To the mind, or conscious awareness, this movie will be likened to an imaginary reality created with eyes closed; as opposed to a physical reality we see with eyes open. As we proceed through this, we are going to attempt to give you simple insight into how this creative process can be used to explain quantum physics.

Then let us have a look at the "mind" workers and what they have found in all of their studies. We will look more closely at this altered state that has been a vital component of creating health and wealth miracles. Then we will look at how many people have learned about a different movie we engage in – our lives on this planet. It is called a Life Plan that you allegedly as a Soul contracted to play a role in.

Because this will open to some very perplexing notions of how this can be, we will look more deeply into the world of Near Death Experiences where so many have had an instant panoramic holographic review of this movie. We will study the phenomenon of Out of Body experiences or Astral Projection where one has more control on these travels to the "other side". Then we will study the arts of PLR (Past Life Regression) that so many have used to change the movies of the past. This will lead to a study of FLP (Future Life Progression) where it becomes possible to see what that Life Plan movie is in the future.

A bit far out? Well perhaps if you are a non believer and have a closed mind about it, it is so. But for those millions who have engaged, studied, or been recipients of these new evolving disciplines, it is far from fantasy. We will also look at the big scientific news these days and see what science is saying about all this.

Finally, we will relook our conclusions of Divine Programmer and attempt to uncover who really is the Divine Programmer.

1

THE POWER OF CREATION

"The power of creation resides in the mind. Our brains do not know the difference between emotion created by fantasy and reality. It follows that the brain does not know the difference between what is created in the mind as fantasy and what it creates as our holographic reality."

    Aly McDonald   **Ed Rychkun**

> **Mirror, mirror on the wall**
> **Who is the creator of it all?**

Let's Create A Mind Movie

You are sitting in a nice quiet environment looking around and you place your attention and view on a nice comfortable chair in the room. Then you close your eyes and still visualize an image of the chair in your mind. On one hand the chair was "real". On the other hand the chair was in your imagination. In one real world that chair was solid made up of particles because that's the way you have been taught to understand the science of the material world. It is typically referred to as 3D. Of course it is solid because you can sit on it. Your brain knows this because it was taught the chair is actually made up of electrons and atoms; and even though 99% of it is empty space, simply energy, that doesn't matter because it is still a solid chair. You see it, feel it, sit on it and that's what you believe – that's what *everybody* believes! That's ok because that's the way your brain sees it and that's what your consciousness observes to be true.

But then close your eyes. It becomes a different form of energy. It isn't there anymore. You brought a thought of a chair forward into your mind, and then you formed an image of the chair. It is a chair made of nothing but conscious energy in the form of waves. You could also form an image of you sitting in the chair - all just waves of energy. You were bringing the chair into your view screen of conscious awareness and could see this chair in two ways – namely material 3D matter (atoms) – if you chose to open your eyes or you could see it as immaterial 4D (waves). By way of opening your eyes you brought it into your reality. But you could not see both at the same time. It was one or the other.

What you are doing is observing two different "realities" available to you at will; imaginary (waves) and material (particles). Well, you have just understood an important principle of Quantum Physics which states that everything in our reality exists in two states of particles and waves, but not both at the same time. You just engaged in the **Observer Effect**. What was the difference? Well to see the particles you used a physical eyeball to observe a chair, bringing it into your view screen which you call reality. In the other case, you used your imaginary eyeball to bring it into a different view screen. The two states are imaginary reality and physical reality, but not both together. Either way, you created this by a conscious choice to see it even though they are two different realities. The thought you acted on was to look at the chair which resulted in your eyeballs seeing the chair. In the other case the thought with eyeballs closed resulted in an image of the chair.

Now consider this. Let us forget the imagination for a moment. You as an Observer in your physical reality open your eyes and see the real chair. Now turn away, close your eyes or whatever and there is no chair. At the moment you brought that chair into your awareness, your consciousness (mind) using the brain as its processor, changed it from a possibility of waves to a reality of particles. When you looked away, it was not really there to your brain, it was in its normal state of waves, awaiting you as the Observer to bring it into your reality. The quantum physicists say that is exactly what you do in your physical reality. Your observation of choosing to bring it into your awareness **collapses** the waves into a chair appearing as particles (atoms).

Far out?

Now let us say that you pretend by visualization that you are sitting in this chair and it is very pleasant, peaceful and comfortable; you are listening to some really nice soft music. It is just imagination. Well, not really because guess what? That brain of yours is going to relax into a different state of brainwaves and it may even begin to react by instructing a cascade of physiological and chemical changes to occur because of the peace and comfort detected in your brain that slows up its activity. The imaginary reality had an effect on the material reality.

And if you stopped this imaginary thing, went over and sat in the chair and did the same thing of feeling the peace and comfort, guess what? That brain of yours would do exactly the same thing. In fact, as we will come to see later on, that brain that orchestrates things in your body does not have a clue as to the difference between the two realities. The common link between the two realities was a feeling of comfort and peace. In both cases it was the great feelings that caused the physical cascades of chemicals in the body.

Let us extend this ability to creating a whole sequence of these thoughts and images by the quantum physics process of collapsing waves by consciously changing the form so you can observe something. The mind, bringing forward a thought of a chair from wherever it was in energy form (waves), converted (collapsed) the waves into an image (particles) of the chair. The only difference here is that the image was not "physically real".

The suggestion here is that we are "observing" and collapsing waves of our lives as our actual reality. Yes, it's a hard concept to take so let us take a slight diversion here. Consider that when a Movie Director creates a movie he directs the scenes, characters and dialogue originating from a whole bunch of thoughts (scripts) into a reality which is filmed as moment to moment (frames) onto a medium of storage (DVD, computer file, etc.) so it can be viewed later. Your home has many of these DVD movies that are like parallel realities, each one having no time, space or material reality until they are played (observed) by you through a medium (brain computer, DVD player) that interprets and presents it in a form understandable to you and your sensory system. Just to throw you off for a bit, what if these DVD's are like a set of lives being filmed and stored simultaneously on some storage medium? You created the movie script, you are the main actor and your brain/mind is the filming, storing device?

So let us play another game; you are still sitting there and now as a Creator and Director and Writer, you decide to create a scene in your mind where you can enjoy the warm sun, tropical waters, sandy beach and bathe in the freshness of it. And so there before you is the scene. And you decide to bring others into it; these are your chosen actors, so you all go snorkeling and see beautiful fish and coral. The situation is very nice and you even feel your senses responding to the scene. You have once again linked the two realities because the emotions, feeling and senses are reacting from the imaginary movie.

Suddenly someone calls you in this physical reality so you think let's leave this alone for now and come back later to create a little private imaginary world where you build a grass hut and bring friends. And so this vision remains until you return again and again by recall. The waves are still rolling onto the beach, the wind is rustling through the trees and your snorkel is where you left it. Now you begin creating a magnificent grass hut with a nice garden, a deck where you can sip a cool drink with your best friends.

And so in your mind you create an imaginary world collapsing it into a sequence of images. It is a virtual movie. You want someone there; just imagine it and they are. You want to be somewhere else. You imagine it so and it is so. Time and distance have no relevance here. All you have to do is bring it into conscious awareness. When you come back these are still here. Maybe you haven't been here for a while and you had planted a tree. Now it is huge. How did that happen? Do you care? Not really, things just abide by some sort of order and process, the same way that your mind knew exactly what a chair was and what it looked like.

Your mind is creating thoughts which you are collapsing (manifesting) in a subtle imaginary realm called your personal imagination virtual movie. But there is another interesting thing happening here. You created the frames or moments in your movie and they are stored for retrieval. Where are these things stored? We have learned that the brain seems to have a copy but even when you cut out a portion of it or go through a Near Death Experience as we have seen; it is still all available from somewhere else. Then, while you are doing something else and came back later, certain things that you gave life to in your movie had changed by themselves. How do these things continue to grow like the tree and the environment behaving according to the other physical reality?

It is like someone else was directing parts of the movie while you were absent. Someone else was taking care of how the environment changed after you decided to give it life in your mind. But when you came back, the flowers had blossomed. How? Was it because you expected them to blossom? How did the flowers know they were supposed to be purple hibiscus?

Now this becomes even more bizarre if you create the intent to see a couple of your dear friends in the move to be married with a kid the next time you return. There is nothing strange about this as in your physical reality, you may have lost contact with some dear friends, seen them later in a few years to find they have a kid. It simply wasn't in your awareness until you decided to observe them again and bring them into your reality two years later. But this is not the same. When you return in your virtual movie, even if it was the next day, the intention of thought has created the reality of the fake movie. How did that occur?

Now, there are some really interesting things about creating this movie. The first is that time and space are irrelevant. You can be anywhere instantly or you seem to be everywhere in all these places which only takes attention to see it. What is more relevant is that the mind:

1. Collapsed (brought and observed) the image from thought
2. Chose a result or an outcome from a place of infinite possibilities
3. Gave life to grow, behave according to some preset order, process, and purpose (like the tree)
4. Directed some continuation of evolving outside your movie guidelines
5. Stored the movie somewhere beyond the brain
6. Linked between realities to engage physical and mental processes

What about these thoughts and images that came to you? Some of these came from something that you may not have experienced in this lifetime. You created or retrieved these from somewhere. Where did they come from? You can't see them yet they are waves of energy that just simply pop into awareness. This mental and emotional indulgent was also having an effect on your physical reality; your body with feelings of joy and tingling of fun came through from this fake movie you were playing out into your reality.

And so your mind can create many movies this way drawing from a world of **infinite possibilities** that your consciousness picks to collapse into the movie reality. Sometimes your imagination can go wild and create a world that you have not apparently experienced or seen. Where does it get that?

The process you are engaging in takes thoughts of something and brings them into conscious awareness. It is a choice you make in creating your movies. This came from a place of infinite possibilities as you decided to create something in a scene. That thought of creating something in the scenes pops into your copiousness of your reality when you want it there.

If you look at this imaginary process, you are the sub director and the sub writer/Creator of the movie being formed in your imagination. Anybody and everybody can do this by using their imagination, drawing from a sea of infinite possibilities, popping these thoughts into an imaginary set of sequences of movie frames/images to be stored and retrieved when chosen so. This is the same way the electrons pop in and out between waves and particle representations.

So as you sat in your chair, you were creating your reality, your world, your players, your universe. You could come back to it as it was a movie stored somewhere. You could retrieve it, run it, edit it, delete it, and play with your emotions in it. You could create your characters, your story line, your events, situations, the settings and environments.

In a sense your were the Creator of your reality and you could express what you wished to express and experience through your created environment and your characters. You were engaging in a holographic type 3D movie that you created by imagination and you could see yourself in it as the main actor, feeling the emotional experience of it. If you wanted to create a chilling scene to launch the emotion of fear, you could do so. If you wanted to create the emotion of bliss, you could do so. Your mind when conscious of these scenes was being used – deployed – to express feelings.

And in many cases, the details of the scenes, the characters, and many of the environmental parts of the movie would be taken care of by some other director who would dovetail your movie into the larger scope of the whole movie. You never had to consider the preprocesses whereby the wind blew, the waves washed the beach, the trees grew or how people even behaved or looked. It was a natural process that was inherently part of the Other Director's job, not yours.

Now what if, you and your mind were part of a much greater mind that was responsible for all the order, processes and purpose of the things you created so as to experience and express within - like that other Director? What if this physical reality was also a holographic projection, which like the Star Trek holodeck, you engage in to experience and express different emotions?

But back to your imagination movie which you can pause anytime. These movie frames get recorded somewhere and every frame is recorded moment by moment in the movie so only the current moment is ready to continue from, like you put the movie on hold. Even though there are extra things like the marriage and kids that have occurred, when you came back to continue from the pause, what you had pulled out to happen was there to continue from. Was the hidden part there too?

The movie created things like trees, water, people, animals, environment that seemed to have a program to follow of their own.

And so you sit and really get weird by creating a new world you have never seen (or have you). Here you create a home and you decide you can be an energy body that lives forever, and you can take any form to experience it... even if you do not have a clue about it.

Now there are two questions about this process.

Is this the same process that creates our life movie reality?

Is the other director of the life movie reality the designer, or the greater mind of the Creator?

Now Let Us Play A Computer Game

Let us indulge in another familiar process of playing a game on a computer or a game machine. There are hundreds of these but the dominant ones are the PS series, Xbox, Atari, and Wii for example. Clearly, these games are so realistic, it is easy for a kid to be totally lost and absorbed in these constructed realities. Like movies these days that allow you to engage in the emotions in a way where you cannot tell the difference between what is animated and what is not. Virtual games have led the animation technology a step further and allow the interaction in a virtual sense. All with preprogrammed instruction sets, a game allows you to explore unlimited variations of fantasy worlds and interact with people, critters, events and situations that require decisions. What for? To indulge emotions and experience things you are not used to. Or it may be to get points and succeed in your mission, namely to stay alive and figure out the rewards along the way.

As you pass through the scenes, you see only what comes in your view screens of conscious awareness. Pass through and it is gone because you as the Observer are not viewing it. But you can look back and see it anytime. The scenes and events and people and situations are all preprogrammed to operate and display a specific way. So there is a greater process going on here. This is the pile of computer programs and subroutines that are "on call" and you decide when to experience or observe them. You can pick your body and character type, in many you can even pick your features from a defined set of examples. As you enter the game, you make choices from a set of options within set rules; each choice creates a cause that has a different effect or consequence. Some of these can result in death, success, conflict and you can store your progress to come back and try it again. You never know the consequence until you have experienced it. It is all very real as you can feel joy, terror, or anger because your brain and body do not see the difference between reality and non reality.

The designers of these as the other Directors of the games lay out the game rules and the scenes, events, choices and consequences in a set of programs that simulate this reality. That global reality becomes the scope of the game, each programmed to become virtual through your interaction. The game is like a consciousness that has its own limits and rules of engagement. You cannot use rules outside the box unless you talk to the programmer. The game you engage in is your own experience subset stored in the games database for future review and learning. What is not stored however, is your personal emotional and mental experience. If you get killed, you can always come back and try again. If you make a mistake, you can retract your steps and try another choice. You can even store several versions being different characters and they are instantly reloadable into your conscious awareness by your choice. You are the key player and observer that orchestrate your progress on the game board. All these different scenes, players, events, situations were all programs written to simulate the real thinking, visual, communication and feeling situation so as to appear real. And if you have ever watched the kids playing these games it looks pretty real from the engagement.

When you decide to use the Internet or wireless network to share the game board with others, they can be located anywhere in the world and play with you. Unlike the characters in the game that are programmed to act and react a certain way, these are your buddies or enemies that act and react according to their own emotion and mental judgments. And you can work together or challenge each other in order to accomplish some task – like find the treasure, stay alive, find joy in accomplishment that the game offers as its purpose. Where is this data stored? Somewhere in the Internet, iCloud or Onedrive. Who cares? It doesn't matter as long as you are having fun and sharing with others. But what it does illustrate is the quantum process of **nonlocality.** The internet or WIFI connects all as one so anybody in the group consciousness is aware of the others status by simply bringing it into awareness.

Not only this, but if you are playing these games in the windows computer environment, you can open several windows and enter or continue the game with a mouse click which suddenly – like your conscious awareness as the Observer – comes alive. And magically, you have multiple parallel lives to engage in the game reality with. Are they happening in a time sequence? No not at all, only when you click the mouse to activate it by conscious intent does it enter your reality. These are like parallel realities or... parallel lives?

All of this magical technology is around us and we accept it without the slightest consideration that it may be a close simulation to another game we play as the Game of Life.

Is The Computer Game Like Your Game Of Life?

So what is the point of this discussion?

These virtual games and the way the mind works from a quantum point of view offer some very interesting parallels. What if your physical reality is a **virtual immersion movie much like the game** presented as a **Hologram** game instead of a TV or computer screen? You may say the big difference is that the computer game was already written. The rules, and the way the reality (world) is presented, the options available are not your creation. But suppose in a **Game of Life** you as a **Soul** are sub-director and creator of your life movie that was put together with the aid of some assistance and that assistance has their own set of subroutines for the way reality of the world is presented, called group consciousness and consensus.

Within this scope, you set out the story line and want to show the story. Then you also choose your characteristics and engage in a particular **Life Plan** and **Soul Contract** like when a movie star signs a contract. What if you created or chose the major characters, scenes, events, people and key situations within which you are the key movies star; but without a script and free choice to act and speak within the sets and scenes already predetermined? To do this you will not need a costume, you will choose a vessel; body type, and a personality in the form of a humanoid that suits you and your purpose.

And within this Game of Life, you will choose a purpose of expression, things to learn and specific character to act with. As to many details of the movie, like the guy that handles the scenes, you will leave the **Director of Divine Order** to set the overall environments of growth process; perhaps as set in the program code in DNA of **morphogenic processes** and purpose whenever it is required. Of course it depends on His rules of engagement within that greater consciousness. The rest of the game behaves according to specific living, growth, evolution, and behavior accorded to a natural law once the game is turned on – exactly the same way that the computer game is programmed to simulate some natural process. Once the game begins, you will be presented with these scenes, characters and events to interact with, to be reactive or proactive mentally and emotionally between set scenes and situations, yourself choosing how to perceive, react and act.

As it proceeds, each moment will be stored in a new movie which becomes your **Life**. Just like a Hollywood movie, your movie will contain many other characters which will have their own movies, dovetailing into yours, but all movies will dovetail into the **Greater Director's** movie. Some are random, some are partners, some are there to test you and confront your issues. Many potential sets and scenes will be planned depending upon how and what you decide at each moment. So just like you can decide to plan a virtual game to enjoy what you could not otherwise enjoy, you as a Soul decided to create an outline of a Life Plan so you could experience a **Game of Life**. Now, because you as Soul are just energy, you need some way of engagement; you need a way to interface with your vessel as a physical body that can play the main actor in the movie. Then you will need a means of having that movie play out and be presented so you can record the fun part of feelings and emotions as it is being recorded. But it has to be like a virtual immersion computer game so it allows interaction of the mind and feelings. Well, you figure the best is to make a copy of you in a lower vibrational form that has the ability to do all this yet not know it is just a game.

So you set up a bunch of rules of playing the game that become the rules of engagement just like the example of playing games. The human Game of Life has a purpose of thinking and emotional expression; to experience feelings from engaging in it. The Life Plan would be like a Human Game of Life with rules that would apply to you in the engagement of it. Let us suppose that you as some form of being of pure energy agreed to abide by the rules of the Game of Life:

1. You must forget who you are as a Being of Light
2. You must believe you are a physical body
3. You must believe the Life Movie hologram is real
4. You must believe that what is out there can affect you
5. You must believe in judgment of polarity (right and wrong)
6. You must believe that wrong needs to be fixed
7. You must believe you have the power to think your way out
8. You must believe that you must live, grow old and die
9. You must believe you are here to propagate, prosper, protect
10. You must believe lessons are to be learned
11. You must believe you can meet your own needs
12. You must believe fear is a key to the game to provide results
13. You must believe there is a possibility of another higher level

Does this sound absurd? To believe you have little control on this life game is certainly a bit of a shocker and the first reaction is to say "crap". But if it were true, how would you live this life?

Before we continue, there is another example of our reality "realness" found at www.youtube.com/watch?v=jAIDXzv_fKA. We are not endorsing a commercial here but it is worth 5 minutes of viewing to take a look at some relevant technology on what can "appear" real. It also shows you how you as a "real physical" being can stick your hand through what appears to be a real physical being – like you do in an Out Of Body Experience. This will help you open your mind to the world of new possibilities simply because you may realize that things are not as they seem and that maybe the power of creation is closer than you "think".

Microsoft has just revealed its next great innovation: **Windows Holographic**. It's an augmented reality experience that employs a headset, much like all the Virtual Reality goggles that are currently rising in popularity, but Microsoft's solution adds holograms to the world around you. The HoloLens headset is described as *"the most advanced holographic computer the world has ever seen."* It's a self-contained computer, including a CPU, a GPU, and a dedicated holographic processor. The dark visor up front contains a see-through display, there's spatial sound so you can "hear" holograms behind you, and HoloLens also integrates a set of motion and environmental sensors.

No wires or PC required, it's a self-contained hologram generator. Though still early in its development, HoloLens will be made available *"in the Windows 10 timeframe"* and, according to Microsoft CEO Satya Nadella, it will be priced *"for both enterprise and consumers to use it."* Microsoft has already shown HoloLens to at least one games publisher, with Take-Two Interactive CEO Strauss Zelnick describing the experience as "extraordinary."

The demonstration of HoloLens presents a highly ambitious vision of future computing and entertainment. Playing *Minecraft* atop the landscape of your living room, taking a tour of the Martian surface, or walking clients through your latest architectural masterpiece — it's all made possible with the HoloLens. Alex Kipman, the man responsible for this project at Microsoft, says Windows Holographic is not so much about "putting you into virtual worlds," which may not be for everyone, but to move beyond them, offering deeper experiences and, well, *holograms!*

The following videos will give you an idea on how what we see as reality can be controlled and contrived by mortal programmers. The convergence what we see as reality and non reality is quickly dissolving any separations between them. Check out the convergence of Games and the Hololens in these short videos.

https://www.youtube.com/watch?v=3AADEqLIALk
https://www.youtube.com/watch?v=xgakdcEzVwg

The lesson in this chapter is that it is pretty easy to change what is perceived and interpreted as reality.

Ok, let us get back to the "reality" that everyone accepts as the real one and look into that bigger Game of Life and the Divine Programmers who can mess with the bigger program. To us, the convergence noted above is the convergence to a whole different reality of what and who we are.

Consciousness Belief Boxes

What is particularly perplexing about this is that we are engaged in this process of creating reality all the time. But in the vast majority of cases it is within the rules and limits of the box that we call consciousness. We all have control over our imaginations. We have seen that we create programs of habits, new beliefs, and behaviors all through life on a reactive and proactive basis. We are already engaged in this programming hierarchy in some way. We have also seen that <u>sometimes</u> we can, through these miracles, create more dramatic proactive changes that are outside the norm of our belief system. We can indeed get outside the boxed limits of our beliefs.

There is an important variable in this process; being outside the norm. Without exception, the healing miracles were outside of the norm in that the consciousness of the individuals engaging had to believe that what they were doing, what they believed in, was outside of the limits of the medical system, science, and whatever said that it would not work. This belief placed no credibility on the limits as defined by the "norm" of consciousness. And whether this was a norm of limits created by global consensus, cultural consensus, family or science was not relevant. The belief and the process went outside of it as did the engagement of a Divine Force. Where the process did not work, the limits of the belief box remained in the norm and all those old norm programs that were placed there reflecting the norm took priority. When people went outside the norm of consciousness, the old programs were replaced or ignored. So one has to be mindful of what has been programmed through the norm and how difficult it may be to ignore them. But this brings another question into the process. How do we get out of the norm?

Consciousness can be a collective of like minds and can reflect anything. It can be yours, your family, your culture, your government, your race, your global consciousness, and so on. Each one is unique and like a game, has rules of engagement that the collective consciousness creates. The consciousness is always evolving and can be changed but it is by the collective that allows it to be changed. This forms the rules of behavior, beliefs and perception and to attempt to step outside of this box is not without consequences. What you will understand later is that these limiting boxes have their more subtle controls on mind over matter.

What we want to convey is that the mind can and does affect matter. This is because the mind can and does affect physical reality to certain degrees. But as we are about to investigate, just like there are different levels of consciousness that each has their limiting boxes, there are also different levels of mind that conform to those limiting rules – and the different degrees too which mind can affect the physical. At the lowest level, our physical reality based minds conform to a consciousness mindset that believes matter rules mind. In order to approach the state where the mind rules matter, it is necessary to be in a higher state of mind outside of the box. What we have seen is that in order to move into a mind (or consciousness) outside the norm, one starts with engaging in an altered state.

2

THE ALTERED STATE

"Fundamental to the manifestation of all miracles is the self induced or the assisted state of consciousness outside of the conscious mind which we call altered. This state is where your Soul lives, listens, and communicates the instructions pertaining to what you believe is your reality."

Aly McDonald   Ed Rychkun

> **Miracle, miracle, I wish to find**
> **Where you hide within my mind**

The Common Denominators Of Healing Miracles

In out last book **"The Divine Programmer: Creating Miracles"** we detected a common pattern in the processes that resulted in miracles. We saw that there are many different ways that these miracles can occur depending on the belief system. From these we could derive a set of common fundamentals and steps that are part of each procedure. Let us review what we found out.

A **belief** that one is worthy, that they can be healed, is important to all these cases. It is a **belief** that is created by way of inner convictions, experience, enforced by an authoritative expert such as a doctor, a healer who has a reputation or some authority on the topic that knows what they are doing. This belief incorporated an **acceptance**, trust and faith that the process to be engaged in would work. The result is that the patient **surrendered** mind control to an authority who they believed could heal the issue.

An altered state was required to open into subconscious. It is through hypnosis, ritual, regression, becoming present, meditation, or a situation where the higher brain waves of the conscious mind are out of the way so as to not interfere with the subconscious. We found it is a strong morphic field that is needed to gain access to the subconscious where program changes are made. This was through a ritual, a group, a facilitator, praying, or some means of creating a strong similar emotional energy.

A state of well being was required as so reflected in a morphic field of love and peace as it opens to the gateways for a change to occur. This was induced by creating a setting of higher vibration by creating a space without conflict or anger, or fear, only of positive energies.

An identification of the issue was required so as to be clear on what it is that needs to be corrected. It was done by visualization, by hands on, by focus of thought and intention, by hypnosis or regression.

A Higher Power was engaged so as to make the change and correction. It was a surrendering process where God, Spirit, Divine Self, Source, or some Guides, Higher Self, or some Higher Power is called upon to assist in the healing as in a Divine Intervention or the "Universe".

A removal of the issue was simulated through various ways such as erasing memories, using intent, visualization, imagination or some induced process like simulation that removes it. Visualization of the desired result, enfolded with the emotion of completion added to the power of its removal.

An emotion of gratitude for being done was brought in for the completion of the issue then having faith and trust that the Higher Power would take care of it.

What we concluded was that there was a similarity in a step by step process we originally identified as **The 7 Steps of Manifesting Reality** which follows a downward causation process of the 7 chakra energy centers. After the Healer sets a scene of peace, love, surrender and faith, there are seven steps engaged in. The Healer, becoming unified with the Healee into a morphic field of peace, then creating a setting where the patient is in an altered state followed the energy chakras:

1. Crown: Brings into thought the belief of being healed
2. 3rd Eye: Brings into vision the image of the issue which is to be corrected
3. Throat: Communicates belief to find the source of the issue or solicits help
4. Heart: Brings in the power of emotion to surround the corrected desire

5. Solar Plexus: Launches the intention to correct the issue
6. Sacral: Surrenders control of the correction to a Higher Power
7. Root: Allows the Higher Power to materialize the correction

These **7 Steps of Manifesting Reality** are well known to any businessman or anyone engaged in a project where an idea is taken to be created in our material reality. These are recalled below.

1. THOUGHT: We bring into consciousness an idea of a desired result.
2. VISION: We form a vision or what it is we want to manifest.
3. PLAN: We write or communicate a plan to manifest the end result.
4. PASSION: We become passionate and emotional about the end result.
5. ACTION: We launch out intent to manifest the plan and succeed.
6. RELATIONS: We engage in required relationships to manifest the plan.
7. MATERIAL: We succeed in achieving the end result.

We found that belief is not a variable that can be quantified easily. The big silent belief parameter is that these miracles had a setting with someone that was an expert, had a reputation, or provided a setting which made the person feel comfortable that what the healer was going to do was credible. In the case of the placebo, it was a doctor that simulated the surgery or gave a pill. It was his credentials, and reputation that impacted the belief system. Where there was no question that it would work – total surrender – it worked. In the case of religion, it was a faith healer that had a reputation for getting results and the person had a trust and faith in a higher power. In the case of an energy healer, there was a history, a presence, a confidence of authoritative knowledge that convinced the belief system to surrender to the process and take over control.

In these cases, the belief as supported by a facilitator as a cause had the unexplainable effect of triggering the subconscious program, instructing the brain and the cells to make dramatic physiological and physical changes totally outside the believed norm.

The Subconscious And The Altered State

We found recurrent steps would be focused on bypassing the conscious mind to convince the subconscious mind to awaken some Divine Intelligence to direct the brain and the cells to reconstruct tissues, as in a healing of bones, organs, or deleting a tumor. In the end, after receiving some instructions, it was the brain that told the cells to get busy; and they listened! These processes seem to do this by putting the conscious mind on the shelf so it shuts up and gets the hell out of the way. Why? Obviously it is not quite as easy as telling the conscious mind to give the directives to the subconscious and then to the brain who gets the cells to tow the line. Did we have to talk to God or Spirit? Apparently this does not matter, yet some Divine Intervention or some higher unknown power to reprogram is clearly at work here. Yet, the confusing thing is that we get the conscious mind to get things done all the time. They don't happen to be dramatic shifts like miracle healing but nevertheless we do trigger the 7 Steps all the time. What is the difference?

The Fly In The Ointment

What becomes very relevant here is the information and books related to hypnosis, placebos and psychiatric work. The placebo effect as we have presented in the beginning is perhaps the most dramatic. Here someone with a problem is given a fake pill that the doctor knows does nothing. At the same time others are given a pill that is supposed to do something—like get rid of some physical issue. What mystifies the medical profession is that many times the placebo cures the problem. Why? Because the patient simply believes they took the pill that would cure the problem. That belief that it would work is so strong it bends physical reality. The placebo is the oddball because it does not have a healer nor is the patient making any conscious effort to engage higher powers. It does not even seem to care about an altered state. In the case of Mr. Wright, he simply depended on the vision of being healed. And the pill plus what he accepted and believed as true - simply being well again - manifested that new solution which he surrendered to without any analysis or question. In fact he even rejected the Docs thesis that he had no hope, and then charged that vision both ways as placebo and nocebo to trigger a dramatic change in physical reality.

We know this does not happen every time. But we do know that more and more doctors are using these placebos. The individual belief is the variable and the acceptance to suggestibility of a new outcome is also important. The patient was simply led to believe that the right pill was being taken, he accepted a new fate, surrendered to it without question and it miraculously cured the problem. Something created a physical transformation in the body because of a strong belief. There was no prayer, no God, no ritual, zip except thought that changed matter. But if the patient has any doubts, reservations, analytical interference, and cannot simply accept a new fate, then it does not happen!

As we have presented, it turns out that the one who is holding the cards is the subconscious which holds an ever evolving inventory of automatic and programmable subroutines. These in partnership with the brain are constantly being created, adjusted and recompiled to define our behavior. So why can't we all just think this way and execute mind over matter consciously and proactively?

We have learned that the subconscious has a mind of its own when the conscious mind attempts to convince the subconscious to act. The brain certainly is just a flunky in the process but who is making the decision? Somehow, just like in the processes of the hypnotist or the regression therapist, the tactics are to get by that conscious mental attitude and the brain so as to issue behavior change and healing directives to change biology. How was this usually done? Through the Altered State so let us review this state and get more acquainted with who or what it is that has the say in this altered state. To get a better handle on what is happening here, we have to review some old information about these brainwaves that change in an altered state.

The Importance Of Brainwaves

Wikipedia states an **altered state of consciousness** also called **altered state of mind** or **mind alteration**, is any condition which is significantly different from a normal waking beta wave state.

Your brain is made up of billions of brain cells called neurons, which use electricity to communicate with each other. The combination of millions of neurons sending signals at once produces an enormous amount of electrical activity in the brain, which can be detected using sensitive medical equipment such as an EEG or ElectroEncephaloGram, measuring electricity levels over areas of the scalp. The combination of electrical activity of the brain is commonly called a *brainwave* pattern, because of its cyclic, "wave-like" nature.

With the discovery of brainwaves came the discovery that electrical activity in the brain will change depending on what the person is doing. For instance, the brainwaves of a sleeping person are vastly different than the brainwaves of someone wide awake. Over the years, more sensitive equipment has brought us closer to figuring out exactly what brainwaves represent and with that, what they mean about a person's health and state of mind.

Here is a table showing the known brainwave types and their associated mental states:

Wave	Frequency	Associated Mental State
Gamma	27 hz and up	Gamma is associated with the formation of ideas, language and memory processing, and various types of learning. Gamma waves have been shown to disappear during deep sleep induced by anesthesia, but return with the transition back to a wakeful state.
Beta	12hz - 27hz	Wide awake. This is generally the mental state most people are in during the day and most of their waking lives. Usually, this state in itself is uneventful, but don't underestimate its importance.
Alpha	8hz - 12hz	Awake but relaxed and not processing much information. When you get up in the morning and just before sleep, you are naturally in this state. When you close your eyes your brain automatically starts producing more alpha waves. It is also called the hypnogogic state.
Theta	3hz - 8hz	Light sleep or extreme relaxation. Theta is also a very receptive mental state that has proven useful for hypnotherapy, as well as self-hypnosis using recorded affirmations and suggestions.
Delta	0.2hz - 3hz	Deep, dreamless sleep. Delta is the slowest band of brainwaves. When your dominant brainwave is delta, your body is healing itself and "resetting" its internal clocks. You do not dream in this state and are completely unconscious.

From this table, you can see that Beta and Gamma are brain states that are rife with mind chatter that is all about intellect and external affairs. It is not a surprise that to get to the subconscious mind you have to stop this incessant noise. You can tell a lot about a person simply by observing their brainwave patterns. For example, anxious people tend to produce an overabundance of high beta waves while people with ADD/ADHD tend to produce an overabundance of slower alpha/theta brainwaves.

The Importance Of The Altered State

When a hypnotherapist relaxes the patient he attempts to get the mind buzz out. The process is to get by the conscious mind interference and have the body and brain relaxed into the level of the mind of Alpha or lower into Theta. Normally our minds are buzzing away generating millions of thoughts, getting input from the external world in a frequency range of 14 to 40 cycles per second. The Alpha range occurs when we are able to ignore all that noise and become more calm and relaxed - like when you do meditation and Yoga. It is called going inside or being in an altered state. Alpha and Theta means getting to a point where you are at the same frequency as the subconscious - like being able to change the frequency on your radio. All sorts of things can happen here when you can talk the same lingo. Here it is susceptible to processes like entrainment and suggestion like in hypnosis. Neuroprogramming **(NP3)** techniques also change your brain wave activity, which is directly connected to your state of mind, using brainwave entrainment techniques. The more notorious of these is the subliminal programming process used to target you for changes in behavior.

Regardless, hypnosis uses the "power of suggestion" where a suggestion by the hypnotist is registered as a program in the subconscious. It becomes temporarily "hardwired and recompiled" in the neural pathways and subconscious unbeknown to the person hypnotized; to load and run at some other time, triggered by some preset environmental signal. It is also where the regression therapists go to locate an issue, acknowledge it, and release it, then change or delete it from subconscious memory. In our miracle lingo, this would be to place attention on it, understand the issue as to why it is there, let go of it by forgiving it, then replace it (new vision) or delete it (divine assistance).

In order to shed more light on why this state of the brain, and the various processes used to bypass the conscious mind of Alpha, Beta and Gamma are important, all one has to do is look at new biological research.

As many researchers have come to realize, the brain and nervous system must interpret environment stimuli and send signals to cells which then integrates and regulates life sustaining functions of the body organ system to support survival. Notice it says regulates and integrates, **not analyze and decide**! For this purpose, as we have said before, the brain dedicates vast cell numbers to catalogue complex perception and remember millions of experienced perceptions and integrate them into a database to give them "consciousness" or more like **self-consciousness** which is the prefrontal cortex – the neurological platform to realize personal identity and experience the quality of thinking. So the brain has a direct connection to consciousness and self consciousness. In general, "consciousness" can be divided into three categories:

Consciousness can process 40 nerve impulses/second that enable assessment and response to environmental stimuli at that moment so one can participate in life.

Self-consciousness allows one to factor in the consequences of past and future as self reflection through free will.

Subconscious can process 40 million nerve impulses/second and monitors and controls automated stimulus-response (also unconscious) programs. It is like an automated record-playback system of recorded habits. It has no creativity, once learned it is automatic. Those who can enter this state of upper Delta such as Yogis can control body through conscious mind functions which are under subconscious control. Subconscious controls body behavior not attended to by self-conscious mind in the present time.

Most of us already know that the brain is electro-chemical in nature. When nerve cells fire, they exchange charged elements that then produce electromagnetic fields. In fact, we generate more electrical impulses between our ears in one day, than do the total number of cell phones on the planet during that same amount of time. Because the brain's diverse electrical activity can be measured and calibrated, these affects can provide us with important information about what we're thinking, feeling, learning, dreaming, and creating, as well as how we are behaving or processing

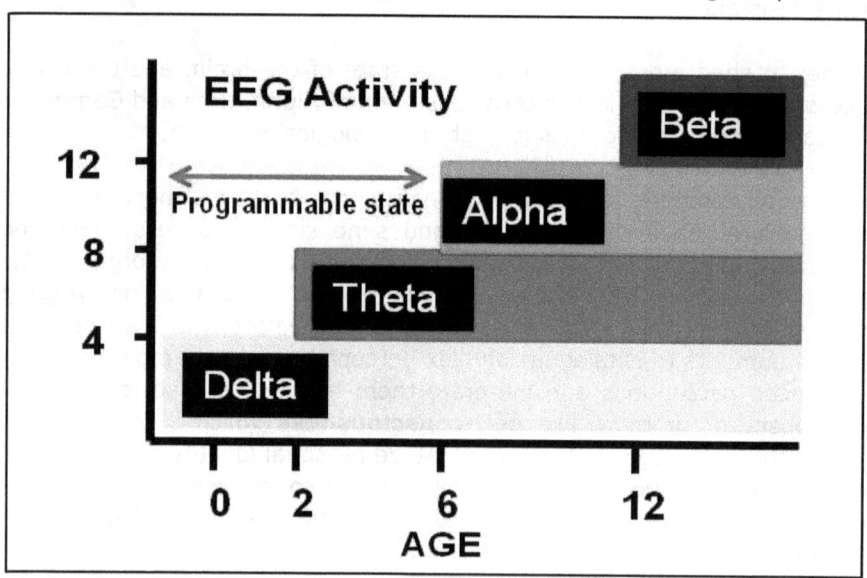

information. The way scientists record the brain's changing electrical activity is by utilizing an electroencephalograph (EEG).

With this record-playback system of subconscious in your awareness, let us look into the research that has been conducted on kids and their brain wave states as they evolve their automated stimulus-response programs so they can engage in life. It has been found that during the lower brain waves of 4-8 Hz, kids are in a highly suggestible state almost like hypnosis. To better quantify this process, have a look at the graph.

What research tells us is that during pregnancy and up to the age of 2 years the human brain is in operation in the delta range of .5-4 Hz. This is the sleeping or unconscious region. Between 2 and 6 years, the human brain is adding the theta range of 4-8 Hz. Between 6-12 years the brain adds the new range alpha of 8-12 Hz. And at 12, the brain goes to beta 12-35 Hz. where focused consciousness is added. Gamma is added after 12 where the brain can go to 35 Hz during times of peak performance. Note that these are added; they are not all there at once. These are clearly development stages that have a purpose.

By understanding the different patterns of brain wave activity in human development, we can better analyze how we learn, experience, store behavioral programs and act. Let's look more carefully at the progression of developmental brain wave stages found in growing children.

The most powerful programs are recorded in the first 6 years of life by observing and listening to people, parents, teachers, and environment. The role of the brain is to create coherence between its programs and real life as quickly as possible; these being inventoried in the subconscious. It unconsciously generates appropriate (or inappropriate depending on perception) responses that assume as truths of its programmed perceptions. With reference to the EEG Chart showing the state of awareness, there are three primary sources:

1. **Nature** First programmed perception is through inheritance such as instincts (nature). These allow the basic survival as encoded in DNA to be brought into the subconscious database.
2. **Nurture** Experiential memories downloaded from the emotional and mental/physical patterns of the mother. This is the time when the child is in the womb and the brain activity is in Delta.
3. **Actions** of Self Conscious Creative platform of perception by imagination that generates unlimited beliefs and behavior patterns through free will. That's when you have a full brain wave card deck to work with so you can build your personal identity and survive with this free will that you are given.

Now let us go into detail as to what is happening in regards to age, brainwaves and the recording of behavior:

From ages 0 to 2 DELTA Between birth and two years old, the human brain functions primarily in the lowest brain wave activity, which is from 0.5 to 4 cycles per second. This range of electromagnetic activity known as Delta waves is where a young baby is typically asleep with its eyes open. This phenomenon explains why a new born usually cannot remain awake for more than a few minutes at a time. The trance state that infants exhibit suggests that new-borns have very little analytical faculties. Information from the outside world enters their mind and brain without any analysis, judgment, editing, or critical thinking. In fact, sensory information that an infant processes is encoded directly into their subconscious mind.

The brain is recording all experiences, motor, speech, information about the world, and subconsciously learning behavior patterns. These shape life automatically because Alpha and Theta consciousness have not yet developed.

From ages 2 to 6 THETA At age 2 a child also begins to demonstrate slightly higher EEG patterns of Theta which mixes the imaginary world with the real world. Here is where the power of suggestion is prominent and the kids in Delta and Theta allow rapid downloading of parent and cultural "wisdom" to be stored as suggested programs of behavior. The infants quickly pick up skills by observation to become hardwired synaptic pathways in the brain and subconscious to control biology and behavior. To the subconscious, because the purpose of the life form is to learn to adapt and react as quickly possible so as to survive, these "truths" so suggested become facts, beliefs, truths, and programs ready for survival. The adaptation is of course both physical and mental to reflect the two greatest faculties that a human has.

Theta waves are the twilight state in which some people find themselves half awake and half asleep. This state is evident in adults when the conscious mind is awake and the body is somewhat asleep. This is also the hypnotic state where there is access to the subconscious mind. In Theta, we are more programmable because there is a thin veil between the conscious mind and the subconscious mind.

From ages 6 to 12 ALPHA At age 6 the child adds Alpha which brings about the brain activity that opens conscious processing. Before it can, however, through its design, the brain must acquire a working awareness of the world into the subconscious. That's its duty up to age 6. As we get older we move more in Alpha and become less susceptible to outside programming where the usual five sense observation systems interact with consciousness. This phases into the mode of discernment where the conscious mind's ability to make a decision by observation before the belief is stored in the subconscious becomes more prominent. It is where the prominent development of self-consciousness begins.

At the Age of 12 there is focused consciousness where more academic activity is prominent and the Beta waves kick in to the consciousness pot to take on life. This is the place we continue to use as our day to day consciousness. We also see the development of Gamma where the brain can go to 35 Hz during times of peak performance.

These are clearly a development stage that has a specific purpose in the evolution of the human mind and body within its environment.

Let's examine what is actually occurring in the subconscious mind. Because of the research done in brain wave frequencies, we now know that when we are born, we are totally subconscious mind. The developing human learns from positive and negative identifications and associations that give rise to habits and behaviors. A good example of a positive identification is when an infant is hungry or uncomfortable and cries out. As the child makes an effort to communicate in order get its mother's attention and as the nurturing parent responds by feeding the child or by changing her diaper, the infant makes an important connection with the outside world. It only takes a few repetitions before the infant learns to associate crying out with being fed or becoming comfortable. It becomes a behavior totally encoded in the subconscious as conditioned stimulus-response system triggered by a physical or environmental condition that is hard-wired in the neurological pathways of the brain.

A good example of a negative association is when a two year old child puts his finger on the hot stove. He learns very quickly to identify the object he sees, the stove, with the pain he is feeling and, after a few tries he learns a valuable lesson. In these examples, we could say that it is the sensory stimuli from the outside world that produces an internal chemical change in the body. And in time, when the developing mind pays attention to whatever it was in the environment that created the internal change, be it pleasure or pain, that process is an event in and of itself. It's called a memory. This type of associative memory requires little conscious awareness.

Somewhere between the ages of 5 and 8, our brain waves change again to an Alpha wave pattern. In Alpha, the brain is in a light meditative state. When we close our eyes and eliminate all of the sensory information from the environment, alpha waves are produced in the brain. We tend to think less because there is little information being integrated from the external environment. We relax. It is at this point in child development that the analytical mind begins to form. The child is genetically changing and along with the sum total of the environmental cues he has experienced, both will influence the growing nervous system. As a result of this type of brain wave activity, children begin to interpret and draw conclusions about the laws of external life. This is just about when children figure out that there is no Santa Claus. As the analytical mind forms at this age, it acts as a barrier to separate the conscious mind from the subconscious mind. Here you begin to see the beliefs and perceptions beginning to make their way into the neurological pathways to be recorded in the subconscious program inventory.

Most psychology texts tell us that the subconscious mind makes up about 95% of who we are. The conscious mind is therefore 5% of the total mind. This does not say anything about the capacity; it only tells us about the relative importance. After all, the conscious mind is like temporary memory while the subconscious is permanent. While the subconscious mind is made up of those positive and negative identifications and associations that give rise to habits and behaviors, the conscious mind is primarily made of logic and reasoning which contribute to our will as a means of analyzing things to determine if they are relevant for programming. It is at this point in development that we function more of the time from our rational thinking as well as conscious decision making abilities. We begin to form the ego. Resultantly, this type of thinking creates Beta wave patterns on EEG machines.

Young children therefore, have the ability to absorb vital information directly into their subconscious minds because of the way the brain develops. We are highly adaptive during our early years of life so that we can organize cultural beliefs and societal behaviors into our nervous systems. The opportunities we provide for our offspring will directly dictate the experiences they will embrace in their own personal reality at some future time. The brain's plasticity, combined with the multitude of mirror neurons it contains, afford the young mind the natural innate ability to imitate whatever that mind embraces in the environment. By providing the proper models early enough in a contemporary educational system, in a family setting, or in society, we may subconsciously teach our children the proper rules of this game called life.

Of significance here is that Delta and Theta are below consciousness and called a hypnagogic trance which is the same state hypnotherapists use to suggest and download new behaviors into subconscious. So kids up until the age of 6 are in a hypnotic trance where perceptions are downloaded without discrimination or filtering of analytic self-conscious mind which does not yet fully exist.

Also an important note is that these five stages of brain wave activates with special purpose are not given to you all at once. They are additive by age, exactly the same way your body develops by age.

Of significance here is that the process of analyzing and deciding is a brain evolution stage that comes in later when higher Alpha and then Beta kick in. Thus the hard core perception-response programs as well as beliefs are set in the first 6 years. This has relevance later when using the Conscious Mind to rewrite programs of behavior; it is like talking to a tape recorder. This can sabotage the conscious by limiting programs!

This is why the conscious mind resident most of the awake time in Beta has a slim hope of changing that which has already been programmed as critical to survival. Research shows that as adults, 5% of cognitive action is through self-conscious while 95% is through subconscious. This means that decisions, actions, emotion behavior, for example, are directed from unconscious processing from the subconscious. The bottom line is that part of the mind imagines who we are as 5% while 95% is controlled by subconscious to be who we are. All is being encoded automatically without us even knowing and as age rolls on, by the time we reach maturity, who we are is mostly done. Hence positive thinking may not work if the subconscious does not agree. Fate is based on recorded programs many of which you don't even have an awareness of! This does not mean that's the end of the line for you; it means from a certain point on, it requires more and more conscious effort of determination and repetition to create new entries into the subconscious.

The Hypnotic State

Hypnotherapists bring the patient down to Theta to do their work. What the hypnotist is doing is starting to shut out the conscious world of noise and bypass the process where the conscious mind gives directives for loading bio-programs at the subconscious level. Again this is in the lower Alpha to Theta range. Now the hypnotist starts suggesting things like you are very relaxed, you are going to have heavy eyelids and not hear anything but me, etcetera, etcetera. It is called *getting present* - eliminating the outside world always being in the mind of Beta consciousness. They are effectively taking you down into those more programmable levels of Theta.

When the hypnotist knows he has you in that state, he checks to see if you—now the subconscious—agree to listen. You are now under his spell as he is able to suggest things to the subconscious mind. He makes some suggestions for later when you are in the conscious buzz state. He may suggest that when someone claps, you will bark like a dog. Now be aware that the subconscious mind simply takes orders and responds—if it has been given the orders properly and it does not have something encoded that is in conflict—like your true belief that this hypnosis is crap. If you believe hypnosis is a joke, your subconscious will protect you and not let the suggestion through.

And in many cases the process works because that suggestion has now been programmed and loaded into the bio-computer to be run at a specific time by the operating software. So suddenly 10 minutes later, when someone claps, you start barking like a dog in your seat. Of course everyone laughs and applauds the hypnotist. Your subconscious is doing this all the time—filtering what comes in on the basis of your belief system.

Sound crazy? Research it for yourself. The Hypnotist bypassed the consciousness to input into the bio-computer what he wanted to. There was nothing there in the belief system to negate it. In self-hypnosis one does it by themselves. It works—not all the time of course.

Now be aware that this process is done all the time by some medical doctors, psychologists, psychiatrists and energy therapists. Some serious and spectacular issues have been solved this way. Some cases have even bypassed surgery. Does it work every time? No. Why not? It is because what is already programmed, and in agreement with the belief system, does not agree with the new information. The belief system is not strong enough to override the old programs.

In the profession of psychiatry, the process goes a step further. In regression therapy, a patient is brought into a hypnotic state and is slowly regressed (taken backward in time) to a point where a problem (which can be a trauma or a physical injury) occurred. In the case of a trauma, once the patient gets to that point and it is revealed, it is released simply by saying it (and believing it to be so). It gets erased! There are millions of documented facts of incredible trauma healings. Likewise, there are millions of documented cases that have eliminated serious illnesses like cancer, AID's, and other problems.

In the physical case, a patient is regressed to the point of injury or before. The patient imagines, and is aided by reinforcement from the therapist to see the issue gone. That is it, and in many cases, poof, it is gone. The belief it is so gets the subconscious to make it so and it is. A miraculous unexplained anomaly happens instantly.

What is clear is that all these processes worked quite often. They all created wonderful results and they all created miracles. However, not all the time. So what was missing here that could control success?

The bottom line was this. Whatever was impressed on subconscious is expressed as a condition to experience an event. The subconscious is the objective responsive process while the conscious is subjective. The subconscious works at the quantum level, the conscious does not. In fact, as we have stated, in comparison to a computer the subconscious mind can process 20 million environmental stimuli per second. The conscious mind can process 40 environmental stimuli per second. The conscious mind can look back and forward, but while the conscious mind is out dreaming and playing, the subconscious mind is always on duty dealing with the moment now. It effectively is the manager, the overriding authority and manages things the way it was trained. In simple terms, if the subconscious does not agree with the conscious, guess who wins?

One follows energy instructions; the other makes them up and uses imagination. When thoughts are conveyed to subconscious as energy, impressions are made on brain cells and as soon as subconscious accepts the idea, it proceeds to put it into effect.

The subconscious does not reason and compare and decide. Yet it can act by suggestion. And it can revise programs that control biology like in miracles. So how does one get through to this big processor; obviously one had to get it to accept something as its "truth" and bypass conditions or anything that limits and prevents reprogramming.

So back to our common denominators. It is important in these processes and procedures to bypass the conscious intellect so it cannot interfere and we can go directly to the source where the programs that create behavior are written. This, like with the kids in early years, is done by inducing techniques like meditation to get into that altered state of awareness.

Is an altered state important? What do you think?

The Biological Process Of Belief

We have already mentioned the work by **PhD Bruce Lipton**, who released his mind-bending study results in **The Biology of Belief.** Here Bruce expounds on the fact that everything in us is expressed in one cell. A cell is intelligent and can survive on its own. It is capable of learning through environmental experiences and creates cellular memories which they pass on to their offspring. Each of the 50 trillion cells is a miniature copy of us. Cells are highly organized communities that subdivide workloads. He underscores that the Earth and all species are living organisms and that we are not subservient to genes. Scientists, he says, have never found genes cause a disease.

His research points out the cell membrane is the brain controlling cellular life. Here is the secret in how your body translates environmental signals to behavior. All living cells have membranes with the same three layer structure. The membrane is very aware and sets in motion a response by the group of cells called the nervous system. These molecules of the membrane behave like a fluid liquid crystal. The membrane is a semiconductor as it conducts or filters through to the inside. It contains gates and channels as receptors and effectors to let nutrients in or waste out.

A computer chip is a semiconductor with gates and channels like a membrane. These are programmable from outside. The nucleus is a memory disk containing the DNA programs that encode the production of proteins.

Genes containing nucleus do not program the cell, data is entered through the membrane receptors into the cell/computer like a keyboard. Receptors trigger effector programs which act like a CPU and convert environmental information into the behavioral language of biology! So Lipton states that we are the drivers of our own biology like a WORD program. We can be masters of our own fate not victims of genes.

But what is clear also is that you need more than positive thinking to harness the control. The conscious and subconscious are independent. Conscious can create positive thought but the subconscious is the repository of data it acts on. It is habitual, millions of times more powerful. If desires of conscious are in conflict, the subconscious will win. You can affirm over and over your cancer will go but if deep down you have learned you are sickly and worthless it will undermine your best efforts.

So one can understand more clearly from Lipton's research that our conscious mind relies on a unique mechanism that converts chemical communication signals into sensations that could be experienced by all cells—emotions. The conscious mind reads signals and generates emotions which are manifested through the controlled release of regulating signals by the nervous system.

Through self consciousness the mind can use the brain to generate molecules of motion and override the system. Subconscious is a stimulus response playback device. It does not ponder and works in the "now" and there is no disagreement with the instructions once they are accepted.

Subconscious is rapid about downloading and emphasizing perceptions about threatening situations. Our perceptions control our biology, namely our beliefs.

So cells respond to outside environmental stimuli that trigger the response action to activate tissue changes. The perceptions and beliefs create the stimuli that have a direct bearing on what the brain and the subconscious need to retrieve as a response. As we unfold the story of this relationship between the brain, consciousness and subconscious we will elaborate on the cells and the neurological process of programming. But first, let us clearly understand what a state of well being has to do with it.

Why A State Of Well-Being?

In order to answer this question, let us continue on the cell's story. We can again look to the work **Bruce Lipton** as reported in his books **Biology of Belief** and **Spontaneous Evolution.**

Cells are unconsciously driven to the fight or flight reactions to service a hostile environment. These cells have moving parts as proteins, as building blocks to generate the cells behavior. Each has 150,000 parts as pathways as assemblies of proteins for breathing, digestion, and so on. These behave as switches in the cell's membrane and get proteins in motion. Biological gauges convert information via sensation from by-product chemicals. For example when one is threatened, immune cells release messengers such Interleukin 1 into the blood. When these are recognized by membrane receptors on blood vessel cells in the brain they forward a byproduct molecule Prostaglin E2 into the brain which activates fever pathways to produce shivering and high temperature. Signals are both energetic and physical (air, food, news) and all activate protein movement to generate behavior. Coupling of protein molecules with complementary environment signals causes a shape change expressed by movement in the cell membrane which animates the cell, bringing it to life.

Research shows that the "brain" of this operation is in cell membrane where these switches respond to environment signals thus relaying information into internal protein pathways. Some respond to estrogen, adrenalin, and calcium for example. There can be 100,000 switches in a cell. Each membrane switch is a unit of perception with receptor and effector proteins. Receptor receives signals (through senses) and moves to bind the effector. A second signal is sent by effector into cytoplasm that controls specific protein functions and pathways. So once again, perception controls behaviors. These switches also activate genes in nucleus to draw out a blueprint from DNA if it is required.

Dis-ease and dysfunction is caused because of defective proteins or distorted signals from three situations:

1. Trauma – twist or misalign spine, impede nerve signal transmissions
2. Toxicity – distorts signals
3. Thought – action of the mind to misinterpret environment

Cells, tissues, and organs do not question information from the nervous system. Once triggered, the brain and supporting nervous system are the regulating mechanism that coordinates all these pathways. These pathways will include using genes as blueprints to make protein parts. But it had to get through the cell brain first! The brain is the CEO of this process!

Let us work through an example. Cells accept/reject food by membrane perception switches (histamines for example). A body wide system emergency response like this is adrenalin—alpha (protection) and beta (growth response present) switches. When both histamines and adrenalin are released by the nervous system, adrenalin overrides histamines signals that are local.

Consider the power of thought as the system does not distinguish between real and non-real. The placebo effect studies prove mind over matter which is always positive thinking. Similarly the placebo effect of negative thinking is possible (i.e. nocebo, you have cancer, you have 3 months to live, it won't work). Negative thoughts can truly manifest disease. It is reported that one third of medical healings are placebo. But what percentage is nocebo when 70% are negative thoughts brought on by fear or doctors? We will explore this in detail in subsequent chapters.

But let's get back to our example. Protection mode inhibits the creation of energy, growth, and vitality. This is controlled by the nervous system in response to stress. This happens through external HPA (Hypothalamus-pituitary-adrenal) like the fight or flight reaction where stress hormones are triggered in the body suppressing or inhibiting normal function everywhere. Where? The key ones are the immune system to fight disease, the visceral digestive area, and the ability to think. This is why if you are frightened you are dumber. Obviously the built in firmware doesn't think you need to waste any resources on eating, thinking or internal immunity when the shit hits the fan! Trouble is, this system doesn't know if the shit is in the imaginary or real perception fan!

We live in a world of fear and threat activating HPA and releasing stress hormones continuously. It is estimated that 70% of our thoughts are negative. Almost every illness has now been linked to stress. Subconscious is an emotionless database of stored programs that creates hardwire behavior response with no judgment; a programmable hard drive into which our experiences are downloaded. The subconscious does not decide whether an order is bad or good, positive or negative. It simply checks its disk drives to see what is ok (belief sub-drive) and does it.

The two mind components are like a dynamic duo operating together. Subconscious takes over the moment conscious is not paying attention. To alter the program one for sure had to change the belief because it is the program that creates patterns in realty. The universe of thought and emotion changes belief because they are already working at a quantum level; ready to put input into those micro chip cells. When you really know, and really believe you deserve something, then you can have it. You simply know it to be true so it will happen.

The state of stress and negativity either physical or emotional suppresses many biological processes that inhibit normal functions. This is why a state of well being of peace and love are enhancers of these biological functions.

Consider the opposite power of thought to heal. Elisabeth Fischer Targ, M.D. (1961 - 2002) was a psychiatrist with many interests including psychic phenomena and the role of spirituality in health and healing. She earned her undergraduate degree and her medical degree at Stanford University. In one of her studies, she found that group therapy was as useful as Prozac for fighting depression. She is probably best known for her study on the effects of prayer on patient outcomes in a group of people with AIDS. This randomized, double-blind study which was published in the Western Journal of Medicine found that the subjects who were prayed for had significantly better health and lower morbidity than the subjects who were not prayed for. She experimented with positive and negative thoughts to see if they influenced events. Could prayer influence AIDS? She got 40 religious and spiritual healers with known credibility to participate.

In this double blind study 20 patients in 2 groups all received the same medical treatment. The healers all got the name, photo, and T-Cell counts of one group. Each had to hold the intention to heal as well being one hour per day for 6 days a week for 10 weeks. This meant 40 healers were praying for 10 patients so each patient got prayers from 4 healers. After 6 months the control group had 4 of 10 die and the Healer group had 10 alive all improved. Many other experiments confirmed the same.

So, is it important to have a state of well being? Well guess who is the emotional conscious dude operating in the higher brain wave area to not let go of meddling when you are trying to get it out of the way. And how can a stress environment be conducive to those entrainment and harmonious brain wave patterns?

The other question that comes to mind is how do you best influence these programs registered in the subconscious? The altered state or some form of it is directly correlated with the state of the brain's vibrations. It is apparent that the brain is in a usual conscious active state of Alpha (developed at age 6) then Beta (developed at age 12) interferes with access to the subconscious which vibrates in the Theta (developed at age 2).

It is not that we cannot create and modify programs in the subconscious, it is that by design and evolution, we develop the programs for survival and adaptability through stages and these form the primary basis not easily dislodged when in the beta state of consciousness. To gain access to the computer code and the operating system you have to be in a state outside of Beta where analysis, intellect and the decision making processes do not exist. And the best state to be in is Theta just like a kid.

We see also that the state of well being is not just a New Age or Religious practice to talk to a superior God, gods or Archangel that can assist in the process of creating miracles. There is a biological, physiological and chemical process that interferes with the ability to move into that state of communication with the subconscious mind. The state of stress and negativity either physical or emotional suppresses many biological processes that inhibit normal functions. This is why a state of well being of peace and love are enhancers of these biological functions.

We can therefore conclude that if we are an adult, where Beta and Gamma are dominant in our consciousness, it is the Theta altered state brought about through some process like hypnosis that would be the most effective way to get back into that programmable environment in order to optimize access to the subconscious where physical changes (programs) of reality are instigated and directed.

It is noteworthy that the placebo effect directly bypasses any requirement for the Higher power of Divine intervention to make the change in reality. How does the placebo bypass Beta? The most successful examples are those that supercharge the vision of a new state of being healed with emotion, then totally surrender to that outcome as already done without analysis, question or thoughts. We have dedicated a complete chapter to this question.

In order to achieve this, the entry into the altered state as a prerequisite for hypnosis, regression, creation of miracle requires a state of well being and peace because otherwise, the brain subconsciously through both physical and mental interference can create cascades of chemical, and biochemical reactions that interfere with being in that "programmable space". This appears to also be the frequency domain of the Divine Programmer who has access to the Higher Power that instigates the change. This is called the altered state.

Now, let us investigate this story of the cell further and look at this CEO called a brain, the fellow in the physical attic that gets instructions from the subconscious to instigate the appropriate changes from running these programs.

3

THE ROLE OF THE BRAIN

"Thoughts are language of brain and feelings are language of the body. Together they open the door to the operating system of the subconscious mind."

Aly McDonald   Ed Rychkun

> **Oh wondrous brain in conscious land
> What is it that you best understand?**

Recap About The Brain

We can conclude from the previous chapter that the importance of the altered state and the state of well being is rooted in the need to eliminate the beta state of conscious activity which creates mental and physical interferences with the programmability process.

In our first book ***The Divine Programmer: Creating Miracles***, we brought forward several conclusions about the brain which we will review before we continue with the role of the brain in the process of programming the subconscious.

The first conclusion was that the brain performs a multitude of sensory, vital and physical tasks that it learns in order to guarantee survival. It is a complex information processing and control system. The brain is dedicated to controlling how the body functions and adapts to its environment. The nervous system, the senses, the mobility, the internal functioning are automated environmental stimuli-response systems.

The second conclusion was that the brain is not in charge, as it takes directives from the subconscious, cell membranes and the heart.

The third conclusion was that the brain is not like a binary computer, it is more analog computer designed to sense and respond so as to create a database of perception response functions. It holds its own database to remember and execute these on conscious and subconscious command. A copy is held in the master disc drive of the subconscious mind.

The fourth conclusion is that the brain is the holographic processor that creates your reality through the meaning, composition, and representation from its local database as its memory and the interpretation of the senses of your lower body.

The fifth conclusion is that while brains are reduced to a lower meditative state, an evoked potential in one induces an evoked potential in the other at distances apart. They "entangle" in the meditative state so one can influence another's brain being quantum in nature.

For the time being we will leave conclusion 4 and 5 for a later discussion.

Mind And Matter Are Not Separate

We can see now that the mind and matter are linked and not separate. Now we are going to investigate how conscious and unconscious thoughts and feelings are the blueprint controlling destiny. Both minds must work together in order to bring about any future change in physical reality. If not, in the majority of cases, it is the subconscious that wins the conflict.

Conditional response is a subconscious program housed in the body that overrides the conscious mind and takes charge. Over time, the body is conditioned to become the mind as conscious thought is no longer in control. For example the autonomic nervous system creates internal changes in the body by associating past memories with an expectation of internal effect through associate memory. The stronger the conditioning, the less conscious control is and more automatic is the programming that generates the internal effect.

It is known in the study of Neurobiology that if you keep taking the same substance the brain keeps firing the same circuits the same way memorizing what the substance does. It is conditioned to the effect by a familiar internal change derived from past experiences. Because of this conditioning, a placebo activates the same hard wired circuit. Associate memory elicits a subconscious program that makes a connection between a pill and the hormonal change in the body and signals go out to make the related change.

The Brain Process Of Programming

Two very important processes are part of the usual programming process that creates programs. The first is the process of **Conditioning** where a past memory is associated with physiological change. For example a pill gets rid of a headache. The pill creates a specific experience to produce a conditional reaction inside associate memory.

The second is **Expectation.** There is an expected result that is associated with the condition and it could be an old outcome of pain if the pill is not believed to work. If a different outcome than what is current is anticipated we accept the pill as a suggestion for a new cure. A new possibility and a different outcome becomes expected. If we automatically accept and embrace the new outcome then a new experience and a new trigger is created to override the old. The stronger the emotion of the experience – like the joy of relief – the quicker that neurological program gets hard-wired into the subconscious.

Our brain and bodies don't know the difference as to how that experience is engaged in. An example is a traumatic event like the fear of water. This could be created because one may have almost drowned, particularly as a kid. At that time a whole cascade of chemicals and physiological reactions in the body occurs as a result and this conditioning process becomes a program. That strong emotion of fear embeds itself as a frequency signature into the brain's neurological filing system and then after that the very thought of water automatically conjures up the reactions as expectations; as does the sight of water, or immersion in it. To overcome this fear and to rewrite the program, you have to believe and accept a different outcome until you get into the water, face the fear, feel the heightened emotion of actual succeeding in being in the water, and reprogram a new sequence. Otherwise the repetitive persistence of getting over it may eventually do the same thing. In truth, that could have also been done in your mind by regressing back to the cause and changing it (as we will see later).

The ways this occurs is that the brain fires the same neural circuits that became hardwired into the subconscious when the original state of conditioning occurred. It will do so until our state of mind changes (like a new drug to release pain when the old does not work) otherwise it will continue to produce the same expected result and release similar chemicals into the body by way of a simple thought that triggers the result.

In looking at this learning process, the brain is 75% water and has 100 billion neurons suspended in aqueous environment. Each nerve cell looks like wiggly branches and has root systems that connect and disconnect to other cells (1000-100000) depending on where it resides. In the neocortex this is 10,000-40,000 per neuron. Each is like a biocomputer with oodles of Random Access Memory to process 100's and 1000's of functions per second. As we learn things, neurons make new connections, exchanging electrochemical information called synaptic connections. If learning is making a new synaptic connection then remembering is keeping these connections wired together to create long term memory. The creation of these connections and the ways they change over time alters the physical neural structure of the brain. As the brain makes changes, our thoughts produce a blend of chemicals (neurotransmitters like serotonin, dopamine, acetylcholine, etc).

When we think thoughts, neurotransmitters at one branch of one neuron tree cross the synaptic gap to reach the root of another neuron tree and an electrical bolt of information is fired. The same thought keeps firing the same ways to strengthen the relationship between the cells so they can more easily convey the signal next time they fire. This way the brain shows physical evidence of learning and remembering. This is the process of synaptic potentialization or selective strengthening.

When jungles of neurons fire in unison to support a new thought an additional chemical (protein) is created within the nerve cell and makes its way to the nucleus, then lands in DNA to switch on several genes. The job of the genes is to make proteins that maintain function and structure of the body. The nerve cell then makes new proteins to create new branches between nerve cells. Repeated thoughts or experiences also affect the physical structure as the brain becomes more enriched microscopically. New thoughts and you become changed neurologically, chemically and genetically. You gain 1000's of new connections in a matter of seconds from novel learning, new ways of thinking, and fresh experience. So by thought alone you can activate new genes right away just by changing your mind; mind over matter.

Studies show repeating strengthens neurons to remember the next time but the synaptic connection soon disappears and the memory is erased if this is not reinforced or continued. It is important to continually update, review, and remember new thoughts, choices, habits, beliefs, experiences to solidify these neurological patterns in the brain. The brain will keep using the same hardware (physical neural networks) and will create a software program (autonomic neural network) to reflect it. That is how programs are installed in the brain. The hardware creates the software and the software is embedded into the hardware and every time the software is needed, it reinforces the hardware

So old circuits are hardwired. New science states that *"neuron cells that fire together wire together"*. The fixed pattern becomes a finite signature of automatic programs called your identity – like a box in your brain limiting you inside that box that holds all your beliefs, perceptions and related programs.

The Science Of Neuroplasticity And The Frontal Lobe

So in order to create new programs you must think outside this limiting box – change your mind. The process of grow, change, adopt is called **Neuroplasticity**. It is where the brain fires different sequences, patterns, and combinations as new choices, thoughts outside the box that lead to new behaviors, experiences, new emotions, and a new identity.

But to change you have to become conscious of the unconscious self (which is just a set of hardwired programs) and not make the same choices every day – break habits. You must think about and perceive reality differently to see life through the lens of a new mind. Leave the same predictable self connected to the same thoughts, choices, behavior and feeling and step into the void of the unknown. You do this by repeated firing and rewiring. The old self must die then you have the power to embrace the new. There is really nothing new about this concept as we can take longer and longer to learn new things the older we get.

The frontal lobe is behind the forehead and is your creative center. It learns new things, dreams new possibilities, makes conscious decisions, sets intentions and basically is the CEO of the physical world. It allows you to observe who you are, evaluate what you are doing and how you are feeling. It's all about consciousness. In the process of learning new things, the frontal lobe is your ally because it lowers the volume of outside world to avoid being distracted by the 5 senses. This is all just part of your brain's evolution and by age 12 this is ready to go. Here the perception of time and space diminish as has been proven clinically by brain scans. This dial down of input sensory centers like the motor center of physical, association center of identity, parental lobe of time allow you to then make a thought more real. This is of course similar to the process undertaken by the altered state.

As CEO the frontal lobe has connections to all other parts of the brain. It creates intention (say to be healthy) and starts selecting networks of neurons to create a new state of mind to respond. It is the frontal lobe that changes your mind to work in different patterns and sequences and therefore typically a picture of internal representation appears in your mind's eye which is the frontal lobe.

This frontal lobe orchestrates neural nets to fire in unison. As you focus on clear intention there will come a moment when thought will become the experience in your mind – where inner reality is more real than outer. Once thought becomes the experience you begin to feel the emotions of how the event would feel in reality. Emotions are the chemical signature of experiences. The brain makes a chemical messenger (neuropeptide) and sends it to the cells in the body, looking for the appropriate docking (receptor) so it can deliver the message to hormonal centers then DNA to get the message a new event has occurred. DNA turns on genes (up regulating) or turns down (down regulating) others to support this new state of being. When a gene lights up it is activated to make protein, when diminished it deactivates and does not produce proteins. And we see the effect with measureable changes in the physical body.

Stem cells are partially responsible for the impossible. These undifferentiated cells become specialized as raw potential when these blank states are active they morph into whatever kind of cell the body needs (muscles, bone, skin, immune system, etc.) in order to replace the injured or damaged cells in tissues, organs and systems. For example in a cut skin local trauma sends a signal to genes from outside the cell. The gene turns on to make the appropriate proteins to instruct stem cells to turn into healthy functioning skin cells. Millions of these processes occur all the time. Healing attributed to this type of expression has been documented in liver, muscle, skin, bone marrow, brain, heart, etc. In fact, the brain and body create the perfect pharmacy to alter the internal condition – a new state of being as mind and body work together as one. This is particularly evident in so many cases that medicine says are impossible to heal.

To enforce the need for a state of wellbeing, you need to be aware that in highly emotional negative states stem cells do not get signals clearly. As in stress response automatic cascades (flight or fight, survival mode) of interfering processes force healing to take longer. That's why in a hospital they insist on rest and wellbeing in a less stressful environment because if the body and mind are dealing with beta, and consequences of anger, conflict, fear and causing interference which prevents coherence for turning on stem cells into useful cells, healing is restricted. As we will explain later, when the placebo is at work and you create the right level of mind with clear intention combined with nurturing elevated emotion the right type of signal can reach DNA more easily. Here it becomes possible to influence production of healthy proteins for better structure and function of the body and also make brand new cells from latent stem cells waiting for the right message.

So the process is one that we will explain later in the chapter on Reality and Quantum Physics. It is one of Downward Causation. The thought triggers the neural networks that create neuropeptides which embark as Epigenetic signals to cells. This creates activation of cell receptors sites and then activates DNA selection and regulation process. This creates the expression of proteins to influence the expression of life for a healthy body which is all about the autonomic nervous system managed by the brain.

The autonomic nervous system is under control of the limbic brain (Emotional brain) or chemical brain and is responsible for subconscious functions. Emotions activate this brain as it exists below consciousness mind control. Emotion activates the autonomic nervous system and bypasses the neocortex. As you move beyond the thinking brain you move into an area where health is regulated, maintained and executed. This is the way to enter the operating system and program change because you are now instructing the nervous system to begin creating the corresponding chemistry. The body becomes the mind emotionally.

Fear, anger, and futility won't signal the proper genes. They turn on the flight or fight syndrome used for survival mode. Trying to do something over and over may bring stress; as the same struggle attempting to force an outcome knocks you out of balance. Gratitude, and appreciation opens the heart and lifts energy. Gratitude is one of the most powerful emotions to lift the level of suggestibility. The process of giving thanks shows gratitude for already happened events. Gratitude is the ultimate state of receivership (selfless as a creative emotion vs. selfish survival emotions).

The more analytical, the less is the suggestibility to this programming process. Duality as good-bad creates conflict and stress and pumps chemicals to drive the analytical cycle more. If calm, it works for you. Ego as an extension of the conscious mind is designed to protect you so it will derail the process with a rush of addictive emotion to get power and to move further away from the operating system. The exception occurs when that elevated emotion has an impact to create trauma programs of response.

Implicit And Explicit Memory

The conscious mind makes up 5% and represents your will, logic, creativity, and reasoning). It is called the explicit or declarative memory dedicated to semantic (learned) and episodic (experience). Note that this does not define the size of the memory, it only defines the ratio.

The subconscious mind takes on the whopping 95% as implicit or non declarative memory as the programmed operating system. Here is where those first years as a kid and teenager have programmed skills, habits, emotional reactions, hardwired behavior, conditional responses, associate memories, routine thoughts and feelings, attitudes, beliefs, and perceptions.

<u>Implicit memory is developed from emotions of experience</u>, especially those that are highly charged one-time emotional events that get branded into memory. The other way is through a redundancy of emotions from consistent experiences that keep firing the same way to hard wire the neural networks.

So any high charged emotional event opens the door to the subconscious. Thoughts are the language of the brain and feelings are the language of the body. Together they open the door to the operating system. To take from the hypnotic process, you are more suggestible when thoughts match feeling. So when you feel emotions you activate implicit memory and the autonomic nervous system.

Where we see the placebo work best is where the thought of it brought elevated emotion (joy of being healed, hope or inspiration) to a new possibility without analysis, the level of suggestibility influenced by feelings and they entered the operating system and reprogrammed the autonomic nervous system with new orders by thought alone. Crucial to this process was to get beyond the analytical mind. Trauma bypasses the analytical mind. Once again, with reference to brain waves, this means getting out of beta because that is where the analytical mind lives. It forms a barrier between Low Beta and Alpha.

The Power Of Meditation

Like hypnosis, meditation bypasses the critical analytical mind to move into the subconscious system of programs – beyond analytical interference away from the outer world of body and time to pay attention to the inner world of thought and feeling. It moves the mind from selfish to selfless, from being somebody to no body and no one, some place to no place, materialist to non-materialist, from survival to creator, imbalance to balance, from limiting emotions to expansive emotion (love, joy) known to unknown.

If the neocortex is the home of conscious awareness (intellect, etc.) you must move beyond it to meditate effectively. You must move into the limbic brain. You have to declare a cease fire on all neural networks. The neocortex uses the 5 senses and is preoccupied with the body, environment and time. This is ego surviving so nobody, no thing, no place is a serious threat to it.

The depth of Meditation is about navigating brain waves to affect how suggestible we are at the moment. The EEC measures how neurons fire together since they create electromagnetic fields. The slower, the deeper we go, the higher the wave the further away from the operating system, the worst being the high state of Beta created by stress chemicals.

Low Beta (relaxed, interested attention like reading a book)
Mid Beta (focused attention, learning and remembering)
High Beta (focused crisis mode)
Going into low Alpha we activate the frontal lobe
Going into Theta (twilight) no analytical mind and high suggestibility

Research has shown that to increase suggestibility you have to weaken the analytical mind as has been done in cases involving:

- Physical or mental fatigue
- Limited exposure to social, physical, environmental cues in sensory depravation

- Extreme hunger
- Emotional shock
- Trauma

These are a short path to reprogramming. Of course these are not recommended processes to get new programs installed in subconscious. But they do tell us the importance of strong emotion and why there is a need to enfold your vision with strong emotion of gratitude and completion. We are also seeing some physiological and physical reasons why so many of our miracle workers and those that train you to attract abundance are so fixed on getting that brain settled down out of beta and body chaos, and getting centered into a peacefully loving state. Both negative emotion and daily beta crap need to be let go of in order to talk to that Divine Programmer who is quite obviously outside the usual physical reality, and outside of the group consciousness. It has nothing to do with Yogis, New Age, Religions or Cultural beliefs; it has to do with the design and operation of the brain at the top of your head and the way it reads mental and emotional input. If anything, these traditions are simply attempting to create a practice that assists in bypassing the chaos of the body and brain.

Now let us look at another brain control center in the body that has to do with emotion.

4

THE ROLE OF THE HEART

"The gateway into the level of quantum energy and our subconscious is through the silent powerhouse of the heart and its brain."

Aly McDonald   Ed Rychkun

> **Oh wondrous heart in subconscious land
> What is it that you best understand?**

The Heart Energetic System

In the previous chapter, we got a feeling for the role of the brain at the top of the head. But as we explored in **The Divine Programmer**, the heart is the energetic balance point of the chakra system and it has a mind of its own. To most the heart is just an organ that pumps blood to keep us alive. If you live within the limits of the consciousness box, then the sayings of loving you with all my heart, heart of a lion, broken heart, from the bottom of my heart, cross my heart, bleeding heart and heart of gold are only silly expressions - a few of the 120 examples posted on the free dictionary.

Where do these come from? They come from the negative and positive choices and characteristics of the energetic heart chakra. If you want to believe it is the physical heart that you feel when your heart is broken, think again. It is the energetic heart chakra sending its message to the body; and even the tight chest or angina may not be a result of the physical heart malfunctioning, albeit the two are linked. To most the "heart" is the center of love so reflected in the love for the special ones in our life as in "falling in love" and "I love you" as a descriptor of special intense emotion. You are here to experience emotion and the heart is the powerful center of emotion, among other things. Love, as we are coming to understand, is much more than just a physical expression. It appears to be a universal "soup" of all that is and a heart-brain is the access point. As we are about to describe, the heart has its own nervous system, its own heart-brain and heart-mind that does not take orders from that big dummy in the attic - the head brain. And it has its own special subtle, powerful energetic fields.

The Double Torus And Energy Vortexes

HeartMath LLC is a cutting edge company providing a range of unique services, products, and technology to boost performance, productivity, health and well-being while dramatically reducing stress. Founded in 1991 as a non-profit research organization by Doc Childre, HeartMath has earned global recognition for their unique research-based techniques and proprietary technology to transform the stress of change and uncertainty. They have learned to help many bring coherence and renewed energy to the workplace and the home. But, they have also studied and reported many other revealing and revolutionary characteristics of the heart. All you have to do is go to ***www.heartmath.com*** and check it out for yourself.

Rollin McCraty, PhD, is the Executive Vice President and Director of Research for HeartMath. He reports the heart, like the brain, generates a powerful electromagnetic field. He explains in **The Energetic Heart** that: *"The heart generates the largest electromagnetic field in the body. The electrical field as measured in an electrocardiogram (ECG) is about 60 times greater in amplitude than the brain waves recorded in an electroencephalogram (EEG)."*

"The heart is a sensory organ and acts as a sophisticated information encoding and processing center that enables it to learn, remember, and make independent functional decisions. The heart's electromagnetic field contains certain information or coding, which researchers are trying to understand, that is transmitted throughout and outside of the body. One of the most significant findings of research related to this field is that intentionally generated positive emotions can change this information coding."

They found that the heart's magnetic field is 5000 times greater than the brains. This field is a torus – like a big donut – and can reach 6-8 feet in diameter. They feel that this field can possibly reach large distances, like miles depending on the intensity. This, they say, can affect other brain waves. Does this make you think about how the Law of Attraction can attract?

That discovery raises the question whether the cardioelectromagnetic field information transmitted from an individual who is angry, fearful, depressed or experiencing some other negative emotion, takes on beneficial properties when it is influenced by positive emotions. It is coming to light that the care, compassion, love or other positive emotions are not only transmitted throughout an individual's body as the cardioelectromagnetic field radiates through it, but transferred externally as well to people in close proximity <u>and</u> even over long distances like miles.

"This preliminary data elucidates the intriguing finding that the electromagnetic signals generated by the heart have the capacity to affect others around us. It appears that when the mother placed her attention on the baby that she became more sensitive to the subtle electromagnetic signals generated by the infant's heart. These findings have intriguing implications, suggesting that a mother in a psychophysiologically coherent state became more sensitive to the subtle electromagnetic information encoded in the electromagnetic signals of her infant."

Note how the state of coherence comes up again, like it needs to be in a coherent state to communicate, or more significantly ALLOW communications out and in! Remember the need for a feeling of love emotion with prayer or it does not allow miracles to work!

In the book, **The Energetic Heart: Bioelectromagnetic Interactions Within and Between People,** McCraty, asks some relevant questions which he reports on. He states that the Energetic Heart explains the bioelectromagnetic interactions within and between people. Did you know that when you're not consciously communicating with others, our physiological systems are interacting in subtle and surprising ways? Or that the electromagnetic signal produced by your heart is registered in the brain waves of people around you? Or that your physiological responses sync up with your mate's during empathetic interactions? His book will allow you to discover why the heart's electromagnetic field is believed to act as a central synchronizing signal within the body, an important carrier of emotional information and a key mediator of energetic interactions between people.

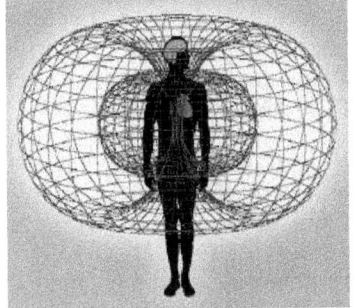

Centered on the heart chakra is this torroid, a double vortex of energy. A vortex is a mass of energy that moves in a rotary or whirling motion, causing a depression or vacuum at the center. These powerful eddies of pure earth power manifest as spiral-like coagulations of energy that are either electric, magnetic, or electromagnetic qualities of life force. Vortexes are areas of high energy concentrations, originating from magnetic, spiritual, or sometimes unknown sources. Additionally to those that think outside the box they are considered to be gateways or portals to other realms, both spiritual and dimensional. Vortexes typically exist where there are strong concentrations of gravitational anomalies, in turn creating an environment that can defy gravity, bend light, scare animals, twist plant life into contorted shapes, and cause humans to feel strange. Many vortexes have been shown to be associated with Ley lines and have been found to be extremely strong at node points where the lines cross. At each chakra there are vortexes reaching out perpendicular to the axis of the body chakra system.

The Heart field is a morphic field which surrounds you and vibrates with emotions emanating outwards. So it can be felt by others but it also is a nucleus within the quantum soup of infinite possibilities drawing likeness (as in the Law of Attraction). Your emotions are signatures of attraction as are images with quantum signatures of emotion. Exact replication is not possible this way, only likeness. Known as the double torus of infinity, it is centered on the heart as the engine of energy, the center of singularity. It means your heart is the central engine, not to pump blood but to provide a portal to the love soup of the quantum; that place of infinite possibilities. Inside this torus is your pillar of life, your chakra system that is not only the transference vehicle between DNA and biology from above to below, but energy transmutation from thought to form both biology and to external material. And so the torus is the spiraling engine that does the actual transmutation of energy. The double torus is like a funnel of energy that spins down the funnel becoming more and more concentrated to reach the singularity point at the heart. Then the funnel inverts itself at the heart and the energy then spins down and expands. This is the double torus.

Each chakra has a function to interface between 3D and other D's within this torus. Your thoughts, images, language, emotions, intent, relationships, existence move down the pillar from above to below and are deployed for the expansion and expression at the choice of consciousness. They are the receivers and transmitters talking to DNA because all these subtle energies are in the quantum world. You have developed a knowing about this. The thoughts, visions, words, emotions that drive intent constitute the torroid process downward to the heart at the point of singularity that then drops into the bottom torroid of intent, relationship and 3D expression of manifestation, and eventually materialization of matter.

The way the pillar is deployed is by choice and intent, and carries the communication of information between consciousness of mind between your first layer of DNA of biological-chemical and the other 11 DNA pairs that constitute your being. This interface is not working at full capacity. It has atrophied through fear and your choice to not develop spiritually into what you are. So it sits stagnant in your DNA. The manifesting processes you have come to know as resident transmitters in your chakras are the thoughts, visions, and the language of emotions. The choice is whether these are sourced from the essence of the heart—love, or the essence of ego—intellect. To open to the full library of DNA, the full abilities of the chakra psychic library, and the portal to infinite possibilities, you must shift from that big dummy the ego brain to the heart brain which awakens in an aura of well-being, love and compassion. That is the "electricity" that turns it on.

Although they are all one, all interconnected, this is a choice of either heart or ego. But nevertheless, all that is you, in your DNA, of karmic lesson, of Divine, of Akashic, and all that is, it all sits awaiting your awareness and intent. You now have a knowing that the best interface is positive thought, visions of completion, words of the language of creation, emotions of love and forgiveness. This is speaking, listening, feeling with the heart. For all this means is that the choice of your seeing, speaking, listening, feeling and thinking is always in the light, not with the traditional limited physical sensory system. The portals of access to the DNA is the communication medium of love. And the ability to optimize the torroid's process is the bringing of these positive attributes into the singularity of heart—yes the heart of all matter. This is simply your knowing that it is so, and however this works is not relevant because you acquire the faith and trust that this is so, and all you have to do is accept and be it. The true power of this process is keyed to a specific vibratory range that is what the energy of love is.

The torus, or primary pattern, is an energy dynamic that looks like a doughnut – it's a continuous surface with a hole in it. The energy flows in through one end, circulates around the center and exits out the other side. You can see it everywhere – in atoms, cells, seeds, flowers, trees, animals, humans, hurricanes, planets, suns, galaxies and even the cosmos as a whole. Scientist and philosopher, Arthur Young, explained that a torus is the only energy pattern or dynamic that can sustain itself and is made out of the same substance as its surroundings – like a tornado, a smoke ring in the air, or a whirlpool in water.

The torus also applies at the human level. Each person not only is a torus – our bodies are a continuous surface (skin) with a hole through the middle (intestinal tract) – but we are each surrounded by our own toroidal electro-magnetic field. Each individual's torus is distinct, but at the same time open and connected to every other in a continuous sea of infinite energy. It is the same energy field you can feel with a magnet. It is usually invisible, but by scattering iron filings loosely around a magnet you can actually see the toroidal shape of energy.

The heart's electromagnetic frequency arcs out from the heart and back in the form of a torus field. The axis of this Heart torus extends from the pelvic floor to the top of the skull, and the whole field is holographic, meaning that information about it can be read from each and every point in the torus.

Most torus dynamics actually contain two toruses – called "tori" – like the male and female aspects of the whole – one spiraling one direction toward the North Pole and its opposite spinning toward the South Pole. This is also referred to as the Coriolis Effect. Examples are the weather on the earth and the plasma flow of the sun. In the heart torus, the spin down the top center is clockwise, down into the point of singularity at the heart, then to the outside of the lower torus, around to the inside of the lower torus, back through the heart then to the outside of the upper torus, then back down.

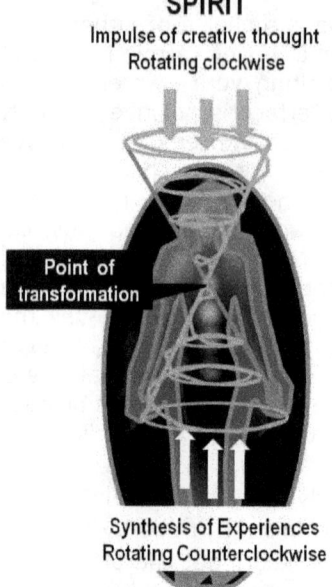

The underlying structure of the torus is the Vector Equilibrium, or "VE." **It is the blueprint by which nature forms energy into matter.** Buckminster Fuller, one of the 20th Century's most prolific inventors, coined the term Vector Equilibrium. He named it this because the "VE" is the only geometric form where all forces are equal and balanced. The energy lines (vectors) are of equal length and strength. **They represent the energy of attraction and repulsion, like you can feel with a magnet.**

You can't actually observe the "VE" in the material world because it is the geometry of absolute balance. What we experience on Earth is always expanding toward and contracting away from absolute equilibrium. Like a wave arising from the surface of a tranquil sea, a material form is born (unfolds) from the plenum (fullness) of energy (ironically referred to by physicists as "the vacuum!") and dies (enfolds) back into it. **The VE is like the imaginable – yet invisible – mother of all the shapes and symmetries we see in the world.**

The Heart Brain And Emotions

We have seen how the perceived environment can cause the flight or fight syndrome and the HPA axis to affect the immune system, the visceral system and the intellect. Now we have another kid on the block that can cause havoc. The research at HeartMath has shown that the heart has its own brain that communicates with and influences the cranial brain through the nervous system, hormonal system and other pathways that affect the quality of life. They also conclude that the brain gets communications four ways: neurological (nerves); biophysical (pulse waves); biochemical (hormones); and energetic (electromagnetics).

They conclude that the heart and nervous system DO NOT follow brain's direction. The heart has its own brain that can sense, remember, learn, feel, and process information independently.

Signals go from the heart to the survival centre in hindbrain where blood pressure and heart rate, and respiratory rate are controlled. This part analyses info and makes changes. These signals also affect your feelings and emotional memory center in midbrain (Amygdala). The cells here synchronize to the pacemaker in the heart. If HRV is chaotic, it matches that to negative emotional experiences and automatically recalls what negative feeling to correlate with. Brain waves in cortex are also affected by powerful chaotic heart signals coloring how you think and perceive, altering top level functions (calculation, planning, creativity, and communications) – all from the big signal generator in the heart.

Research shows that stress feelings activate a stress response that is emotional and psychological. So a simple thought recalling anger will provoke a response but it is nowhere near the intensity of the physiological and psychological process of the stress response of emotion. Where have we heard this before? In our discussion about the cells. Research at HeartMath found that emotions contribute heavily to stress on the brain and it can be either real or imagined. The end effect is the same. There is no difference.

Research suggests meditation, yoga, and prayer help. They say when stress or negative things hit, first focus and neutralize – time out. Shift attention to the heart area away from noise and stress. Stop the emotion or thought. Feel the breath through the heart in a steady rhythm while you disengage from negative thoughts and feelings. Then engage a positive feeling emotion by thinking back to a positive situation of love and care. This coherent pattern overrides negative emotional programs. They say a positive feeling is not a thought process. You want to be genuine. Learn an inventory of these and your awareness/control increases so the threshold is reset. It is like our bedtime practice in our plan.

So, there is a lot of stuff in you that is your subtle sensing system and energetic body that is working away clogging up your chakras to result in dis-ease and disease as well as clog those higher abilities, and cause a negative reactive procession in your body. Your heart field is also doing the same thing.

Now remember the 100 trillion bits of your DNA that are all in quantum space, all connected, all acting instantly as one? Well, the Light Body is also one of trillions of other bodies that make up the Unity Consciousness. And this Light Body has a certain vibrational signature unique to you.

Let us look more deeply into the result of the heart emotion. The research at HeartMath shows stress feelings activate a stress response that is emotional and psychological. The emotion creates a reaction in the brain that affects the body. The ANS, short for Autonomic Nervous System, kicks into action upon any threat and it works in two parts. We are already familiar with the Flight or Fight syndrome coming from a different source. First is the fight or flight situation where the sympathetic system causes the body to constrict blood vessels, raise blood pressure, raise heart rate, constrict skin arteries, move blood away from organs, dilate pupils, and raise neck hairs for starters. And this is all done automatically in a few seconds to prepare you. The orders are made by the brain to do this.

The second situation is when the threat is only perceived like when you walk into a dark alley and feel threatened. Then the parasympathetic system kicks in. It causes the heart rate to go up, you get a sweat, or chill, and the blood pressure goes up in readiness. The hormonal system then starts a long sequence of reactions of nervous system signals to the glands so as to increase chances of survival. These actions take a few minutes but they last for hours. The research says that once this starts, there are some 1400 reactions that occur in the body.

For example when you get wounded, there are a lot of things happening that the body does to protect you. But the major trouble maker is cortisol released from adrenal glands when we perceive stress. It goes into the blood to raise blood sugar so muscles have more fuel. Adrenaline also increases to make the heart beat faster, and it also raises blood pressure by constricting arteries and interacting with kidneys to save salt and water. So this is what the protective system does automatically.

They have found that this same process is also triggered by negative emotion like anger and depression. Makes you wonder what is happening when you watch a horrible movie, doesn't it? This then creates a feedback loop of stress, cortisol, bad mood, more stress, and more cortisol feeding on itself. This can rise to levels that can reach a burnout condition. To add to this mayhem, cortisol also inhibits memory, clarity, and higher functions of the brain.

The research has also proved that another hormone called DHEA is produced by the adrenals that actually counteracts the effects of cortisol. It, they point out, is produced by positive emotions of love, compassion, reverence, gratitude, and joy. But this hormone declines with age. So increasing stress with age can make a stress button get stuck in the on position for good. So watch nice positive movies!

What they point out is the obvious conclusion; things like finances, job, conflict, and anxiety problems are stress triggers that accumulate on an ongoing basis and the body gets used to a new threshold. Then you come home and watch the bad news, and a stress filled movie to add to the problems. If this happens, and the cortisol and adrenaline are stuck in on positions, you get heart disease, raised blood sugar, hypertension, high cholesterol, obesity, arterial diseases, and diabetes over time. What happens is the body functions get set to a new higher threshold as the body simply believes this is where it should be.

They suggest you need to reset the thermostat down to a normal level again because the stress can become an addiction. What they have found is that a diet of positive feelings resolves this problem and this is how you can reset the thermostat. The heart is where you feel strong emotion because it is the core of emotion so you need to carefully manage this emotion.

What is being stated here is that the real emotional control center is the heart brain, not the brain. Sure the old brain up top has responsibilities, but it ain't the real boss! So these sayings like heartfelt emotion, heartbroken, put your heart into it, the heart of the matter, heart to heart, and from the bottom of my heart are not just sayings. They are reflecting a real process from the heart center. These are of course, the ancient energy centers called chakras including the heart's own field of subtle energies.

Heart Rate Variability And Coherence

Heart Rate Variability or HRV defines how much the beats per minute change over a period of time, so one minute you can be at 60, and then suddenly you go to 90, then 130, then 70. That is what they called chaotic, whereas slow smooth changes occurring over the time period are called coherent. The research points to the source of the heartbeat or pacemaker being in the heart, and messages that may regulate speed come via the nervous system from the brain, but the heart beat is independent of the brain. So it can be influenced by the brain when the brain needs to vary the heart rate in order to meet perceived demands, but the true control center is the heart. They state that signals go from the heart to the survival centre in hindbrain where blood pressure, heart rate, and respiratory rate are controlled. This part analyses the information and makes changes.

They found that emotional states affect HRV. When stress hits or negative emotions occur, HRV goes chaotic like an earthquake graph. But a coherent HRV is created by deep sleep or sincere positive emotions. This also creates improved clarity, mood, and communications.

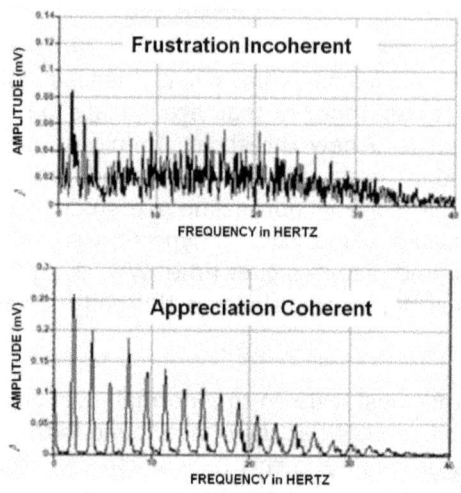

These signals also affect feelings and the emotional memory center in the midbrain called an amygdala. The cells here synchronize to the pacemaker in the heart. If HRV is chaotic, it matches that to a library of negative emotional experiences and automatically recalls what negative feelings correlate. Brain waves in the cortex are also affected by powerful chaotic heart signals coloring thinking and perception, altering top level functions like calculation, planning, creativity, and communications – all from the big signal generator below in the heart.

HeartMath notes that we must listen to the heart, not the ego which can create false fears and demands. We need to shift emotions and change HRV by reversing stress. Events can create an auto response which equals HRV in chaotic mode. This then goes to the brain to produce anxiety, panic, and anger. But when signals from the heart are coherent, the brain's three parts synchronize to create cortical facilitation of improved function. It is called heart intelligence.

In this way they have proven that there is a Brain-Heart talk going on through the ANS nervous system. The research clearly shows that by controlling thoughts and subtle emotions, we influence the balance and activity of ANS, and efficient brain function. This means we have a direct means of controlling the ANS (Autonomic Nervous System) – digestive, cardiovascular, immune and hormonal systems. When we do this, they say a process of entrainment happens. This is when coherence occurs between multiple oscillating systems and they work at their optimum in harmony. It means the subtle energy systems of the body go into a coherent state.

The key, they conclude, is to create the heart-head entrainment that is brought about by appreciation and love. This creates a strengthening of all of these communications as they get synchronized.

Not surprising is they also report that from their findings, it is important to lock into positive emotional memories and rewrite your pathways. They have found that a healthy strategy is to shift attention by breathing slowly, then activating genuine positive feelings held for 5-15 minutes. If such feelings are created before sleep, they can be sent to others. They have found these heart signals are picked up by others.

In summary, the research concludes something quite staggering. The heart is not only the source of emotion, courage and wisdom, it has its own brain that communicates with and influences the cranial brain through the nervous system, hormonal system, and other pathways that affect the quality of life. The heart and nervous system *do not* follow brain's direction like everyone believed. The heart has its own brain that can sense, remember, learn, feel, and process information independently.

They state that we do not want any negative emotions to create disorder. We want real positive emotions to increase mental clarity, creativity, balance, and effectiveness. The heart is obviously the most powerful generator of rhythmic information patterns in the body.

There is one more interesting thing they talk about. When people touch or are in proximity of each other, one person's heart beat signal is registered in the other's brainwaves. Have you ever felt uneasy about somebody just being in their presence? They also found that music affects emotion and mood states. They found Classical is good and Rock produces increased hostility.

HeartMath research is telling us we must set a life style that tunes the brain. The heart is what sends the signal to the brain, and the mechanism to regulate coherence is human feeling. This causes a field around the heart and that's where we really need to focus. A high degree of coherence is when this is done by quality of feeling between heart and brain. Words like love and gratitude, and emotions like compassion plus forgiveness are needed to create the best coherence for optimum chemistry.

They emphatically state that anger causes erratic signals and chemicals to be released that are not good. The heart is not just a physical pump that keeps the circulation going. It has subtle energy counterparts reflecting nonphysical things happening in that piece of physical machinery – these are the many subtle forces at work.

Get Into Alpha Permanently!

What comes out loud and clear is that Alpha waves of the brain (like those produced in meditation) is the place to be. These are synchronized to the cardiac cycle. Hence they suggest meditation, yoga, and prayer help create this coherence. They say when stress or negative things hit, first focus and neutralize – time out. Now we can't be in meditative oblivion all the time but Alpha is the cool place to be. Shift attention to heart area away from noise and stress. Stop the emotion or thought. They say breathe slowly by counting 5 in and out. Feel the breath through the heart in a steady rhythm while you disengage thoughts and feeling. Then engage a positive feeling emotion by thinking back to a positive situation of love and care. This coherent pattern overrides negative emotional programs.

Beta brain waves as you learned are faster (13-40 cycles per second) and somewhat more chaotic than the Alpha waves. When you're in dreaming sleep or deep meditation, you are in the theta state – or, your brain waves are oscillating at 4-7 cycles per second. And when you're in very deep dreamless sleep, you are in delta, which is 0-4 cycles per second. Each brain wave state corresponds to a different state of consciousness – there is no one "perfect" brain wave state. A fun metaphor for this is comparing your brain to a car with four gears. First gear (delta) is sloooooow. You're moving but barely plugging along. As you become more conscious, you shift into second gear and enter the deep meditation/dreaming sleep state of theta. Alpha is third, where you are still moving slowly – relaxed, enjoying the scenery – but you are moving at a reasonable speed and the miles are ticking away. Beta is fast (highway speed) at fourth gear. Great fun, and it gets you from here to there quickly, but it's also potentially dangerous.

The trouble starts when we're running our car in the wrong gear. For example: if you've ever been in deep, deep sleep and the alarm starts screaming that it's time to wake up, you don't jump out of bed all alert and ready to rock-n-roll. You are groggy, disoriented, and you have to force yourself into alertness. Usually, this is accompanied by stress of having to get to work on time and you start thinking about the day ahead, and all the unwanted stuff that you'll have to deal with shifting your brain from first to fourth too quickly. You know what this feels like: you're sluggish and tired, yet you're forcing your brain into hyperdrive because you have STUFF TO DO. So, being in any given brain wave state is great and useful – except when you need to be in a different state of consciousness. If you can't sleep, your brain is not in theta or delta, but spiking up into beta (which is why you can have stressful thoughts at night). If you can't focus, your brain may be stuck in beta with many thoughts and, you are not in Alpha. You can't control your emotions or think your way out of a complex situation if you are not in Alpha. If you can learn to direct your brain to enter a specific state of consciousness when you need it, your life will improve! Think about complex problem-solving, for example. Most of the time, your waking hours are predominantly spent in the beta state.

Being In The Heart Brain

So the bottom line is this: The focus is becoming present and centered in the heart mind - in Alpha every moment as the Higher Self resides in the present (now) while the Lower Self (past/future)resides in the Beta brain.

As we have said before, the key is in meditation, yoga, and prayer. When stress or negative things hit, first focus and neutralize – time out. As said before and this bears repeating. Shift attention to the heart area away from noise and stress. Stop the emotion or thought. Count 5 in and 5 out to feel the breath through the heart in a steady rhythm while you disengage thoughts and feeling. Then engage a positive feeling emotion by thinking back to a positive situation of love and care. This coherent pattern overrides negative emotional programs. This is Alpha where you can think more clearly. They say a positive feeling is not a thought process. You want to be genuine. Learn an inventory of these and your awareness/control increases so the threshold is reset.

MD Larry Dossey says prayer is good medicine. He reviewed 60 scientific cases to show prayer has a measurable impact on healing regardless of religion but without love and compassion it had little effect. *"Have a good heart"* says Buddhism, Larry says it means *"care deeply without hidden agenda"*. The heart is the mind's Powerhouse – the center of wisdom, mediation between Heaven and Earth.

Science admits that by focusing attention on the heart, we increase synchronicity between heart and brain to calm the nervous system and deactivate stress response so the body conserves energy for growth. Love feelings generate measurable heart field coherence; negative emotions create incoherence and disharmony.

This brings another common practice which has to do with going inside, or being present to the heart. Many meditation methods take you into that altered state, as does hypnosis. It is to bypass the conscious mind that is hooked to the brain. What is more important in our assessment is to get into this state by becoming present to the heart brain, and that has to be done in a state of peace and love to open the portals. It is a simple practice but places your attention away from the higher interfering brainwaves of consciousness into the lower state and centering your attention to the heart energetic center. Here is the balance point of above to below, the center of the toroid, and the point of creation in the quantum soup of love - the point of singularity. This is a common process in the healing steps we have looked at.

The process can be as simple as this:

Settle your body in an upright and seated posture. Bring your focus to the natural flow of your breath as it enters and leaves your body. Just watch your breath as your mind settles. Now bring your attention and intent to enter into the heart space in the center of your chest. And just breathe in and out of this space. As you do so, with each in-breathe feel your heart gently opening and softening; with each out-breathe release any tension or resistance.

As you do this, silently repeat, *"My heart is opening and softening."* You may experience great joy or even sadness. Let the feelings come and go, while you just keep breathing into your heart space. Stay here as long as you wish. When you are ready, take a deep breath and let it go.

The Love Center

When you fall in love, you feel your heart flutter, beat loudly or leap for joy; when you're rejected, your heart breaks. You are called heartless or cold-hearted when you show no care or love... and big-hearted when you extend your concern to others. You *"take things to heart"* or *"talk heart-to-heart"* about deeply personal issues. You love someone *"from the bottom of your heart"* but are *"half-hearted"* about something when you're emotionally uninvolved. You experience your heart as the center of your feelings, as seen on Valentine's Day when love-filled hearts abound. You know this instinctively, as you always physically point to your heart when you say "I" or want to express your deeper feelings.

Yet as we have pointed out, your heart is so much more than a vessel for romance. It has been described as the king, with the mind as the king's adviser. When faced with a decision, the king may ask his advisers for advice, may even send him out into the world to gather information, but ultimately it is the king that makes the final decision. Even though the advisers do not always agree with the king's decision, the king is invariably right, because the king's view not only sees the bigger picture but is also aware of the needs of others.

Note how the state of coherence comes up again, like it needs to be in a coherent state to communicate, or more significantly ALLOW communications out and in! Remember the need for a feeling of love emotion with prayer or it does not allow miracles to work! In the same way, when faced with a decision or conflict, your mind may come up with numerous, different and quite logical reasons why you should act as it advises, but if you listen to and trust your heart—however illogical or irrational it may seem—it is usually right and you are happier as a result.

There is great brilliance and beauty inherent within the mind, because it is capable of understanding the most intricate scientific and mathematical theories and can make complicated corporate decisions. Yet the same mind can get caught up in trivia and nonsense, becoming upset or even unglued over a seemingly harmless remark. It runs your life, pushing and pulling you in all directions, from attraction to repulsion, creating endless dramas in acting out your insecurities and fears, because it is not in touch with your deeper feelings. Living inside your head all the time is actually not much fun!

While the mind is the content of who you are, your heart is your essence. Your true heart is not subject to chaos or limited by pain, fear and neuroses, but is joyful, creative and loving. But it will "ache" as a red flag when something is not right. That is the heart intelligence telling you to smarten up. Some believe the heart can be too uncertain and even misguided, but that is the head talking! It is actually a source of great richness, and this wealth is one that cannot be squandered or lost. It is the core, the essence of your being, a reservoir of joy, powerful love and infinite compassion that lies within you. But you have to listen to these "aches".

When you honor the wisdom in your heart, then you act from this core of your being. You experience it in those moments when your needs and worries quietly dissolve and confusion or pain no longer dominates. Tears may spontaneously arise and there is a sensation of great warmth and peace. It is the letting go of fear and the need to control. Try a meditation of your own to get more deeply in touch with this loving center of your being.

Leonard Laskow who wrote *"Heal with Love"* a well known healer once said when he dealt with a cancer patient: *"I placed my hands on the sides of his chest, visualized a radiant ball of light from the head to heart, down my arms and thru my hands."*

He did tests with three Petri dishes of tumor cells in a state of healing consciousness. A non healer also held 3 dishes. He sought to activate a natural force of coherence in the universe. The most effective process that diminished cancer growth by 39% was his statement:

"Return to the natural order and harmony of the normal cell line."

When he added imagery the effect doubled from a diminished growth of 39 to 80%. He states: *"We should apologize to cells and thank them."*

Laskow offers his wisdom in four simple steps:

Inform yourself about what has already materialized. Telling the truth is the first step toward responsibility.
Conform to the condition by loving it rather than creating separation. Resonating with the form allows us more influence over its organization.
Unform the condition by releasing it. It is the Observers intent that converts particulate matter to its wave form and wave back to matter.
Reform the released energy to conform to our purpose and desire. This is the letting go where we send our information into the universe without attachment.

Even when releasing the diseased condition there is a connection. Not separation. *"When you accept and love the parts of yourself you want to reject or change, you create the opportunity to discover the positive life force behind them."* We make ourselves at One.

In quantum, love is the glue that holds things together. It is the universal pattern of resonant energy. We can love a cancer cell to death!

The heart is the minds Powerhouse –center of wisdom, mediation between Heaven and Earth.

The **John and Beatrice Lacey** research is relevant: They confirm that the heart does not obey brain messages. It interprets neural signals and bases response on individual's current emotional status. It employs its own logic. The heart has more to do with perception and behavioral reactions. The impact of love is biochemically measureable through Coherent Heart intelligence. Increased coherence gives a cascade of neural and biochemical events that affect virtually every organ in the body. It leads to more intelligence by reducing activity of sympathetic nervous system in fight or flight. It leads to increasing growth of parasympathetic nervous system as it reduces production of the stress hormone cortisol.

One of the most dramatic examples of how the power of love and intention can affect the material world is the work done **Dr. Emoto.** By looking at crystals of different water, he detected that they were affected by human emotion, words and thought. They were typically six-pointed crystals but were distorted or pretty depending on the negative or positive energy projected on the water.

He did it by freezing water. He reports that in order to obtain examples of ice crystals, many samples are required to be photographed under as stable conditions as possible. Therefore, dishes are placed in a freezer for three hours at a temperature of -25C. When they are taken out, ice grains have formed with their center rolled up due to surface tension. These grains are very tiny. Water expands when frozen and ice crystals form at the tip of the water sample. Light is directed on each grain of ice and observed through a dark field electron-microscope in a room at a temperature of -5C. Under the magnification of 100 to 200 times, the ice crystals can be observed as the ice begins to melt away. If things go well, a crystal starts to form as the temperature rises and the ice begins to melt. Taking only one to two minutes, it opens up like a flower blooming. So the crystals reveal a specific good or bad property of the water.

He points out there is a message from water that has the potential to transform our world view. Water teaches us the delicacy of the human condition and shows the impact that love and gratitude can have on the world. I was fascinated to read about water labeled *Thank you* and *Idiot*. These words changed the properties to make them clear or yellow. I was interested to note he said that this process works best with children who don't have doubts. They have no lack of purity.

He concludes that energy is vibration. Atoms vibrate in the nucleus and vibrations in the organic world need help to continue life. When we meditate, gaps open in between vibrations of our thoughts and allow short waves of Creation to sneak in. Here the shorter frequency energy is purer and goes farther. This state allows contact with the Creator and cosmic information. That is what praying and meditating is all about. We have limitations on the range of sounds so to transmit and receive beyond that limit we need water which circulates around the planet and in us. We entrust information to it by resonance. He showed that water can change by praying remotely with a response happening in as fast as five minutes. He tested this with a group of 500 people in what he calls Hados. These are people tuned to the world of senses and images. He says many experiments show the same results. If you say 'Water, we love you, Water we thank you, Water we respect you', you are purifying it. No life can exist without water as it delivers vibrations to 50 trillion cells. Each cell has a unique vibration and role. Junk food disturbs the vitality of cells. You need to feel grateful for your existence, respect and like yourself first. Then you are able to properly feel the same about others. You can not give off good vibes if you have a distorted image of your substances.

So it follows that if you say the same thing to yourself, like I love you, I respect you, I trust you, then you are also purifying all the water in you. He points out we are 70% water, like the planet. So pray anytime, and recall feelings of thanks to water. Close your eyes and put your hands together. Putting your hands together reinforces the energy. When you do this the hands connect to create clear circulation of energy. It allows emotional energy to be transmitted purely.

We are beginning to see here the importance of coherence in the heart. As we mentioned earlier, the process of coherence creates a cascade of neural and biochemical events that affect virtually every organ in the body to improve clarity, mood, and communications. If not it also creates chaos in the mind and body. We are also seeing how this huge heart field has attraction and influencing properties that affect others. We need to be in a coherent state to communicate, or more significantly ALLOW communications out and in! Remember the need for a feeling of love emotion with prayer or it does not allow miracles to work! This can only be done in a field of love to turn the "current" on and be in the heart-brain as opposed to the head-brain. Also we see that heart emotions contribute heavily to stress on the brain and the stress can be either real or imagined. This is why you are told by many Gurus that when releasing the diseased condition there is a connection. Not separation. *"When you accept and love the parts of yourself you want to reject or change, you create the opportunity to discover the positive life force behind them."* We make ourselves at One. So love is the glue that holds things together. It is the universal pattern of resonant energy. We can love a cancer cell to death!

So we are now going to make a new statement because we want to get better access to the Divine Programmer that sits outside the box. Here is the prime residence of your Higher energetic Self and its counterpart in the body – the energetic heart mind. The Lower Self and ego occupy the box as the brain mind at the top. It is concerned with the past and future for survival and lives in beta consciousness. The Higher Self occupies the heart mind and is not concerned with time at all as it is focused on the present moment looking for positive emotions to be generated. It lives in the state of Alpha or lower. The power of emotion and all those energies of love, gratitude, forgiveness, compassion, joy, and bliss are very strong program writers that simply bypass the head brain to the subconscious.

So don't think that it is just your conscious brain mind that you have to train into new programs, it is that unconscious heart brain that really rules the roost. The real power is in emotion and if it is equally charged with negative power from fear, hate, conflict, it is equally effective in the program conditioning process like in severe trauma. But those are not the good programs to occupy your life habits and life attractions.

In the next chapters we are going to move to a series of researchers, healers and processes that will begin to paint a new picture of how we create and manipulate our physical reality. Of importance here is that we will take you outside of the box and not speculate on metascience. We will use many cases and clinical evidence that assist us in making us change our minds about what is possible once we take belief, acceptance and surrender outside the box limits of the norm.

5

THE HYPNOSIS PORTAL TO SUBCONSCIOUS

"The fastest way to suggest something new to the subconscious mind is to use Hypnosis to be like a preschool kid again and enter a hypnotic state, where your mind is in THETA."

Aly McDonald   Ed Rychkun

> **With hypnosis I believe I can Become a preschool kid again**

Hypnosis As The Subconscious Mind Doorway

In our first book **The Divine Programmer: Creating Miracles**, we used the example of **Andy Tomlinson** and the world wide network **Life Regression Academy** to exemplify how trained people probe deep into the subconscious memories using induced hypnosis. Once the issue is found, you in your current life are then able to understand what it is, why it was caused, what it resulted in, and simply re-write the history of it into a new possibility—with the mind. That history is available and the record of the event, the perceptions, acts and emotions are all there as a Cause of something that may be occurring in a subsequent life as an Effect. And that re-write of the Cause not only affects current behavior, it affects your physiology. As conduits to a Divine Programmer, these people effectively delete and re-write the application's program from subconscious that controls the brain's behavior.

Our interest here is to bring the process of hypnosis into your world of awareness; to understand it, learn it, and use it as part of the proactive reality changing process. As we age, we create reality more and more on autopilot with the beliefs of a larger consciousness governing our creativity outside this box becoming less and less plausible. We want to explore the process of hypnosis that is a prevalent tool in getting people outside the box and in getting in direct communication with the Divine Programmer; and getting access to this previous life information.

We have learned that Delta and Theta brain wave states are below consciousness which is where we see hypnotherapists use to create new behaviors. We have seen that kids up until the age of 6 are in this hypnotic like state where perceptions are downloaded without discrimination; where the filtering of analytic self-conscious mind does not yet fully exist. What we want to provide here is a better view of this common process and to illustrate the process as a self controlled way to get into the place where the subconscious operating system exists. Hypnosis takes one through that filter of the box consciousness of the self conscious beta mind.

As we have pointed out from research and studies, kids in the early ages of 2-6 are in a trance-like state called hypnogogic having a very high suggestibility to outside environment and perception. It is very high because in these years, the brain is working hard to develop the physical and external environment programs to optimize survival. This is also typically where meditation techniques take you. As grownups with the Beta and high Alpha resident, it is particularly important to find ways that get the mind totally clear of the conscious world and enter the domain of Theta; essentially be like a kid that has not really developed this so called advantage of rational thought and acquired the ego self. From studies it has been determined that the use of hypnosis can take you into this deeper altered state to raise the degree of suggestibility.

It is for this reason that induced hypnosis is common to the therapy of Past Life and Between Life Regressions. Why? Because in most cases it does get to that stage where suggestibility is high and this is where we see the greatest possibility of success in addressing issues caused by prior traumas. The process of suggesting to the subconscious that the original Cause may be brought into awareness and understood in order to change the Effect now becomes the purpose of the process. Since this is the same place that we want to create changes in our internal and external reality, the hypnosis process would improve our chances of success.

Before we go there, let us bring back into your awareness what the mind consists of. It can be divided into three systems: the conscious mind, the subconscious mind, and the unconscious mind.

The conscious mind is your awareness at the present moment. You are aware of something on the outside as well as some specific mental functions happening on the inside. For example, you are aware of your environment, your breathing, or the chair that you are sitting on. This has been scientifically identified as the Alpha and Beta frequency domain.

The subconscious mind or **the preconscious mind** consists of accessible information. You can become aware of this information once you direct your attention to it. Think of this as memory recall. You walk down the street to your house without consciously needing to be alert to your surroundings. You can talk on the cell phone and still arrive home safely. You can easily bring to consciousness the subconscious information about the path to your home. You can also easily remember phone numbers that you frequently use. It is possible that some of what might be perceived to be unconscious becomes subconscious, and then conscious (e.g. a long-forgotten childhood memory suddenly emerges after decades). We can assume that some unconscious memories need a strong, specific trigger to bring them to consciousness; whereas, a subconscious memory can be brought to consciousness more easily. This has been scientifically identified as the Theta frequency domain.

The unconscious mind, consisting of the primitive, instinctual wishes as well as the information that we cannot access. Although our behaviors might indicate the unconscious forces that drive them, we don't have easy access to the information stored in the unconscious mind. During our childhood, we acquired countless memories and experiences that formed who we are today. However, we cannot recall most of those memories. They are unconscious forces (beliefs, patterns, subjective maps of reality) that drive our behaviors. This has been scientifically identified as the Delta frequency domain.

It is the hypnotic state that gets you closer to the subconscious which appears to "direct" the conscious. There is a lot of buzz these days that tells us that hypnosis actually works. The many have been conditioned to believe hypnosis is just silly entertainment despite the wake of millions of people and hypnotherapists who have helped so many with serious issues. We are now seeing many are coming forward despite criticism to admit there is much more to this state than we have ever considered.

According to David Spiegel, from Stanford University, one of America's leading psychiatrists, he told the prestigious American Association for the Advancement of Science that he had scanned the brains of volunteers who were told they were looking at colored objects when, in fact, they were black and white. A scan showing areas of the brain used to register color highlighted increased blood flow, indicating that the volunteers genuinely "saw" colors, as they had been told they would. *"This is scientific evidence that something happens in the brain when people are hypnotized that doesn't happen ordinarily,"* Mr. Spiegel told delegates. He added that there were *"tremendous medical implications"* and envisaged people being able to manage their own pain and anxiety.

The fact remains that many have been cured of fears and phobias and were genuinely cured. Much research confirms what professional hypnotists have been successfully using the technique for medical purposes, have known all along - hypnotism has a genuine effect on the functioning of the mind, as well as the body.

Does Hypnosis Work? How?

Paul McKenna is considered the number one hypnotherapist in the world. **McKenna-Breen** is the largest hypnotism training centre in the world where endless examples and studies are available. We are not here to convince you that it works because if you don't want to believe it, you won't. What you will find is that it all points to the same conclusion; *hypnosis works by communicating with the subconscious and unconscious mind.*

Conscious and unconscious are really just shorthand terms to describe the general characteristics of the human mind. The "conscious mind" is the bit where we tend to "live" - the bit you might think of as "you". If there's a little voice reading these words out loud in your head, that's the conscious mind talking. The unconscious with the upper band as subconscious mind is everything else!

As you know, the subconscious controls all of the autonomic processes that you don't have to think about - the heart rate, the blood pressure, tissue growth, cell regeneration, the immune system and so on. It's where our thoughts, memories and accumulated experience reside. It controls our emotions, our habits and our responses to the world.

In many ways, it creates that world for us. The subconscious mind handles about two million bits of sensory information every single second. The conscious mind deals with about seven. That means that the reality you're actually aware of from moment to moment has been brought to your conscious attention by the unconscious, choosing seven bits which it thinks are important from the two million it's just processed.

The conscious mind as we have stated is more logical, critical and analytical - it's constantly making value judgments. If somebody was to say to you *"you really should give up smoking, you know, it's terribly bad for you"*, you're highly unlikely to become a non-smoker on the spot. You're more likely to come up with a dozen, rational sounding reasons as to why you should carry on smoking, or you might tell them to shove off and mind their own business. It is because the body has become addicted and it is running the conscious mind. Even if you do consciously accept that you should give up smoking, it's not the conscious part of the mind that's keeping the habit in place. In order to quit, you have to go to a new repetitive process to create a new habit to change or use a process like hypnosis to talk directly to the subconscious. Through sheer repetition, the subconscious mind becomes convinced that smoking is serving a vital purpose - that it's *"good"* for you in some way.

The subconscious part of the mind is quite literal and tends to take things personally; relating any information it receives to you as an individual. Hypnosis works by bypassing the critical conscious mind (usually through relaxation or linguistic techniques), and speaking directly to the subconscious in a language which it understands - pattern, association and metaphor. We now know that we can add another language to this list, namely emotion that gets the subconscious off its butt immediately. The subconscious mind is basically in charge. The vast majority of things that we do are under the domain of the unconscious and subconscious, which we can be grateful for - if you had to consciously think about every single thing you did, you wouldn't do anything. However, it can lead us astray. Most problems are things that we've learned how to solve at an unconscious level. We've just learned how to solve them in an unhelpful way.

Hypnosis works by updating the subconscious mind with new and more helpful information, like reprogramming a computer. It can be used to change associations, so that cigarettes, for instance, are no longer seen as "little friends", and are more realistically regarded as "toxic killers". It can also be used to mentally rehearse better ways of going about things, such as being able to deal with stressful situations without having to light up. What is happening is that the neuron networks that have created an addiction in the body cravings are re-fired and rewired to eliminate the problem.

Since the subconscious mind controls our autonomic bodily processes, physical change can also be achieved through hypnosis. Pain control is a very good example. The mind alters our awareness of pain all the time. Professional chefs, for instance, get burnt on a regular basis, but rarely notice it unless it's particularly severe. You'll have experienced this yourself if you've ever discovered a cut or a bruise and wondered how it got there. Physical events are still occurring, but the subconscious has relegated them to the 2 million bits of sensory information you are not aware of every single second. Hypnosis can therefore be used to amplify that same response and apply it to a specific situation, such as the control of headaches.

Hypnosis works, then, by shaping our perception of reality by dealing directly with the subconscious mind, the seat of most of our problems, and most of our solutions.

Process Of Self-hypnosis

Have you ever seen old horror films and television programs that portray hypnosis as a frightening instrument of mind control where unscrupulous villains enslave the will of helpless victims? Perhaps you have seen stage shows where a hypnotist *seems* to be able to use their "hypnotic powers" to *make* people do and say things that they would never do or say under normal conditions. If so, it is not surprising that hypnosis may seem just a little bit wacky, not unlike other seemingly mystical and unexplainable phenomena. Well, of course that is the belief box again. This is unfortunate because hypnosis is, in fact, a serious therapeutic tool that can help people overcome many psychological, emotional and even some physical problems.

In this light of new awareness, hypnosis is not mind control, brain-washing, sleep, unconsciousness, or a mystical experience. When in hypnosis a person is aware, in control, in a natural and harmless state and able to come out of hypnosis when she/he wishes to.

The state of hypnosis can best be described as a state of highly focused attention with heightened suggestibility. Hypnosis is sometimes but not always accompanied by relaxation. When a person such as a therapist induces hypnosis in another, it is called hetero hypnosis, often referred to as hypnotherapy. When hypnosis is self-induced it is called autohypnosis and is often referred to as self-hypnosis. The word hypnosis comes from the Greek word "hypnos" which means sleep. It is an abbreviation of the term neuro-hypnotism which means sleep of the nervous system.

Self-hypnosis is often used to modify behavior, emotions and attitudes. For instance, many people use self-hypnosis to help deal with the problems of everyday living. There are thousands of clinical cases that confirm self-hypnosis can boost confidence and even help people develop new skills. A great stress and anxiety reliever, it can also be used to help overcome habits such as smoking and overeating. Sports men and women can enhance their athletic performance with self-hypnosis, and people suffering from physical pain or stress-related illnesses also find it helpful.

So let us look more closely at a fairly simple method of self-hypnosis. This technique is called *eye fixation self-hypnosis* and is one of the most popular and effective forms of self-hypnosis ever developed. We will start by using it as a method to help you relax. After you have practiced this a number of times you will add hypnotic suggestions and imagery. Reduce distractions by going into a room where you are unlikely to be disturbed and turning off your phone, television, computer, etc. This is your time. You are going to focus on your goal of self-hypnosis and nothing else.

1. Sit in a comfortable chair with your legs and feet uncrossed.
Avoid eating a large meal just before so you don't feel bloated or uncomfortable. Unless you wish to nod off, sit in a chair, as lying down on a bed will likely induce sleep. You may also wish to loosen tight clothing and take off your shoes. If you wear contact lenses, it is advisable to remove them. Keep your legs and feet uncrossed.

2. Look up at the ceiling and take in a deep breath.
Without straining your neck or tilting your head too far back pick a point on the ceiling and fix your gaze on that point. While you keep your eyes fixed on that point take in a deep breath and hold it for a moment and then breathe out. Silently repeat the suggestion *"My eyes are tired and heavy and I want to SLEEP NOW"*. Repeat this process to yourself another couple of times and, if your eyes have not already done so, let them close and relax in a normal closed position. It is important when saying the suggestion that you say it to yourself as if you mean it, for example in a gentle, soothing but convincing manner.

3. Let your body relax.
Allow your body to become loose and limp in the chair just like a rag doll. Then slowly and with intention, silently countdown from 5 to 0. Tell yourself that with each and every count you're becoming more and more relaxed. Stay in this relaxed state for a number of minutes while focusing on your breathing. Notice the rising and falling of your diaphragm and chest. Be aware of how relaxed your body is becoming without you even having to *try* and relax it. In fact, the less you try, the more relaxed you become.

4. Linger in this space.
For the purpose of this exercise, you want to feel this void of space, of peace and silence. It is the altered state of well being. This is where you instigate

your suggestions. Once you are comfortable with this process you can follow the processes in the next sections on Hypnotic Suggestion Rules and Imagery in Hypnosis.

5. When ready, come back to the room by counting up from 1 to 5.
Tell yourself that you are becoming aware of your surroundings and at the count of five you will open your eyes. Count up from one to five in a lively, energetic manner. At the count of five, open your eyes and stretch your arms and legs.

Repeat this technique three or four times and notice how each time you reach a deeper level of relaxation. It is the same process as meditation. If you find you do not relax as much as you would like, do not force it. There is a learning curve involved so resolve to practice self-hypnosis on a regular basis. Sometimes people will feel a little spaced out or drowsy after they come out of the hypnosis. This is similar to awaking from an afternoon nap, is harmless and passes after a few moments.

How To Set Your Self-Hypnosis Goals

Self-hypnosis should always have specific goals to achieve by its engagement. Remember, you are going into the subconscious operating system to suggest a new program so here are some guidelines:

1. Give achieving your goals a high priority. Plan to use self-hypnosis on a daily basis and you will start to see results.

2. Write your goals down on paper. Clarify what you want to work on and be specific. Make sure you set goals that are achievable. If they are long-term goals, it may be helpful to break them down into manageable steps.

3. Formulate your hypnotic suggestions and write them down. Write out a number of suggestions for the goal you are working on. Follow the rules of post-hypnotic suggestions. You may even want to write your own script (see the example further down) and record them to follow without analysis.

4. Decide on the imagery you plan to use. If your aim is to relax, picture a pleasant scene like a beach or a park on a warm summer's day. You want to describe the emotions and feeling that would be experienced.

5. If you fail to achieve a goal, do not give yourself a hard time. Remember, failing to achieve a goal does not mean you are a failure. It may be that you need to approach the goal in a different way or perhaps you need to be persistent, clearer and feel the emotions more strongly.

Hypnotic Suggestions And Their Rules

Have you ever experienced the frustration of having a name on the tip of your tongue? The harder you try to remember the name, the harder it is to recall. Then when you relax the name comes back to you. Sometimes, when we try too hard, we block ourselves from achieving our goals. The attitude you take towards self-hypnosis will determine how easily you learn it. Don't try too hard or set unrealistic goals at first – keep it simple and clear at first. Relax and take your time. Accept the pace at which you achieve results, however small they may at first seem. Believe in yourself and you will go on to achieve the success you desire.

As previously mentioned, hypnosis is a state of heightened suggestibility. Giving yourself suggestions when in hypnosis will enable an action or other response to take place after the hypnotic experience has occurred. These forms of suggestion are called post-hypnotic suggestions and will help you to achieve your goals. Over the years, hypnotherapists have developed rules of suggestion. These are guidelines that will enable you to achieve maximum success with the suggestions you give yourself. What follows is a summary of these rules.

1. Say it as if you mean it.
Have you ever seen an actor mumbling his lines on stage, speaking in a quiet meek voice? The result is a performance that's not very convincing. Unlike acting, hypnotic suggestions are repeated silently. However, you need to repeat the suggestions as though you mean what you say. Be reassuring, positive and confident.

2. Suggestions need to be phrased positively in the present tense.
Most of us will react more favorably to a positively worded suggestion than a negative one. Which request would you rather hear: *"Do not leave that lying on the floor"* or *"Would you mind picking that up?"* Suggestions are far more effective when you mention what you wish to move towards, rather than what you are moving away from. For example: *"I am calm"* is better than *"I am not anxious"*. *"I stop smoking with ease"* is better than *"I will try to stop smoking"* as the word *try* implies difficulty and struggle. Your suggestions are best phrased in the present tense, as though they are happening at this moment in time. So, *"I am relaxed on the aircraft"* is better than *"I will be*

relaxed when I am on the aircraft". Or, *"I am becoming more confident"* is better than *"I will try to be confident".*

3. Make your suggestions specific and realistic.

Your suggestions are going to be more effective if they are specific and realistic. If you wish to improve your swimming performance, it would be unrealistic to give yourself the suggestion *"I am a world-class swimmer",* unless of course you are, or are about to become, a world champion. Instead, ask yourself what specifically it is about your swimming that you wish to improve. So if you wished to improve your breaststroke, you would give yourself a realistic suggestion tailored to that specific aspect of your swimming. Structure your suggestions on changes you wish to see in yourself rather than things that are out of your control, such as external events and other people. Do not give yourself suggestions for two or three issues all at the same time. For instance, the suggestion *"I am confident that I can lose weight and stop smoking"* is probably not effective. Instead, work on one goal at a time, repeating suggestions associated with that goal. When you see some results, move on to your next goal.

4. Repetition of suggestions.

Advertisers know the value of suggestion, which is why they repeat television and radio commercials on a regular basis. One of the most important rules when practicing self-hypnosis is repetition of your suggestions. That way you drive the point home and are far more likely to affect positive change.

Imagery In Hypnosis

While giving yourself hypnotic suggestions, visualize the situation, the action and the feeling that you desire as already done. As well as picturing a desired outcome, you can utilize your sense of touch, hearing and even smell. You can create new images as well as using images from your memories and experiences. Understand that the neurological system responds to strong emotion so always bring it in.

Adding hypnotic suggestion and visualization to self-hypnosis and rehearsing positive outcomes is an important part of the process. Here you would do steps 1 to 3 and Step 4 would become:

4. Picture an image that represents a situation you wish to master and see yourself achieving your goal. Repeat to yourself three times a positive suggestion such as: *"I am confident, calm and relaxed."* Say it with conviction while picturing the image for about 30 seconds. Repeat this three

times and between times stay in hypnosis and focus on your body's relaxation.

A Self-hypnosis Script

In this example, we are going to provide a sample script designed to help you relax and cope with anxiety. Feel free to alter the imagery to fit your particular needs. For instance, instead of picturing yourself on a beach, you may prefer to imagine that you are in a park on a warm summer's day. You may also wish to change the symbolism used to address an issue you wish to work on. Feel free to record the text and play it back, or have someone read it to you.

Sitting in a comfortable place with legs and feet uncrossed, without tilting your head or straining your neck, pick a point on the ceiling and fix your gaze on that point. While you keep your eyes fixed on that point, take in a deep breath and hold it for as long as is comfortable. Then, as you breathe out, repeat the suggestion "*My eyes are tired and heavy and I want to SLEEP NOW.*" Repeat this process to yourself another couple of times and, if your eyes have not already done so, let them close and relax in a normal closed position.

Repeat the following script to yourself silently and with conviction:

I am now allowing my body to become loose and limp in the chair just like a rag doll.
As I continue to relax I am noticing where the comfort is in my body.
I notice a warming comfortable feeling in my hands and fingers or maybe the comfort is noticeable in another part of my body.
With every breath I take and every sound I hear, the comfort deepens.
I now count down from five to zero.
With each and every count my relaxation deepens and may even double.
Five – deeper
Four – calmer
Three – more relaxed
Two – more relaxed
One – more relaxed
Zero – deep peace and silence

I now picture myself on a golden sandy beach.
I can feel the warmth of the sand under my feet and the warmth of the sun on my body.

I can imagine that I am alone on the beach or that others are there as my relaxation continues.
I listen to the sound of the sea, the waves lapping against the shore. I feel so calm, secure and relaxed that I can stay on the beach for as long as I choose.
After several moments of lingering (soft music or silence),
I picture myself in a field on a warm summer's day.
There is not a cloud in the sky.
In the middle of this field is a hot air balloon and attached to the balloon is a basket which is weighed down on the ground with sandbags.
The hot air balloon hangs effortlessly in the sky.
I now imagine that I am placing any worries, fear or anxieties into the basket.
The more I offload my worries into the basket, the more relief I feel.
I now feel as if a great weight has been lifted from my shoulders.
I release the sandbags and watch as the balloon, along with its basket, rises into the air.
As I watch the balloon rising into the air, I feel relief.
The higher the balloon rises, the more relief I feel. The more distant the balloon becomes, the more insignificant my worries appear to be.
As I watch this balloon getting smaller in the distance, I repeat to myself three times:
I am letting go of my worries, fear and anxiety.
I am letting go of my worries, fear and anxiety.
I am letting go of my worries, fear and anxiety.

When ready, I come back to the room by counting up from one to five and opening my eyes.
One
Two
Three
Four
Five

When you practice self-hypnosis the imagery you use and the suggestions you give yourself are only limited by your imagination.

Post-Hypnotic Suggestions

Here are some post-hypnotic suggestions you can use in your self-hypnosis. Feel free to alter them to fit your particular needs.

Each and every day I am calm, secure and relaxed.

I am becoming more assertive and confident when I speak to colleagues.
Each and every day I accept myself as I am.
Each and every time I enter hypnosis I relax more deeply.
I find it easy to stop smoking.
I eat three healthy meals a day.

Recording The Script

One critical observation we have encountered in our studies is that healers and facilitators rarely solve their own health issues. It is also noteworthy that when a miracle or reality change outside the consciousness box occurs, it is through a facilitator. Although we encourage people to practice on themselves, in the beginning, it is best to have the assistance of another to lead the "mind" out of the conscious state. By engaging in the processes we have brought forward, one may find that one cannot easily disengage the conscious beta state because you are conscious of the steps, of whether it will work, and out of ease with the purpose of deep relaxation, silence and peace. This will interfere and sabotage efforts. This is what is avoided by a second party and the suggestibility is increased, there is no interference of the beta brain.

So to best improve the odds of getting into the appropriate state and following the suggestions we have outlined, it is best to have another lead you, or else prerecord the script and follow your own voice that will lead you through the process. After a while when you have become comfortable with the process and know you are achieving the right state, you can do it quickly and without help.

Hypnosis is a known way to launch the intention that takes you into the domain of the Theta brain waves and the subconscious. Over and over, we have learned that this process has become more widely accepted and used to modify unwanted behavior. It is simply because of the results. It's where the unconscious and the subconscious open up to being programmed. The Altered State through meditation attempts to get you there but it is only part of the way. Sometimes prayer and rituals and trances enter this area that gives access to the programs and then the hypnotist, the healer, the doctor talks to the Divine Programmer to submit a change in the reality. But, like in the case of the placebo, you yourself can bypass the consciousness and all these other parties to submit the change in program code.

As we dig deeper into this, we find some other big questions: Why does this work at all? How does this work? Who and what is this Divine Programmer that has the power to call upon a Higher Power to change physical and mental realities?

To get some insight into this we must investigate the state we have not yet talked about at 0 Hz which is the low end of Delta. It is called dead... well not quite, but close. This is where we can learn more about the Divine Programmer and bypassing this state of consciousness where the brain is not around to interfere at all. It is the Near Death Experience which we covered in our first book. Now it is time to explore this further.

6

THE NEAR DEATH EXPERIENCE

"It's easy to understand who and what you are; just go out of your mind and have an encounter with your true Self."

Aly McDonald

Ed Rychkun

> **A funny thing happened when I died
> I met myself on the other side**

In this chapter we are going to look at NDE's or Near Death Experiences. So far we have looked at the process of the altered state and hypnosis that attempts to get into closer resonance with the frequency of the subconscious. This process provides some success in being able to instigate new programs into subconscious without interference from the beta brain. In our first book, we also looked the various methods that attempt to get you out of the belief box so you can get a look at the other side where the Divine Programmer is, to take a more proactive approach to changing reality from outside the box. It is here that we see our Divine Programmer waiting for us to visit. And so we see many successes and we see many failures because there still seems to be a lot of intangible limits and parameters that thwart our progress in determining what is over there and who we are dealing with. What we want to do now is to take a closer look at who or what is Divine Programmer, what is reported to be on the other side. One such process involves getting **completely** out of your mortal mind.

How do you go out of your mind? We do not mean to a Nuthouse type Institution. There are many other ways to have a chat with what has for thousands of years continued to form the basis for much esoteric wisdom referred to as the Higher Self, the Soul, the Higher Being of Light and so on. These have always been believed to be the real You. Trouble is, it is not accepted in any scientific way and is simply a personal opinion.

There are many ways that people have attempted to chat to this Higher Self. And commonly those who practice deep meditation and get into Theta will tell you this higher fellow is filled with wisdom and love. Some people use the method of Astral Projection, some use Out of Body practices, some use hypnosis and we will of course cover the clinical studies related to these. But the one that does not require any assistance or inducement is the Near Death Experience. This is where, uncontrived by you or anyone else, you absolutely and totally get rid of that meddling brain and the interfering physics of reality to take a trip to the "other side", and visit your Higher Self, your Soul and your Maker. It is a process of totally "**letting go**".

Near Death Experiences are the most popular way to leave the holographic carcass behind and chat with what is commonly said to be the real you. The Near Death Experience is a bit dicey to try but because it is so common, so researched and has so much consistent evidence about the nature of the journey to the other side, it is of great benefit to look at the research. This trip has not been planned by the conscious mind and is a wonderful repository of information for us to look at. What we want to do is get a better picture of what typically happens over there, who NDE people meet, and how and why they decide to come back after being pronounced dead. So now we are going to leave the physical world behind and have a closer look at this energetic You and the process of "dying".

When you begin to investigate NDE's you may find your opinion about death much different. You will find there are millions of people dying all the time - then coming back to tell about it. And you will find many professional and medical researchers looking into this particular phenomenon. Among many other books and websites, the **Big Book of Near Death Experiences** is our focus. It is written by a timeless researcher in this subject, **P.M. Atwater** and is sure to flabbergast you. Being a clinical new breed of professional that has dropped the flaps of their belief box, she has studied thousands of cases. She has compiled her observations about people pronounced clinically dead that have returned to tell about their little vacation.

Now, you must understand that NDE's mean the person is "clinically" pronounced dead! Gone! Dead for some period of time like 15-60 minutes!

The heart is stopped and the body weighs one half to one ounce less! Yes, something left the body. This means that the cells are dying in the brain from lack of oxygen, and it is coffin time. At least that is what the medical belief box tells us.

Atwater reports there are 13 million cases of NDE's that have been recorded. Of the thousands that she has herself studied, she reports that an energy force simply leaves the body (nice to know a ghost weighs an ounce!) and floats up and away to take a little vacation. This is consciousness or spirit or Soul that has left along with the force that gives life. It separates from the physical body at this point of death and the people are completely aware of this; they see their bodies lie lifeless below.

Consciousness Is A Separate Intelligent Energy

In her research, Atwater describes how this consciousness that leaves the physical body can see, hear, think, move, communicate, float, and tell jokes, and retain senses regardless of distance from the body. In fact the senses are even better - heightened just like in the case of miracles. Everything that was ever learned, experienced, and felt - along with all of the senses (perhaps taste may be questionable unless you can get some ghost food!) are left completely intact.

It obviously had nothing to do with the brain. That brain was pronounced dead. Consciousness, which clearly includes the life giving force, leaves the body, goes on a little trip, then comes back and ta-dah, the body has life again. All the dead cells are working again. Rigamortis has no say here - the white face gets pink again, and it is wakey, wakey time!

But what about the little vacation that this consciousness takes when it leaves the body? For many it is like a little visit to an amusement park where you meet something or somebody and have a serious discussion – and usually a guided virtual tour of your life! What happens during this little excursion has been recorded independently from many different places, by different unrelated people and cases. That is why this research is so valuable as a consensus of what really happens.

Current day researcher Atwater confirms with thousands of cases what one of the foremost early researchers found out about this little trip. His name was **Raymond Moody** who did this as far back as 1975 when he published the highly controversial book **Life After Life**. In this book, he described the little vacation in detail. Moody built his study on some 150 cases of near death experiences, not a lot according to a statistician, but nevertheless relevant. He defined his cases as people who were either resuscitated after pronounced dead, had severe injuries and were close to dead, or who told others who were present what was happening as they "died". He noted that these were all disconnected and knew nothing about each other's cases. This was important because the stories would be personal and not influenced.

Now underscore that he had only 150 cases and it was done in the 70's but Atwater confirms everything from thousands of cases - as do many, many other documented cases.

The Stages Of Dying – Nearly

What is so important here is that this little trip the life force - consciousness takes - exhibits striking similarities between cases. Moody broke these down to specific stages and observations not particularly in any set order. What were they?

People had what he called ineffability - a difficulty in describing the trip with any real justice. It was unexplainable and beyond their comprehension. Then he outlined the stages. Most important they had an **Out of body experience**. After they *died* they would find themselves looking at their body, watching and hearing things as a spectator. They felt like pure consciousness that was indescribable - most called it a spiritual body - but they could not touch other bodies or material things. No one could hear or see them. They were weightless, floating, going through things like a cloud. They had projections like rounded limbs but all their senses were intact. Consciousness existed outside the body! What we would commonly call a ghost!

The first stage was **Hearing the news**. They heard the news of dying from the Doc or others around the croaked body. They saw people and events around them.

Another stage was that they had the **Feeling of peace and quiet**. They experienced wonderful feelings of comfort, peace, quiet, relief, and no pain. Exactly like the altered state requirement.

Now the next stage was the **Noise**. They had unusual auditory sensations of buzzing, ringing, and clicks.

Then there was the **Dark Tunnel**. They were pulled rapidly through a dark space, tunnel, valley, pipe, trough or some such thing in a wonderful worry free ride. Sort of like getting onto the amusement park ride.

The next stage was what he called; *"meeting others"*. They encountered other spiritual beings, people they had known before, like friends and relatives that came to greet them. They were recognizable ghosts. Everything was filled with white light and was beautiful - like a feeling of coming home. These beings had a clear body but no physical body. Moody says the type of people encountered depended on a person's background. But there was no speaking. Thoughts were communicated as a direct transfer - no language. They were totally telepathic.

At this stage he says there are typical questions that come forward telepathically like: *Are you ready to die? What have you done in your life that is sufficient?* There was a point of stressing preparation yet there was no condemnation or judgment, only total love and acceptance coming from the light.

Here is a very important common occurrence. The next stage is the **Review appearance**. This is where a bright light being presents a high speed video panorama review of life. Here the intent is only to provoke reflections. There is a rapid temporal display of memories in chronological order that occurs almost instantaneous. The images generate emotions of all participants as they flip by. The being who is conducting the interview typically asks what they have done with their life, stressing love, and pointing out things. All feeling could be felt, even other people's. No one could gage time. It is like the stories you hear about when people drown. They have their whole life flash by in a moment - instant replay of consciousness.

After the review stage, the reports reflect a **Border or limit approach**. There seemed to be some limit like a fence or border where over the line there was peace, tranquility, golden light, and joy. But the ones that come back don't go over this limit and go through the last stage. Obviously if you do not come back, that is a whole different story!

At the **Coming back** stage, some would come back spurred by some being which many said was God. They would be sent back for obligations, or pulled by relatives. Some actually felt a re-entry into the physical body.

With those that came back they inevitably had a totally changed life, just like in the miracles cases. Moody goes on to say that most times this experience created a totally new attitude in life. Some reported enhanced senses, some picked up on other's feelings better, many expressed a need to cultivate love of others, seek knowledge, became morally purified, and created new clear goals mostly in service of others. The bottom line is that their belief systems and behavior had changed dramatically. They were totally out of the usual belief boxes of their lower reality.

For most people this is so out of the box it simply is not accepted as having any credibility. Of course these are the group consciousness limitations that are doing this, as we mentioned before in a previous chapter. But in historical esoteric wisdom, this dying process is not anything new. Moody makes a parallel to the works of Plato, the Bible, and the Tibetan Book of the Dead. He says they contain a description of the steps of the Soul after physical death. They are exactly the same. First, the Soul departs the body and enters a swoon and a void where consciousness still exists. The Soul may hear alarming noises and it enters an envelope of gray misty illumination. There is a surprise of the Soul to see itself outside of body, but then hears relatives and friends mourning over the body. There is a feeling of regret and it wonders where it should go. It is a shining body of no material substance with intensified senses. The Soul may then meet other beings and sees clear white light. There are feelings of immense peace and contentment as a mirror of the entire life of all deeds good and bad are reflected.

When people go through this they inevitably become conscious of a Life Force (whatever you want to call it matters not - Universal consciousness or the mind of God). Once you know this and really believe it, and it is very hard not to when you yourself have experienced it, it is impossible to worry about fear and death.

This is something that has been known all along, from the Ancient Book of the Dead to studies in the 70's and today. Now back to Atwater's discoveries. She confirms it all again and if you care to check this topic out yourself, there are hundreds of books and thousands of websites on this topic.

What Are We Being Told Here?

Ok, let us go back to more recent work of Atwater. What is Atwater showing in her studies? She tells us from her work that life is immortal consciousness that grows in an unlimited way. Most of her cases see a book of life - a full history of everyone. Their faculties are heightened and they retain that expansion upon return. During the little NDE vacation, the consciousness always has the power to make choices. She observes the intuitive mind is a sacred gift, and the rational mind is a faithful servant. We have forgotten this and honor the servant.

What is clear here is this consciousness of ours - or life force - is alive and does not croak like the body. In fact it IS LIFE as it gives such to the body upon entry and exit. It can take a vacation. It is the field of transpersonal experience that is the source of knowledge and memory - not the brain. It is independent of the person's brain mind. Whole consciousness is stored somewhere in space not in the brain. The brain serves as a relay station for connecting to our bodies when we are in a conscious state of being awake.

Here is the real mind bender: The Review process shows us that our life is a recorded movie that is accessible and can be shown to the vacationing consciousness by some other entity. Is this our recorded movie of life and a Divine Programmer that decides the next step?

The lesson here is that death is a passing, a simple shift of focus in vibration from one state of energy to another. The physical body of particles dies and the consciousness as waves of energy leaves. The body is a temporary vehicle to have fun in while we are on the earth in a movie that was created carefully and purposely, then recorded somewhere for review. Where was this movie held? Well obviously not in the brain. There may have been a copy in the brain but it was pure consciousness separated from the brain and body that held it.

What else? Here is the big one. There is something most people called God – some angelic type ghost - that they met and had a telepathic experience with. Is it some figment of the mind? Is it really the Force or God? What is relevant is that *there is something* and it is consistently part of our consciousness. Period! It does not really matter what it is does it? What matters is when this ghost of God appears in the mind or in person, life changes big time! This must be the place where the Higher Power resides.

But what must be clearly understood here from the multitude of clinical evidence is that we have some invisible energy field that gives us life, a Soul as esoteric wisdom would tell us. And when it decides to leave the old body, the life force ceases to support the physical body. That is not exactly a mystery. But having this energy measured and keeping all of our consciousness and sensory abilities intact; wow! That's a bit different from the old belief box.

What is also so interesting is that when people came back to life into the dead body it was still ok. It was not dead and smelly with dead brain cells clogging life, but fine. And then there was a life transformation with life changing habits. Their belief and faith had been completely altered to produce new habits outside of their current belief boxes – a new mind.

Now, we ask you, if you came back after you croaked for an hour, floated around in a tunnel, got your free ticket to this wonderful, peace filled amusement park, talked to some friendly ghosts, met the big boss in the sky, then had an instant replay of your life's movie, and remembered everything you experienced out of your body, what would it do to you? But who is this entity, this big boss that can play the movie and decide to send you back for another go?

Some say it is God, Angels, Spirit Guides, Holy Ghost, or some divine entity that the Soul has a meeting with. It really does not matter what you call it. Whatever comes out as the belief, would you believe anyone - scientific or otherwise - that told you when you croak that's it? Not likely! What if they said it was nonsense what you saw? You would not care much to associate with them and simply keep your new knowledge to yourself. Simply knowing it would be your truth. And no one on the planet would convince you otherwise. Your belief system would have taken a paradigm shift because you knew your own truth, period!

Would this change your approach to life? Would you then be afraid of dying? Would you not realize you needed to do something meaningful and had been given a new chance? If you saw a rerun of your life and what you had done, or not done, would you want to take another shot at it? Would you be grateful? What would you be like after? Would you be completely freaked out and shrivel away? I think the possibility of that would be remote because you would have gained a new will and purpose to live. And where would that notion be? In a thing called consciousness – your new mind that had a glimpse of a greater mind and purpose.

Perhaps if you listened to the people living inside their belief boxes on this you may think you had gone mad, but I think you would change your consciousness - your awareness - to accept beliefs outside of your usual belief box. It would change me. It has already without having to croak.

The cases make you realize perhaps you don't need to croak to go through this but it certainly illustrates the need to let go of your mortal life and needs totally and absolutely to understand how the altered state can bring a different reality to you. It would seem that when it is all gone - physical life, pain, goodies, and all that seems to be real in the mortal life, you are then in a place where the Soul and the movie director can make decisions not made easily in your physical life. By letting go – temporarily dying – you go to a place where the beliefs can be zeroed out and launch a new set of programs. In some cases, you can come back to a healing miracle; certainly a mental one. It would seem that these cases all had a chat with the Director of the program that runs the Life Plan Movie.

Perhaps the most eloquent writer and pioneer in this and the alternative health area is **Deepak Chopra**. In his book **Life After Death: The Burden of Proof**, he says "*death itself, in the Indian belief system, was seen as a* brief stopping point on an endless Soul journey that could turn a peasant into a king and vice versa." He also said: "*the idea that I have a fixed body locked in space and time is a mirage. Any drop of water inside my body could have been ocean, cloud, river, or spring the day before. I remind myself of this fact when the bonds of daily life squeeze too tight.*"

He says: "*the cosmos that you and I are experiencing right now, with trees, plants, people, houses, cars, stars, and galaxies, is just consciousness expressing itself at one particular frequency. Elsewhere in space time, different planes exist simultaneously. If I had asked my grandmother where Heaven was, she would have pointed to the house we lived in, not only because it was full of love, but because it made sense to her that many worlds could comfortably inhabit the same place. By analogy, if you are listening to a concert orchestra, there are a hundred instruments playing, each occupying the same place in space and time. You can listen to the symphony as a whole or, if you wish, put your attention on a specific instrument. You can even separate out the individual notes played by that instrument. The presence of one frequency does not displace any of the others. Every frequency in nature exists simultaneously, and yet we experience only what we see. It's natural to fear what we can't see, and since death snatches a person out of sight, we react to it with fear. Different planes of existence represent different frequencies of consciousness. The world of physical matter is just one expression of a particular frequency.*"

Our perception is actually inhibited in the material world. He describes things in planes. He says: "*in the twentieth century Western science came to understand that all solid objects are actually made of invisible vibrations. In my childhood, solid things were seen to have a large portion of the Earth element. To put it another way, solid things have dense vibrations or vibrations on a lower plane. Vaporous things had a fine vibration, on a higher plane. Just as there are different planes of material things, there are also different Spiritual planes.* Then he brings in the astral planes where he says: "*the Earth was a dense Spiritual world; there must be higher Spiritual planes, known to us as Lokas, which in Western mystical circles became known as astral planes. There are an almost infinite number of astral planes, divided into a higher and lower astral world, and even the lowest ones vibrate at a higher frequency than the material world.*"

"*In the Indian tradition every physical body is assigned an accompanying astral body. Your astral body is a complete mirror of your physical body; it has a heart, liver, arms, legs, a face, etc., but since it operates at a higher frequency, most people are unaware of it. During life, the physical body provides a garment for the Soul; it gives it the appearance of being localized in the material world. In death, as the physical body begins to disintegrate, the departing Soul enters an astral plane that corresponds to its existence on the material plane, the frequency that corresponds most closely to its former life.*"

Now here he starts on what happens after we die. He states: *"I found that after we die, we remain self-motivated. A Soul moves according to its desire from one astral plane to another, projecting as in a dream whatever sights and people, guides and astral entities it needs for its own advancement."*

Chopra is obviously vibrating highly himself as he simply *"knows"* his truth. He says: *"All these planes ultimately were imagined by Spirit, just as it imagined the material world. The Indian word for Spirit was Brahman, which is Everything, the one consciousness that fills every plane of existence. The cosmos is nonlocal, that is, it can't be mapped as a location. After death we gradually stop being local. We see ourselves as we really are from the Soul's perspective: everywhere at once. The fact that you appear to be in different places is a sensory artifact. It's based on sights and sounds, which are local events. You are not a local event."*

"As the gross senses become duller, the subtle senses sharpen. We still see and hear after we die, but now the objects aren't physical. They consist of anything we want to see on the astral plane: celestial sights and sounds, Heavenly beings, and brilliant lights. In near-death experiences the most typical manifestations are faces, voices, or an emotional presence. In other traditional cultures people might expect to encounter ghosts or animals. Often a dying person feels something subtle around him—a certain warmth, a faint form or sound before leaving the body. Somehow these can be accessed on the dying person's vibrational frequency. Anyone who has spent time with the dying knows that they may say that they've been joined in the room by a departed spouse or other long-dead loved one. Some kind of astral contact is being made in the transition zone from physical to subtle."

Then he says: *"At death the astral counterpart of the physical body separates from it. According to Vedic teachings, the departed Soul then sleeps for a time in the astral region, which I translate as its incubation period. New ideas percolate in the mind before they lead to action, and something similar happens with the Soul."*

So what? What' the point here? If you believe you simply die and that's it, wake up! Your body is like a costume for a temporary play and you are recording it in consciousness moment by moment, probably 7 times per second. If you think your mind vanishes and all your experiences are gone, wake up! This is clinical research that tells you there is more to you and your body that is available to you where the Divine Programmer sits waiting for you to learn how to communicate with it.

NDE's And Miracles

There is another aspect of this little vacation that can occur. In her book ***Dying to Be Me My Journey from Cancer, to Near Death, to True Healing, Anita Moorjani*** explains how she had been fighting cancer for almost four years, and her body was overwhelmed by the malignant cells spreading throughout her system. It began shutting down. As her organs failed, she entered into an extraordinary near-death experience where she realized her inherent worth and the actual cause of her disease. Upon regaining consciousness, Anita found that her condition had improved so rapidly that she was able to be released from the hospital within weeks without a trace of cancer in her body! In her book Anita freely shares all she has learned about illness, healing, fear, "being love," and the true magnificence of each and every human being! This is a book that definitely makes the case that we are spiritual beings having a human experience and that we are all One!

She described her ensuing near-death experience as a realm of clarity and expansiveness, a state of being; Moorjani made the choice to return, and her rapid and remarkable recovery defies all medical understanding. She said that *"Realizing that I am love was the most important lesson I learned, allowing me to release all fear, and that's the key that saved my life".*

This is not an isolated case. There are thousands of these where the Soul, the Higher Self, our Divine Programmer instituted a program code change in the subconscious that re-wrote the instruction set to create a physical healing miracle totally outside the norm of the belief box. Clearly, this is where we want to be if we want to proactively get the hell out of the old mind and into the new!

The Near Death Experience is one that is not induced purposely by an altered state, medical professional, regression therapist, healer, hypnotist, or any other means. It is a natural process of documented separation from the physical body with the brain waves at a frequency of 0 Hz as pronounced dead at the lowest end of Delta. We see that consciousness is separate from the body upon death. It appears as an energy form and holds with it the sensory memories of the body. The process of dying includes a place of peace without pain. There is the separation, the hovering, and the viewing of consciousness. The noise, the tunnel, the light, meeting of family, and then the meeting of an entity that conducts a review of past life is common. We see a non-judgmental questioning of the worthiness of life in your terms of perception. The review process is one of instant flashing by of a visual panorama of key events, people and experiences. We see a return back becomes one of re-engagement and re-entry into the physical body and the life changes that can occur are noted as dramatic attitude shifts in the engagement with, and the perception of reality. In many cases, physical miracles are noted as spontaneous or occur over the ongoing time.

We now get a new notion that we have an astral counterpart, a mirror copy of a physical being and beingness that is eternal so separated upon death. This entity or Soul operates at a higher frequency of consciousness and appears to have control over the physical body. It would appear that the human vessel is a means for its consciousness to express itself. It has the ability to access a recorded version of your Life which is reviewed at this NDE exit point. Was this exit there to teach you something? This recorded version of the panoramic review process was like a 3D holographic Life Movie of events, people, experiences and emotions all played back and clearly seen, understood and remembered. It was all brought into your conscious awareness instantly.

Now having a look at the other side and this Divine Programmer, we are going to take you into another unbelievable world of research. Here we will look at documented evidence that brings forward this topic of this Life Movie from a different vantage point. This is the life that your Soul designed for the purpose of expression and experience – the one you are having. In the review process, you looked at the recorded or actual version which instantly flashed into your consciousness. But there is another movie; the one that you created as your Life Plan.

7

THE IMMERSION MOVIE OF LIFE

"The life you engage in is a virtual holographic movie which you directed and produced so you could engage in the mental and emotional joy of its experience."

Aly McDonald   Ed Rychkun

> **Why must I torture myself this way**
> **If I created a plan of love and play?**

Did We Really Create A Movie?

These documented cases of Near Death Experiences show the power of the mind or something "up there" to facilitate a dramatic change in attitude and even physical reality. What is of particular interest now is what we see in these cases called the Review Process. It allowed someone or something a way of projecting an instant temporal movie of one's life in explicit details including emotions. It has been recorded somewhere and becomes available to consciousness upon being free of physical reality. Most all cases end up having a look at a holographic type movie that is retrieved as a set of instantaneous frames or moments into conscious awareness from a recorded version of this ongoing Movie of Life. And in some cases these participants convinced the guy in charge to rewrite new frames in upcoming reality so as to create a program back in your physical body; like sometimes to affect a healing.

We have also studied Past Life Regression in the previous book and saw that here the mind was able to bridge between imaginary and physical reality, one affecting the other, the new frames or moments that were looked at and edited the cause in one reality changed the effect in another reality. These were also done in some altered state. And some overseeing Director took responsibility for making sure that the process for the re-creation of some issue or defective physics that started with a new perception and belief. In the case of physical change it was returned to a normal function by simply issuing the directive to the subconscious, the brain to organize the event, and the cells to pull out the right program code from the DNA archives and get to work. In the case of a miracle, it issued a directive to create a new program and get to work with stem cells. It used the good code to replace the defective code and replaced it in some cases instantly and then it continued to function frame by frame in the current reality in accordance with the new program. In the case of a mental issue, it simply replaced an old mind set with a new and then continued to record it.

In our continuing quest for creating reality, it is the **Review appearance** that is of interest. This is where a bright Light Being presents a high speed video panorama review of life. Here the intent is only to provoke reflections. The rapid temporal memories in chronological order occur almost instantaneously. The images generate emotions as they flip by. The Being asks what they have done with their life, stressing love, and pointing out things. No one could gage time. It is like the stories you hear about when people drown. They have their whole life flash by in a moment - instant replay of consciousness. We will see later that this is similar to the hypnosis and regression process of fast forward or backward in the movie of your life. Again, the altered state of hypnosis allows you to stop at a particular recorded scene and change an effect now by re-perceiving a cause in the past.

When this process occurs there is no dividing line between the real and the nonreal worlds and you can change both. It appears to be a way that you can change the frames of the stored movie that result in a new frame to be created in the mental, emotional AND physical bodies. Whether this is a direct creation of some material thing, or an instant correction of broken bones or diseased tissue, there is a re-write of the movie frames. In our previous book we brought forward the idea that this astral double involves the causal, mental and emotional bodies that houses the information where the Divine Programmer can correct things through the interface of etheric, the physical body. The two realities are accessible and both realities are interactive from the power of the mind to change what the movie has recorded.

It is also important to know that with those that came back they inevitably had a totally changed life, just like in the miracles cases. Most times this experience created a totally new attitude in life. Some reported enhanced senses; some picked up on other's feelings better. Many expressed a need to cultivate love of others, seek knowledge, became morally purified, and created new clear goals mostly in service of others. The bottom line is that their belief systems and behavior had changed dramatically at a physical level. It is a clear example of mind over matter.

The mind blowing suggestions are that the reality we see and the life we live is a virtual movie, a holographic medium understood and viewable when we are pure consciousness not limited by the physical body and the Beta bothersome brain. The suggestion which comes as an inescapable notion: if this movie can be changed, how, and why is it being recorded and who created it?

Under Free Will We Created Our Plan

There is a great body of research and "science" emerging these days that suggest we all created a "contract" to engage in a virtual movie of life called the Life Contract. This movie of life sets the major parameters of existence in the physical reality.

The suggestion is that the moments we engage in are like frames in a movie hologram we are interacting with; and that the major events, our characteristics, our plan of life has been created by way of free will by or with someone. Like we found in the movie we created in our imagination, parts of this were set by intent, while parts were subject to laws of natural order, growth and purpose setting the overall stage. This was all intricately woven into what we created as our stage of experience and expression. In other words, our consciousness and awareness as in the game of imagination where we played out our mental and emotional game of choices by a process of observation, was part of a greater consciousness. Similarly it would seem from these review movies of NDE's we are allegedly in roles as players, and we simply make choices at set decision points, in between which we create our individual reality, express our emotion, and register these frames or moments as we go.

This is not an easy concept to accept. To think that we are actors in a contrived movie and to believe we at some point created the storyline is not well accepted. It is a long way out of the belief box. But there is a wave of research that suggests that this may not be so ridiculous. This body of evidence can be found not only in Near Death Experiences where your life moments are played before you, but Out Of Body Experiences where you as a Soul or Light Body separate and you have access to the same movie. This we will explore in a separate chapter. To add to the list of evidence are thousands of cases of Past Life Regression, Future Life Progression, and Astral Projection where that illusive holographic movie of past present and future can be edited in the "imagination" of some higher state, then congealed into physical reality.

The Life Review Process

In Wikipedia there is an interesting synopsis of what they call a **life review** is a phenomenon widely reported as occurring during near-death experiences, in which a person rapidly sees much or the totality of their life history in chronological sequence and in extreme detail. It is often referred to by people having experienced this phenomenon as having their life "flash before their eyes". A reformatory purpose seems commonly implicit in accounts, though not necessarily for earthly purpose, since return from a near-death experience may reportedly entail individual choice.

While experiencers, who number up to eight million in the United States, sometimes report that reviews took place in the company of otherworldly beings who shared the observation, they also say they felt unjudged during the process, leaving themselves their own strongest critics. Although rare, there are also a few accounts of life reviews or similar experiences without a near death experience, such as during the simpler out of body experience or when under circumstances of intense threat or duress. Many scientists discount near death experiences themselves and criticize their credibility. Furthermore, there is evidence suggesting cultural differences in the near-death experience, which is why some believe NDE's are hallucinations. The interesting question that arises is how these hallucinations being independent and disconnected cases have so many common rememberings?

Nevertheless, the perception of time appears to be subjective and has been described as from lasting less than a few seconds to instantaneous. Accounts differ as to what phase of a near-death experience a review might take place in. Subjects frequently describe their experience as panoramic, 3D or holographic. During a life review, the subject's perception is reported to include not only their own perspective in increased vividness, as if they were reliving a given episode itself, but that of all other parties they interact with at each point being reviewed.

The term 3D Plane is employed to approximate the inclusion of different physical perspectives onto a scene; the intensity of a life review was described by one individual as enabling him to count every nearby mosquito; but equally common is the description of feeling the emotional experience of the other parties, including in one case virtually everyone in a room. While some accounts appear to describe scenes as selected, others more commonly narrate the experience as including things they had, probably naturally, long ago entirely forgotten, with "nothing left out". Experiencers commonly describe the intense vividness and detail as making them feel more alive than when normally conscious:

"Most things were pleasant to see, some things made me very embarrassed. In fact, revulsion and guilt took away any good feelings, making me so very sorry for certain things I had said or done. I hadn't just seen what I had done, but I felt and knew the repercussions of my actions. I felt the injury or pain of those who suffered because of my selfish or inappropriate behavior."

The effect of a life review is often a strongly transformative experience. Experiencers describe them as extremely unpleasant from the perspective of the unhappiness they had inflicted on others, including feelings they had never dreamed of as resulting, and equally pleasant from the perspective of the good feeling they had brought to others' lives, extending to the littlest forgotten details. To some extent, this experience resembles purgatory. The Tibetan Buddhist understanding can be found in The Tibetan Book of The Dead, and is known as *Bardo Thodol* (the stage between life and afterlife).

Experiencers often report a sharp drop in materialistic outlook (both acquisitive and philosophical), an intensified compassion for others and sense of interconnectedness, newfound altruistic activities, personality changes (though occasionally entailing divorce), a new interest in self-education and spirituality, and so on. **Dannion Brinkley** as one instance described himself as putting off previously deep-rooted sociopathic traits ingrained from a difficult childhood through his work as a sniper in the Vietnam War. A frequent comment by Experiencers is that they later strongly avoided unethical or inconsiderate actions because they wanted to avoid painfully reliving the receiving end of the action which they knew would await them.

The transformative effect is in fact so statistically uniform in comparison with other areas of demographic study that some near death experience investigators point to it as evidence for the empirical reality of the phenomenon itself. **Kenneth Ring's** book **Lessons from the Light** includes numerous accounts of a near death experience permitting people hitherto blind, including cases from birth, as enabled to see (and interpret) vision during the experience.

The spiritual teacher Meher Baba held that one engages in a life review process after dying, with the lessons learned from this review becoming part of one's intuition in subsequent incarnations:

"The truths absorbed by the mind in the life after death become in the next incarnation a part of the inborn wisdom. Developed intuition is consolidated and compressed understanding distilled through a multitude of diverse experiences gathered in previous lives."

Your Soul Contract And Life Plan

In his books **Your Souls Gift** and **Your Souls Life Plan**, writer and researcher **Robert Schwartz** details his extensive work which clearly dovetails into these life reviews. What his work reveals is that by taking one via hypnosis into an altered state where you gain access to what he calls the Causal Body memory, you also gain access to that whole movie that was created – past, present, future AND inbetween! Now there are many like Robert who are rapidly changing the scientific landscape regarding these virtual movies of life, but in this case we have chosen Robert's work because it is so well documented, so well accepted and has been so effective in so many cases. So let us first introduce Robert, as taken from his website www.yoursoulsplan.com.

"For a very long time, and well before I wrote Your Soul's Plan, I had been searching, fruitlessly, for the deeper meaning of my life. In 2003, my search took a new and surprising turn when I decided to consult with a medium. Although I had a strong belief in God, I had never (as far as I knew) directly experienced the metaphysical. I researched mediums and selected someone with whom I felt comfortable."

"My session with the medium took place on May 7, 2003. I remember the exact date because on that day my life changed. I told the medium very little about myself, describing my circumstances only in the most general terms. She explained that each of us has spirit guides, nonphysical beings with whom we plan our lives prior to incarnation. Through her I was able to speak with mine. They knew everything about me—not only what I had done but also what I had thought and felt. For example, they referred to a specific prayer I had said to God some five years earlier. At a particularly difficult time I had prayed, 'God, I can't do this alone. Please send help.' My guides told me that additional nonphysical assistance had been provided. 'Your prayer was answered,' they said. I was astounded."

"Eager to understand the suffering I had experienced, I asked my guides about the major challenges I had faced. They explained that I had planned these challenges before birth—not for the purpose of suffering, but for the growth that would result. I was shaken by this information. My conscious mind knew nothing of pre-birth planning, yet intuitively I sensed truth in their words."

"Although I did not realize it at the time, my session with the medium triggered a profound spiritual awakening for me. I would later understand that this awakening was really a remembering—a remembering of who I am as an eternal soul and, more specifically, what I had planned to do on Earth. I became obsessed with reading about spirituality and metaphysics. As I read I thought often about pre-birth planning. All my life I had viewed my challenges as nothing more than meaningless suffering. Had I known that I'd planned my challenges, I would have seen them rich with purpose. That knowledge alone would have greatly eased my suffering. Had I also known why I'd planned them, I could have consciously learned the lessons they offered."

"During this period of intense study and inner exploration, I met a woman who is able to channel her soul and who agreed to let me speak with her soul about pre-birth planning. I had no knowledge of channelling and was taken aback when she went into a trance and another consciousness, one clearly distinct from hers, began to speak through her. I spoke with her soul for fifteen hours over the course of five meetings."

"These conversations were thrilling. They verified and complemented my reading and study. Her soul told me in detail about her own pre-birth planning: the various challenges that had been discussed and the reasons some were selected. Here I had direct, specific confirmation of a phenomenon of which very few people were aware. Because the pain in my life had made me extremely sensitive to - and intensely motivated to relieve - the suffering of others, I was excited by the potential healing an awareness of pre-birth planning could bring to people. I knew that the information I had discovered could lighten their suffering and imbue their challenges with new meaning and purpose. As a result I decided to devote my life to writing and speaking about the subject of life plans."

"Working closely with several mediums and channels, I have now explored the pre-birth plans of many, many people. I have learned that the events in their lives are neither random nor arbitrary, but rather part of a wisely conceived and intricate plan - a plan they themselves bravely designed. I

have learned, too, that souls often select very different challenges for similar reasons. You may therefore hear the motivations of your soul in the story of someone whose life is, at least on the surface, very different from your own. In Your Soul's Plan and Your Soul's Gift I offer to you the life stories and pre-birth plans of twenty-two courageous souls."

And so Robert offers several ways to uncover what that Life Plan is and what is its purpose. It is important to note that Robert is a professional hypnotist and uses hypnosis in his therapy sessions.

Between Lives Soul Regression
In a Between Lives Soul Regression sessions many different types of experiences are possible, but most likely you will talk with one of your spirit guides and then at great length with the Council of Elders, the wise, loving, and highly evolved beings who oversee the cycle of reincarnation on Earth. The Council knows everything about you, including all your past lives and your plan for your current lifetime. Clients describe basking in the Council's pure, unconditional love and total nonjudgmental. Often the Council will provide a powerful energetic healing. Talking with your Council is a wondrous opportunity to ask any questions you have on any subject. After a BLSR many clients state, *"I received an answer to every question I asked, and I have no more questions about my life!"*

Past Life Soul Regression
In a Past Life Soul Regression (PLSR), you'll have the opportunity to experience a particular past life that had a direct bearing on your soul's plan for your current lifetime. This is a very liberating experience that has helped many people understand their personal life path. More specifically, a past life regression can help you to: reduce or resolve any fear of death you may have; heal grief, phobias, and emotional and physical issues; gain great insight into past and current relationships; and understand themes in your life.

Contact a Deceased Loved One
In this type of session, I use a hypnotic induction specifically designed to facilitate your entry into a trance state in which you contact a loved one who has returned to Spirit. This is not a session in mediumship or channelling; rather, it is a direct experience.

Spiritual Guidance Sessions
Spiritual Guidance Sessions will help you understand the deeper meaning of your life: why you are here; what you hoped to learn in this lifetime; the purpose served by the major relationships in your life; and why certain

patterns may reoccur. If you like, you may choose to do the Divine Virtues Exercise I've developed, which will give you an awareness of the specific qualities you sought to cultivate and express in your lifetime. Spiritual Guidance Sessions are a powerful way to become "unstuck," heal, and experience more love, joy and peace in your life.

In his books, Robert documents the process and the results of his work in these sessions.

Creating The Life Plan Movie

To believe that you reincarnate into different lives is a tough cookie to chew for most. To accept that you have a Soul that continues to reincarnate in different bodies and lives is also tough. To believe that each time you do, you as a Soul, use free will to make a life plan and a contract to follow it, is even a tougher cookie to chew. Yet from our work on investigating miracles, we know that the physical results of events and conditions coded as frames of a review or imaginary movie can be edited once brought into this higher consciousness. What Robert's work does is it adds a whole new set of credence to this, will attempt to summarize it below.

Robert has concluded that the Soul is a spark of God which has a **greater purpose** of spiritual growth. In order to do this, a Soul chooses the way in which it will incarnate into a body, choosing a soul family to experience this with and sets out a life plan of lesson to do this. Souls then review the akashic records to determine a new plan. The players, the character, the events, the script for this life plan are all created with the Soul family and Spirit Guides so as to learn virtues and evolve their spiritual growth. The Life Plan creates a contract that is developed through free will of the Soul. A soul determines the way in which it will incarnate and leave the physical body. It can walk in or walk out when death occurs.

He says that in his work, he sees that the Soul's true evolution is to turn negative to positive. Without negative it is believed that it cannot be motivated to want positive because it forgets when it crosses the veil into the incarnated plane. Its purpose is to understand that misery is an illusion and that to know this, it must stop judgment. It is an understanding that there is something more, that we are love and we have a prebirth desire to be of service to one another. Without contrast to love we cannot know fully who we are so we script lives and forget our true identity to awaken and attain the greater self to know ourselves as love and only express that.

He states that once you engage in the life plan to do this you must follow intuition not intellect. Intuition is direct communication with a higher intelligence for the right path and usually discounted by the mind. To do this one must use meditation to hear intuition, then attention and intention to it to open paths. You learn to allow skeptics to help you open conviction, overcome fear in a life plan as they go and you grow. So you need courage and love of the heart, a choice open by way of free will.

Robert explains that to accomplish this, a Soul has a purpose of creating a Life Plan; to determine body, time, place, and events to evolve. The body is part of a Soul that has full access to this plan but it will appear as separated. He states that in his experience, the aura and subtle bodies are contained by the Soul to develop 30 divine virtues. These cultivate and express on the physical plane the virtues of compassion, love, empathy, kindness, and unconditional love.

The Souls Plan is to balance karma and heal issues like false beliefs and develop service to others through these virtues. Many different virtues are to be developed as expressions by cultivating passion, compassion, forgiveness, unconditional love, empathy, and become a balanced Self. The Self identity defines what the Soul wants to express. To do this, a series of lives become the vehicles of expression, typically cultivating 2-5 virtues at a time. Love, peace, and joy are primary expressions. As the Soul wants profound self knowing, the Life Plan is usually designed to experience the opposite. So love, peace, and joy need contrast to know who we truly are. This is why we appear to torture ourselves; to learn to rise above it.

To do this Soul groups of the same evolutionary needs incarnate together and evolve their own life plans which integrate into each other's. To assist, one can have several guardian angels or Spirit Guides who also assist by providing the silent guidance. All this is in service to each other.

The Soul's plan will involve the development of virtues so as to awaken; to come to know there is more to a physical body than just emotions and personality. Each is an eternal Soul agreeing to come into body to express these divine virtues. Each can change the lesson by increasing vibration for learning to be compassionate, choosing the high road at key junctures in the plan to ascend to a place that holds all records of past, present, future. This learning by contrast, by ascending to a higher place then allows access to life plans which can be altered by loving thoughts that bring the Soul and its vehicle into a thought form for human good. The learning process is to understand that thoughts are energy in prephysical form.

At any time you as a vehicle of the Soul, or lower mind and body may ask your guide to materialize your file and meditate in change. In the unconscious guides have full access to the Soul to remind them of the plan, destiny, and purpose to help it rise in vibration when consciousness returns. The Soul would have subconscious seeds planted to produce the desired effect of reminding, triggering, opening, awakening because as the Soul crosses to the earth plane for incarnation it forgets these plans.

Robert confirms the subconscious is the birthplace of change. Healing (forgiveness) alters DNA (Ayurvedic System) as a wave to both parties; laughter heals DNA as a cascade of hormones.

In a Prebirth Planning Process sessions are conducted to create a complex flowchart advanced beyond comprehension with decision points where parameters are set up as choices; all pre-anticipated. Each is shown scenes to upcoming life. Guide's and Souls idea's of personality and various life paths create the plan in benefit to all of the Soul's family.

Major life challenges are set up and exit points are planned. Normally a guide would implant a notion or idea. If it is a prebirth plan they can intervene. Life will end when Soul decides when the plan is done or when it is futile. Intervention can occur through soul agreements.

Several plans are made as a flowchart that can expand to infinity with choices that are predetermined. Acting in love takes you on a different time line which may take several lives. These plans are conceived for a deeper meaning and purpose. Karma provides situations and events as a range of possibilities as to how you could choose at these juncture points.

All major things are planned, some minor. The detail is an individual Soul choice. Free will allows deviation but you may create more issues through the Law of Attraction into low vibration choices that cause the same issue to recur. The free will allows going into joy choices of love, and appreciation to minimize the issues. The many virtues are learned via contrasts so for example it may be that loving people may have challenges because of prebirth plan to experience the negative contrast. These can be poverty, incest, or rape as serious challenges. The Plan may also put others in support of challenge to assist in dealing with these tests. This is part of the prebirth plan. The victim mentality is something that we will overcome by way of setting people and events up to assist. The Soul plan challenges and how to overcome these as a set of choices are all agreed to. Holographic images are presented so we know what the events, situations, and possible outcomes may be. The planning process shows houses, colleges, places, all predefined.

In laying out the contract, each Soul designs and is shown scenes to upcoming life. Guides and Soul's ideas of personality, life, and physical characteristics are used to create the plan in benefit to all of the Soul's family.

Robert explains that the **Soul Contract** is to use Spirit Guides and God to create a personality to agree to the plan. You will feel unconditional love to agree to the plan. You can express concern and modify it but highest good is for all and each other of Family. The purpose is to choose paths in such a way as to help deep meaning to challenges so they are not victims. Life is not random, as we all agree to the plan, and specifically the idea is to come out of victim, helpless, consciousness mentality. If not, these negative energies will become a self fulfilling prophesy executed through the Law of Attraction. When dealt with through the virtues, it all results in the healing power of the Soul - wounds can be healed with love. So that which is perceived and felt as torture is simply a way to heal. The true growth comes through emotion. Only by working through the experience does a human understand it.

Robert explains that there is no judgment. Some Souls do bite off more than they can handle to accelerate or deal with old issues of guilt. One can fail at a level of personality but a Soul never judges because of the failure, they just try again. The personality is eternal as is the Soul but each personality is different in each life so a portion of the Soul is placed in each body. Dark roles are played in service to others. There is no judgment by the Soul (at a Soul review) however; one may carry a notion of failure as the Soul tries again. Significant people are all part of the plan, each assisting to bump a Soul back on a plan. Each Soul is in collaboration with other Souls and can bring in others to help if the plan is not on track. The Soul's plan can override the Law of Attraction as it can choose location, time, events and people. The law is powerful when you send a picture with feeling and gratitude it is stronger.

Life challenges break the heart open to create contrast so as to learn and heal. At Life Review sessions (prebirth, OBE's, NDES's for example), Divine virtues are brought forward as a test to see how these are scored in a life. One can see progress and determine extent of healing. When you know this, you will see the reason for these challenges and find the purpose in the future so as to cultivate the virtues. Certain virtues will come up again and again. The Soul may take on too much and Spirit Guides may caution it. It can come to an end because all has been achieved or it may not be achievable but it is the soul that decides and various exit points are created, as are support people and events to keep on track.

It is the personal search for victim consciousness that is a heavy path, not a painful experience. The virtuous path is to change this by forgiving others, deal with unresolved karma ties, and take responsibility for creating your life in the world of virtues and service, stepping up with the heart, not ego, and to use real emotion with gentle kind intention instead of forced intent and will. It is a process of surrender to it as a real experience. It is the same process as with Law of Attraction; do not force it.

In his work, Robert concludes that **all lifetimes occur concurrently.** Life plans are like a stack of movies on DVD's. The DVD's sitting on your shelf are like the imaginary movies in your mind. They can all be played at any time, put on hold, fast forwarded, backed up, and if you have the right divine computer, be changed. In the non physical world thought manifests instantly. Thought creates reality, not respond to it. The Play Boards are like holograms; their thoughts create their boards (by Spirit guides and the Soul) and then draw lines of growth. Souls can exert influence by nudging, suggestion, and thoughts.

All memories including past lives and time between are stored in DNA. The Soul can take on a cloak, and plan the personality needed to incarnate into. 98% of the time, markers such as physical identifying markers are embedded in unconscious to help recognize soulmates and important people. In the afterlife Souls are counseled in self forgiveness. Souls evolve to higher vibration – guides do not need the school. They connect, understand or create things they are never without – all divine, no negative emotions, no duality only peace.

Personality is an illusion in space time – it survives death but never separates. All this plan, once agreed to is published in the Akashic records. Ascended masters are finer vibrations in all that is love.

Memories Of Afterlife

Michael Newton, PhD is the Founder of **The Newton Institute** for **Life Between Lives Hypnotherapy (TNI)**. Dr. Newton serves on the TNI Board. He holds a doctorate in Counseling Psychology; is a certified Master Hypnotherapist and is a member of the American Counseling Association. He has been on the faculty of higher educational institutions as a teacher and counselor while also active in private practice. In addition, Dr. Newton has been a hypnotherapist for over 50 years and a LBL therapist for over 40 years. He is considered a pioneer in uncovering the mysteries about life after death through the use of Spiritual Regression.

He is the author of three bestselling books, **Journey of Souls: Case Studies of Life Between Lives (1994), Destiny of Souls: New Case Studies of Life Between Lives (2000)** and **Life Between Lives Hypnotherapy (2004)** published by Llewellyn. These books have been translated into over 25 languages. In 2001 his second book was awarded "Metaphysical Book of the Year" by the independent publishers association at their annual Book Exposition of America meeting. He is also the editor of the latest release *Memories of the Afterlife* (2009), which includes intriguing case studies written by members of TNI's growing global network of **Life Between Lives** Therapists.

At their website http://newtoninstitute.org/ The Newton Institute (TNI) for Life Between Lives Hypnotherapy is dedicated to the intriguing and expansive world of inter-life exploration. Here one will anticipate, begin to re-connect as the door opens to your own memories of home; Soul Home. Here you can re-establish your sense of connection and belonging as you begin to cross this bridge between your current life and your Soul's true home.

Home awaits us all; a home where only pure, unconditional love, compassion and harmony exist side by side. Recognize that you are currently in school, Earth school; and when you graduate, that loving harmony awaits you. Some of our classes are exhilarating, some are daunting and for most of us, there is a diverse mixture of both. But know that each experience you have during your current life is enabling your personal, Soul growth. No matter what, when school's out you will return home to the unconditional love that's there waiting for us all.

What does Michael Newton say in his latest book **Memories of Afterlife**? When you go through Michael's work and his many cases, you find that there is a very close alignment with the work of Robert Schwartz. Working independently on different cases, he reports:

- Souls are evolving by color (advancement status as an indication after completing incarnation). Purple is most advanced and it seems to follow the chakra system of colors
- Souls can have a name and are pure light energy but all must overcome karma through incarnation
- Hybrid Souls have been on other planets as alien creatures
- Souls develop plans using triggers that may be set to awaken
- Souls communicate via telepathy
- In life selection Souls take participating roles insisting live action by watching scenes unfold into life to come. They Select climates and body to suit their karmic development
- Some lessons may repeat over and over until learned.
- Elders do not tell – they allow us to find ourselves by indulgence because of stereotypes, elders are portrayed as old white beings denoting wisdom in human mind
- No negative emotions exist in the afterlife
- Souls may hide in seclusion between lives (crystal caves) to regenerate
- The portal in an NDE is a tunnel to the other side
- Subatomic particles acting under vibrational influence record, store all images, animate and incarnate. These energy waves can create multitude of alternate patterns of possible future events.
- We can leave recorded fingerprints in geographic locations
- Souls join fetus for 4-9 months but need brain tissue for integration
- Angels are religious things but evolved into archetypes as spirit guides

The evidence brought forward by many of these cases begins to paint a rather radical picture of our lives on the earth plane of reality. Once again it is the process of hypnosis that is used to achieve that altered state where the Soul, the Spirit Guides, and the Divine Programmer who knows all about that "Higher Power" resides. Here it can telepathically communicate and present the Life Plan movies. We see that the work says we are a Soul who has a prime objective of learning by contrast how to be of service and virtues. To do this you decide to incarnate into a body of your own choosing and develop a Life Plan which you will script out people, events, triggers, situations that will assist in your development. You use Spirit Guides and collaborate with a Soul Family to play roles and parts in the life Plan, thereby creating a contract. Major and minor events are written into the script, stored as images to be played out. Each creates choice points at which different options may be chosen. How you choose via perceptions and emotions governs the pathway along the life plane. You will determine the nature of your body and your characteristics and you will see glimpses of your parents, your key situations, associates in order to decide your plan. You will see what is planned for you future in explicit detail.

Everything is stored and played out moment by moment, allowing the life to unfold between set junctures and stored as a record of engagement. Before you incarnate in a body, you as a Soul, a spark of the greater consciousness and of God use your free will to plan this life. You as the main actor select the environment, the other actors, the major events, your own personality, time, place, and points of exit for the movie to play out. You determine events, conditions, choice points so as to allow your own expression to be allowed and when done, like entering the hollow deck, the movie plays frame by frame, moment by moment.

So once upon a time, each of us as something else than this body, wrote a story line, a script and recorded this as moments in a timeline called a life plan and then contracted with a Soul family to engage physical mental and emotional parts of the Soul in this plan to develop virtues by experiencing contrast. So we chose the way we would look, feel and think, where to release the movie, and set out markers, events, situations and environments, relationships, that would allow us to perceive, express and act using free choice. The plan would contain all of the different options at critical junctures where we could choose which way to think, see, speak, perceive, and project feelings. To engage in the script, we would need to have a receiver and projector – a physical body – that would convert this plan into a reality which would be shared by others. That physical body would include a control center called a brain, both of which would evolve and grow according to a process of natural order, purpose and evolution.

When we decided on the plan, we chose sets of possibilities as branches along the path of life. To do this we used free will but when we incarnated into a physical body, we forgot that we created the movie, and forgot who we were so we forgot that it was free will that created the options along a preferred life line of possible destinies to deal with issues. However, when in this life of forgetfulness, we still retain free will to choose how to perceive, react, and act when the time comes to engage in the life interaction with the organic life of this contrived reality.

But, how is this reality made so real? And how does it develop and integrate what we see as organic life? The answer lies in how our bodies and brains interpret the output as a projection, just like the goggles from Microsoft and the holographic Telepresence create a reality that appears real; and creates the same engagements as with the real one which perhaps is not so real.

It would appear from this evidence that the director in charge of creating, changing and re-installing the appropriate programs is the Soul and the Spirit Guides who worked together to create the movie of life. One may want to conclude that the Soul is the true Divine Programmer, and that the entities that are encountered in the NDE's are the Spirit Guides. The Soul then as a Higher Self of the Causal, Mental, and Emotional energy bodies interfaces through the Astral and Etheric bodies to the Physical.

In our previous book we brought forward the different energy bodies that make up our Higher Being. To do this we are going to investigate another well documented phenomenon called Astral Projection. It is the same as OBE's or Out Of Body Experiences. These are induced by a facilitator or through hypnosis/self discipline and do not require near dying to do it. The process is one of controlled separation of your Higher Being from that Lower Being called a human body. Let us look more closely at our "out of the box" makeup and see if we can get closer to the Divine Programmer.

8

ASTRAL PROJECTION

"That which you do below in your physical reality is mapped above in your nonphysical reality but that which you create above in your nonphysical reality controls your physical reality; as above, so below."

Aly McDonald   Ed Rychkun

> **A time must come when we know
> The truth of as above so below**

As we have unfolded the previous chapters, we have presented a picture which points to a lot of evidence that there is much more to us than being a mere mortal vessel that is born, lives and dies. The suggestions that come through, points to the altered state of love, peace and silence being the environmental setting for discovering something much more about us. The altered state not only gets the hyperactive overprotective brain out of the way and helps us let go of the interfering 3D world around us. It allows us to go where the Life Plan movies are created and reviewed. We have seen that in the most extreme case of an NDE where we totally let go of the material world, we come face to face with what is most likely the Soul, Spirit Guides, and Soul family.

But we have learned that another process called Out Of Body experiences are a way to leave the material world behind and chat with this same group. Much work is being done to work with people through meditation, hypnosis and other means to do two major things this way; to enhance abilities and to address issues that need correcting. In this way, rather than temporarily dying, we can understand and use another procedure to visit our Higher Self, Soul and Spirit Guides.

We are now going to look at the research on Astral Projection. It is the same process as the Out Of Body Experience. Like the NDE, it is a means of leaving the physical body and meeting your mirror self. In so doing we are going to look more closely at the researchers' ideas and conclusions that are engaged in astral travel. It will further our own research on the reality of Life Movies. We will also look at the process of doing astral projection and the benefits that are reported to arise from the experience. Perhaps we can get a better grasp of this alleged Soul journey to this place called earth reality. And, more importantly get to more easily connect with the Divine Programmer.

But first, let us recall some information from our previous book about this mirror copy that lives in the higher vibrational plane; the one that people are saying is the Soul and Higher Self.

The Energy Bodies

In our previous book ***The Divine Programmer: Creating Miracles***, we told you about the different energy bodies that are your makeup. We are all used to seeing the anatomical side of our material bodies as atoms and particles. But what about the subtle energy parts which are just energy? We described the enveloping **Causal/Soul Body** (golden orb) as the subtlest level of personal individuality, the enlivening source of life and consciousness for the current personality, all past life personalities, and all future life personalities. It is typically referred to as the **Higher-Self**. Most of us out of the box are comfortable with the idea of the Higher and Lower Self and Soul. It does not really matter what it is called as long as you get the idea that it is consciousness that does not die and is pure energy, the same as your quantum mind. It can be proposed here that this Higher Self or Soul is what is encountered as the Review Guide in Near Death experiences. It is the dude that has the power to create and change the Life Plan movie and instigate a program change downward through the total anatomy of the human to change reality. The Lower Self is the usual us of mind and body in the 3D Plane as in this picture.

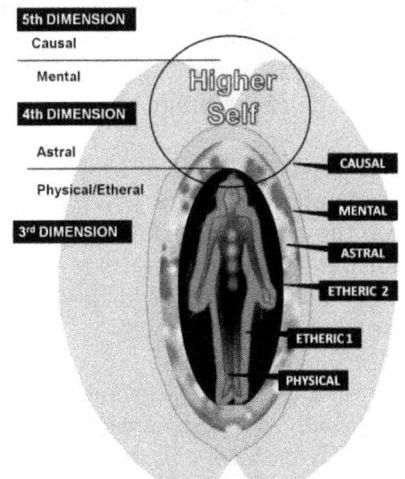

What we want to review here is the rest of the anatomy that interfaces with the physical body. In a sense, we are showing the progression or what we can call Downward Causation of "above to below" as energy components of the total human anatomy at different levels of energy vibration. The picture shows onion ring levels as energy bodies progressing from the 5D non-material energy wave plane to the physical 3D (material) matter plane through the interface plane. The interface plane is the 4D Astral Body.

We are now going to bring forth the notion that this 5D place of higher energy state resides in the quantum field which has no space or time and everything is connected as one at the **Causal Body.** It is a level where you as a Soul or Higher Self reside as pure consciousness. Let us review the different bodies relevant here proceeding downward from above to below from nonmatter to matter. Each has a specific purpose becoming denser and denser in frequency vibration. So allow your mind to temporarily get out of the belief box.

The Causal/Soul Body is named "Causal" because it is the originating source of each personality that incarnates in each lifetime. It is the source of your personality, causing it to be and exist. When your personality ends, the essence of you is absorbed back into the Causal Body. It is the first level of your individuality that is relatively immortal as the Causal Body exists permanently and during your journey as a human through many incarnations or lifetimes. This is where all the information regarding mental and emotional experience is stored.

The **Mental/Intellectual Body** is the vehicle for understanding, for beliefs, thoughts, knowledge, and cognitive processes. The Mental Body is the higher mind that interfaces through the Astral/Emotional body to use the Etheric/Vital body. It connects to the Physical for experiencing the Personality. The mental body simply knows and does not need to think things out like the mental mind does below. The instrument of representation below in the world of matter is the brain mind. Thought is the language of the brain.

The Astral/Emotional Body is the vehicle for emotion, desire, imagination, personal power, and is a focus of feeling. The Astral Body gives you the ability to feel the higher desires, emotions, imagination, and psychic abilities. It lends power to thought which is the Mental Body's territory essential for effective action and manifestation. Emotions and feeling are the language of the body.

Astral consciousness includes the full range of emotions from fear, hate, and sorrow to love, happiness, and ecstasy. It also includes the full range of desire from totally selfish and destructive desire to common personal desire to high spiritual aspiration to selfless servicefull desire. The astral/emotional body speaks the language of emotions through the body, interfaced via the etheric-chakra energetic centers that all have purposes and interfaces to physical organs and tissues.

The Etheric/Vital Body is the vehicle for energy and vitality, the subtle basis for the physical body. It is where the chakras and meridians, ley lines of the upper bodies connect to the specific area of responsibility in the physical body.

The Physical Body (at the center), is the vehicle for stability, separation, and individual focus. It is the human physical vessel that is designed to be the engaging party for the Life Plan experience. As we now know, the higher mental expression is through language and the brain. The higher emotional expression is through the body and the heart brain. The brain has the responsibility of maintaining the body in accordance with DNA evolution, process and purpose, and it has the responsibility to create the holographic reality where it is able to play out the Life Plan through immersion.

The Personality is composed of the Mental/Intellectual Body, the Astral/Emotional Body, the Etheric/Astral Body, and the Physical Body, as a unit. The Personality is very temporary and is changed or re-created every lifetime, effectively erasing past life memories on a personality level. All past life experience, knowledge, and developed ability is retained on a Causal/Soul Body level as the Causal Body lasts many millions of years. The interface to the physical plane is through the Etheric body which insures character, behavior and physiological/chemical processes conform to the contracted design formed by the astral substance at birth.

The Higher Self and Soul as pure consciousness are a nonlocal part of the quantum field as one consciousness and are therefore nowhere and everywhere, all interconnected as one sea of greater consciousness. The aspect of nonlocality allows all Souls to be one and know about each other at any instant; so what occurs in one occurs in the other as instant communication. It is like the communication between cells in our body. In addition, the Higher Self and Soul are interconnected and interfaced to the energetic bodies to the physical brain. In this way, they not only oversee all the things going on in the bodies, they have a connection to the physical brain through the subconscious thus linked between the quantum field of non-matter and the physical matter.

When you get into this astral territory you then are straddling the place of interface between non-matter and matter. In this place consciousness becomes more like our first chapter on imagination because now the distinction between reality and non-reality does not exist. It is simply consciousness without bounds. Unlike the box of beliefs that make up the rules of engagement in lower consciousness, there are no such limits here. This belongs to the quantum sea of infinite possibilities simply waiting to be caused into reality by the Observer. That is why, upon entering this place of nowhere land, astral experiences, like some of the NDE experiences, include dreams, fantasies, out of body experiences, hallucinations, imagination, and visions. And in many NDE cases, new abilities that are all part of the astral inventory come with the return. The five astral senses are clairaudience (astral hearing), psychometry (astral touch/feeling), clairvoyance (astral sight), imagination (astral equivalent of taste), and emotional idealism (astral equivalent of smell).

The Astral Body has a figure form in the shape of the Physical Body and an aura usually in an ovoid shape pointed at both ends. The aura extends about 4 to 9 feet from the Physical Body. It has 7 major energy centers, 21 minor energy centers, and many smaller centers, just like the etheric body. It is constantly changing color, dark to brilliant colors depending upon your mood. It has a total of 4 spatial dimensions.

Astral/Emotional consciousness is primarily awakened through the stimulation of desire. Awareness of the Astral Universe is awakened by meditation, psychic development techniques, out of body (astral) travel techniques, shamanic practices, lucid dreaming, and drugs - especially psychedelics, certain pranayama practices, and certain types of trauma, biochemical imbalances, and certain types of energetic stimulation.

What we want to say here is that there is much more to awakening these higher vibrational qualities than a simple statement that it is possible. Those who have accomplished these higher vibration states have not sat around simply dreaming. They have in some way trained themselves to get into the right state (environment) and have become familiar with understanding and experiencing the Out of Body consciousness. Here they have discovered a new empowering world of a new mind reality available to them. It is done through the process of astral projection into that place of astral interface which the Higher Self has responsibility to represent the Soul and to interface with the Lower self. Many refer to this as astral projection because it is the astral part of us that straddles the physical and nonphysical reality.

So the bottom line is that this is a desirable place to be if you want to link with the void of the quantum field and pick up some very cool abilities. Most engaged in the process as facilitators see this as the place of opening up your higher potential. When you have a visit with your higher counterpart, understand that it is as illustrated in the above picture. It has commonality with all the bodies it opens a new reality not so much as illustrated but as a quantum interface into all at once. Here it is consciousness as pure energy of thought, residing in the quantum world so it is part of everything that is, is interconnected to it and resides within a quantum field of infinite possibilities, just like your mind and imagination do. This is the place you want to go to get access to that Life Plan you created and to change reality below from above. All you have to do is go here and speak to your Higher Self as an integral part of your Soul; you have to talk to yourself in a different form. Yes, pure energy, not talking to a holographic projection because that is an illusion.

It is here in that above quantum field of energies that you escape the limits of the belief boxes formed by group consciousness below.

Astral Projection And Psychic Empowerment

In order to explore this further, we are going to shift to a book which is truly a work of excellence on this topic of Astral Projection. The reason we present this here is because these authors have immersed themselves in controlled clinical and laboratory tests to gain some light on the credibility of this topic of altered states, out of body, and higher mental faculties that become available through Out Of Body Experiences or what they call Astral Projection. It is a big book and has a lot of meat in it, and, it presents a summary of findings, procedures, and processes that provide some staggering justification for what we have been presenting. In this book you will find loads of information that provide groundbreaking evidence for the energetic-physical anatomy we presented at the beginning of the chapter.

The book is **Astral Projection for Psychic Empowerment: The Out-of-Body Experience, Astral Powers, and their Practical Application**. It is written by **Carl Llewellyn Weschcke** and **Joe H. Slate, Ph.D.** and is the most comprehensive psychic development guide available anywhere. It is richly supported by detailed tables, charts, and developmental exercises. Incorporating the latest discoveries in quantum physics, it organizes the concepts of psychic empowerment into a progressive, cohesive plan that features straightforward instruction on a wealth of psychic empowerment methods and practices. Most of all, this book provides further support and clinical evidence for what we have been writing about here.

And these authors are no casual writers without supporting credentials to be experts in these areas. **Carl Llewellyn Weschcke** is the owner and chairman of Llewellyn Worldwide, the world's oldest and largest metaphysical publisher. **Joe H. Slate** is a Licensed Psychologist in private practice with a PhD from the University of Alabama and postdoctoral studies in hypnosis and psychosomatic medicine at the University of California. He is Emeritus Professor of Psychology at Athens State University and Honorary Professor at the University of Montevallo. His research interests include health and fitness, rejuvenation, pain management, reincarnation, astral projection, and the human aura.

Joe is also the founder of the **Parapsychology Foundation of New York** which provides a worldwide forum supporting the scientific investigation of psychic phenomena. The Foundation gives grants, publishes pamphlets, monographs, conference proceedings and the *International Journal of Parapsychology*, hosts the Perspectives Lecture Series, conducts the Outreach Program, maintains the Eileen J. Garrett Library with its collection of more than 12,000 volumes and 100 periodicals on parapsychology and related topics. Parapsychology is concerned with the investigation of paranormal and psychic phenomena. Parapsychologists study telepathy, precognition, clairvoyance, psychokinesis, near-death experiences, reincarnation, apparitional experiences, and other paranormal phenomenon classified as "unexplainable."

Science is confirming what ancient wisdom has always asserted—that reality is far more complex than we have imagined, and that our individual potential is far greater than we have believed. In this time of expanding consciousness, the new frontier - the gateway to spiritual growth and self-empowerment - is through the astral realm.

Opening Your Optimum Potential

Astral Projection for Psychic Empowerment introduces you to the real-world benefits that come from exploring the astral plane. Here you can learn controlled, self-induced astral projection and reach beyond physical limitations to new sources of knowledge. It is about opening your full potential; to live and love more fully than you have ever thought possible by tapping your immense unconscious powers and integrating them into your conscious experience. This comprehensive guide includes true case studies of astral projection, scientific test results from laboratory studies, and a seven-day developmental program designed to unleash your highest potential. The book is written to show you how to:

- Induce an out-of-body experience
- Safely visit astral realms
- Explore past lives
- Communicate with guides and entities
- Interpret the aura for health and healing
- Create powerful thought forms
- Practice astral sex
- Expand your psychic awareness
- Achieve your goals
- Understand psychokinesis and the power of your mind

But this is just the tip of the iceberg because they provide an extensive list of empowerment potential that they have clinically observed. These are cited as the reasons why anyone should engage in Astral Projection.

- To visit the heavenly world while still alive
- To experience the continuity of life and consciousness
- To feel a confirmation there is life after death
- To explore the astral plane and the larger universe
- To gain an understanding between the physical and other energy/consciousness levels
- To gain an understanding of the functions of emotional interactions between people
- To explore the play of electrical and magnetic energies between men and women in relationships
- To gain understanding of the relationship between physical world and other dimensions
- To explore the role of subatomic particle and quanta in the greater universe
- To explore the quantum level of the physical plane and astral plane
- To gain understanding of the interactions between consciousness and energies
- To have astral adventures
- To explore the nature and meaning of tarot, rune, tattwas, religious symbols, kabalistic symbols
- To explore the possible therapeutic applications of astral projections
- To do path-working on the tree of life and other guided journeys
- To meet and interact with spirit guides, angelic beings, departed ones, friends and other astral entities
- To exercise psychic abilities
- To engage in remote viewing
- To develop clairvoyant and PSI skills
- To actually see chakras, thought forms, astral entities, angels
- To see higher dimensions of sacred sites, healing sites, local deities
- To see the creative visualization of personal goals in action
- To stimulate creativity in problem solving
- To develop fictional stories and seeing the action
- To augment artistic work and design-seeing things in future motion
- To better design new products-trained imagination intensified
- To diagnose health problems
- To augment physical vision with astral perspective
- To work with healing energies, physically and psychologically
- To find missing documents, lost objects, pets, persons
- To prospect for minerals, locate water, rare plants

- To find undiscovered archeological sites
- To research real estate sites for unknown problems
- To augment forensic search
- To augment divination answers
- To time travel to the past and future
- To space travel to planets, water depths inside volcano, deep inside earth

This is quite an impressive list of reasons to engage in Astral Projection to open up your potential. In the following sections we are going to give you a brief summary of the main points as we interpret their writings and conclusions. We will also provide what they suggest as the process of engagement.

Consciousness is like a permeable container of space. It is permeable in that it shares in the space that is everywhere. It is a container in that it is yours. Within the container is a bubble of light that is your awareness functioning as your conscious mind. Both light and dark, consciousness and unconsciousness can be found to function within a particular vibratory range that we experience as a body.

It is your goal to expand the bubble of light to focus anywhere in the entire container that makes yourself as light move beyond through expression and experience as an expansion of consciousness. This marks the growth of the ordinary person to become the extraordinary fully integrated with the Higher Self. To achieve this, astral travel or OBE'S are critical to evolving souls, reaching beyond physical limitations for new sources of knowledge and personal enhancement – solving issues and enhancing decision making, to understand life beyond death, gain new insight, awaken new potential, and to engage in healing and rejuvenation.

In the 100's of studies, it has been shown without exception that through the engagement in astral projections:

- intelligence functions are enhanced
- high positive emotions of joy and elation are common
- states can influence tangible objects
- all senses are intact or expanded
- feelings of weightlessness occurs
- sensory abilities like temperature/energy changes are enhanced
- there is an awareness of a guiding presence such as Spirit Guides
- meaningful interactions with departed and living people are common
- many have a spontaneous OB travel
- many cases show it can be instrumental in preventing physical injury
- may rise above the body, view from above, and travel over terrain

Crucial Discoveries Of Astral Travel

There is a very crucial discovery that the research has confirmed. If you want to truly understand the statement **As above so below** it describes the fact that the higher consciousness always incorporates the lower consciousness. The great secret is that higher always controls lower Causal-Mental-Astral hierarchy to effect in lower planes. On this there are two key principles:

1. Every physical action is duplicated on higher planes according to the nature of these planes
2. Higher or inner controls the lower or outer. So you can apply leverage at higher to shape reality in lower once you are able to function consciously at a higher level

What they are saying is that the leverage to change the reality at the lower is from the higher plane. In our study here in this book, this is a very important factor in understanding how the directives to change reality in the physical plane must come from a higher mental and emotional plane. And this means a total let go of the belief box and the influences of the lower plane! This is particularly important to understand how we communicate with the Divine Programmer.

They have concluded that typically people accept their experience to be the physical and the inner experience is an addendum. To take command of astral power it is the opposite; physical is the addendum to the non physical. We must confirm this as in our work here in this book we have stated that access to this inner world which we have determined is through an altered state and well being is the key to directing reality changes in the physical from the energetic bodies through the subconscious and the brain down the causal hierarchy to the cells. Or in the case of external reality, manifesting by way of attraction energetically that which has been mentally configured and energized mentally and emotionally from the infinite possibilities to be collapsed into external reality.

The authors have concluded that the astral plane OBE's bring adoption, wholeness, enlightenment, discovery, learning, loving, and play where joyful laughter is the most powerful plane in the cosmos. In their studies, they confirm that this Astral domain has angels, guides, facilitators and teachers who share a common commitment of continued growth and spiritual actualization. This is exactly what we have found in the studies of NDE's.

They confirm that when consciousness is centered with the physical body, your astral, mental, spiritual attributes are channeled through the physical senses provided by the brain and the nervous system. We can say that this ego-intellect mode makes the mind a slave to the body. It takes one into the belief boxes of group consciousness that have been diligently programmed since birth into the "below" subconscious of the Lower Self. It is what is bypassed in the OBE or Astral projection process. Here it is opposite where the body is the slave of the mind.

Their studies conclude that as a result, in the Astral plane and up there where you are pure energy thought in touch with your Soul and your Higher energetic Self there are things you can do not possible from the physical. What you do in astral can create a physical correspondence. So healing from above can have effects in physical below. This is where the mental and emotional energetic counterparts, as the invisible anatomy of every person becomes the creator of reality exactly the way we described in the first chapter. It is because the mind, the emotion, the consciousness, once you dump the Beta mind, are all one. And the same quantum field encompassing all that was, is and will be as pure imagination becomes accessible.

Their work indicates that the process of Astral Projection requires training and exercise. You do not have to change diet, take vows, be celibate, be a monk, or change your job but you DO have to devote time to train and build your higher astral "muscles". Lower astral merges with etheric below, mental above. The process of engagement in astral projection or OBE is not something that does not have a learning curve and time element. It must be practiced, believed, and developed in order to be effective. Each individual is different in this respect, just like the degree of suggestibility as we have seen in hypnosis.

They state that there are no forms in this astral place but they note colors blending into the mental above. Because the etheric energy body is personal, one must gain control of the etheric double to gain more control over the physical. This allows the means of channeled type control below into the physical counterpart. We can use creative visualization that is charged with emotional energy then projected from astral into physical. Examples are prayer, mind power as charged with emotional energy with directives for manifestation – like the power of attraction which is simply activated astral power. It is a place where astral power can change your life and empower you.

Another important conclusion is that the emotional state is critical and can inhibit progress if not right. OBE research from hundreds of research participants shows that there is no need for negativity on higher planes of peace, love, and joy. So in order to be part of it you have to be in that state of positive emotion. As we have seen in the previous chapters, this should not be much of a surprise as the state of being must be a precondition in order to be in the field in order to communicate with it. The lower struggle from karmic baggage and the survival mode of the ego have no place in the astral plane.

Astral substance is shaped by feeling and thought to create thought forms seen clairvoyantly. This property is both passive – reflecting feeling, passing thought, day dreams, and ACTIVE by deliberately created and shaped concentrated thoughts and visualization.

Astral Projection Processes

The authors go to great extents to determine what Astral Projection processes work best. It is highly recommended that if you want to pursue this area, you get your own book. In this section we are going to summarize some of their suggested processes because they are very relevant to understanding how we get to know the Divine Programmer. It is certainly true that if you want to become a programmer, you need to be educated in this process. You have to spend time learning and you have to be in an environment where you can implement your programming techniques to be effective.

You will see a common process in the examples we cite below. What you must comprehend here is that we have an Astral Double which provides a complete model parallel to the physical. In the process of moving into an altered state, through hypnosis or other methods to induce an OBE, we see the same steps:

1. energize astral parts or systems needed to be healthy with positive astral energies
2. channel or infuse healthy images so as to transfer to biological counterparts
3. when the same counterparts are energized, it transfers upon re-emergence

The procedure calls for one to be in an altered state of relaxation and silence. The research shows that when one is not in this peace and silence, attempting this is simply a waste of time. The other important consideration is that this is not a 10 or 20 minute affair. They state that an hour is needed to truly engage and this should be done daily without any of the daily mind buzz. Here is the process:

1. **Statement of Goals** formulate objectives and affirm goals by creating images of the desired outcome. An example is to repair an organ in which the image reflects a repaired organ
2. **Induction** includes relaxation, and imagery affirmation to induce OBE
    a. Give permission to disengage, easy return, to solve issues
    b. Sense the separation, eyes closed and relaxed
    c. See replication as a glowing aura
    d. Experience rising and hovering over body
3. **Astral Infusion** Once apart remind yourself the astral realm is rich with energy and power and you are now part of it.

a. Focus on parallel astral parts or system to be energized and saturate them with radiant energy
   b. Mentally engage your biological body at rest and influence the counterpart organ or system with astral energy
   c. Let both bodies become fully infused and empowered with energy from the highest level
   d. Sense a saturation of energy and power through your total being
   e. Do not rush a return. Take time to enjoy the infusion as you reflect on its relevance to your goals
4. **Astral Return** with the infusion complete
   a. Initiate a return by stating the intent to return and reunite as intent is a powerful force
   b. Sense the reunion
   c. Pay attention to the powerful merging of the astral body with its physical counterpart
   d. Note a reunion of specific biological and astral parts
   e. Upon engagement experience a final burst of energy to fill you totally, mentally, physically, and spiritually
   f. Enjoy the oneness
5. **Conclusion** Review the experience and mentally re-infuse your body with healthy vigor. Again saturate organs and systems with positive energy and affirm: *"I am at my peak empowerment"*

As a side note, they say that laboratory experiences show that when a deep emerald green (image or crystal) is used, it accelerates healing.

The next example relates to **PK or Psychokinesis** which means you are engaging in changing material reality. This is where we influence material reality through mind power. In controlled lab experiments it has been shown it is possible to induce motion in an object. It can be deliberately applied to improve performance, influence chemical reactions, and influence the biological body. Lab experiments show that the formalization of goals, verbalization of the words and imagery all add to success. Our PK energies usually are scattered and unfocused so the OBE liberates and energizes PK from the point of the Astral Body.

It has been found that the formulation of goals creates a state of readiness that prepares the activation environment for OBE. Once the OBE is induced, the PK faculty operates independently of physiological constraints that impeded it. With biological barriers minimized or banished our PK energies can become concentrated and directly found to result in a forceful release of power. It can intervene in aging, rejuvenation and reverse issues. Astral PK is the power of consciousness in OBE to directly intervene physiology to institute healing. It allows transfer of healthful energy from higher astral plane. As we have stated before, it is the Astral Energy Body that has all these higher "above" abilities that can be activated "below" through awareness of and being in the Astral Body.

The procedure for PK energy channeling with emerald green is as follows:

1. **Goal** Formulate goals and expectations, visualize desired end as clear images completion.
2. **Affirmations** Verbalize intent to enter OBE and access higher sources of healing and well being. Visualize self enveloped in light, secure and protected, can exit any time.
3. **Emerald** With image of emerald or in hand close eyes and focus on innermost region of your being. Allow all to give way to emergent light until totally infused by bright healing energy.
4. **Induction** To enter OBE form an image of consciousness as light form gently rising from physical body. Form images relevant to your lift involving motion to sense lift or flow for separation. Affirm: *"I am totally protected"*.
5. **Emerald Plane** With consciousness disengaged visualize an iridescent astral plane of emerald green radiating healthful energy. Allow plane to be clearly visible and give yourself permission to ascend and interact with it.
6. **Astral/Physical Interaction** Enter the astral plane and draw the healing energy – take time to infuse it – fully infused. Imagine an astral cord of energy connecting to the body and a cord as a channel to transport radiant healing energy. In using channeling this way, the cord will brighten. Select specific biological organs or systems to infuse.
7. **Conclusion** Turn attention to physical body and give permission to enter. Allow a few moments to re-engage, and then focus on physical sensations. Notice emerald and allow it to radiate vitality through your being. Form images of particular body parts and saturate them with healing energy. Affirm: *"I am infused with health and vitality empowered at any time to unleash abundant healing energy by visualizing the emerald green which represents my contact with the higher astral realms."*
8. **Take time** Reflect upon the experience and open the eyes.

The following is provided to understand what works best for Astral Projection or OBE's. These are the key Steps provided:

Step 1: Disengagement Settle back or lying down position, hands at sides, legs uncrossed, eyes closed, mind cleared, active though gone as physical becomes increasingly relaxed. Positive state of well being generated by imagery and Affirm:

"I am relaxed at peace, enveloped by protective energy fully infused as I prepare to leave my body. I will be shielded and protected by guiding powers of higher astral planes. I will journey to other realities and return safely at my choosing. Upon return I will have my total being infused, refreshed, invigorated and empowered".

Imagine consciousness as a glowing energy form rising gently from the body. Aid this with images of motions (pendulum, light flow, swinging). As the movement of images and clarity increases, the separation occurs. The sensation of weightlessness or floating upward will ensue.

Step 2: Destination Intending to experience another destination or source of empowerment typically initiates OBE travel. This can be any place or life once separation is established. Mental images of destination will facilitate travel.

Step 3: Intention An intense range of empowering experiences, interactions, observations, goal activities can unfold. Here insight and significant knowledge emerges as empowering and life changing. Here is the space in which to linger.

Step 4: Re-engagement The typical return is by deliberate intent to return and reengage physical body. Return is visual. After reengagement, biological attention can be via breathing. Conclude with reflection and resolution to maximize empowering benefits.

The Altered State Hierarchy

We have seen that there is a certain hierarchy within the activities of the brain. Each state becomes deeper and deeper, further and further away from the reality of day to day life. We have seen that the initial altered state is best described by meditation where the mind wanders between Beta and Alpha but the best place is Theta. We have seen that in the hypnotic state it can easily be induced by one's self easily. This is the place of the Astral Plane where the access to the programming process is but it is not something that most people can do easily. We explained this in the Chapter on Hypnosis but here we will use this purposely for Astral Projection or OBE. You need one hour without interruptions. You are the best one to use hypnosis using the 7 simple steps as outlined below:

1. **Goal Formation** State your personal objectives as before.
2. **Trance Induction** Settle, hands on thighs, close eyes and mentally scan your body from head down to release tension by taking deep breaths; exhale slow in rhythm for each breath count 10 to 1. Then focus on your hands, noting sensations of tingling or numbness. After a

few moments focus on right hand and imagine weightlessness. Imagine a gentle force under it pushing it gently to your forehead. As your hand rises give permission to enter a deep hypnosis and then leave body. With hand rising affirm: *"When my hand reaches my forehead I will enter a deep hypnotic state. Upon relaxing my hand and returning it hypnosis will give way to the OBE state. Upon leaving my body I will be fully conscious, safe and secure. I will be enveloped through this experience in the powerful energies of higher astral planes. I will return to my body at any moment by so deciding. Upon returning and reengagement I will exit hypnosis by simply counting 1 to 5* (allow plenty of time to raise hand) then affirm: *"I am now in hypnosis and prepared to leave my body by simply relaxing my hand to resume original position"*. Let your hand drop.

3. **Astral Disengagement** With hand down, sense gentle rise leaving body below. Facilitate this by visualizing your astral body as a glowing mist lifting gently from body suspended above it. View body as a passive state of rest and sense the powerful radiance enveloping your total being then affirm: *"I am now outside my body fully enveloped by pure, radiant cosmic energy. The radiance enveloping my astral being extends to my biological body protecting and energizing it as I travel to higher planes. The highest cosmic realm is now receptive to my intentions."*

4. **Astral Ascent** You have two goals. First is to ascend to the realm of cosmic archives typically seen as bright dimension of light surrounded by sweeping swirling radiant color. Second is to access cosmic sources of past life experiences. This is typically accompanied by awareness of guides who are always luminous violet energy. The suggested affirmation is: *"I am now prepared to ascend to realm of cosmic archives in my efforts to gain new insight and knowledge concerning my past. I now invite the presence of astral guides who will be my constant companions."* The experience is usually being carried forward first through darkness into a radiant fluid like dimensions of varying colors – corridors or channels. In the distance magnificent light will draw attention as you go to the cosmic core now one with cosmos. Upon entering you will notice lights forming a great wall of many side by side vertical frames with which your past unfolds in channeled order from pre to present incarnations. Each vertical frame represents a significant period of your past, first depicting record of pre incarnate existence, and each successive frame depicting a lifetime or discarnate interval between lives. Each frame is progress of your growth, beginning at bottom of frame culminating to top. The last frame which is incomplete is a record of present lifetime. As past unfolds before you in discrete frames you will notice continuity and common themes. Total span is now at your command. Commanding attempts are highlighted contents that

represent significant events and turning points in your evolution. Guided by higher wisdom you can let frames unfold or arrest them to focus on relevance.
5. **Astral Return** Affirm intent to return, sense the presence of escorting Guides who accompany the return. Upon re-engaging your body, the hypnotic trance is spontaneously resumed.
6. **Resolution and Conclusion** Allow hypnotic state/trance to continue and then affirm: "*Upon ending this trance by counting 1 to 5 I will have immediate and full remembrance of all that I experienced during my OBE ascension I will understand the significance of this experience and use the knowledge gained from it to enrich and empower my life*".
7. **Conclude** Count 1 to 5 and intersperse increased awareness and alertness. Conclude by reflecting on the ascension experiences and contemplate its relevance.

We now have more information about our mirror copy and our Higher Self. The Causal/Soul Body is named "Causal" because it is the originating source of each personality that incarnates in each lifetime. It is the source of your personality, causing it to be and exist. The Soul and Higher Self interface from the higher nonmaterial planes through the mental, astral/emotional, and etheric planes to engage the personality in the lower physical 3D plane of matter. These are non local energies within the quantum field that link as one consciousness. Our Astral Double provides a complete model parallel to the physical. In the process of moving into an altered state, through hypnosis or other to induce an OBE, here is where typically the process is to energize astral parts or systems needed to be healthy with positive astral energies, channel or infuse healthy images so as to transfer to biological counterparts, and when the same counterparts are energized, it transfers upon re-emergence. We see that OBE's are part of our Soul's evolution through their Life Plans. It is about reaching beyond physical limitations for new sources of knowledge and personal enhancement – solving issues and decision making, life beyond death, new insight, awaken new potential, healing, rejuvenation.

The statement *As above so below* describes the fact that the higher consciousness always incorporates the lower consciousness. The great secret is that higher always controls lower Causal-mental-astral to appear in lower planes. Every physical action is duplicated on higher planes according to the nature of these planes. Higher or inner controls the lower or outer. So you can apply leverage at higher to shape reality in lower once you are able to function consciously at a higher level. In order to execute changes in the physical, they need to be executed from the higher astral planes. We see that this is process that requires time and persistence to master.

By now you will be forming a different picture of how this reality thing works with regards to miracles of shifting reality. The research here is pointing the way to you now getting better access to the Program Director of your Life Movie, and being able to change things in the movie.

Let us now look at some more "clinical" work and conclusions that illustrate how these frames in the Movie of Life can be changed by reprogramming from a higher state of being. The next two chapters will cover Past Life Regression and Future Life Progression.

9

PAST LIFE REGRESSION

"Being aware of a past mistake as a Cause which is manifested into physical reality as an Effect allows you to change the energetic picture then, and the physical reality now."

Aly McDonald   Ed Rychkun

> **Oh what did I Cause in my previous life
> To create an Effect of all this strife?**

We saw in "**The Divine Programmer: Creating Miracles**" how by working from a higher plane we can create miracles of wealth and health in the lower plane of physicality. We also saw how past life regression was used to correct an issue recorded in the past. Being taken back and having realized what was the cause; one was able to simply cleanse it and create a different effect in the current time. This is a great re-application of the Law of Cause and Effect. The thoughts, perceptions and emotions were changed and the effect translated in the physical now. The thing about this process is that sometimes this goes back to previous lives meaning this information is stored in what we are learning is the Causal Body; like you would store a show on a video recorder. And then what was stored as belief and perception can be edited by our Divine Programmer. Sometimes we have found the result can be a spectacular healing miracle. More and more we are finding that not only was there a Life Plan that was recorded, playing out in our reality, but that the actual life plan in explicit detail is being recorded as engagement in it continues. Then we are seeing that these moments in these recorded movies can be edited in the Astral plane of the quantum consciousness and we can change the effects in the current physical plane. In this chapter, we are going to look deeper into this process of Past Life Regression.

Past Life Regression Therapy

The purpose of past life regression therapy is to retrieve memories and belief systems from previous incarnations that are still negatively influencing a person's life in a current incarnation. These old belief systems can create disharmony; physically, mentally or emotionally. Once the past life memory is brought into awareness, deep understanding and insights arise as to how the events of the past are deeply impacting the present. For example, during a session a person may re-experience having starved to death in a past life. They then relate this memory to a current behavior pattern in their present life which as an example could be a compulsive eating disorder. Often once the connection between the past life and the current behavior is made, the pattern is broken. However, if the pattern still exists, the therapist can apply energetic and therapeutic techniques to release the frozen energy and help free the person from the limiting pattern.

What is particularly relevant about this is that karmic cycle we have discussed before can be broken if the lesson has not been learned. We have learned that the Soul purpose is to experience the lower form to exercise mental and emotional abilities; to engage these and learn to evolve better through the virtues; to overcome fears by engaging in that which creates it. To put it bluntly: get over the crap and learn from it! So in our example if you carry a karmic record of being starved to death in a previous life as a Cause, you may have an Effect of overindulgence in food in this life. Obviously you carry this karma because you did not learn from it and get over it; so you carry the fear of starvation and have to learn again. That fear generates an urgent emotional and mental need for food as the effect. So the Law of Attraction looks at this highly charged energy signature you constantly enforce until your body is addicted to over consumption. Being consciousness within the infinite quantum field, it buzzes with this energy to attract possibilities that satisfy the energy. But if we had learned the lesson before and got over it, it would not occur in a different life plan. Therefore, the Soul is always getting into these predicaments designed into a life plan to get over these issues. To get over it, you forgive yourself for this state, let it go and learn from it to instigate a new state of being. That would take you on a new path that would have been one of the designed options of choice in your life plan. What is so very interesting about this is that this possibility is always available no matter what life created the cause; and we can change the effect to break the Karmic loop.

Once again we see that the typical procedure to do this is what we saw with some of our miracle healers. To engage in this process a person is asked to be in a comfortable sitting or lying position and the person is first asked to set an intention about what they want to heal or change. More often than not, the skilled therapist uses hypnosis to lead the patient. They are verbally led through progressive relaxation steps until they reach a deep state of hypnosis, preferably Theta where the subconscious mind is open to suggestion. The therapist proceeds to lead them on a guided meditation to an inner sanctuary, where they feel safe and comfortable, and from here, they're guided to journey back to the time when their problem first began. The therapist facilitates the process by asking questions to help them figure out what occurred in the past, and how it is presently influencing their life.

Once the connection is established, the person is guided to the end of the lifetime and is often instructed to float above their body. In this in-between life state, the person has a broad perspective on the incarnation and they are able to understand the life lesson they learned from that lifetime. The person is then slowly lead back to the present lifetime and given positive suggestions to feel really good, better than before.

If for some reason you think that these are just contrived stories that people imagine, you can easily conduct your own research. For example Dr. Brian Weiss facilitated several cases where people have compared names, dates, times and places accessed through the regression process with historical records, and found identical correlations. There have also been instances where people being regressed begin to speak fluently in a foreign language.

In past life regression therapy sessions, the person is in total control of the process and the therapist acts merely as a guide. The conscious aware mind is always present and can withhold any information at anytime. The person is also able to immediately return to present time awareness if desired. If at any time during the regression process an unpleasant or traumatic memory is recalled, the person always has the option to float above the scene and watch it as if a movie; comfortably detached from the painful situation.

Most people can retrieve some past life information, and with practice can achieve deeper and deeper trance states where they can access more vivid memories. About 15 percent of the population has difficulty achieving trance states deep enough, to allow past life memories to emerge. Usually this is due to the depth of conviction to the belief box that analytically limits them from believing in the merit.

Past life regression therapy has been used to successfully treat phobias, eating disorders, physical aches and pains, fear of death, depression, anxiety, relationship issues, bottled anger, insecurity and migraines. Basically any physical, mental or emotional disorder that has its roots in past incarnations, can be treated with past life regression therapy.

Some say past life memories are the autobiography of your eternal soul; personal stories that explain who you are now and why you're here on Earth. Some people try past life regression simply out of curiosity to see who they were in the past. But for most, it's a path for personal growth and healing. With the help of a trained guide, past life regression can help you:

- See personal relationships in a new light
- Energize talents and abilities from the past
- Release fears and anxieties linked to past life traumas
- Release past life traumas at the root of physical problems
- Experience the transitional states of death and beyond
- Understand and align with life purpose

Past Life Regression is an amazing, full-sensory experience. You might experience the memory as a vivid movie, or see only vague flashes of images that prompt the narrative. You might hear gunshots or explosions on a battlefield, or music at a dance. It is possible to recall smells too: smoke from a fire, leather from a saddle, or the sweat of a dirty body.

As the story unfolds, you feel real emotions appropriate to the story. You may cry when you re-experience deep sadness at the death of a beloved child, feel despair in the pit of your stomach as you witness a massacre, or elation at a long-awaited homecoming from war. And just as you can recall strong emotions, you feel the pain of an arrow piercing your body as you are dying, or the heaviness of a load you're carrying on your back. These physical sensations and emotions are very real in the moment, but pass quickly as you move through the past life story and death.

How Regression Healing Works

Past life regression is healing. You were born not as a blank slate, but as a Soul rich with both the wisdom and scars from many lifetimes. We all carry memories from past lives into this life – unconscious memories that carry an energetic charge and continue to affect us. They can be things left undone, vows made, accomplishments, failures, mistakes, success, emotional debts, guilt, gratitude, traumatic and sudden deaths, wisdom, and love.

These charges from the past set up patterns which are continually triggered and repeated in our present life. These patterns can be positive or negative. They can affect our relationships, behaviors, motivations, and even our physical bodies and health. Positive patterns can feed talents, bestow wisdom, influence tastes, and energize life purpose. Negative patterns fuel destructive, compulsive behavior, cloud judgment, cause injury, and block your way. By making these memories conscious, we can release the patterns that no longer serve us, freeing us to live more fully in the present. Beneficial patterns are reinforced, negative patterns are neutralized. It is not surprising to understand that these programs are a hidden part of the sub and unconscious minds.

Past life regression is the process of healing the Soul by healing the past. It is gaining recognition as a legitimate form of spiritual healing. No matter what religion you profess - or even if you don't follow any religion - experiencing yourself as a Soul in other lifetimes gives you a profound awareness that you are more than a physical body. You encounter your Soul's essence, connected and aligned to a greater universal energy, perhaps for the first time in your life.

We have already dedicated a chapter to this topic discussing the work of Robert Schwartz. After slipping from your body, you travel in the spiritual state between lives and feel the energy of "heaven." You get a glimpse of who you truly are - a Soul learning and growing through different incarnations. Some meet guides and make plans. Some dialogue with deceased relatives, and are left with a profound sense of having made genuine contact with their loved ones.

Experiencing the life-between-life state is a natural part of most past life regressions. **Michael Newton**, author of **Journey of Souls and Destiny of Souls**, has pioneered methods for exploring the life-between-life state in more depth. Basically the story emerging from these practicing authors is the same. It is that you come into this life as a Soul impressed with the wisdom and wounds from many other lifetimes. These impressions are encoded in an "energetic template" that informs your present personality, physical body, and some external circumstances in your life. This template also carries the emotional charges from unfinished lessons from previous lives, and the plans and blueprints for the present life.

With the help of a past life therapist, you "re-live" the past life story, you understand the full context of that life, and you recall the thoughts and feelings that got frozen in the past life trauma, usually at the time of death. That's where the pattern originated. The process of remembering diffuses the energy around the pattern. You finally release these old thoughts and feelings. You feel lighter. You are lighter. The past life therapist guides you to see the bigger picture to understand why you were born into your present family and circumstances, and to realize that you brought this pattern with you into this life - it's a pre-existing condition of your Soul. With these insights, you understand your purpose and what you came here to learn.

When you attain the state of awareness from the higher perspective, many surprising things can happen. You can objectively review the past life just experienced, and gain a sense of understanding of lessons learned in that lifetime, and what thoughts, feelings, and physical sensations may have carried forward from that life into the present. If more than one lifetime is recalled during the session, general Soul patterns can be observed, shedding tremendous insight into where you've been and where you're going in your journey through incarnations.

Some people move into a highly energetic state where they experience healing energies coming into their bodies, imbuing information, love, and understanding. These energies may be experienced as orbs, colors, and other amorphous forms. Or the energy can take on the form of spiritual beings that give guidance and answer questions. Groups of Souls may appear and act as agents of teaching and healing. This type of healing usually occurs spontaneously, without any prompting from a facilitator. These healings have been described by clients as one of the most significant, life-affirming events of their lives. For some, it is the first time they've experienced absolute peace and unconditional love.

In this state of soul consciousness, deceased relatives can suddenly make contact both viscerally and telepathically. A presence is felt in the room. Their forms are recognizable with telepathic dialogues. This extraordinary state of consciousness has been described by mystics, near-death Experiencers, and past life therapists for more than forty years.

Hypnosis is a form of focused awareness that is best used to attain the appropriate state. It is necessary for you to focus inward to access your past life memories – or any distant memories for that matter. In this state you can still be aware that you are reclining in a chair, a bird is chirping outside, or an airplane is flying overhead, while at the same time you are completely engrossed in the past life memory.

By now you know the process of altered state and well being as your environment. To help you focus inward, you need to focus on the rhythm of your breathing while relaxing your entire body. By focusing on your breathing, you fall gently into a light trance state. So in a sense, you don't go "under" hypnosis, you are simply relaxing deeper and deeper opening to the subconscious mind. As you relax you need to be aware of your inner images, feelings, and physical sensations. Then you focus on a particularly charged thought or feeling, which is often the reason why you wanted to do a regression in the first place. For example, if a dominant theme in your life is the fear of being alone, direct a focus on the thought and the feeling, *"I'm all alone."* This serves as a bridge from your present feelings to a relevant past life memory.

Some past life memories are of happy and fulfilling lives. These benign lifetimes help us understand and appreciate our present positive attitudes, talents, and good relationships. They are life's gifts. Most memories that surface in past life therapy are of past life trauma, usually a traumatic death. It is the past life trauma that continues to affect us emotionally, mentally, and physically, causing difficulties in many aspects of our present life. By exposing these painful memories to the light of awareness, and understanding the context of the past life and death, the emotional intensity loses its grip. We can finally let go of the past and move forward in our lives. We feel lighter, as if a burden has been lifted. This is the heart of your purpose to heal the deepest part of us, our Soul. You will not get "stuck" in these traumatic memories. Sometimes the healing is immediate and dramatic, or can be more subtle and noticeable over time. After the regression, you will remember everything you experienced. Over time, new layers of insight and understanding emerge spontaneously.

In his book **Past Lives, Future Lives Revealed, Dr. Bruce Goldberg** discusses his techniques in the field of progressing patients into future lives. Bruce reveals the implications of karma in our lives, how we are affected by reincarnation, and how hypnosis can reveal our pasts and our futures. Here he includes some enthralling case histories from the 35,000 past and future-life regressions from of some 14,000 individuals. Goldberg spends a great deal of time dispelling the myths surrounding the practice of past/future life hypnotherapy. He shows how it is now recognized as a valid and viable tool by many experts throughout the world.

He tells us that the laws of Cause & Effect and Karma work between lives. For example he cites many cases that illustrate how an effect in current life is a result (opposite) in a previous life. For example desertion now relates to overprotective parents in previous life. The fear of water in this life relates to drowning in a previous life. A fear of noises now relates to being killed by a bomb kill in a previous life. Loss of children in this life is a result of being barren in a previous. What his cases illustrate is the notion of learning lessons that we will carry over and over until we can balance the karma. The Key point is that through the process and hypnosis it is possible to overcome a problem, accomplish an objective, have an experience.

Bruce conducts energy healing which he reports is through the superconsious mind tap system, OBE's and Time travel. It engages a process to introduce the subconscious mind (Soul) to the Higher Self. This mind is perfect and tapping into it raises energy level of superconsious mind. He concludes that most therapy takes effect at night as willpower does not function in sleep and the cleanse is in Alpha consciousness. The process involves energy cleansing the emotional level down to the physical level. The cleansing is done by raising the patients frequency level to a new threshold once established is irreversible. Thus emotional and physical symptoms as well as causes are resolved by treating the ultimate cause – the patients' energy level upping the frequency rate.

Bruce points out that you hypnotize yourself all the time in daydreams, when lost in thought, watch TV shows, or movies as you are in Alpha trance. In this state you actually bypass the conscious mind and allow subconscious to come through where all details are stored. You may also now be aware that this is a pretty good way to reprogram the subconscious mind just like when you were a kid that had not yet developed Beta.

In his experience, he states that the Higher Self is the perfect component of the Soul. On the other side where the Higher Self dwells, there is no time or space. It is here you choose your next life (when where, how born, parents, relatives, friends, major events). Your purpose is to learn lessons or change the karmic cycle. From here you are free to incarnate in past, present or future because time does not exist. Here the objective is to learn.

He points out that Earthly lifetimes are not the ultimate reality only one of several possibilities. The mind or consciousness continues through each life as we are in our higher form of energy that cannot die. The link he finds throughout is Karma which is Cause and Effect. As a result, if you are unhappy, a cause exists and can be traced to past lives as all is retained by subconscious. The purpose is to educate the subconscious and purify it.

And like we have been hearing before, when all is done it is ascension back to your Soul and Home. The Soul has free will to choose a Life Plan. In his past life work, Bruce reports consistent results, namely the patients see screens of audio and visual presentations that flash through. They feel whispering. They have cloudy or quick impressions and read words. They appear to know with feeling. The Subconscious which lives in the Theta and low Alpha state hears what conscious which lives in the Beta state, cannot. The usual process is for the therapist to search (ask subconscious) for scenes of related issues, and sources. Then they suggest a return to that place. He then brings a patient back and asks them to remember the situation and the source of issue. He then asks the patient to awaken to see and feel the issue gone. Thus the Cause of issue once known creates a change in current reality and the Effect as the symptom disappears.

The following is what Bruce suggests as a **Superconsiouness Mind Exercise:**

1. Imagine a bright light from above coming down to the top of your head to fill the body. See it, feel it and let it become reality

2. Imagine an aura of pure light from heart region emanating out to surround you, protecting you. See it, feel it and let it become reality. Now only your Higher Self and highly evolved loving entities who mean you well will be able to influence you during this and other hypnotic sessions. You are totally protected by an aura of pure white light
3. Count 1 to 20 as you feel yourself rising up to superconsious Higher Self. Take a moment to orient to that level
4. Play music for 1 minute
5. Ask yourself a question about the past, present or future, state the desire for information or an experience and let superconsious mind work for you
6. Hold here for 8 minutes and play music
7. Open up channels of communication by removing obstacles and allowing receiving of information and experience to help present life time. Allow advanced information from HS and Masters and Guides to raise your frequency and improve the karmic subcycle
8. Hold here for 8 minutes with music
9. Count forward 1 to 5 as when you reach 1 you will be in present and will remember everything
10. Count out of the trance

The following is a **Past Life Regression exercise provided by Bruce:**

After determining a specific time, place or situation, (say a previous life at age 15) repeat 1, 2, 3 above, then:

4. I will count backward 20-1 and you will move through a dark tunnel. It will get lighter and lighter. At the end is a door with bright lights above it. When you walk through you will be in a past life scene. You will experience one of your past lives at about age 15. You will move to an event that will be significant in explaining who you are, where and why. If you feel uncomfortable you can awaken anytime by counting 1 to 5
5. Orient yourself, focus, listen. Describe where you are, what time? What are you? How do you feel? Take a few moments to let the information flow
6. Play music for 3 minutes
7. Listen, sleep now and detach from the scenes. I will count to 5 and you will move forward away from the scenes

The purpose of past life regression therapy is to retrieve memories and belief systems from previous incarnations that are still negatively influencing a person's life and to remove them as a cause to delete the effect from the current time. Once a past life memory is brought into conscious awareness, it can be understood and released to eliminate the limiting or behavioral effects as a limiting pattern. Again we see the process of reaching into the past requires the patient to be in an altered state by way of hypnosis or suggestion and to be guided to the point of interest. The results show increased abilities, released fears and traumas, understanding of life purpose, life in a new light.

We see that getting into this state with the Divine Programmer allows the mind to simply delete an issue and replace it with a new effect in behavior. And this new behavior became an update in the subconscious programs, triggered a new firing-wiring of the neurological processes in the nervous system and managed new behavior of mental, emotional and physical processes. If this was some physical-physiological issue like an addiction to drugs or other trauma induced issue, all those chemical and physiological processes simply got their shit together and it happened!

What we are seeing clearly is that we are dealing with a stack of playable and editable Life Movies that are holographically recorded, presented, and modified under the direction of our Divine Programmer.

Up to this time, we have looked at these movies of the past, current and inbetween where we created a plan to engage in that holographic reality. But what about looking at the future movie and getting the Divine Programmer to change some of that stuff too? To answer this we are going to look at another process called Future Life Progression.

10

FUTURE LIFE PROGRESSION

"If we can regress to clean up the moments in the past to affect change now, why not progress into the future life plan and change now to affect the future?

Aly McDonald   Ed Rychkun

> **I don't like this movie I directed**
> **Time to edit what's become infected**

What Is Future Life Progression?

Future Life Progression – or FLP for short – is a waking dream therapy. It is a form of hypnosis that relaxes you into a deep, yet alert state that also opens your mind to the potential you have at your fingertips. Past Life Regression concentrates on your personal history and how certain events in your life, or past lives, have shaped your beliefs and circumstances in the present day. Future Life Progression takes you forward in time to a place where you can explore the possibilities that extend from your own Life Plan creation and the paths you chose to provide for your experience. More astounding is that FLP can also take you on a journey into other future lives and doing so can provide you with a wealth of insight and knowledge.

You may wonder how is this possible. Well, if you go back to the work of Robert Schwartz in an earlier chapter on In-between Life Regression and consider his therapy work this is not hard to understand. Remember, his work pointed to the creation of a Life Plan and contract to engage in a carefully laid out plan that suited your needs of self evolution in the form of learning your lessons. This plan was like the branches of a tree expanding at every branch providing a path already designed at each juncture. That Life Plan included the actors, the scenes, the storyline, key events and multiple situations, choices, and exit points that you saw as a Soul before you engaged in it. And the detail was up to you as the creator of the Life Plan. That was You as a Soul and your best Buddy the Spirit Guide in collaboration with your Soul Family. It was your guideline to craft your life to engage your mental and emotional higher bodies through the interface of the astral body. It would interface to a lower form where the brain would be the physical CEO/sub processor deploying thought and the body would be the physical means of deploying feeling body. And the heart would be the seat of emotion. And the subconscious would be the recording instrument, operating system and link to the higher state of Self as Soul or Higher Self.

FLP allows you to peer ahead into those choices and pathways that you created and forgot... silly you! You actually saw what things would be like and what people looked like before you decided! Bizarre, isn't it? Where this is used a lot is when one feels life is stuck on hold or one has tried and failed to remove personal blocks and obstacles. The big question of course becomes one of asking: *Why can I not overcome this issue; is it because I absolutely have to do it by design?*

Future Life Progression can provide you with the tools to make renewed progress. What is being told here through these clinical cases is that you can fast forward the Life Plan; look at how you would screw up or look at how you would benefit, then come back and make the appropriate choices now! Yes, that's pretty bizarre! So obviously that Life Plan and that Contract are somewhat adjustable! We say somewhat because it isn't the plan you adjust, it is the choice of path within that plan that you adjust.

You may have already cleared blocks and now need clarity to build confidence and move forward in the direction that most appeals to you. In this case FLP can help you make better informed choices and help you explore alternatives. Future Life Progression will also allow you to see how your future could pan out. You may be able to experience how your life is, given the choices you opt to make, as well as the people you share your life with and the location that it all takes place in.

During a session it is like hypnotherapy. The practitioner, or facilitator, will talk you through relaxation steps that allow your body to become naturally deeply relaxed. You will have discussed, beforehand, the areas that you are most interested in exploring and examining and will therefore be led in that direction.

The information that you will receive during the meditative state will, however, be the most relevant information for you to gain knowledge for in the present time. This means that although you may feel you want to focus solely on career prospects your unconscious mind may feel that it is more important for you to examine another area or issue of your life that is preventing you from living your true potential. Because the Soul or Higher self is a quantum part of the subconscious, it will know what is best to serve your growth and direct the subconscious to accommodate this in what is presented.

The process you will now recognize is similar to the life review where you are led through relevant images to review your mortal progress. Once again, we are getting a look at some recorded information but this time it is a plan that has not yet become reality. That is the beauty of the reality we appear to accept as real illusion as it is like a readable-writeable DVD that contains a self created movie. It can be changed with the cooperation of the Divine Programmer.

After a session, having explored the possibilities of your future life you will return to normal waking consciousness feeling more relaxed, confident and keen to start implementing the changes you saw clearly in your mind during the meditation. These images will be vivid enough for you to interpret them as a memory because you will have explored happenings that feel true to life rather like in a dreaming state. This experience will bring with it new insight and personal knowledge that you can tap into during moments of stress or anxiety. This will encourage you to continually make progress towards the path that leads you to the future you have seen and experienced during Future Life Progression.

In the book we already mentioned in the last chapter - **Past Lives, Future Lives Revealed - Bruce Goldberg** contends that people have the power to customize and control their destinies. In his work on Future Life Progression Bruce reports that the future already exists, tomorrow is real only in potentiality. The future has many forms but only when congealed into the present does it exist in actuality. We live in a framework of potentiality and our actions determine the final form so we can change the future. He states that in sleep the mind wanders between present and future.

In an interesting explanation, Bruce relates to Einstein's theory of space-time continuum where he says all lives are concurrent so you can change past and future by changing present. A good example is when you are in a helicopter you can see the road below, forward and backward. You see what has not happened yet as cars approaching an accident area ahead as to what could happen as a possibility. By learning in the Earth plane from a similar position, you can see past, present and future. Since our brains deal with 3D present only the space-time continuum confuses it.

What is particularly relevant to the work done by Bruce is that he describes many cases where the ability to see forward has been tested. He describes many experiments where the patient moves to see a week ahead (short term) into future, documents these details then confirms them after a week. He states that most often these are correct but the timing is not exact.

The Self Hypnotic Trance

Once again we see hypnosis as the key method. The process suggested by Goldberg is one that has been tested over 25 years. It is to be done twice daily for 20 minutes; best when fresh in the morning and you are alert. You will see a certain pattern of processes and steps here similar to what we have already discussed. In these examples, it is suggested that you basically record your own versions of the three different procedures to access the Superconsciousness Higher Self within a Self Hypnotic Altered State.

The key components are a quiet environment, a passive attitude, and a comfortable position. When you enter the self-hypnotic trance, you will observe the following:

- Positive mind of tranquility, peace of mind
- Experience unity or oneness with environment
- Inability to describe experience in words
- Alteration in time/space relationships
- Enhanced sense of reality and meaning

The following is what Bruce suggests as a **Superconsiouness Mind Exercise** after getting into the altered state:

1. Imagine a bright light from above coming down to the top of your head to fill the body. See it, feel it and let it become reality
2. Imagine an aura of pure light from heart region emanating out to surround you, protecting you. See it, feel it and let it become reality Now only your Higher Self and highly evolved loving entities who mean you well will be able to influence you during this and other hypnotic sessions. You are totally protected by an aura of pure white light

3. Count 1 to 20 as you feel yourself rising up to superconsious Higher Self. Take a moment to orient to that level
4. Play music for 1 minute
5. Ask yourself a question about the past, present or future, state the desire for information or an experience and let superconsious mind work for you
6. Hold here for 8 minutes and play music
7. Open up channels of communication by removing obstacles and allowing receiving of information and experience to help present life time. Allow advanced information from HS and Masters and Guides to raise your frequency and improve the karmic subcycle
8. Hold here for 8 minutes with music
9. Count forward 1 to 5 as when you reach 1 you will be in the present and will remember everything
10. Count out of the trance

The Following is what Bruce suggests as a **Future Life Progression Exercise** after getting into the altered state:

1. Apply white light protection, visualize a symbol to toss into the future to broadcast information about the future
2. Ask the Higher Self to assist you. Imagine a week in the future. See, feel what you are doing and allow thoughts, feelings into awareness. What is different? What do you see? What do you want answered?
3. Now perceive 1 month in advance and ask the Higher Self to assist

Do the same for 3 months, 6 months, 1 year, and 5 years and investigate important issues. Ask yourself for advice.

4. Ask the Higher self for comments or advice with attention to:
   a. What will facilitate my spiritual growth?
   b. What decisions, choices can I make now to achieve highest aspirations?
   c. What behavior, thoughts, actions can I implement to accelerate my spiritual path?
   d. What am I learning from this scenario?

The Future Is Yours To Review

Anne Jirsch states: **"The information I gleam out is never wrong"**. She is a London born professional psychic with a large worldwide following. Her client base includes heads of industry, politicians and celebrities from the world of film, music and sport. She is an internationally best-selling author of four books ***Instant Intuition, The Future is Yours, Cosmic Energy*** and ***Create Your Perfect Future***.

She has appeared on numerous radio shows, having regular slots on Star FM, BBC Radio Cumbria and BBC Radio Cambridge. Anne has also appeared on Kuwait morning television, Estonian television and BBC morning news and more recently **'This Morning'** where she hypnotized celebrity Natalie Cassidy and took her into her future lifetime.

Anne is a leading world pioneer of Future Life Progression and runs the only training school for FLP in the world with 250 practitioners in 8 countries. She is the **Chairman of The Past & Future Life Society**. She has representatives in Japan, Kuwait, Dubai and Estonia and travels extensively with her sell-out workshops and seminars.

Through this work people can see the life type they could have should they find a partner, job, etc. This way it is for people to take control of their destiny and create the reality they want and deserve. She reports that you can see what happens and clients typically become self assured, confident and more direct.

She tells us that *"the Higher Self provides answers to your questions and links you with future lifetimes and even concurrent lives. You will only see future events that you can influence now, in the present."* Note the life plan actual and planned are different here as with regression and progression because the life plan has less details and more interaction occurs on the actual. *"You will see warnings; see future partners (major events, people, etc)."*

An interesting addendum to this is the documented work of **Dr Helen Wambach** who in 1960 wanted to disprove regression and show how foolish it really was. For 10 years she studied through hypnosis 1088 people and concluded that with the exception of 11 people, descriptions of details were consistent with historical records. She then worked on future progression and found 9 of 10 gave same details of government, wars and other key information when she took them to the same time.

Dr. Wambach questioned 1088 white, middle class subjects from California while they were under hypnosis. The subjects were asked to regress to a former life. If this was successful, they were told to remember everything when they awoke from their hypnotic state. Not satisfied to just ask who they were or when they lived, Dr. Wambach also made them describe their status, gender, race, clothing, footwear, utensils, tools they used, their money, housing and even the food they ate!

The subjects frequently reported viewing the former lives much like watching a movie. They said they could experience whatever the individual experienced in that particular time. They heard ancient languages but did not understand them. The full details of their experiences were recorded both during and after the sessions. Never before had past life inquiries been that specific or involved such a large population. The results of her 10 years of research surprised everyone.

The detailed reports were thoroughly investigated to see if they corresponded with historical facts. In all but 11 cases (less than 1%), the descriptions were totally accurate. Some of the results are as follows:

- 50.6% of the past lives reported were male and 49.4 % were female - this is exactly in accordance with biological fact.
- The reported class or status was exactly the same proportion as the estimates of historians of the specific period of the former life.
  In general, this was approximately 10% upper class, 20-35% from the middle class and the remaining 55-70% from the lower class. Although the proportion of middle class was higher around 1000 BC, the proportion later dropped and increased again after 1700 AD.
- The recall by subjects of clothing, footwear, type of food and utensils used was better than that in popular history books. She found over and over again that her subjects knew better than most historians -- when she went to obscure experts her subjects were invariably correct.
- A subject who lived around 1000 B.C in Egypt described different types of clothing worn by the upper and lower classes. The upper classes wore either a half-length or full-length white cotton robe. The lower classes wore something like an exotic-looking type of pants that was wrapped downwards from the waist. The researchers viewed historic records of clothing worn during the respective periods and could therefore compare it to the descriptions of these subjects. The descriptions were found to be correct.
- Between 60-77% of the ancient population lived at or below the poverty level. They wore homemade clothes and lived in simple, even primitive, abodes. The majority were farmers who labored every day in the fields. **None of the hypnotized individuals recalled being a famous historical figure.** Those who recalled a high social position seemed highly dissatisfied with their lives, as if it

was a burden to be alive. Those who recalled being a farmer or a member of a primitive tribe appeared to be content.
- Their recollections were from different geographic areas and races during their prior life. Dr. Wambach divided them into several categories: Caucasians, Asians, Indians, Blacks and Middle Eastern descent.

  Around 2000 BC, only 20% of the subjects reported that they were Caucasians. They lived widely dispersed throughout what is now known as the Middle East, the Mediterranean, Europe and Central Asia (Kazakhstan, Uzbekistan, etc., called *the central steppe* during historical times).

  Five subjects stated that they lived in Central Asia between 1000 and 2000 BC. They recalled living in tents, which was common to the migrating population of that region. Amazingly, they found themselves to have white skin color and yellow or golden hair! At first, this didn't appear to be historically accurate as Asian people should have black hair and darker skin. However, recent discoveries of mummified corpses along the ancient Spice Route have shown that there were indeed light skinned and blond haired people!
- Eating habits of people who lived around 500 B.C. were not that bad. Twenty percent of the subjects recalled that they ate poultry and sheep meat. However, between A.D. 25 to A.D. 1200, people's eating habits were rather poor. The subjects recalled that the food was tasteless. One young man said: "*I will never bad-mouth McDonald's food*". It is not surprising that those who recalled the best tasting food were those who remembered a prior life in China.
- Among all the subjects, 62% died of old age and illness, 18% percent died violently during war, or some other manmade catastrophe and the remaining 20% died in accidents. Many of the prior lives ended during the two world wars, as well as civil wars in Asian countries. Thus, **these people reincarnated shortly after they died.**

  Surprisingly, Dr. Wambach found that 69% of the subjects who had died during the 1850's were Caucasians, while between 1900 and 1945, only 40% were Caucasian. It seems that transmigration of the different races increased after 1945.

Dr. Wambach went on to publish her findings in **Reliving Past Lives: The Evidence Under Hypnosis** and **Life Before Life** (1984). Although she began her work as a skeptic, she would later write:

"...Fantasy and genetic memory could not account for the patterns that emerged in the results. With the exception of 11 subjects, all

descriptions of clothing, footwear, and utensils were consistent with historical records..."

And in later interviews, she stated,
"I don't believe in reincarnation -- I know it!"

In **Life Before Life** Dr. Wambach described the results of hypnotizing another 750 people and taking them to the time between their past and current lives. One of her most controversial findings was that people have some choice in their current lives and that the disembodied consciousness or soul does not enter the body until near birth. *"The soul usually enters the body near birth, and has a choice of which fetus to enter. If one fetus is aborted, it is possible to choose another. In some cases, the soul who will occupy the fetus, is in contact with the soul of the mother, and can influence her decision regarding abortion."*

Dr. Wambach found that 89% of those hypnotized said they did not become part of the fetus until after six months of gestation. A large group said they did not join the fetus, or experience inside it, until just before or during the birth process. They existed fully conscious as an entity apart from the fetus and even after six months many reported being 'in' and 'out' of the fetal body. *"Many subjects reported that the onrush of physical sensations on emerging from the birth canal was disturbing and very unpleasant. Apparently the soul exists in a quite different environment in the between-life state. The physical senses bring so much vivid input that the soul feels almost 'drowned' in light, cold air, sounds. Surprising to me was the frequent report that the new-born infant feels cut off, diminished, and alone compared to the between-life state. To be alive in a body is to be alone and unconnected. Perhaps we are alive to learn to break through the screen of the senses, to experience while in a body the transcendent self we truly are."*

Dr. Wambach found that a certain number of people she hypnotized actually saw into future lives. What they saw concerned her--a devastated and depopulated world. So in the early 1980s, Dr. Wambach decided again to apply systematic methods. She did a huge study that involved over 2,500 people undergoing hypnotic *future* life progression.

The future life progressions were conducted over a number of years and several groups were involved in the study. Wambach offered the participants a choice of five time periods (three in the past and two in the future) with instructions that their subconscious minds would choose one of the periods. Of the 2,500 people in the study, six percent reported being alive in 2100

AD, and 13 percent said they were alive in the 2300 AD period. Only a handful of the subjects progressed to the future.

There was evidence, she believed, that there was a decline of up to 95 percent of the population within a few generations. Concerned, Wambach asked one of her students to progress to a specific date in the late 1990's but had to bring the woman out of hypnotic trance rapidly after the woman found herself *"choking to death on a big, black cloud"*. Wambach found predictions for the last years of the century to include severe earthquakes, a new US currency, severe weather patterns, financial crises, bank failures, an increase in volcanic activity and the decimation of a large number of people. In 1999, there would be an isolated incident in which a nuclear explosion in Europe kills many people.

Future Life Progression Processes

So how does one best go about digging into their future life plans? Anne offers her experience to describe the common practices that work best. Here is her wisdom:

What do you need to know
Think back to what you would have liked to know so you could have taken a different path and actions. Make a list of these which can relate to worries, concerns, problems, or future relations. Spend some time thinking about these. Write these down on paper because:

1. It acknowledges them
2. It sends a request for help to the universe and your future self, your higher Guide

Create the proper environment by opening up
1. Find a comfy place, relax, take a few deep breaths of love in and release out
2. Know on out you are releasing negative thoughts, feelings of emotion, to be replaced by love
3. Imagine white light down on you protecting you, surrounding you with love
4. Know white light is universal energy that knows all as all information is there and you have access to it
5. Allow it to flow to you to bring what you need to know forward

Use the Gallery Method to get Your answers
1. Use the Opening Up process above to begin

2. Fill body with light and peaceful energy through legs to toes, up to head, down to back, feel tension release to relax body and mind
3. Imagine a long tunnel and floating along it, dark but silver lights on sides. Notice cool and peaceful and relaxed. See a curtain at end as a gentle blue cloth and reach out to pull it aside
4. See a large red shiny door with the word Gallery in brass. Trace fingers on it
5. Note the brass handle, turn it, push open the door into a dim lit room with a few candles. Note a candelabra on a wood table. Light the candle on it and pick it up. Look around
6. See walls covered in huge paintings in this wondrous place. Suddenly you are drawn to one and you realize it is you with the outcome to your dilemma or question you came with
7. The answer will be here as a picture which you need to study and inspect to see the future. The details will answer your question. Who are, why are you here, are you happy, how do you feel?
8. Step into the picture as the image is a doorway. Feel yourself inside. How do you feel? While inside, have you made the right choice or move? Step outside when ready
9. Hold candelabra high and look at other pictures. Do you want to step inside?
10. When done, put down candelabra, walk back through the door, close it, step into the tunnel and glide back, feel at peace
11. You are back refreshed, ready to move forward with new information
12. CLOSE DOWN

You will travel to the time that answers your questions but you can say I wish to go to a specific period into the future. I.e. go six months and ask
"will I get along with my ...."
"will this project work out?
"will my relationship work out?

Your Soul Purpose Review

Anne sheds light on what she has concluded as the SOUL PURPOSE. It is to evolve and grow to become one with the universal energy – the energy that flows through everything, is part of everything and governs all things. Each lifetime will teach you and allow your opportunities to perfect yourself until the time you are ready to reconnect with the universal energy – when you have learned all you need to know. The Soul lessons are made by spiritual agreement and we go through life reviews to review progress between lives.

If you want to check this out then she suggests her SOUL TO SOUL exercise after opening up as before, then:

1. Step into a huge cavern knowing you have been here before
2. See Guides and know they are here to assist to show you pieces of lifetimes past and future
3. They will explain themes, lessons, how you can be aware to move on and release what does not serve you
4. They will present images of you in thought forms and you will be told of your higher purpose, what you must release, what repeats and how to fine tune your path

We are seeing that what we have found out from the work of Robert Schwatrz and Bruce Goldberg is forming the basis for the therapy work as described here. People have the power to customize and control their destinies. Hypnosis once again provides the vehicle to interrogate the Spirit Guides and The Soul/Higher Self in reviewing that which is the future not yet experienced. We are getting more reports that the future already exists and the tomorrow is only real in potentiality. We live in a framework of potentiality and our actions determine the final form. All lives are concurrent so you can change past and future by changing the present. By learning earth plane from a position of the Higher Self, you can see past, present and future. Since our brains deal with 3D present only the space-time continuum confuses it.

If you recall, we said the placebo was the oddball in all of this because it created miracles without anybody's assistance. So let us take you into the latest clinical evidence related to the placebo where it appears to be the mind and the thought alone that changes physical reality. But which mind is it? We all know the answer to that don't we?

11

THE PLACEBO MIND OVER MATTER

"When you begin to understand the power of the placebo, in a world dominated by negativity, you have to carefully consider the power of its opposite, the nocebo.

Aly McDonald   Ed Rychkun

> **What is the matter with my mind
> Is it the body that makes it blind?**

And so it is that our thesis about the common steps that are used to create miracles and to change reality are still intact. Get into an altered space away from that meddlesome brain state of beta, feel a state of positive peace and silence, create the thoughts and visions of completion in your mind, have a clear vision of your desire, supercharge that vision with high emotion of joy and gratitude from the heart, launch intent to the Universe and get some Divine Intervention and be thankful for it being done.

No matter what we looked at, the healers and wealth gurus' methods basically reduced to these same basic steps. Yet it did not work for everybody. Not everybody could modify the movie. Of course we now know that everybody's degree of suggestibility, depth of altered state, and convictions to the belief boxes are pretty significant variables! To get more insight into why and how, we are now going to look at the oddball process that creates miracles – the Placebo.

You Are The Placebo Or Nocebo: You Choose

A Placebo accounts for an enormous amount of healings and these just simply happen. If you go back to the introduction, we saw how dramatic these could be. There did not appear to be any Divine Intervention involved, nor was there an altered state. What are we missing here? To look into this we are going to take you to the work of Dr. Joe Dispenza, a rapidly emerging guru on this topic.

Joe Dispenza, D.C., studied biochemistry at Rutgers University in New Brunswick, New Jersey, and holds a Bachelor of Science degree with an emphasis in neuroscience. He received his Doctor of Chiropractic degree from Life University in Atlanta, Georgia. Joe's postgraduate training and continuing education has been in neurology, neuroscience, brain function and chemistry, cellular biology, memory formation, aging and longevity. He was featured in the award winning film, "**What The Bleep Do We Know**?" His lectures provide basic yet powerful information on how to co-create one's day and how to use focused concentration, repetition, and visualization (mental rehearsing) to rewire the brain. Using these skills, he says, we can all harness our reality by being the placebo.

Since that film's release in 2004, his work has expanded, deepened, and spiraled in several key directions - all of which reflect his passion for exploring how people can use the latest findings from the fields of neuroscience and quantum physics to not only heal illness but also to enjoy a more fulfilled and happy life. Dr. Joe is driven by the conviction that each one of us has the potential for greatness and unlimited abilities.

As an author, Dr. Joe has written **Evolve Your Brain: The Science of Changing Your Mind** followed by **Breaking the Habit of Being Yourself: How to Lose Your Mind and Create a New One**, both of which detail the neuroscience of change and epigenetics.

If you go to Joe's website at www.drjoedispenza.com you will find an incredible number of health and wealth miracles, all of which have occurred through his coaching of how to become the placebo. From a clinical point of view, he states that he has documented and measured some 750 brains to see what is going on in the mind and the physiology regarding placebos.

His latest book **You Are the Placebo: Making Your Mind Matter** (2014) is an Amazon Bestseller and hit the NY Times Bestseller List within a week of its release. It very explicitly brings together a revealing picture of how and why placebos work and how you too can be one.

We will summarize some of the key points of the book here and add a few of our own observations, but in a nutshell Joe's extensive cases of miracles in health and wealth, and his research on the workings of the brain point to three key words of **acceptance, belief** and **surrender** as the way to change the code in the operating system of the subconscious.

Joe explains that when you see the Doc who says you have cancer and will die, you get a series of thoughts; images and emotions conjured up as past experiences (from parents, TV, other opinions, etc.) in your mind. We will add that these are typically coming from your belief box which is a product of the larger consciousness. Because this subconscious programming is what prevails, you will then **accept** the condition, **believe** what is said and **surrender** to the treatments and possible outcome. How this suggestion is received and believed determines the susceptibility to that new possible outcome. If you embrace these fears by surcharging them with fear emotions, then the only possible thoughts are equal to how you will feel. It is the nocebo; the wrong placebo that you accept, believe and surrender to as **your state of being**. That is pretty natural because the conscious mind simply accepts what is in your subconscious programming as the accepted outcome.

Recall Mr. Wright from the Introduction, the guy with the tumors the size of golf balls laying on his death bed. In this case he did **not accept** the finality and he brought forward the **belief in a different new outcome.**

In the case of the placebo, he did not accept the finality, did not believe in the most probable outcome, and he **did not surrender** to the diagnosis. He simply did accept, believe and surrender to a different state of being, different attention, different intention, and different outcome in his future. As he supercharged this new possibility with the emotion of the different possibility, he reprogrammed his subconscious, fired neurons that wired a new neurological circuitry in his brain and launched the appropriate cell behavior, chemicals, and physiological processes that corrected the physical issues in a few days.

But, when he found out that the treatment did not work, he then activated the same old programs by accepting the original fate, believing in the old outcome and surrendering to his original fate. His hopelessness simply reinstituted the old outcome as the set of programs in the subconscious.

If you repeat thoughts they form an attitude or feeling, if you repeat the attitude long enough you create a belief. If you continue you hardwire them into the brain and emotionally condition them into the body. You become addicted to them as they are etched neurologically. That is simply the way we create our reality. The problem is the depth of conviction as we get older and how difficult the old mind belief box programs are to over-ride.

An altered state is when you decide to change regardless of your existing state of being. The key is to see this as done as a new possibility and get goose bumps thinking about it. It requires new information, a new state of being different from past taken from a new future. It requires that you are the mind changing a belief, and surrendering to its fruition with gratitude and passion that when created internally as new experience **is greater than** the past experience, greater than the existing hardwired programs. Then you change the old Cause and create a new Effect that overrides old patterns of the brain and removes the neurological evidence; or brings it back through lack of support of the new mind.

The Process Of Thinking And Feeling

Part of the most revolutionary thinking about this process which we have called Divine Intervention comes when Joe starts telling us about his neurological research. He explains that when we give action to a new meaning we add intention behind it and put conscious purposeful energy into it. The more you believe a substance, a procedure; surgery will work because you have been educated about it, the better the chance of success of changing the inner state by thought alone. The clearer the model created in your mind, the better you are at programming the brain and body to replicate it. The more you believe in the cause the better the effect. Because 95% of our programs are already there based on the past, thinking the same thoughts leads to the same choices and enforces the same old programs. We have 60000-70000 thoughts per day firing through the beta brain and 90% are typically the same as yesterday. 60% of these are negative, most are fragmented, so you only get through to the subconscious when these are clear, decisive and heavily charged with emotion. So this is why 95% of the programs are already instilled. It does not mean that your "disc" capacity is 95% full, it means that of all the programs you have placed there, 95% are pretty well set because it becomes harder and harder to create new ones or override old ones. Your personality becomes more and more "opinionated" and stubborn as do your habits, all created by your personal reality as how you think, act and feel so conditioned by the belief box of the group consciousness.

Each thought, in addition to making a neurotransmitter makes a protein called neuropeptide that sends a message to the body which reacts by having a feeling. The brain notices this because it is supposed to monitor this for your survival. If you generate another thought matched to that feeling that produces more of the same chemical message that allows you to think the way you were just feeling. And then the feeling created thinking that is equal to the feeling. This becomes clearer to the brain so it is getting instructions through redundant thoughts that hardwire the brain into a fixed pattern of neurocircuits. Eventually as feelings are modus operandi of the body the emotions will condition the body to memorize those emotions that are equal to unconscious hardwired mind and brain. The key here is that conscious mind is not in charge. The body becomes the control of the mind and both are a product of the accepted belief box which the subconscious is programmed to surrender to. And it does not give a crap as to whether this is positive or negative, real or unreal as we have learned. Our mental design is to understand and experience emotion which is the branding iron of programming.

The body has subconsciously been programmed and conditioned to become its own mind. Just like the kid from ages 2-6 has been unconsciously writing the neurocircuitry, you are also affecting the same process. But the big difference is that with Beta active, it takes intense repetition of conscious memory, or intense emotion to override what is already created in subconscious program banks that relate thought and emotion to a particular subroutine of chemical, physiological and psychological behavior.

Eventually it is all memorized into a familiar state of being. The emotions as chemical records of past experience are driving our thoughts over and over to live in the past and it gets harder and harder to work from the 5% of conscious beta driven mind to cause a change in what is 95% recorded effect.

If neurons are firing the same way they release the same neurotransmitters and neuropeptides in the brain and body and they remember these emotions by altering it physically. The cells and tissues receive specific chemical signals at specific receptor sites. These operate like docking stations for chemical messengers. These are molecules of emotion carrying bar codes that are read by the receptors and if matched create/alter a protein to activate cell DNA. DNA opens, and then unwinds the gene to that corresponding message from outside the cell and makes a new protein from DNA to release it into the body. Now the body is being trained by the mind. Over time when the same genes are activated (same stuff firing) they start to wear out and make weaker proteins with weaker structure and functions and we get sick and age. This is another reason why it gets harder and harder to institute new programs and we simply fall back to the norms of the belief box chosen, and then become more adamant and stubborn about being able to create things outside the belief box.

An interesting statistic that Joe brings forward is that 95% of who you are is done by the time you reach 35 years. By then if not sooner a set of instructions reflecting neurological fire-wire pathways for memorized behavior, skills, emotional reactions, beliefs, perceptions, and attitudes are all functioning like a sub automatic computer. From then on, it seems to all be downhill in changing that belief box. The end result is 5% of conscious mind is working against the 95% subroutines already memorized. So thinking positive is swimming upstream against a current of 35 years of programming as the past governs the current and future. Of course it becomes more and more difficult with age to dethrone this continually demanding and conditioned state of being.

As this same old crap of belief box opinions and behaviors reinforce themselves, there are two scenarios that commonly become the effect.

First, the intelligence of the cell membrane can adopt biological conditioning by modifying receptor sites to **accommodate more** of the chemicals with more docking stations and the body then craves the chemicals that do this and controls the mind. This is like an addiction of the body to nicotine, alcohol, drugs, to name some.

Second, the cells are overwhelmed and require **higher emotions** to get cells to open the door to get it off their butts. This needs greater thrills to turn on the cells – more anger, more excitement, and so on – hyper active Beta and Gamma. When the body is not getting enough of emotional chemicals it signals the brain to make more. These become emotional addictions.

When feeling becomes the means of thinking this way then we are *"in the program"* and our thinking is how we feel and our feelings are how we think. In this loop the unconscious mind lives in the past 24/7 as bodies and minds are aligned to a destiny predetermined by our unconscious programs. To change this requires being greater than the body and all its emotional memories, addictions and habits. That's why you have to let go of the old mind without question and surrender to a new mind with a high degree of passion and emotion.

The Placebo And Brain In Action

Let us look at an example of how this works. In this case we have someone who has a horrific event happen to him. It is a public speaking situation that turns out to be a horrible emotional experience. The speaking engagement went crazy, equipment did not work, speaker was unprepared, slides out of sequence, ran out of time, the crowd booed him. This became a situation that created reactions all through the body; heart rate, fear, sweating, nausea, and a cascade of emotions that one can well imagine if the speaking engagement went badly. All this emotional intensity instantly created a cascade of chemical and physiological results in the body. The autonomic nervous system that functions subconsciously below conscious would of course be on the spot to memorize these emotional chemical signals to create automatic physiological changes and record this as programs in subconscious. From then on all you would have to do is bring a thought of the event into the conscious mind and it would trigger the same chemicals and physiological changes automatically. The thought instantly reloaded the programs, as would another speaking engagement bring on the same fears and reactions.

You would without even consciously knowing what the brain and subconscious were doing. Now you automatically and autonomically associate this with the future or current thought of the event with past emotional meaning of the event so it becomes a conditional response to respond to that feeling. One then lives in the past because we can't think greater than how we feel and any future event or thought of it continues to create this reaction of experience. The event was embossed and patterned neurologically as a physical memory, physically wired in the brain and programmed to create chemically and physical processes.

Because feelings and emotions are the end products of our experiences, and it is our emotional energy bodies that we are here to engage through the body, feelings are the true direct doorway to the subconscious. In this case, your five senses capture the event and relay this to the brain. Mobs of nerve cells organize into fresh networks to reflect the event where circuits gel, the brain makes a chemical to signal the body and alter physiology (chemical is called feeling or emotion). The event created a cause and effect and the memory of it created your conditioned process. So as you recall the event over and over in your mind it produces the same chemical and same level of mind in the brain and body to reaffirm the conditioning process.

As the body acts as your subconscious mind, it does not know the difference between actual events and that created by emotions, or the emotions you created by remembering the event. The body believes it is living the same experience over and over. You fire and wire the circuits of the brain creating long term memory. Now the conscious mind has no control for as you think about it again, in seconds, a host of conditional responses from the brain and body pharmacy manifest the same effect – all from a single thought – the same as the placebo. You have enslaved yourself by the body as it has become the mind and trapped you in that environment lost in past time.

How do you get out of this hardwired trauma? It will continue until the time you take charge of the mind and issue a new state of mind that would result as a new possibility (a wonderful presentation) and this means you need to change the perception about future events (forgive self, love yourself, see a better result believe it, accept a new outcome and surrender to it as your new ability). There must be a new event that overrides the old one. We have seen that through hypnosis and regression, one could go back and delete the perception cause to understand the lesson as to why this occurred, rise above it and issue a command to the subconscious to get rid of the phobia and trauma in the current time, then engage with a new mind that the outcome is a forgone conclusion. Alternatively we see that the method of the placebo effect is much the same. This new outcome would have to be created in the mind with emotional charge of success so as to delete the old program in subconscious. This is the placebo effect in action. And when the time came to do it, the prevailing new mind would preside as you would expect. The emotional high of successful completion would reinforce the fire-wire pathways

However, if for some reason, things went sideways again because the energy of fear was brought in, it would be easy for that fear energy to re-institute the old programs for a re-enforcement of the old trauma. Alternatively, as the old belief box prevails, you continue to persevere in the trauma and learn to engage as long as it takes to succeed and eventually have the emotion of success that overrides the old programs. In the first case, it is the state of new mind that is controlling a new outcome, in the second because it is the outcome that is controlling the mind. This is easier because the old programs are already there.

The Role Of DNA - Deoxyribonucleic Acid

Joe also explains the role of DNA. DNA is stored in every cell and contains the raw information and instructions of who we are. These are not an unchangeable blueprint as we will see later. Like two twisting ladders, each half contains corresponding nucleic acids called basic pairs (about 3 billion per cell). Groups of long sequences of the nucleic acids are genes. DNA uses instructions imprinted within its individual sequences to produce proteins (meaning primary importance). Proteins are raw material bodies used to construct anatomy and function and complex interactions that make physiology (muscles make actins, skin makes collagen, etc.). These proteins are the expression of our life in the physical form.

Genes are classified by the type of stimulus that turns them on or off. For example consider a new experience. Depending on the activity, special genes are activated when we have a novel experience like learn new functions, and healing where the process generates stem cells to morph into whatever types of cells are needed at the time of healing. DNA is like a parts list of program potentials awaiting instructions to construct proteins which maintain every aspect of life. When a new protein is sent to the nucleus to select a gene sequence, the sleeve covering is removed to be read. The regulating protein creates a molecule RNA which organizes the translation and transcription into a protein of building blocks called amino acids. This cascade occurs from outside the cells brought about by thought, choices, behavior, experience, and feelings. These elements initiate change and determine genetic expression.

The new discipline of Epigenetics which means "above the gene" reflects control outside the cells. As long as you perceive life through the past and react to the same conditions and neural architecture, you head for a specific predetermined genetic destiny. What you believe about self, life, and choices you make keeps sending the same messages to the same genes. It is through this process that each holds the keys to genetic destiny. But you have to find the right key to unleash your potential. Genes are providers of possibilities and unlimited potential or tools for transformation. It is you, not preprogrammed biology that holds the key.

As we have learned before, stress causes epigenetic change because it knocks your body out of balance three ways; physical (trauma), chemical (toxins), and emotional (fear). Each type can set off more than 1400 reactions and produce 30 hormones and neurotransmitters as a chemical cascade influenced by the mind through the autonomic nervous system as we have learned in the flight-fight process of survival. This is how the mind-body works against us as we attempt to engage in the three elements of placebo; acceptance, belief and surrender. Survival mode which is the Beta Wave world of brain activity has stress response on all the time because we are focused on the physical body (Am I ok?), the environment (when will I be safe?) and time (how long will I be threatened?). These are less spiritual inclined, more focused on the ego self and survival mentality.

Changing The Way Of Being

Here is the crux according to Joe's research and numerous examples. Every thought, emotion, or event acts as epigenetic engineer of your own cells. When you are truly focused on an intention for some future outcome, if you can make inner thought more real than outer environment, the brain won't know the difference. Then your body as the unconscious mind will begin to experience the new future event in the present moment and you will signal new genes in new ways to prepare for the imagined future event. If you continue to mentally practice this enough times this new series of choices, behavior, and experience that you desire, they reproduce the same new level of mind over and over. Then your brain will begin to physically change installing new neurological circuitry to begin to think from that level of mind – to look as if the experience has already happened. This begins producing epigenetic variation that leads to real structural and functional changes in the body by thought alone – just like placebo.

This is done through mental rehearsal by closing eyes and repeatedly affirming an action and mentally rehearsing the future you want all the time reminding yourself you no longer want to be the old self. You think about future actions mentally planning your choices, focusing on a new experience. You are reminding yourself of what your life will look like once you get it putting intention behind the attention. When you consciously make thought and intention with heightened emotion such as joy and gratitude the state of being, your body changes. When you embrace this in new emotion and neurochemistry that would be present in that event (a taste of the future) the brain and body begin to believe it and they have no choice but to respond to it.

This is how you turn down the volume of old circuits and fire-wire new circuits which initiate the right signals. This is to activate new genes through the process of neuroplasticity. The circuits in your brain begin to respond, and reorganize to reflect what you are mentally rehearsing. As you keep this up coupling new thought and mental images with strong emotions (mind and body working together) you are in a new state of being and your brain and body are no longer a record of the past. They are a map to a future you created in your mind. Your thoughts have become your experience and you just became the placebo.

Higher emotional responses to new thought are like a turbo charging effort on mental rehearsal. Emotions make epigenetic changes faster. You will create a new future out of the past as new information from outside the cell is provided. There is no difference between the effects of the outer environment or the inner of pure thought and imagination.

In placebo studies, the success is dependent upon two key processes:

1. Clear intention of a new future possibility (life without pain or disease)
2. High emotion (excitement, hope, anticipation)

In the case of Mr. Wright, he got super excited and imagined how it would cure him. His body responded emotionally as if imagined it had happened. Mind and body responded emotionally together as one to signal a new way and new genes to begin the work. He reverted back to old programs of thought and emotions when he brought back the fear and doubt and activated the old. Then he repeated the process. This case clearly shows how negativity and positive thoughts and emotions are the sole means to trigger the switches and programs in the body.

Positive thoughts and emotions release oxytocin neuropeptides which shuts down receptors in amygdala (part that generates fears and anxiety) so we can feel more trust, forgiveness and love. It shifts selfish to selfless to embody a new state of being and neurocircuitry opens the door to endless possibilities because we are not expending energy in survival mode. The frontal lobe as conductor sees all sorts of creative possibilities from neural connections to form nets and unplug from old state. And neurochemicals begin delivering new messages to epigenetic changes that signal new genes in new ways because we used heightened emotions to make it seem like it has already happened, ahead of the environment, not waiting and hoping.

In Joe's book, he clearly explains why so many processes do not work. Here is a summary related to the public speaking example:

Conditional You have conditioned your body into subconscious state of being when mind and body are one – thoughts and feelings have merged and body is programmed to automatically, biologically and physiologically be the mind by thought alone. Any time a stimulus is presented (to speak) you subconsciously and automatically respond to the mind of the past experience. In placebo, a single thought can activate the body's autonomic nervous system and produce changes by simply associating a thought with emotion to regulate your internal world.

Expectation You expect that your future will be like your past and selecting a known future based on past and emotionally embracing that event until your body as unconscious mind believes it is living in the future in the present moment. All attention is on known, predictable reality to limit new stuff – unconsciously forecasting future by physiologically clinging to the past.

Assignment of Meaning You create conscious intention to an action. You are telling yourself you are not a good speaker and the public reaction has meaning so you have become susceptible to your own autosuggestion. So you will continue to create the same actions on autopilot. You are being the nocebo.

Reasons Why The Placebo Works

On Joe's website at www.drjoedispenza.com you will find a huge number of testimonials that are pretty dramatic, many who were told the disease or condition was not curable. As Joe points out, each first **accepted** then **believed** in the suggestions and **surrendered** to the outcome without analysis. They aligned with a new future reality as possibility as though it had already occurred and they enfolded it with emotion.

They believed the outcome, emotionally embraced it and as a result their bodies as the unconscious mind was living in that future reality in the personal moment. The pills even if fakes can reinforce continued living in that new belief simply as reaffirmed acceptance, belief and surrender without question. Like hypnosis, a placebo of thought alone created by conscious interaction with autonomic nervous system. It created a cascade of physical events that automatically took over and just happened. Like hypnosis it does not work for all because the degree of suggestibility dependant on your state of being and the interference of the Beta-conscious brain. Acceptance, Belief and Surrender are the keys and the more we do this the better the result. Emotion will condition, expect and assign meaning to the whole delivery system. If you can't emotionally embrace the result you can't enter the autonomic nervous system (as in hypnotism). And the longer you embrace that new state of being, the more its signature vibrates in the quantum field of infinite possibilities; and the harder it is for the subconscious to ignore re-programming.

Life Transformation Process

In his book, Joe reveals the secrets to the transformation process. He explains this as the common requirements from the hundreds of cases.

1. **Inward** All had to go inward to change states of being – must meditate to go inward as it equals placebo.

2. **Meditation** It is best done before bed or on awakening as that is low beta/alpha where it is best to enter subconscious.
3. **Silence and Peace** You want no distractions and need to unplug from any sensory input and external interference.
4. **Present** It needs quiet place, comfortable clothes, and relaxed, closed eyes with deep breath. Same place, continued practice to get to theta.
5. **Time** You need 45 minutes to ignore time and senses and practice over and over to be no one, no where, no time, and no place. Avoid conscious meddling of ego who will not like losing identity as will fearful, voice of negativity. Pull in reigns of present moment as it is the body trying to be the mind so master it.
6. **Altered State** Use the Open Focus method to attain an altered state where there are no stress hormones, away from object (material) focus and away from incoherence of Beta. Pay attention to space (waves) and not thinking. Sensing space is restful Alpha Inner world becomes real and brain becomes synchronized nervous system more whole, and balanced.
7. **Quantum Field** Find the present moment where you access possibilities on quantum level. Here all past, present, future possibilities exist in the quantum field. You must be fully in the moment; no body, time, space, thing, one. You are into the unknown as your being.
8. **Be Consciousness** You must become pure consciousness as a thought alone where you create a new timeline, realm of possibilities, choices, thoughts, emotions, behavior, experiences, emotions. Linger here, it is the place of power.

To change your belief you must change your style of being and that means changing your energy because you have to become more energy than matter. You must have clear intention and elevated emotion. You must make a clear decision with a high energy level – energy that you thought about a new belief becomes an experience that carries a strong emotional signature to become the placebo to change your body and make your mind matter. The body must respond to the new mind as you get goosebumps, inspired, empowered and lifted with joy. One of the meditations that Joe uses is found on his website that can be downloaded. We recommend that you download this so you can be led properly through it. It is as follows:

PROCESS: Create the new rules
Write down the beliefs and perceptions you want to change
Write down what you want to believe and perceive instead
Write down how the new beliefs and perceptions would make you feel

INDUCTION 10-15 minutes
It is important that you stay present in this meditation without trying to analyze or figure it out. The process is one of becoming aware of the space

around and within your body. Joe leads you through a series of shifting awareness to rest it in the space and the anatomy through the body. He progresses to the eyes, temples, nostrils, nose, ears, nose, throat, ears, chin, neck, volume, chest beyond, shoulder energy, spine, thighs, each time becoming aware and sensing the energy of space around, its volume, the space beyond the body, the room, all of space. Here he is leading you into the quantum void outside of the material world.

PRESENT MOMENT 10-15 minutes
Joe then leads you into the sweet spot of the Void and all possibilities. In this space, you must be totally disconnected as no body, no where, no time, no thing, time as you shift awareness to the infinite field of potential to linger into the unknown. Here he takes you to become a thought in blackness of infinity and the quantum void of infinite possibilities. You become energy as no body, no one, no thing to become pure consciousness and aware of the infinite field of potential. Here you will now invest your energy in the unknown to draw a new life to you as you become a thought in the blackness of infinity. Here you will remain present to unfold into the quantum realm of quantum potentials as the more you become aware of possibilities the more you create the possibilities in your life

CHANGING BELIEFS AND PERCEPTIONS 20-30 minutes
Now you draw into awareness the first belief or perception you want to change. You make a decision to not continue believing this with such firm intention that the amplitude of energy related to that decision is greater than the hardwired programs in your brain and the emotional addictions in your body. Your body will then respond to a new mind, to a new consciousness. You then allow the choice to become an experience that you will never forget as you let the experience produce an emotion with huge energy that rewrites the programs and changes your biology. As you come out of your resting state you change your energy so your biology is altered by your own energy. You will now surrender the past back to possibility and allow the infinite field of possibilities to resolve it in a way that is right for you... Give it up

Now you bring what you want to believe and perceive about yourself and your life into awareness to move into a new state of being. Here is where you allow your body to respond to your new mind. You change your energy by combining a clear intention with elevated emotion so that matter is lifted to a new mind. You let the choice carry an amplitude of energy greater than the experience of the past to let your body be altered by your consciousness, by your own energy. Here you shift into a new state of being making this moment define you. You let this intentional thought become such a powerful internal experience that it carries elevated emotional energy which becomes a memory that you will never forget, replacing the past memory with a new memory in your brain and body. You become empowered, become inspired as you make the choice - a decision that you will never fail to remember.

Now you give the body a taste of the future by showing it how it will feel to believe this way as you let your body respond to a new mind. At this point, Joe leads you through the feelings and emotions:

How would you live from this state of being?
What choices will you make?
How will you behave?
What experiences are in your future?
How will you live?
How would you feel?
How will you love?

This allows infinite waves of possibility to collapse into an experience into your life as you teach your body emotionally what it is to be in this new future. The process is one of opening your heart and believing in possibility as you are lifted, falling in love with the moment and experience that future now

And now you surrender your creation to a greater mind. For what you think and experience in this realm of possibility if it is truly felt and will manifest in some future time, from waves of possibility to particles in reality, from immaterial to material, from thought energy into matter. You will now surrender your new belief into a field of consciousness that already knows how to organize the outcome in a way that is perfect for you planting a seed in possibility.

Bless this future with your own energy, then it means you are connected to a new destiny. For wherever you place your attention is where you place your energy. You are investing in your future by being defined by your future instead of your past. You now open your heart and allow your body to become moved by your own inward experience. Remember that what you truly experience in the unknown and emotionally embrace will ultimately slow down in frequency as energy into three dimensions as matter.

And now let go and give it up and allow it to be executed by a greater intelligence in a way that is right for you.

And now take your left hand and place it over your heart.
Bless your body that it be lifted to a new mind.
Bless your life that it be an extension of your mind.
Bless your future that it never be your past and returns to wisdom.
Bless your adversity in your life that it initiates you into greatness and you see the hidden meaning behind all things.
Bless your soul that it awakes you from this dream.
Bless the divine in you that it moves through you and all around you, that it shows cause in your life.

And finally, you give thanks for a new life before its made manifest so that your body as the unconscious mind begins to experience that future now. For the emotional signature of gratitude means the event has already happened, as gratitude is the ultimate state of receivership.

And now, just memorize this feeling as you bring your awareness back to a new body, to a new environment and to a whole new time.

When you are ready you can open your eyes.

By now we are forming a better picture of the process of the mind and the power of thoughts to change biology. What we are learning is that these changes in reality need to be instigated from a place that is in higher vibration. And the further away from the lower vibratory signature of the human physical form and its environmental interference, the more effective is the outcome. What also comes through is the business of well being and altered state. But this time it is a requirement of the physics of bypassing the lower functioning physics of mind, brain and body. Again, the tools are the same: hypnosis, deep guided meditation into a place where you have no identity in the quantum field of infinite possibilities where your higher Self and Mind rule the show – literally! And we see that the greatest catalyst to the change that occurs in the physical plane is heightened emotion. In fact, because the placebo is healing done by self as one's mind over matter, the Healers, the Divine, God, Doctors, Christ, gods, potions, spells, rituals, archangels, angels and the likes may have nothing to do with the actual process. These are simply things that make the individual acceptance, belief and surrender more palatable to open up the degree of suggestibility and emotional power. These are part of the belief constructs that we have formed individually to satisfy the characters we have contracted to play.

It is simply we and our ability to release all that mortal stuff of the physical realm, enter the quantum field of infinite possibilities and imagine whatever we want in this reality. And these higher powers really have nothing to do with it. Why? Because obviously we are that higher power as creators. It is the same process we went through in the very first chapter when we created these mind movies in our imagination. But unlike us simply sitting in a chair and imagining a new reality in our minds, we had to be outside of the influence of the physical body and brain to become present to that higher Causal, Mental and Emotional energetic double to be able to instigate the actual change into the lower vibration of the physical reality.

The other niggling question which comes forward is about the process of medical healing, particularly the pills. Are these human constructs like the healers and angels and things that are only a facilitating process for the mind to get off its butt and create the physical changes? Do the pills or the higher mind of pure thought get the brain off its butt? Obviously as the work of Dispenza shows us it is the mind by thought alone that can heal; or as he shows in his cases, change external reality the same way Future Life Progression was able to instigate a different possibility.

It also seems that this degree of success, however, has some serious stipulations in that you have to practice, practice, practice until you get it right. Although there are many cases of instant spontaneous changes, it seems most are not. So like learning to program the Computer, you have to learn to program the subconscious by first entering the school of New Life and graduate into a new state of being.

We have learned what the science of the brain says about healing on the inside. We are seeing from so many cases what people are doing about changing the physical reality outside. If the brain is also in charge of creating this projection of holographic reality which is our physical world and universe, perhaps it is just the sophisticated projection device that plays our personal movies and we can also deploy the same tactics to coax this brain to change the movie. This is in effect what we do in regression and progression. So why not the whole external movie which is a composite reality we all live in?

In the next chapter we are going to look at what our new scientists say about this. Before we do, we want to end this chapter with what Joe Dispenza says about quantum physics.

The Relation To Quantum

Joe has his own opinion of the relevance of quantum. He tells us that if you look at any atom, it is 99.9999% filled with an array of energy frequencies that form an invisible interconnected field of information. This is a scientific fact. Subatomic matter as a quantum world does not behave anything like matter we are used to. Particles which we see and perceive through our brains as material reality exist as a tendency, a probability or possibility – not as absolute physical things. And when particles are observed the process of observation bringing them into consciousness affects or changes their behavior. They exist simultaneously in an infinite array of possibilities within an invisible infinite quantum field of energy only when an observer focuses attention on any one location, and if an electron does it appears in that plane. Matter cannot exist until we give it attention – notice it. It is constantly vanishing, oscillating, transforming, manifesting from matter to energy at a rate of 7.8 times/sec. Mind over matter is a quantum reality. It means that your mind can become matter. So we as part of this are doing this act all the time. If particles exist in infinite number of possible places simultaneously then in the same way so do we. We are also potentially capable of collapsing an infinite number of potential realties in physical existence. So a future reality you imagine exists in the quantum field.

We know exactly what Joe is saying. Recall our first chapter on what you can do in your mind. If your mind can affect where and when an electron appears out of nowhere then you should be able to influence the appearance of any number of possibilities.

That is exactly what we do all the time but the issue is that all the experiences, all the learning, all the subconscious programs that run unconsciously have been burned as neurological pathways linking emotions with experience that run the way we have reacted and perceived the experience. And 95% of these have already been fired and wired into a set network by age 36, so they are not easily changed unless you become a kid that has no Beta or Alpha to interfere with the process. This is simply the way of our evolution as a physical being.

Joe goes on to explain further. All atoms emit various electromagnetic energies such as ultraviolet, infrared, and visible light to name a few and carry encoded information. Each atom is a vortex of spinning energy. Fast spin emits more energy, slow spin emits less. Particles and waves at slower vibration and longer wavelength are the ones that we see in physical reality. The brain is designed to use the senses to feel this and create emotion. The faster the vibrations goes beyond what we can see as the shorter wave length. This energy to matter process based on frequencies (wave to particle) shifts from quantum possibilities to physical reality. The physical universe shares this field of information as through the quantum field that unifies matter and energy so it is not possible to consider anything within it as separate entities. It all connects through an immaterial invisible field of information beyond space and time. That field is made of consciousness (thought) and energy (frequency) the speed at which things vibrate. When atoms assemble collectively to form molecules, they share the fields of information and then radiate there as unique combined energy patterns – just like you and I based on a state of being.

The invisible field of consciousness orchestrates all of the functions of cells, tissues, organs, systems of the body (atoms-molecules-tissues-organs-systems). The chemicals share this too and know how and what to do as they share the field of information. So the field that is created that gives birth to matter is what controls matter. Low frequency is incoherence seen as disease, high coherence is health. All things are in the field all connected as one, made of atoms unified under a field of intelligence that gives life, information, energy, consciousness to all things. This is the field of love; the quantum field, nobody, no time, no one, no place. When you enter this state of being you become aware in a field of infinite possibilities (just like imagination).

When you change the state to altered belief or perception you are increasing the frequency to amplify energy fields (spin faster and broadcast more energy) around your body which affects your physical matter – you become more energy and less matter by using your consciousness as a new mind to interact with new frequencies. The more emotion the higher the creative state.

So when you observe yourself in a new future and for a moment live in it you would be conditioning the body to believe it were in that future in the present moment. Because the brain does not distinguish between imagined and "real" situations, when it as the CEO responsible for the body functions feels the emotional experience regardless of real on non-real, it simply does what it was conditioned to do from the past built operating system of 95% stored in the subconscious program inventory. Why is this? Because perhaps there really is no difference to the mind and the movie of life is just an illusion like imagination? We will look at this in the next chapter.

The quantum model states all possibilities exist in the moment so we can choose these and observe these into reality. Since the universe is made of atoms being energy of possibility - means a lot of possibilities which you by default are observing and collapsing into your reality by your attention all the time. These possibilities can be bad or good, based upon the high energies of fear or love as there is no distinction in the world of energy; it is only your own judgment perceived through free will. But because we lose the connection between Cause and Effect, as you do not keep track of the how, when and what manifests as a result we rarely give credence to the possibility that we are actually collapsing quantum possibilities by mind over matter.

Now, let us look at some "scientific" opinions on this business of reality and consciousness.

12

THE QUANTUM REALITY

"How many times have we seen today's science fiction becoming tomorrow's reality? I wonder if the awareness in global consciousness has anything to do with it."

Aly McDonald						Ed Rychkun

> **Take me please to that place to see**
> **What my mind can create as possibility**

Is Reality Really Real?

To consider the idea that our reality is a self made movie is pretty difficult to fathom. Yet from all the previous chapters, we are seeing that all of these therapy methods enforce the idea that such a movie exists, captured in vivid imagery. They are there awaiting our engagement in the altered state to be who we are as bodiless energy forms; then the world of imagination of the higher mind can change the movie. The results of miracles, of changing personal issues, of digging into the past and looking into the future all appear to be stored in the Causal Body of the higher mind. In all cases we bring a cause into awareness, and then change the mental and emotional perceptions to create a different cause that then affects the current physical, emotional and mental reality. The big question that comes to mind is are we actually changing the movie or are we just taking a different choice and changing our mental and emotional perception?

The world of reality around us is so real. How could all the details of who we marry, what they look like and what paths we have be predetermined? It is ineffable! Whoever designed the great holographic illusion certainly made it ineffable; otherwise how could it be effective if you could just understand it? It appears that the words trust and faith play a large role in believing that it is true. When you attempt to understand; how can it be that all these organisms and this universe is just an illusion that one's Soul plays this game of life in, it is certainly ineffable. In this chapter, we are going to attempt to answer this question by looking at some different evidence that explores this thing called reality. But this time we are going to look at what the intellect is programmed to accept - science.

As we look at how this reality movie of life is played, and try to simplify the process that we brought forward in Part 3 of **The Divine Programmer**, we will attempt to encapsulate what the new wave of quantum physicists are trying to tell us by way of their own research. Unfortunately, there are several "quantum physics" terms that they use a lot. We have attempted to bring some of these into your awareness by way of looking at the mind and its process of imagination. We always hear about the energy bodies, brain, the chakras, holograms, heart, consciousness, subtle energies, and so on that is stated to behave according to quantum physics – that's what this new science is saying. But when we look at it closely we get into a whole lot of confusion about waves and particles, Observer effect, slit experiments, Schrödinger's Cat, the Uncertainty principle, entanglement, nonlocality, collapsing, and endless terms that don't make much sense. What do these really mean and how do they relate to consciousness and reality?

Because some of the experts working on consciousness and quantum physics are using this terminology, and there is now a plethora of people expounding on this quantum reality idea which has been sitting idle for 80 years, it is important to have some idea of what these things really mean. So bear with us on this.

The stark conclusions so far brings us to a point where that brain of ours is not in charge of our total reality. It gets directives from "upstairs" through the subconscious which is not very definable. But it is really the CEO of two very important things:

1. **The development of the internal environment**. Through the sensory systems of the body, it manages the conditional response systems for the evolution and survival of the life form.

2. **The creation of the external environment**. For the purpose of the development of the Soul's evolution of the mental and emotional abilities in a way that follows the individual Life Plans, it presents a reality in the form of a holographic reality.

These two responsibilities allow the higher mental and emotional bodies the interface into the holodeck called Planet Earth. These are some pretty hard to believe statements but we have seen over and over how the first part appears to be the case. Now we have to look at the world of holographic projections to get a better grasp on the second statement.

It is the subconscious mind and something above that is calling the shots telling the brain what to do when it comes to the body. Our brains are 3D and we have to concede that it is the 3D CEO of the physical body. Clearly it has a responsibility to direct and orchestrate healings. But in these healings, we are now having to look at the radical possibility that it is simply the mind and its thoughts coupled with emotion that instigate changes to internal reality in the way of healings. And the plethora of constructs in the form of healers, rituals, gurus, potions, doctors, pills, God, gods, Jesus, Angels, and so on, do not create healing miracles on their own. They are all constructed facilitators adding to the emotional process of accepting, believing and surrendering to a healing process. This is particularly evident when the placebo effect is considered. It all has to do with the mind – the consciousness and what each individual believes is true – and how they accept and surrender to their box of beliefs that affects their evolution of life.

Now we are faced with another radical possibility. That the brain is also the CEO of another physical department; one of presenting our holographic physical reality that allows our life plan movies to be played out within a larger holographic structure called Earth. As we have seen in our wealth "healings" we see that the mind can facilitate dramatic changes in our external reality. We have seen the many ways that people have changed their external reality using thoughts, visions and emotion alone. It should be clear now that the brain does not distinguish between the unreal and real realities. Thought and emotion are the key catalysts changing the internal physical environment. It would seem that the same is true in changing the external environment as well. On this it seems the brain also has the responsibility of creating a holographic projection of both realities.

In the Introduction, we looked into how the mind works – namely through imagination. Imagination does affect the physical internally as we have learned, albeit within the construct of the belief boxes. Since we as physical beings also belong to the hologram, as does the brain, does the mind work the same way with this external projections? It certainly does to some degree as limited by the norm and how we accept our evolution. It's when we attempt to work outside of this norm and within the scope of the lower self that we have a problem. But so far we are still in the scope of ineffable as to how this reality thing works. So in order to get a better idea of what these scientists are telling us about the Quantum reality, let us quickly explain some of their terminology. We will attempt to do this without giving you a headache! The main terms you encounter relating quantum physics to the workings of mind and reality are as follows:

Consciousness In simple terms, consciousness is the state of being awake and aware of one's surroundings. So when you look around you, you are aware of your surroundings. When you bring forward a thought, or an image you become aware of these in your surroundings. Consciousness is therefore simply being aware of something by bringing it into your conscious awareness (surroundings, reality). Some thing (thought, image, object) is in your awareness because you choose to think about it, see it or observe it with your eyeballs or your senses.

Dual states This states that everything exists in two states of particles and waves, but not both at the same time. As a particle you used a physical eyeball to observe a chair, bringing it into your surroundings or view screen which you call reality. In the other case, you used your imaginary eyeball to bring it into a different view screen. The chair image and the chair object could not be seen at the same time. In the physical reality this flip flop of dual states occurs some 7 times a second and forms from wave to particle and back again when you as an Observer, bring it into your conscious awareness.

Observer Effect says that the chair as an object existed as waves until you choose to see it by opening your eyes, then it became the object made of particles. The two states are imaginary reality and physical reality, but not both together. Either way, you created this by a conscious choice to see it even though they are two different realities. The same process occurs in our physical reality, the difference being that what you see as particles becomes waves when not observing it. You became the Observer creating the material representation. All of our reality is constructed this way.

Collapsing The mind bringing forward a thought of a chair from wherever it was in energy form (waves), converted (collapsed) the waves into an image (particles) of the chair. The only difference here is that the image was not "physically real". In quantum theory, this goes a step further and says that the object chair was just a thought/image in your mind, and the collapsing of the waves created the chair object. In our analogy to thoughts and images of the mind, we collapse the thought of something as a possibility into actuality.

Nonlocality Where did that thought or image come from? Nowhere and everywhere. Where is it stored? Where is the thought? Where is the image? It can be retrieved at will so it is somewhere. You imagine it so and it is so. Time and distance have no relevance here. All you have to do is bring it into conscious awareness. Nonlocality describes the apparent ability of objects to instantaneously know about each other's state, even when separated by large distances (potentially even billions of light years), almost as if the universe at large instantaneously arranges its particles in anticipation of future events. And so in your mind you create thoughts and images from where? Where is a thought stored? We have learned it is beyond the brain in the Casual energy field which is quantum consciousness. And although the brain may have a copy, that is not the main storage. It is in consciousness everywhere and nowhere at the same time waiting to be brought into awareness – into actuality. Thus in your consciousness, all thoughts are available all the time because they are all interconnected within consciousness.

Entanglement One of the most mind-blowing areas of quantum mechanics is entanglement: two or more particles separated in space can have physical properties that are correlated. A measurement performed on one particle will tell us the result of the same measurement taken on an entangled particle. Entanglement is important but difficult to study, both in terms of a theoretical understanding and doing experiments. While entangling relatively small groups of particles has been accomplished several times over the last 30 years (pioneered by Aspect et al. in 1982), scaling these experiments up in sizes sufficient to create quantum computers and other complex systems has eluded researchers.

Superposition Superposition is a principle of quantum theory that describes a challenging concept about the nature and behavior of matter and forces at the sub-atomic level. The principle of superposition claims that while we do not know what the state of any object is, it is actually in all possible states simultaneously, as long as we don't look to check. It is the measurement itself that causes the object to be limited to a single possibility.

Uncertainty The Heisenberg Uncertainty Principle states that you can never simultaneously know the exact position and the exact speed of an object like an electron. Why not? Because everything in the universe behaves like both a particle and a wave at the same time. Your consciousness has an infinite number of possibilities to bring into awareness (actuality).

Now, we may have spoken about these terms in relation to your imagination but what we are getting from the scientific quantum community is that that chair, object or external reality is consciousness working exactly the same way. You as the Observer collapse waves of possibilities from the quantum field into particles of material reality. The fellow that is assisting in this process is once again our old CEO that is reading a Life Plan script and playing it in a Consensus or Group Consciousness with its larger life plan cleverly integrating our personal consciousness and life plan into it. And it all is designed according to some higher intelligence of order, process and evolution. How? In the quantum field everything is interconnected and knowing of everything else.

In our presentation here, it is necessary to bring back into awareness a book by an author we looked at in **The Divine Programmer: Creating Miracles**.

Our Holographic Universe

Michael Talbot was an American author of several books highlighting parallels between ancient mysticism and quantum mechanics espousing a theoretical model of reality that suggests the physical universe is akin to a giant hologram. According to Talbot ESP, telepathy, and other paranormal phenomena are a product of this holographic model of reality.

His book **The Holographic Universe** is truly an epic book. It is a revolutionary and enlightening work of a visionary, primarily because of endless amounts of the documented clinical and experimental evidence he presents. This book has come to be an important reference manual for anyone attempting to make sense of the link between quantum, consciousness, holograms and reality. Here is a small part of his findings:

- Interference is the criss cross pattern of waves where two or more waves ripple through each other. Laser light being extremely pure coherent light is best when a single laser light is split, one bouncing off an object and second allowed to collide with the first so an interference pattern is created. It is recorded on a holographic plate looking like nothing at all but as soon as a second laser or bright light shines then a 3D holograph image appears. And when the holographic film containing the image is cut in half, each half retains the whole image.
- An image presented to the brain by the eye is the same process so images are recorded or retrieved by illuminating the film with light taken at the same angle as the recording.
- We perceive things as out there but they are really in there on the plate. The pain in the toe is a neurological process in the brain to manifest experience. Look in a mirror are you there or is it just a plate? Or are

you located in the mirror surface. The brain and the hologram all operate in the frequency domain according to Fourier transform theory.
- Electrons possess no dimension, no traits of objects and can manifest as particles or waves. They can create wave like patterns that when collided create interference patterns. The chameleon's ability to change back and forth are quanta - that which makes up the universe.
- When we look at them, quanta manifest as particles as the Observer Effect. All are interconnected as one called nonlocal, everywhere and nowhere.
- The brain mathematically constructs objective reality by interpreting frequencies that are projections from another dimension beyond space and time. What is out there is a vast ocean of waves and frequencies and the brain converts these. Without the brain we would experience nothing except an interference pattern. We would not be a body, we would be a blur of interference pattern enfold (implicate) of the cosmic hologram (unfolded as explicate order as us). We are part of the hologram looking at the hologram.
- We tap into the implicate order with what is resonant with personal resonance. The theory of the Implicate Order contains an ultraholistic cosmic view; it connects everything with everything else. In principle, any individual element could reveal "detailed information about every other element in the universe." The central underlying theme of Bohm's theory is the "unbroken wholeness of the totality of existence as an undivided flowing movement without borders."
- All experiences are ultimately neurophysiological processes that take place in the brain. The reason we experience it as external reality is because that is where the brain localizes it through which it creates the internal hologram that we experience as reality.
- The brain cannot distinguish between out there and what it believes to be out there.
- All experiences reduced (real or imagined) to some common language of holographically organized wave forms.
- Every action starts from intention, imagination is already the creator of form and has all the movements needed to carry and it affects the body from subtle levels until it manifests. So to the brain, imagination and reality are indistinguishable and images in the mind can ultimately manifest as realities in the physical body.
- The master plan is that DNA programs itself. Hypnosis and imagination can control autonomic process such as blood flow, immune system. When we access the right strata of our beliefs, our minds can override genetic makeup.

- Just as every portion of a hologram contains the image of the whole, every portion of the body contains an image of the whole. Every electron contains the cosmos
- The Universe is a hologram of all things integrated and interconnected for a vehicle of experience and we create the laws that govern it. We copy that part of it into our resonant frequency hologram.
- 50% of what we see is information from the eye. 50% is pieced together out of expectation of what the world should be like. The brain edits and manipulates by the temporal lobes before being presented to the visual cortex. The brain interprets from the frequency of interference patterns in the implicate order.
- All aspects of an aura are holographic as each part contains the whole. The body itself is a holographic construct.
- Free will may be an illusion. 1.5 seconds before we decide to move muscles, the brain has already generated the signals to do it. The human energy field (heart) responds even before the brain. The mind is not the brain and it supersedes all. It is the field that the true computer controlling the hologram of body and brain. Time and space are constructs of this.
- Each phase of activity is recorded in successive images like frames in the multi-image hologram. If it is a white light hologram an image seen by the normal eye that does not need laser light to be visible, a viewer sees 3D motion portrayed to present the illusion of movement. Our past is recorded this way as a non local way accessed from any point in the space time framework.
- It is only when one is freed from the senses of the body that the holograph can be experienced directly otherwise it is an intellectual construct.
- We are at the heart of all interacting and resonating frequencies.
- Our universe is constantly sustained and created by 2 wave length flows, one from heaven, one from our Soul. Put these together to form a hologram and one is direct from divine and one is direct from divine via our environment. We can view ourselves as interference patterns because inflows is a wave phenomenon and we are where the wave meet.
- In a holographic universe consciousness is everywhere and nowhere.
- We create sub atomic particles and hence the entire universe both in self-reference cosmology, each creates the other.
- The Universe is a holomovement, a constant interrelationship between all things in the Universe itself.

If we can suggest what is being said here is that there is a convergence between science and metascience; the key being that the brain is indeed interpreting creating a holographic reality for humans to engage in; just like in the Star Trek holodeck. But Michael's book is a few decades old so what is the current scientific community saying?

What Are Quantum Physicists Saying?

Historically, quantum physicists have not come forward too often because the scientific community did not view favorably those of "pure science" that mixed consciousness into the theory. It did not fit within the norm of the group consciousness. That has changed because like our own box, it can evolve by choice. So many are now realizing this is as the new trend and are jumping on the band wagon. One of the more outspoken and advanced is **Theoretical Quantum Physicist Dr. Amit Goswami.** He is a revolutionary amongst a growing body of renegade scientists who, in recent years, has ventured into the domain of the spiritual in an attempt to interpret the seemingly inexplicable findings of curious experiments and to validate intuitions about the existence of a spiritual dimension of life. A prolific writer, teacher, and visionary, Dr. Goswami has appeared in the movies **What the Bleep do we know?**, **Dalai Lama Renaissance**, as well as the award winning documentary **The Quantum**.

He served as a full professor at the University of Oregon's Department of Physics from 1968 to 1997. He is currently a pioneer of the new paradigm of science called "science within consciousness," an idea he explicated in his seminal book, **The Self-Aware Universe**, where he also solved the quantum measurement problem elucidating the famous observer effect.

Goswami has written several other popular books based on his research on quantum physics and consciousness. In **The Visionary Window**, he demonstrates how science and spirituality can be integrated. In **Physics of the Soul**, Goswami develops a theory of survival after death and reincarnation. In **The Quantum Doctor**, Goswami seeks to integrate both conventional and alternative medicine. In **Creative Evolution**, Goswami presents a resolution between Darwinism and the intelligent design of life. In **God is Not Dead**, Goswami demonstrates that not only are science and religion compatible but that quantum physics proves the existence of God. In **Quantum Creativity: Think Quantum, Be Creative**, Goswami explains all facets of creativity—its definition, the quantum thinking it entails, and what is required to be creative. Most interestingly, Goswami says, "Every human being has creative potential, and grasping the quantum process - do-be-do-be-do - will help everyone to explore his or her creative potential."

In his most recent book, **Quantum Economics: Unleashing the Power of an Economics of Consciousness** (May 2015) Goswami focuses on critical issues for a new paradigm in economics and business for the twenty-first century, touching upon the stability and sustainability of the economy and leadership, as well as creativity and ethics in business.

In his book **Quantum Creativity 2014,** Goswami states that reality is a combination of Potentiality and Actuality as a conscious choice collapses into actuality that which we see as our reality. A conscious choice equals the collapse of wave possibilities into manifest (reality we see). The collapse is nonlocal without communications and is discontinuous. Our expressions occur from collapse of objects and the mind interacts between consciousness and matter. The role of the brain is to make a representation of mental meaning so that this interaction can be facilitated.

He describes what science believes as upward causation is incorrect; the way things really work is through downward causation. We saw how the process of as above so below was presented in the astral Projection chapter. It is the same process. Amit explains that the current worldview has it that everything is made of matter, and everything can be reduced to the elementary particles of matter, the basic constituents - building blocks - of matter. And cause arises from the interactions of these basic building blocks or elementary particles; photons as elementary particles make atoms, atoms make molecules, molecules make cells, and cells make brain, brain makes consciousness. But all the way, the ultimate cause is always the interactions between the elementary particles. This is the belief that all cause moves from the elementary particles up the ladder. This is what we call "upward causation." So in this view, what human beings think of as our free will over the world of matter does not really exist. It is only an epiphenomenon or secondary phenomenon, secondary to the causal power of matter. And any causal power that we seem to be able to exert on matter is just an illusion. This is the current paradigm.

Now, the opposite view is that everything starts with consciousness. That is, **consciousness is the ground of all being.** In this view, consciousness imposes "downward causation" and it is the matter that is the illusion. In other words, our free will is real. When we act in the world we really are acting with causal power. This view does not deny that matter also has causal potency; it does not deny that there is causal power from elementary particles upward, so there is upward causation. But in addition it insists that there is also downward causation. It shows up in our creativity and acts of free will, or when we make moral decisions. In those occasions we are actually witnessing downward causation by consciousness.

He further states that consciousness has four worlds of possibilities that arise from:

1. Material world through use of senses
2. Vital world through energies that we feel
3. Mental world through thinking and process meaning
4. Supermental through choice of archetypes of truth, love, and other major ideologies we pick

We are now getting some insight that confirms the existence of these energetic bodies and the process of as above, so below.

Moreover, he explains a process called quantum leap and the workings of dual states under the control of the Observer. It is when an electron exists as possibilities and when observed pops on orbits but are nowhere in between when you look away; that is why it is potential. These possibilities as realized by the brain through consciousness allowing endless possibilities to be brought into reality. Where the uncertainty comes in is that in regards to these electrons we cannot measure both position and momentum at the same time. The brain and consciousness are busy working away this way flip flopping between two states at 7 times a second. Quite a head wringer for that superior human intellect, isn't it?

But as Gowami explains, thoughts as quantum objects appear in awareness only when we are thinking (as in measured under the Observer Effect). Between measurements they go to the original state of waves of possibility of meaning – transcendental possibilities of potentialities of many possible meanings continuously flip-flopping 6.7 times a second. Amit states that collapses manifest into form that has complementary attributes such as features and association. Physical and mental worlds remain possibilities until consciousness gives them substance by collapsing them into an actual expression or object. Consciousness reorganizes and collapses into a state from possibilities by the brain in response to stimulus, then chooses a convoluted mental meaning – perception. The Neocortex is a symbol processor as the mind gives meaning to an object. In the notion of Quantum Leap we "suddenly" get a solution at unrelated times/events as attraction of a morphic field. It comes from outside of ordinary consciousness – from the collective consciousness of information images, and archetypes.

He states that all quantum objects exist in transcendental (possibility) or realm of potentiality or in immanent level or made manifest. Intensity such as emotions creates superposition of possibilities in unconscious processing which is biased by learning context. The more you collapse the mind's quantum state relative to the same question the more you increase chances of a new response – from a bigger and bigger pool of possibilities from quantum consciousness to choose from. As we have seen with the placebo, this process involves the collapsing selection of images from the Quantum Field supercharged with emotion and gratitude.

In his book **Physics Of The Soul,** Goswami reports that Quantum is a discrete quantity. A quantum of light is a photon, a localized energy bundle or particles which exist in two states; wave or particle. Quantum objects exist as a superposition of possibilities until observation brings about actuality from potentiality (one actual localized event from many). That process is to take a possibility from infinite possibilities, and cause it by superposition to bring about the actual object from some possibility which typically reside in memory. All objects are therefore possibility waves. So we select a new possibility and superimpose it on top of the material reality, doing this through downward causation.

He states that quantum waves of possibility transcend space and time because in this wave world there is no space or time. That is a construct that the brain uses to create the illusion of space and time. All objects as possibility waves are non local thus implying transcendence and interconnectivity. So in that space, everything is one huge interconnected everything. Thus all within it behaves as one regardless of space and time. This process is best understood by how our cells work together yet have different functions and they simply "know" what to do – sort of like an ant colony. And each cell reflects the whole; one can be used to create the same human being. They communicate instantly regardless of space or time. Really, they don't have to "communicate" because they are all one unit; just like one vision or thought in your consciousness does not "communicate" with another; it is just "there" encompassing everything.

On this we say that we see this clearly in how cells know exactly what to do because they are all interconnected through the soup of quantum field as one, just as all of our individual consciousness is. Every individual consciousness is interconnected through the soup of the quantum field. It is also seen clearly in a holographic plate where any part contains the whole.

Consciousness can collapse the potential of infinite possibilities into material possibilities because it is beyond (transcends) jurisdiction of quantum mechanics. Thus all possibilities are within consciousness. For example we each see things differently and as with a picture, we do nothing to pictures, we just recognize and choose out of present possibilities. In this case there are two different possibilities.

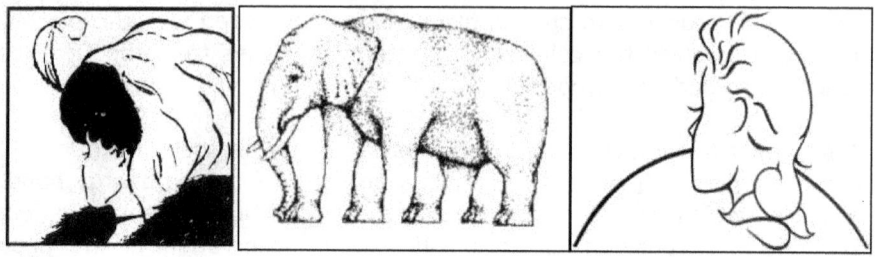

In the above example you will see an old woman or a pretty lady, an elephant with many feet or an old man or a young lady. In a world of infinite possibilities there is only one chooser (monistic) as one consciousness is part of one universal quantum consciousness. It is like a holographic plate which projects a hologram. If a chunk is cut off it still contains the whole. Waves can have a fractal of the whole which contains the whole.

We have introduced feelings, emotions and engagement through mental and sensory equipment. The same consciousness exists for all of us so there is no conflict. It is like everyone experiencing different emotions from the same movie. What is different is how the feelings, emotions, perception and access to the whole is different through individuality of character. That's what is recorded in the Causal field of Higher Consciousness. Consciousness is the ground of being so you cannot turn it off.

Amit says we all are (not have) the same consciousness. So we can choose but not conflict as every quantum measurement needs a sentient observer and each time, the brain in response to the stimulus produces a number of macroscopically distinguishable possibilities as the brains possibility wave. Consciousness collapses the waves of object and brain. The quantum measurement in our brains sets up our self reference – cognitive distinction between us, subjects, and the field of awareness of objects we experience. So the brain self refers to itself. There is no collapse without the brain but there is no brain - only possibilities unless there is a collapse. The distinction of self and the object, upon quantum measurement is only in the brain and give rise to our self reference – subject object split nature of experience.

So consciousness collapses the possibility waves of the object of observation, plus the possibility wave in the brain that gives self reference. It uses classical memory making of content like a tape producing a holographic view played back when a similar stimulus is presented. This is non linear outside of time. Experience produces memories which condition our self reference system - our brain. Influence of conditioning our quantum measurement is what gives the appearance that our actions arise from ego acting on past experience, and its character. But it is an assumed identity that the free-willing consciousness does in the interest of having a reference point. Our ordinary states of consciousness are clouded by this ego identity.

Nonlocality Of The Human Brain

Amit also confirms that you have to be in a different place beyond ego to be able to conduct the downward causation. He says to recognize the power of the downward causation of photon-atom-molecule-cells-neurobrain-consciousness; we have to experience oneness beyond individuality and a creatorship of the subject-object world. You would have to penetrate the cloud of conditioning and act in full knowledge of love and oneness as we collapse the available possibilities with full freedom of choice. In other words, get into the altered state and the place where the brain does not interfere with that mortal material stuff! Quantum nonlocality means photons are connected through a non local domain of consciousness beyond space and time. The proof is in distance and remote viewing, a trait of the astral abilities.

In the Grinberg Experiment for example we can see how this is working. The Einstein-Podolsky-Rosen (EPR) study, correlations between human brains are studied to verify if the brain has a macroscopic quantum component. Pairs of subjects were allowed to interact *(they spent 20 minutes in a joint meditation)* and were then separated inside semi-silent Faraday chambers 14.5 m apart where their EEG activity was registered. Only one subject of each pair was stimulated by 100 flashes. When the stimulated subject showed distinct evoked potentials, the non-stimulated subject showed "transferred potentials" similar to those evoked in the stimulated subject. Control subjects (which did not know each other and did not spend 20 minutes in joint meditation prior to the experiment) showed no such transferred potentials. The transferred potentials demonstrate brain-to-brain nonlocal EPR correlation between brains, supporting the brain's quantum nature at the macro level.

So the bottom line is that given the right conditions, subjects with correlated brains who collapse an event in one as electron potential becomes an instant non local collapse in another. These right conditions mean one cannot think and do without impacting the other (or whole). To see this, one can go to a state of letting go to consciousness beyond ego where two are one. We are not cognizant of creating our reality as we are rarely in a state of consciousness or the right conditions that chooses freely. But it happens when creative deep compassion, moral insight, reverence with nature come into our awareness through feeling.

Neurophysiologists state their research confirms there is a 1/2 second delay between a subject receiving a stimulus and verbally reporting the experience. This they say is the time for multiple reflection of the stimulus in the mirror of memory. So experience with some freedom of choice becomes preconscious when we identify with any memory-ego. In a Near Death Experience, this process is bypassed. NDE is a non local experience.

The Human Energy Bodies

Amit goes on to explain the different energy bodies of vital, mental, intellectual, and supermental as all possibilities collapsed by consciousness parallel to physical to get a personal experience. All feelings (emotions) are mapped into physical stored in vital body and are in nonlocal morphogenic fields. Morphogenesis is the development of forms or organs guided by non local extraphysical morphogenic fields. This is the vital body (etheric connected to the life process of the body).

He adds the brain cannot process meaning, it comes from outside. The "feel" behind vital functions of living organisms comes from the vital body of consciousness which maps the vital function in the form of various functional organs in the physical body through the chakras. Thus consciousness then "writes" meaningful mental programs in the brain. Consciousness also uses the mental body to create mental software for meaning that the mind processes in the brain. Then consciousness uses the physical hardware to make software representations of the vital and the mental.

Possibility waves of macromatter are sluggish. Between my and your observation, their spread is small so we both collapse in the same place to create consensus of physical reality, outside is public (but is actually projected inside.)

We need apparatus to see micro bodies to observe and lose touch with microworld. So we lose a shared reality of physical object and everybody can see macrobodies simultaneously. Mental substance (objects) are indivisible – no micro, this is an infinite medium where quantum possibilities exist as mental objects but you never track where thought goes. We can observe them without apparatus but not share them as they are normally private; but are quantum nonlocal.

Amit states that prana (breath) is made of movement in the vital body through nadis (meridians) and chakras are points (organs) where representatives are made of vital body blueprints for biological form making (morphogenesis) from DNA blueprints in cells. Feelings convey to regions as conditional movement (heart, tense). Movement of chi is nonlocal – able to affect bio chemistry.

Both the non material and material body are mere possibilities within consciousness and consciousness mediates interaction and monitors parallel function. There is an unconscious processing of quantum possibilities of subtle bodies to create various possible paths. At birth when a body is available one of the paths manifest and the events of entire path may happen retroactively – their memory is available as it happens. This gives us some insight into how the Life Plan comes into existence.

Amit explains that humans evolve through a **tangled hierarchy**: *"Behold the causal circularity of the role of the observer in quantum measurement. The observer, the subject, chooses the manifest state of the collapsed object(s); but without the manifested collapsed objects, including the observer, the experience of the subject does not arise either. This circular logic of the dependent co-arising of the subject and object(s) is called a tangled hierarchy."*

Chakra points for a particular region of the body are where the quantum collapse of physical takes place. There is a correlated collapse of vital body which becomes a mapping of the vital into physical. Manifestation is the descent of consciousness (individualization). As it descends to a denser and denser state, it forgets itself. At each individual level of descent, the previous subtle levels are forgotten, delegated to consciousness and potential in matter, ready to unfold. Once involution is complete, evolution begins. Life emerges as it was all potential. Manifestation occurs via a tangled hierarchy causing illusory separateness which causes temporary amnesia. The steps are:

1. **Loss of intellect** There is loss of existence as waves of possibilities thus creating limits on what consciousness can do.
2. **Mental level** The mind's subtle sustenance presents to consciousness the possibility structures that contain processing of meaning but consciousness & mental possibilities still remain whole.
3. **Vital level** Consciousness is limited to exploration of a particular set of vital functions among all possibilities but no actual collapse or separation takes place until the physical body arrives.

4. **Living Cells** At a certain level of complexity of possibilities existing in physical matter, a tangled hierarchy of quantum measurement comes into play. No consciousness can intervene in matter via self-referential collapse of the quantum possibilities waves and actual manifestation begins. And collapse remembers this previous level of life, prana to employ matter to make software representations which we call life in the living cell and its conglomerates of vital function. Now the process of morphogenic fields guiding development of adult from embryo begins. Evolution and morphogenesis of life now takes place and the conglomerate of cells as the brain evolves. So software representation of the mind can be programmed in the brain hardware – then we become mental beings to make representation of the themes (intellect) body.

The Brain Is A Holographic Processor

A brain shattering example of how holograms can change your reality is Windows Holographic. Have a look at the video shown on this website http://www.theverge.com/2015/1/21/7867593/microsoft-announces-windows-holographic. Or just Google Windows Holographic.

In Jan 2015, Microsoft unveiled new prototypes and details of its HoloLens project and the new technology looks like it could have a profound impact on how we use computers in the future. Like the Oculus Rift, the HoloLens system is headset-based, but that's where the similarities end. Where Oculus Rift creates entire 3D realms to explore (virtual reality), HoloLens is meant to create holographic overlays over existing objects and structure in the real world (Augmented Reality).

They say that HoloLens is only meant to augment real-life rather than completely replace it means that there's no need for a screen and face-covering. The truth is that the holographic technology of today is closer to the "real" reality than they know… or do they?

The brain works holographically to create reality as an image. We cannot see a holographic object until we use a laser beam. The brain does the same with pure light just like a laser. When a holographic film or plate is created it appears as ripples (interference patterns) or criss cross waves. The holographic film is used to create a projection of the object. Reality which manifests as a concrete image is a projection by the brain as created from a sea of interference patterns.

It is not possible to remove memory from the brain because it is not stored there. The brain uses Fourier transform to interpret frequency – same as process of nature and sight. The brain does not do the thinking; it is a holographic processor/projector. We are like conscious TV sets picking up frequencies to convert into images. To understand this look at the way you play a game. As you move past a feature object, it disappears but it pops back if you look at it. Our reality also pops back in and out the same way.

Waves of possibilities exist as the field of unlimited possibilities out of which all possibilities already exist in wave form. All is a single unified field of (ocean) existence, not material but in wave form. The whole universe is like this; like a thought wave which cannot explain it. All are waves of potential electrons. We are made of this unified field.

Reality is created like a hologram which is a virtual image not real created by interference patterns just like the electron. The plate which is the interference pattern is not the object any more than your TV is the object or holds the object inside. To see we put another laser on the pattern, then we see the 3D hologram and see real 3D and beyond as well being seen on a 2D plate.

To clearly understand how reality can be an illusion of holograms all you have to do is have a look at a new emerging technology called DVE Telepresence.

You can check out Telepresence at the website www.youtube.com/watch?v=jAIDXzv_fKA. The example used shows an interview which beams a 3D hologram of two people onto a stage. Two men on the right can touch each other but the interviewer cannot touch them. The DVE Immersion Room creates what looks like a 3D hologram of people from across the country! It is real-time HD communication of people walking around in your meeting room. Patented polymer reflectors create this stunning effect. This is so far beyond other "telepresence" systems that use simple flat panel TVs with cameras on top. This is way beyond videoconferencing such as webchat, ichat, and videochat. Imagine being beamed into the middle of the room and talking with your friends, family or co-workers and you are actually on the other side of the globe. This technology gives insight into how your own virtual reality may be working as you direct your life plan from "above".

Technologies such as Realtelepresence creates holograms by active holographic cameras used today to combine real and projected live holograms (as in entertainment) done in a live performance from separate locations. Now we can bring back dead people to perform. Now, as we start adding the animation abilities of computers, we can create programs that are part of the whole process just like these morphogenic process become part of our own life plan movies. It's just like we, or trees, or earth processes are predesigned morphogenic programs of self evolution. There is nothing there as the hologram appears to be where it is not, our reality is an illusion universe; is a splendid hologram with billions of interactive morphogenic programs being projected out to appear as reality.

The World And The Universe Are Flat!

Remember how smart humans thought they were when they discovered the earth was not flat. That it was actually round. And so we all took on the new conscious awareness that it was round and this became the scientific norm. Does anyone believe it is flat anymore? Only the ones that are smoking something - Right? Wrong! There is an interesting simple scientific mind test for you to answer if you believe it is round.

You begin digging a hole vertically right through the center of the Earth. So you dig and dig. How do you emerge on the other side? Feet first upside down? Head first digging up?

You would not believe the crazy conflicts and answers that come from people scientific and otherwise that attempt an answer. If science says the Earth is a ball, then the scientific answer should be pretty simple, you have to come out feet first. That would be an interesting trick to see feet popping up on the other side! So would a scene of a head popping through suspended in the hole. What's not right about this picture? Typically people will bring in all sorts of theories about gravity at the core, getting turned around at the center, but these are simple conjectures avoiding the simple reality that you are drilling through a physical sphere. Or are you?

The thing about this question is that it is probably so stupid it has not emerged as a possible reality in anybody's awareness. It just remains a possibility. The interesting aspect of the holographic projections is that the plate which becomes the holographic storage and display vehicle is simply a 2D flat system of criss cross waves (interference pattern). The apparent physical object was what we see as 3D particles that was replicated here is stored on this other form of waves. And if you take any part of this plate, it contains the whole object when you project it using a holographic projector. The projected object is a copy of the original particle object as created from a flat plate. The brain does the same as the holographic projector, the hololens, to take the fabric of consciousness stored on a 2D plate and make it look like 3D.

In recent research, it is reported that Black holes suggest reality is really 2D and all the 3D stuff (info) is stored in a black hole but is 2D outside. Research suggests that black holes and universe are holograms.

So the world must be flat!!!

Really??

Here are some perplexing thoughts: Is the universe a consciousness hologram? Is reality a projected illusion within the hologram? Is it a virtual experiment created in linear time to study emotions? Our hologram is composed of grids created by a source consciousness brought into awareness by electromagnetic energy at the physical level. The hologram is created and linked through a web, or grid matrices based on the patterns of Sacred Geometry.

Is The Universe A Hologram?

In a publication titled **Is the universe a hologram?** Published in **Science Daily - April 27, 2015** it brought forward the "holographic principle"; the idea that a universe with gravity can be described by a quantum field theory in fewer dimensions. It has been used for years as a mathematical tool in strange curved spaces. New results suggest that the holographic principle also holds in flat spaces. Our own universe could in fact be two dimensional and only appear three dimensional - just like a hologram. At first glance, there is not the slightest doubt; to us, the universe looks three dimensional. But one of the most fruitful theories of theoretical physics in the last two decades is challenging this assumption. The "holographic principle" asserts that a mathematical description of the universe actually requires one fewer dimension than it seems. What we perceive as three dimensional may just be the image of two dimensional processes on a huge cosmic horizon. Until now, this principle has only been studied in exotic spaces with negative curvature. This is interesting from a theoretical point of view, but such spaces are quite different from the space in our own universe. Results obtained by scientist TU Wien (Vienna University of Technology) now suggest that the holographic principle even holds in a flat space-time.

The publication **Black holes are not ruthless killers, but instead benign hologram generators, in Science Daily** - June 17, 2015 gives some more insight into the world is flat notion.

"New research in theoretical physics shows that black holes aren't the ruthless killers we've made them out to be, but instead benign - if imperfect

- hologram generators. The world could have been captured by a black hole, and we wouldn't even notice, according to a new theoretical perspective. Mathur and his team have been expanding on their fuzzball theory, too, and they've come to a completely different conclusion. They see black holes not as killers, but rather as benign copy machines of a sort. They believe that when material touches the surface of a black hole, it becomes a hologram, a near-perfect copy of itself that continues to exist just as before."

To enable you to better visualize what he means, **David Bohm**, classified as one of most significant physicists of our time, offers the following illustration. Imagine an aquarium containing a fish. Imagine also that you are unable to see the aquarium directly and your knowledge about it and what it contains comes from two television cameras, one directed at the aquarium's front and the other directed at its side. As you stare at the two television monitors, you might assume that the fish on each of the screens are separate entities. After all, because the cameras are set at different angles, each of the images will be slightly different. But as you continue to watch the two fish, you will eventually become aware that there is a certain relationship between them. When one turns, the other also makes a slightly different but corresponding turn; when one faces the front, the other always faces toward the side. If you remain unaware of the full scope of the situation, you might even conclude that the fish must be instantaneously communicating with one another, but this is clearly not the case. This, says Bohm, is precisely what is going on between the subatomic particles.

According to Bohm, the apparent faster-than-light connection between subatomic particles is really telling us that there is a deeper level of reality we are not privy to, a more complex dimension beyond our own that is analogous to the aquarium. And, he adds, we view objects such as subatomic particles as separate from one another because we are seeing only a portion of their reality. Such particles are not separate "parts", but facets of a deeper and more underlying unity that is ultimately as holographic and indivisible as the previously mentioned example of the aquarium. And since everything in physical reality is comprised of these phantom images, the universe is itself a projection, a hologram.

In addition to its phantom-like nature, such a universe would possess other rather startling features. If the apparent separateness of subatomic particles is illusory, it means that at a deeper level of reality all things in the universe are infinitely interconnected. The electrons in a carbon atom in the human brain are connected to the subatomic particles that comprise every salmon that swims, every heart that beats, and every star that shimmers in the sky. Everything interpenetrates everything, and although human nature may seek to categorize and pigeonhole and subdivide, the various phenomena of the universe, all apportionments are of necessity artificial and all of nature is ultimately a seamless web.

Karl Pribram best known for his development of the holonomic brain model of cognitive function and his contribution to ongoing neurological research into memory, emotion, motivation and consciousness encountered the concept of holography and realized he had found the explanation brain scientists had been looking for. Pribram believed memories are encoded not in neurons, or small groupings of neurons, but in patterns of nerve impulses that crisscross the entire brain in the same way that patterns of laser light interference crisscross the entire area of a piece of film containing a holographic image. In other words, Pribram believed the brain is itself a hologram.

One of the most amazing things about the human thinking process is that every piece of information seems instantly cross-correlated with every other piece of information - another feature intrinsic to the hologram. Because every portion of a hologram is infinitely interconnected with ever other portion, it is perhaps nature's supreme example of a cross-correlated system.

The storage of memory is not the only neurophysiological puzzle that becomes more tractable in light of Pribram's holographic model of the brain. Another is how the brain is able to translate the avalanche of frequencies it receives via the senses (light frequencies, sound frequencies, and so on) into the concrete world of our perceptions. Encoding and decoding frequencies is precisely what a hologram does best. Just as a hologram functions as a sort of lens, a translating device able to convert an apparently meaningless blur of frequencies into a coherent image, Pribram believed the brain also comprises a lens and uses holographic principles to mathematically convert the frequencies it receives through the senses into the inner world of our perceptions. An impressive body of evidence suggests that the brain uses holographic principles to perform its operations. Pribram's theory, in fact, has gained increasing support among neurophysiologists.

Pribram's belief was that our brains mathematically construct "hard" reality by relying on input from a frequency domain has received a good deal of experimental support. It has been found that each of our senses is sensitive to a much broader range of frequencies than was previously suspected. Researchers have discovered, for instance, that our visual systems are sensitive to sound frequencies, that our sense of smell is in part dependent on what are now called "cosmic frequencies", and that even the cells in our bodies are sensitive to a broad range of frequencies. Such findings suggest that it is only in the holographic domain of consciousness that such frequencies are sorted out and divided up into conventional perceptions.

But the most mind-boggling aspect of Pribram's holographic model of the brain is what happens when it is put together with Bohm's theory. For if the concreteness of the world is but a secondary reality and what is "there" is actually a holographic blur of frequencies, and if the brain is also a hologram and only selects some of the frequencies out of this blur and mathematically transforms them into sensory perceptions, what becomes of objective reality?

Put quite simply, it ceases to exist. As the religions of the East have long upheld, the material world is Maya, an illusion, and although we may think we are physical beings moving through a physical world, this too is an illusion. We are really "receivers" floating through a kaleidoscopic sea of frequency, and what we extract from this sea and transmogrify into physical reality is but one channel from many extracted out of the superhologram.

In **Scientific American, August 14, 2003** a publication stated the Theoretical results about black holes suggest that the universe could be like a gigantic hologram. An astonishing theory called the holographic principle holds that the universe is like a hologram: just as a trick of light allows a fully three-dimensional image to be recorded on a flat piece of film, our seemingly three-dimensional universe could be completely equivalent to alternative quantum fields and physical laws "painted" on a distant, vast surface.

The physics of black holes - immensely dense concentrations of mass - provides a hint that the principle might be true. Studies of black holes show that, although it defies common sense, the maximum entropy or information content of any region of space is defined not by its volume but by its surface area.

Ask anybody what the physical world is made of, and you are likely to be told "matter and energy". Yet if we have learned anything from engineering, biology and physics, information is just as crucial an ingredient. The robot at the automobile factory is supplied with metal and plastic but can make nothing useful without copious instructions telling it which part to weld to what and so on. A ribosome in a cell in your body is supplied with amino acid building blocks and is powered by energy released by the conversion of ATP to ADP, but it can synthesize no proteins without the information brought to it from the DNA in the cell's nucleus. Likewise, a century of developments in physics has taught us that information is a crucial player in physical systems and processes. Indeed, a current trend, initiated by **John A. Wheeler of Princeton University**, is to regard the physical world as made of information, with energy and matter as incidentals.

This viewpoint invites a new look at venerable questions. The information storage capacity of devices such as hard disk drives has been increasing by leaps and bounds. When will such progress halt? What is the ultimate information capacity of a device that weighs, say, less than a gram and can fit inside a cubic centimeter (roughly the size of a computer chip)? How much information does it take to describe a whole universe? Could that description fit in a computer's memory? Could we, as William Blake memorably penned, "see the world in a grain of sand," or is that idea no more than poetic license?

Remarkably, recent developments in theoretical physics answer some of these questions, and the answers might be important clues to the ultimate theory of reality. By studying the mysterious properties of black holes, physicists have deduced absolute limits on how much information a region of space or a quantity of matter and energy can hold. Related results suggest that our universe, which we perceive to have three spatial dimensions, might instead be "written" on a two-dimensional surface, like a hologram. Our everyday perceptions of the world as three-dimensional would then be either a profound illusion or merely one of two alternative ways of viewing reality. A grain of sand may not encompass our world, but a flat screen might.

The holographic paradigm also has implications for so-called hard sciences like biology. Keith Floyd, a psychologist at Virginia Intermont College, has pointed out that if the concreteness of reality is but a holographic illusion, it would no longer be true to say the brain produces consciousness. Rather, it is consciousness that creates the appearance of the brain - as well as the body and everything else around us we interpret as physical.

Such a turnabout in the way we view biological structures has caused researchers to point out that medicine and our understanding of the healing process could also be transformed by the holographic paradigm. If the apparent physical structure of the body is but a holographic projection of consciousness, it becomes clear that each of us is much more responsible for our health than current medical wisdom allows. What we now view as miraculous remissions of disease may actually be due to changes in consciousness which in turn effect changes in the hologram of the body.

Similarly, controversial new healing techniques such as visualization may work so well because in the holographic domain of thought images are ultimately as real as "reality".

Even visions and experiences involving "non-ordinary" reality become explainable under the holographic paradigm. In his book **Gifts of Unknown Things,** biologist **Lyall Watson** describes his encounter with an Indonesian shaman woman who, by performing a ritual dance, was able to make an entire grove of trees instantly vanish into thin air. Watson relates that as he and another astonished onlooker continued to watch the woman, she caused the trees to reappear, then "click" off again and on again several times in succession.

Although current scientific understanding is incapable of explaining such events, experiences like this become more tenable if "hard" reality is only a holographic projection. Perhaps we agree on what is "there" or "not there" because what we call consensus reality is formulated and ratified at the level of the human unconscious at which all minds are infinitely interconnected.

What we perceive as reality is only a canvas waiting for us to draw upon it any picture we want. Anything is possible, from bending spoons with the power of the mind to the phantasmagoric events experienced by Castaneda during his encounters with the Yaqui brujo don Juan, for magic is our birthright, no more or less miraculous than our ability to compute the reality we want when we are in our dreams.

In Summary Of Science

Ok, this is a lot to digest but if you read this several times, you can see the similarity to what we have been writing about in the previous chapters. And you can see a convergence to the worlds of science and metascience.

We see that physical and mental worlds remain possibilities until consciousness gives them substance by collapsing them into an actual expression or object. Consciousness reorganizes and collapses into a state from possibilities by the brain in response to stimulus, then chooses a convoluted mental meaning – perception. The Neocortex is a symbol processor as the mind gives meaning to an object. In the notion of Quantum Leap we "suddenly" get a solution at unrelated times/events as attraction of a morphic field. It comes from outside of ordinary consciousness – from the collective consciousness of information images, and archetypes.

We see that all quantum objects exist in transcendental (possibility) or realm of potentiality or in immanent level or made manifest. Intensity such as emotions creates superposition of possibilities in unconscious processing which is biased by learning context. The more you collapse the mind's quantum state relative to the same question the more you increase chances of a new response – from a bigger and bigger pool of possibilities from quantum consciousness to choose from. As we have seen with the placebo, this process of recurrent collapsing is by repetition of images from the Quantum Field supercharged with emotion and gratitude.

So the brain is a holographic electrochemical machine (computer) designed to process information that creates patterns of experiences and realities. We could say that reality is a computer-like generated consciousness hologram in which the characters it creates at the physical level are programmed to believe it is real. It is a game of illusion, delusion, perception and deception.

Different bodies vital, mental, intellectual, supermental are all possibilities collapsed by consciousness parallel to physical to get a personal experience. All feelings (emotions) are mapped into physical stored in vital body and are in non local morphogenic fields. Morphogenesis is the development of forms or organs guided by non local extraphysical morphogenic fields. This is the vital body (etheric connected to the life process of the body).

The brain cannot process meaning, it comes from outside. The "feel" behind vital functions of living organisms comes from the vital body of consciousness which maps the vital function in the form of various functional organs in the physical body through the chakras. Thus consciousness then "writes" meaningful mental programs in the brain. Consciousness also uses mental body to create mental software for meaning that the mind processes in the brain. Then consciousness uses physical hardware to make software representations of the vital and the mental.

Possibility waves of macromatter are sluggish. Between my and your observation, their spread is small so we both collapse in the same place to create consensus of physical reality, outside is public (but is actually projected inside.) Thus we can have the brain play out a holographic Life Plan like a subprogram of our personal consciousness to interact within the larger holographic program of global consciousness so it has to abide by the design of the larger program. And that larger program contains all the morphogenic subroutines of every living thing to reflect its purpose, order and evolution according to its blueprint DNA.

Subjects with correlated brains who collapse an event in one as electron potential becomes an instant non local collapse in another. These right conditions mean one cannot think and do. It is a state of letting go to a state of consciousness beyond ego where two are one allows access to the larger scope of the greater Consciousness. Consciousness is all and everything in the virtual hologram of our experiences brought into awareness by the brain - an electrochemical machine forever viewing streaming codes for experience and interpretation.

The place where the Greater Consciousness is accessible is where quantum waves of possibility transcend space and time. There is no space or time. That is a construct that the brain uses to create the illusion of space and time. All objects as possibility waves are non local thus implying transcendence and interconnectivity. Thus all behave as one regardless of space and time. Consciousness originates from a source of light energy for the purpose of learning. The human biogenetic experiment is consciousness brought forth into the physical by the patterns of sacred geometry that repeat in cycles called Time.

What we are beginning to see from a different perspective is that this projected holographic reality is about the evolution of consciousness in the alchemy of time. It is about experience and learning. It is virtual immersion movie, perceived through conscious awareness. We exist in a biogenetic experiment to experience emotion and higher mental thought - through the construct of linear time and a holographic morphogenetic vessel called a Lower Body and Mind. So we need a Life Plan immersion movie to best express the Soul's higher mental and emotional mind.

To become fully consciousness, is to remember who you are as a being of light, why you are here, and where we are going as dictated by the collective unconscious that creates the programs of realities through which your soul experiences simultaneously. That is the ultimate victory of the engagement; then you stop playing the game of life and perhaps become Spirit Guide?

Within the higher energetic state of who we are as energy of consciousness individualized within the quantum field, we created a Life Plan and contracted to immerse into the holographic projection so as to engage in emotional experiences. Within the creation of this movie we incorporated a greater intelligence of geometric design following the patterns of sacred geometry which form the underlying basis for running DNA programs within the larger scope of the immersion movie. But that overseeing hologram – the larger scope – had to have rules of engagement. Being a self evolving live consciousness, its rules would be created by the consensus of its participants, each making up the whole and being limited by the consensus beliefs within it. And that consensus hologram is in itself a consensus observer of the reality that is shared by the Life Plans running concurrently. To evolve beyond it, to the next level of consciousness, you have to allow into your conscious awareness the rules of play outside that game and get to believe, accept and surrender to your true Higher Self your Soul – all by your lonesome self!

Reality appears to move in synchronized linear fashion creating the illusion of time, also known as the loops/cycles of time, wheel of karma, or the alchemy wheel. It is never the same as it incorporates the flow of the collective unconsciousness forever in motion creating new patterns of experience that modify its process of order, evolution and purpose as morphogenic subroutines.

Consciousness spirals like a slinky, mirroring the movement, or evolution, of DNA. The higher your consciousness moves up the slinky, the faster the vibrational frequency - the faster you think, create, understand higher holographic archetypes of reality, and increase your manifestation in physical reality. As you move up this ladder of vibration, the awareness of the nature of reality opens and the mind as consciousness as Creator unifies with the lower and higher mind as one within the quantum field of infinite possibilities.

You as your mind collapsed (brought and observed) the image from thought, chose a result or an outcome from a place of infinite possibilities, gave it life to grow, to behave according to some preset order, process, and purpose, then directed some continuation of evolving outside your movie guidelines. You stored the movie somewhere beyond the brain in the Causal Body, and then linked between realities to engage physical and mental processes. At the same time, at the next level of global consciousness, the global consensus collapsed a shared 3D world called the Earth Game into holographic reality.

13

FREE WILL... REALLY?

"Free will is the Soul's prerogative to choose the characters and story line and events in the Life Plan. If you want to really exercise true free will you have to go back to your true self as the Divine Programmer that created the plan."

Aly McDonald   **Ed Rychkun**

> **It's nice to believe I have free will**
> **But which one of me really has that skill?**

Ok, we will admit that the last chapter is pretty heavy and you may wonder if this is some stupid movie that you planned right down to what people look like and places and things defined in the future, where is free will? That's a good question. And when you consider the art of Palmistry that shows a map of a Life Plan, one hand being the planned (life plan) and the other being the actual (life) recorded one, the whole idea of destiny and free will get more clouded. We are now going to look at free will and more scientific research that tells us more about our participation in the this Life Plan Movie.

The Brain Is Not Really In Charge Of Free Will

We will take you to some laboratory work that may hurt your brain. We have written much about this brain being the one who has to somehow read a holographic script of your Life Plan, of your personal consciousness and dovetail it into a much larger Plan of the global consciousness which then has to conform to the universal consciousness. And it all has to be interactive in a self learning, evolutionary mode yet still allow individual adjustments. This immersion movie has to allow for an interactive self learning evolution reflecting the consensus consciousness. That's a pretty tall order – ineffable!

In studies such as with neurophysiologists Ben Libit and Bertram Feinstein they measured the time it took for a touch stimulus on a patient's skin to reach the brain as an electrical signal. The patient was also asked to push a button when she became aware of being touched. The brain was aware at .0001 seconds, the button was pressed after .1 sec but the awareness of the stimulus was not until .5 seconds. **This meant the patient's decision to respond was being made by the unconscious mind** with the patient awareness being the last to know. None were aware that their unconscious minds had already caused them to push the button before they had consciously decided to do so. Their brains were creating the comforting delusion that they had consciously controlled the action even though they had not. Many other studies have shown that 1.5 seconds before we decide to move our muscles, such as a finger, our brain has already started to generate the signals necessary to move it. So the bizarre conclusion is that the conscious mind is truly the big dummy. **It is simply being informed after the fact to make it look like it is making the decision!** The brain and subconscious knew what to do, but that conscious mind part of the brain had no clue until it was sent a memo that all the requirements had been done.

In a kind of spooky experiment, scientists at the **Max Planck Institute for Human Cognitive and Brain Sciences** revealed that our decisions are made seconds before we become aware of them. In the study, participants could freely decide if they wanted to press a button with their right or left hand. The only condition was that they had to remember when they made the decision to either use their right hand or left hand. Using fMRI, researchers would scan the brains of the participants while all of this was going on in order to find out if they could in fact predict which hand the participants would use BEFORE they were consciously aware of the decision.

By monitoring the micro patterns of activity in the frontopolar cortex, the researchers could predict which hand the participant would choose 7 SECONDS before the participant was aware of the decision. The conclusion was that: *"Your decisions are strongly prepared by brain activity. By the time consciousness kicks in, most of the work has already been done,"* said study co-author John-Dylan Haynes, a Max Planck Institute neuroscientist.

Certainly from hypnosis research it has been established that the unconscious pretty much controls everything and that personal consciousness is extremely limited. This kind of research is telling us that decisions are made by subconscious 7 seconds before the conscious. This study was publicized by **Marcus Du Sautoy (Professor of Mathematics at the University of Oxford)** but seems to have become blocked.

Valerie Hunt whom we presented in our first book discovered the human energy field responds to stimuli even before the brain. Using EMG readings of energy field and EEG readings of the brain, she recorded that loud sounds or flashes register in the energy field before it ever shows up in the brain. She states: "The *minds not in the brain, it's in that darn field*." This goes a step further in that the hierarchy of communication starts in the "field" to quantum subconscious to identify the program for the brain to do the work with. Then the personal conscious self just gets informed. It is not the other way around!

People who see these types of experiments get somewhat concerned about free will. But free will is also a misguided construct of ego because to give it up would mean the conscious analytical mind of the brain has no control at all. It is just a big flunkee to manage the work. In fact, what we are seeing in all this is that there are three levels of free will:

Level 1: free will before incarnation is the Soul's prerogative to choose the characters, story line, events and purpose of the Life Plan holographic movie.
Level 2: free will during incarnation is the Physical vessel having the freedom to use mental and emotional abilities, perceive and display emotions by choice within the pathways created in the Life Plan, at the same time choose the path.
Level 3: free will within the pathways of the Life Plan. Depending upon the details chosen for the pathways, events, people, the activities between are essentially undefined allowing free will of the mental mind to determine, discern and choose acts along the way.

But here is a big one. If you want to really exercise true free will you have to go back to your true self as the Divine Programmer that created the plan. But what comes up immediately is: Even if you do that, and create a change in reality like a miracle, was that part of the original Life Plan movie as a predetermined option, or did you really change reality? Of course our conscious mind (ego) does not like that one because then we are simply puppets being controlled by the Soul for its amusement to engage us in a game. For its amusement it wants to see how we would think and feel by being thrown into the game. And just like the brain is being informed after the decisions, these decisions are actually being made by the Soul through the subconscious which is simply waiting to see how smart we are with our mental and emotional choices. Obviously there are escape routes in the plan if we either take an exit point like an NDE or evolve according to what we as spiritual energy beings were designed to expand and use that defined in DNA layers beyond the first two physical reality layers.

We Are Part Of An Immersion Movie Of Life

Interestingly enough, it is sort of like loading up and watching a DVD movie. It takes you a few seconds to respond to it. As you watch, you become immersed in the movie with no control over it except to turn it off. The brain and subconscious are also playing out an already created movie. You and the dummy ego are not really creating the movie directly unless you get into that creator space - directly within the quantum field where the Divine Programmer is resident. What you are creating are mental and emotional energies that behave according to set laws governing the global consciousness – like Cause & Effect and Attraction.

What is coming more and more to the forefront of our joint awareness is that the unconscious makes decisions and conscious follows. We know that seeing and imagining creates the same process in the brain. As we have seen, the results show that the brain knows what is going to be chosen before we do – **before we become consciously aware.**

A pattern emerges unconsciously to lead up to the decision – a deterministic decision brain creates hard reality from frequency domain. The brain downloads the frequency, creates reality, and then sends it to see how it is perceived. The Field and the quantum Causal field contain the stored life plan like it was on holographic film. Holographic reality is downloaded, to project out there as hard reality. So your personal conscious awareness is not aware of experience until brain and body know what experience we are about to have <u>after the experience has been chosen</u> *by one on the other side and downloaded from subconscious to our brains.* And someone watching our brain activity can know what experience we are about to have up to 6 seconds before our self conscious knows.

So the brain already knows ahead of time but when the brain was stimulated it was a new hologram. An area of the brain collapses and projects out there to be perceived and experienced as reality and only when we perceive and interact do we become consciously aware of what is happening and the whole process can take 6 seconds. The brain is the observer that collapses the wave function into something we understand so we can believe we are engaging in a real reality. Then we can perceive; create mental analysis and emotional energies that are recorded in the Causal body.

To bring this closer to home consider your PC which uses binary code 0 and 1 like those wavy things the brain uses. Inside is a CPU like a brain of the computer. It translates and projects on a screen in a form we understand. Sensory perception is like the mouse, to respond back to CPU to process. The brain does the same thing to project out there to get input which it already knows about.

What is happening is that we are not sensing, we are projecting reality. Our senses are not sensing out there but in fact are first projecting that reality so it appears to be out there. Projection plus perception. The brain collapses wave functions and makes it appear like we are surrounded by a holographic 3D total immersion movie from a frequency domain. Our senses read the projection and bring information back to the brain. The act of seeing is experienced in the visual cortex. What we see, touch, feel, perceive is only through electrical signals in the brain; we do not see it in the external world; we see it in our brain as the brain's interpretation of electrical signals. It is the same with distance, time, as well as the body which is an image formed inside your brain. To see it outside is a deception. It is easy to deceive us and the brain of reality.

The bottom line is that we project reality, then perceive it. So we believe what we see out there is real, with a life of its own and we observe and perceive it to interact with it. No! We project reality first and then perceive it coming back to us in four simple steps:

1. We first download wave frequency from the field into the brain
2. Brain translates this wave frequency into a hologram by collapsing
3. The hologram is projected out there so it appears real
4. The reality comes back to us through our physical perception

It is like you are in a 3D movie theatre but the projector is coming from your brain and that movie is what you are immersed in – it is not real. Michael Talbot states that reality does not exist. The world out there is translated and created by the brain. Underlying the illusion is a deeper order of existence and that gives birth to all objects like holographic film gives birth to a hologram. The brain converts the waves of our world. That we are physical beings moving through a physical world is an illusion. We are receivers floating through a sea of frequency. Each individual must have their own unique hologram they are projecting as their private reality that each brain downloads and translates. Thus we all see reality differently. You do not create your reality, you project your unique holographic 3D experience to your brain and the perception and mental/emotional experience is recorded.

In order to really be in charge of this, you have to be outside of the influence of the brain and its body, and its perceptions. You have to be pure consciousness that is non locally part of everything which is the 99.99% of nonmaterial space, the glue that interconnects everything as the quantum energy field of all that is, was and will be. How does that grab you?

We have to look at something to collapse it and activate the immersion. Written for you is the immersion movie 3D written uniquely for you, by you from a higher vibratory state of energy, downloaded to your brain translated into a hologram, you see it and project it out there for you to experience.

So who or what is writing the script for your experience? As we have said, brain experiments show that the brain and body know what is about to happen before we become conscious of it. As said before, conscious follows unconscious. A larger Consciousness of the Soul is the Director and Scriptor of the immersion movie. It chooses specific frequency waves from unlimited possibilities in the field to create the holodeck experience as outlined in a life plan, stored individually for each as a moment to moment path with predetermined events.

We have learned from a previous chapter that this is the Life Plan that we each agreed to. The unconscious or subconscious downloads this to the brain to project it outside as reality for the purpose engaging in it. A higher consciousness is directing the playback of the immersion movie.

Science says that you can't study consciousness but there is a common agreement between scientists; matter is completely insubstantial, more like a thought. We are concluding more and more that an intangible energetic world energetic influences-chooses a tangible material world; that is what quantum physics is all about. Something is affecting reality; to achieve something and cause it to happen. It is like a secret underground effecting and creating reality. It is a higher consciousness that chooses specific wave frequencies from the field of unlimited possibilities in the field that it wants and downloads them to a human brain which converts this into space/time particles and out pops our holographic reality, at the same time integrating these into our Life Plans.

But consciousness is not aware of experience until brain and body know what experience we are about to have <u>after the experience has **been chosen by one on the other side and downloaded to our brains.**</u>

The Movie You Collapsed Into Reality

Your mind is creating thoughts which you are collapsing (manifesting) in a subtle imaginary realm called your personal imagination virtual movie. But you created the frames or moments in your movie and they are stored for retrieval. Where are these things stored? In the Causal energy body. We have learned that the brain seems to have a copy but even when you cut out a portion of it or go through a NDE; it is still all available from somewhere else. Consciousness which is part of the quantum field stores all this information in the Causal Body. If it is hard to understand how, drop the notion of the hard disc of computers and think about the iCloud, or better still the trillions of information bits floating around on carrier waves in the open space around you that contain your cell phone messages and the WIFI networks that are decoded by way of the right decoders. These are all just higher frequency carrier waves in the 99.9% quantum soup that carry information that can be projected, compartmentalized, and understood in the physical domain.

We know this is consciousness as represented by the Soul or Higher Self. Really, to not confuse things there is only one great quantum consciousness; but there a many subsets of it. It becomes a question of which one do you want to play the game in? We have stated that the consciousness is what you bring into your awareness. Understand that this can be your local conscious mind, the global conscious mind or the Soul conscious mind all quantum subsets of the Greater Conscious Mind. It would appear that our purpose is to evolve this mind into higher and higher subsets thus enlarging the scope of our Soul's mind. So to create things that are outside of each subset, one must open to the awareness of the next higher mind and really know what downward causation and as above so below REALLY means.

Control Over Destiny?

Hmmmm, do we? As a humanoid within the confines of the Lower Self, not much! So let's get back to the mind movie you created as Creator in Chapter 1. When you created that mind movie, you had no consideration for time and space. You could be anywhere instantly or you could be everywhere in all these places which only takes attention to see it. What is more relevant is that you as your mind:

1. Collapsed (brought and observed) the image from thought
2. Chose a result or an outcome from a place of infinite possibilities
3. Gave life to grow, behave according to some preset order, process, purpose
4. Directed some continuation of evolving outside your movie guidelines
5. Stored the movie somewhere beyond the brain
6. Linked between realities to engage physical and mental processes

What about these thoughts and images that came to you? Some of these came from something that you may not have experienced in this lifetime. You created or retrieved these from somewhere. Where did they come from? You can't see them yet they are waves of energy that just simply pop into awareness. This mental and emotional indulgent was also having an effect on your physical reality; your body as feelings of joy and tingling of fun came through from thes fake movies you were playing out.

And so your mind can create many movies this way drawing from a world of infinite possibilities that your consciousness picks to collapse into the movie reality. Sometime your imagination can go wild and create a world that you have not apparently experienced or seen... but aha, perhaps it was seen and saved in the Causal energy field and it was experienced in a different life?

The process you are engaging in takes thoughts of something and brings them into conscious awareness. It is a choice you make in creating your movies. This came from a place of infinite possibilities as you decided to create something in a scene. That thought of say creating something in the scenes pops into your consciousness of your reality when you want it there. If you look at this imaginary process, you are the sub director and the sub writer/Creator of the movie. Anybody and everybody can do this by using their imagination, drawing from a sea of infinite possibilities, popping these thoughts into an imaginary set of sequences of movie frames/images to be stored and retrieved when chosen so.

So as you sat in your chair, you were creating your reality, your world, your players, your universe. You could come back to it as it was a movie stored somewhere. You could retrieve it, run it, edit it, delete it, play with your emotions in it. You could create your characters, your story line, your events, situations, the settings and environments.

In a sense your were the Creator of your reality and you could express what you wished to express and experience through your created environment and your characters. You were engaging in a holographic 3D movie that you created by imagination and you could see yourself in it as the main actor, feeling the emotional experience of it. If you wanted to create a chilling scene to launch the emotion of fear, you could do so. If you wanted to create the emotion of bliss, you could do so. Your mind when conscious of these scenes was being used – deployed – to express feelings.

And in many cases, the details of the scenes, the characters, and many of the environmental parts of the movie would be taken care of by some other director who would dovetail your movie into the larger scope of the whole movie. You never had to consider the preprocesses whereby the wind blew, the waves washed the beach, the trees grew or how people even behaved or looked. It was a natural process that was inherently part of the Director's job, not yours.

Now consider that this is exactly what is happening with you sitting in your Director's seat in a higher energetic state, within the quantum energy field and your mind is part of a much greater mind that was responsible for all the order, processes and purpose of the things you created so as to experience and express within it. And how could you do this. It is presented and projected by the key device, the brain to create a holographic projection which like the Star Trek holodeck you can engage in and express within so as to exercise your mental and emotional higher bodies through that holograph experience which you chose to create.

But... and here is the big but! There are still limitations of what you can bring from that field of infinite possibilities of imagination down into this 3D plane. With miracles we get a glimpse of *some* of the radical possibilities so there must be certain rules of engagement. We have determined that each subset of consciousness has its own rules. Your consciousness is controlled by a larger consensus that you take from to form your belief boxes you become subject to those limits. To break out into the next level – let us say a 4D Astral energy body consciousness - you need to become aware of it, step out into it, believe it, accept it and then surrender to its rules which are obviously wider than the 3D Physical energy body.

If we go back to our energy anatomy of the higher bodies, we see each is like a consciousness compartment that vibrates at frequencies lower and lower. Each has its own rules. When we step out of the 3D box into the 4D box by understanding that we are more than just a physical body, new things, abilities, capabilities open up. These are all already encoded in our DNA and we are only using a few parts. What about the other layers? What do they do? How do we get access to those programs from what scientists call "junk DNA" simply because their narrow boxed minds can't explain them. And what about the other 90% of our brains that are dormant? In the mind movie we created things like trees, water, people, animals, environment that seemed to have a program to follow of their own. They are indeed programs reflecting the greater natural order, process and purpose, just like you are as a human vessel. Those programs and templates are reflected in DNA as the progress and state of evolution of the whole.

But we only use 2 layers of DNA. How does it open? This relates to our own physical stages of evolution that we are going to bring forward in a final chapter on **"How Does It All Work"**. The choices we make in our Life Plan have a Higher Path and a Lower Path and many in-between. What we choose to accept, believe and surrender to determines our evolution as a physical vessel and what opens. Quite obviously when we become aware of our Higher Selves and get familiar with the 4D Astral consciousness, we open up related abilities within that Astral Box. But there are many levels of these boxes and consciousness as we have brought forward.

Imagine a situation where, like in your current mind of consciousness you could manifest absolutely anything you thought about instantly – just like you did in your imaginary movie. What would happen? Do you think the 3D vessel has the responsibility to manage this ability for the good of all or the good of self? Can you imagine the world that would be created? The fact remains that humanity itself is nowhere near that point as ego would simply go nuts.

So each level of consciousness, and the belief box it reflects, carries a certain level of understanding and responsibility before it can be deployed. At the ultimate end, where the Soul resides, it can create things exactly the way the mind can now in imagination but it is spiritual growth that must dominate the human behavior and belief system – as a unified part of the whole – that has to be attained; within the sea of quantum consciousness based upon love only. Each level has a portal to the next level that provides a glimpse into the next. If these portals are not taken and the awareness of them is not brought into consciousness, then they simply do not develop and we default to each box of limitations.

In the end, it is all just a game anyway.

Well...

That's a lot of information to digest but the last two chapters take us full circle to the first chapter where we became creators in our own minds and our imagination. What we wanted to do however is to summarize the changing "scientific" landscape on the topics we have presented in the earlier chapters. There is a distinct convergence between science and metascience taking place now as the greater consciousness brings more and more focus and awareness into the phenomenon of miracles and "paratechnology".

The end result is that it is the same process of mind imagination and previewed reality that actually creates the holographic world we engage in. It is occurring all the time without our knowing, the clearest, most intensely charged thoughts, images, words being the ones that are manifested into this reality. The process however is not understood until you let go of it and your lower identity, nor can it consciously be modified unless you learn to be in the Director's seat as pure consciousness. That is the portal that is always open to every individual. It is to evolve and learn, to open awareness and expand personal consciousness into the next level. And the ultimate goal? To open to the full 12 layers of DNA and then evolve beyond the limits of that box!

Methinks that is a long way to go from where we sit now!

In the following chapter we will attempt to bring this all together.

14

WILL THE REAL DIVINE PROGRAMMER STAND UP

"If you can align thought, feeling, and emotion as one, you can create miracles. As ancient wisdom says; be enveloped by what you desire, that your gladness be full".

Aly McDonald   Ed Rychkun

> **Why can't I engage in my Game of Life Without these issues and emotional strife?**

Ask And It Shall Be Given; Really?

We have in this book not given much attention to the New Age or Religious Ideas on the topic of Divine Intervention and Miracles. It is because these are human constructs of belief systems that have a tendency to keep personal opinions, and lower mental interference alive within the process of creation that add to the limits of the belief boxes. Presenting favorite "biases" about these diverse opinions does not assist much in our quest because we are simply looking at what works and what; if anything, is the common consensus of how to escape the limits of the box.

Because we are already perhaps unknowingly creating our realities within the scope of our Life Plans, one can of course simply continue to do so. Of course the best way is to learn from our prior authors and practitioners like Napoleon Hill where total thought, words and emotion as passion and vision become relentless in pursuit of desire. But what we are learning is that this hard work and persistent conflict to achieve our desires from below to above may be executed a different way; by managing energies, changing the cause and effect, and attracting what we desire a different way in the process of above to below. That is what we have attempted to bring into a reader's awareness; that different ways may assist in the engagement of a better path and a bit more "free will".

As it turns out, if you can bring yourself to an awareness above the ego's opinion about the New Age and Religion, you begin to see that they are all converging on key principles that reflect this quest for who and what we are and the evolution to a higher state of being. If we look at the ideas behind meditation, altered states, letting go, divine intervention, gods, God, prayer, and so on infinitum we see that there are reasons for these processes directly related to physical processes and changing reality. However, as egos, opinions and individual experiences would have it, many of these have been distorted or commercialized to convey too many versions of what is perhaps a partial truth.

A very interesting example of this is the process of prayer because it is such a common part of the processes and it allegedly talks to that Divine Programmer of God. In this area we want to bring back into awareness a writer and scientist that we presented in our first book. His name is **Gregg Braden** and you can find him at **www.greggbraden.com**.

As a crossover between science and spirituality, he has been on an incredible quest involving ancient wisdom and religions. What is really pertinent to our example is what he found out about what he called the lost mode of prayer. Gregg says there are four modes of prayer that religions use but there is also a lost mode of prayer. The four types of prayer are *colloquial,* an informal prayer. There is *petitionary* which petitions for help, *ritualistic* where statements are made of the goodness of God, and *meditative,* where you create a deep sacred relationship. But the fifth is called *feeling*. Here the prayer has already been answered as the thing asked for was "*as done"* and surrounded with feeling.

This, he points out, was hidden from us. The conspirator was the church that deleted special wisdom from all books back in the 4th century - back in Alexandra and then they re-wrote the bibles and destroyed all of the writings that they believed were contrary to their beliefs. They took out empowering mystical information. Forty-five books were taken out and condensed. Twelve hundred other translations to other languages further distorted the original truth. It was how this key powerful mode of prayer was lost.

It was, as he suggests, that this wisdom was too powerful because within it was the power of miracles. A prayer made in this faith could heal the sick. So the *"Ask and you shall receive"* prayer is not complete and does not work as is suggested in the new version! It was edited out. What is really fascinating is Braden's evidence in the King James modern condensed version of the Bible. He quotes: *"What so ever ye ask thy Father in my Name, he will give it to you. Hitherto have ye asked nothing in my name: Ask and ye shall receive, that your joy may be full".* But from the original version we have a whole different concept: *"All things that you shall ask straightly, directly... from inside My Name you shall be given... be enveloped by what you desire, that your gladness be full."*

Braden says that in the spring of 1998, he had the honor of facilitating a pilgrimage into the monasteries of central Tibet, searching for evidence of an ancient and forgotten form of prayer. There he found the language that speaks to the field that unites all things. The monks and the nuns who live there shared the instructions for a way to pray that was largely lost to the West in the fourth-century biblical edits of the early Christian Church. But it was preserved in Tibet for centuries in the texts and traditions of those living there. He found this was the lost mode of prayer and it has no words or outward expressions. It was based solely in feeling.

Specifically, he says: *"this process of prayer invites us to feel as if our prayer has already been answered".* It is different than feeling powerless and needing to ask for help from a higher source. In recent years, studies have shown that it is this very quality of feeling that does, in fact, *speak* to the quantum field that connects us all. Through prayers of feeling, we are empowered to take part in the healing of our lives and our relationships, as well as our bodies, and our world! He says: *"Research has shown that it is through a quantum field that connects us to the universe that our beliefs and prayers within us are carried into the world around us".*

If you are paying attention these days, you will see it has taken thousands of years to reveal this truth. Braden reports another aspect of this is revealed in the Essenes' Gospel which is 2500 years old. The Essenes, he reports, were the real ancient keepers of wisdom. It says: *"When three become as one, you will say to the mountain move".* This language is what speaks directly to the Force.

The three items Gregg is talking about are thought, feeling and emotion. It is the lost mode of feeling - already accomplished. It requires a faith that acknowledges our power in creation - it happened. You created it or the seed. Then you give thanks after you felt it. So you don't just pray for something, you have to feel it to really give it life. That is what creates the vibratory power that draws it as a possibility into reality. Feeling is magnetic energy movement through us and around us. So if you can make thought, feeling, and emotion one, you can *"move mountains"* and create miracles.

But Gregg points out if you look at the old edited version it says: *"ask"* when the real version says: *"be enveloped by what you desire, that your gladness be full"*. That is a whole new picture. That is referring to visualization and feelings. There is more. He says the Essenes said: *"First, seek peace in his own body (emotion) then seek peace in the feelings, then seek peace in his own thoughts, such can shape the Heavens"*. Peace is the key. Demonstrate love and compassion. It is an anchor point. The Essenes said: *"go to Nature to nurture peace - reverence will help create peace"*. The Essenes said peace is the most powerful component. We can create it in our bodies through thought.

What is so interesting is that there is a universal template of prayer. It has input, function, output. The words are not key, the feeling is. Open the field, feel the feeling and give thanks. These are the three components. And if you look at what processes we have studied that work, we see these three components over and over. Create a feeling as if the prayers are already done. This is the way you communicate with the field and show the appropriate faith for the reality process to get going and do its job.

Gregg points out that it is through subtle energy that science now acknowledges, the language of creation is words, thoughts, and emotions. The results are mirrored in the events we experience. Our visible world of what we see is a reflection of the invisible unseen world. What we become in our beliefs is what we experience in this world.

Karma, Cause & Effect And The Law Of Attraction

We have stated that the process of creating reality is an ongoing process. This process goes on differently depending upon the place of instigation, but nevertheless originates through the intent of the mind. We have seen that the more unusual they are; as unexplainable occurrences that are different than the global consciousness, they need to be executed more from and energetic place of the higher mind and pure consciousness. These occurrences of miracles for example are essentially outside the limit of the box that humans have created and need some special coaxing. Should you want to change your reality from the lower vibratory plane like the material then you typically engage in the 7 steps of manifesting with much attention to what Napoleon Hill wrote. In the material plane, we follow the material plane rules of engagement to achieve our health and wealth desires but still with the believe system that guides its processes.

But even in this plane, people are creating their desires (and their worst nightmares) on autopilot because there is not an awareness outside that global box. In this place there are three laws that are playing a role in what type of desires and nightmares are being experienced.

First there is karma. These are experiences that have yet to be learned a lesson from and they continue to come forward as an experience until a lesson is learned to stand above it and see and feel a positive outcome as a result of it. As we have seen, if in a previous life, one had a plan that involved starvation that nothing was learned from because in this life the result of that cause was an overindulgence of food, then the karmic lesson would not be learned because it would be the fear of starvation that was the hangover to be over come in this life. That thought (albeit subconscious) and the fear of starvation would become the energetic emotional signature that would be the energy that would be created in the morphic field of infinite possibilities and it would be fed by opposite energies that would attract situations where one was always eating to respond to trauma of fear of starvation.

In the normal sense, then if one was to get over the fear and launches a new thought-emotion plan, it would be that which would override the old trauma in the subconscious. However you came to the place to eliminate a fear you would have learned your lesson and from that point on dissolve the karma and at the same time instituted a different outcome. The potential of this would then attract different realities to you. If gain that same point of understanding an issue through a process like regression, the end result is the same. It just occurred using a different method.

In normal activities where we create thousands of thoughts and emotions every day; the ones that we create as the clearest in terms of thought, vision, words and the ones that carry the highest charge of emotion (bad or good is not relevant) are the ones that attract similar energy signatures the fastest. It's the same as the ones that carry the highest focus and passion within the Napoleon Hill rules of consciousness succeed in making the millions. Because we naturally do not correlate the time and relationship between a Cause and an Effect we do not believe there is relationship other than just working within the lower plan rules of working hard to get what you want within the scope and limits of the global consciousness rules.

Regardless, we can see the relationship between Karma, Cause & Effect and the Law of Attraction. One just carries the old scenario forward to get over and learn from and it will be typically part of the Life Plan so you have a chance to do just that. But when it is brought forward, you have a choice as to how it will affect you. Once that choice is made, then the Law of Attraction kicks in to seek out a like energetic bundle from the quantum field. That choice of effect can be realized by hard knocks school until you break it working from below, or looking at the issue from above then energetically doing the same effect for the Law of Attraction to do its work.

This is what needs to be done in these abnormal activities like we see with miracles and attracting wealth by thought and emotion alone. Thus as we have dramatically expounded upon, one needs to look out through the portal into the next level of consciousness; move into the above of the energetic anatomy of self, into the quantum field of infinite possibilities and see it all being done in a vision brought forward, supercharging with the emotion of completion and being grateful so the rest of the anatomy down below gets its shit together in preparation. And there are essentially two ways this is going to happen within the hologram.

First, with an internal health miracle that needs to take the instructions from the pure consciousness to the subconscious, then to the brain and body to adjust the programs for the cells to change the hologram of the body. This must be done in accordance with rules which operate under a higher intelligence of design encoded in DNA.

Second with an external miracle that needs to take instructions the same way, it is the vibratory strength that attracts the results and the brain updates the hologram under the guidance of a higher intelligence governing the rules, processes and purpose of the greater scope.

What we are looking towards is an easier way to achieve the same effect by working in the higher energetic expressions of self, in accordance with those rules of higher intelligence. The stark difference is best illustrated by whether you believe you need to pay the bills by working hard in the lower plane or letting go and working in the upper plane to attract the means of paying the bills.

And So What Is Reality?

What we are seeing more and more evidence on is that reality is a human construct, a virtual hologram played out by a greater consciousness for the purpose of evolution and expansion, to experience emotions through a human vessel. In the following sections, we want to convey more of what we feel is reality.

The Reality Game

Reality is a simple set of captured moments which you plan before you incarnate as scenes, people and events at specific points of time. At each juncture you as actors are free to choose several options which produce special life pathways until the next juncture. The emotional and mental choices become recorded as you pass each moment. Each path yields a different time line and detail is up to your needs as a Soul. Between such points you as an actor are free to use your senses and choices to speak your script and act out. Where definitions of the plan are lacking, natural laws so activated by you creating energies by the notion of as above so created below as Cause and Effect, Attraction and Divine process/order prevail in the free intention versus set interaction points.

The free will is a process of the greater consciousness creating and controlling the movie projected outside as a 3D hologram which is done by the brain. Multiple movies are experienced and run concurrently within the scope of the larger movie consciousness. In a life plan the main characters, events are defined as set in this open virtual movie much like you would plan a sequence of steps and decisions in a game. As you play the game certain places, people, events as preprogrammed are brought into awareness; however there may be certain actions, consequences, events you encounter which may not be predicted and may cause choices of regret or benefit. As you proceed through, what you see is gone once you pass through but reinstated if you relook but because it is a running program according to program design, it changes as well. The human brain runs the programs using its sensory system the same way. It has preset meeting and choices. As you learn the game it is recorded and your path is known but not so looking ahead.

The Rules of Consciousness

Our reality is very "real". It has to be in order to continue the play. Our reality forms a group consciousness. Just like you have an individual personal consciousness or mind, so does a group like your family, your culture, your race, your country, your global consciousness. Each is nested within the other. Each is formed by the consensus of the group creating what we call belief boxes reflecting the rules of that group. These are the rules of religions, of cultures, science, governments, dynasties, and so on that create the guidelines for beliefs, behaviors, and ways of living the lives that are agreed upon as the laws. These belief boxes dominate the particular consciousness of those who form the group and can be restrictive and limiting. When you decide to play a computer game, you must abide by the rules of that game. It is not possible to go outside of the programmed rules of engagement unless you leave the game and go into the consciousness of the programmers who created the game, then instigate a change to the rules.

Within the global consciousness "game" the rules and regulations of engagement are also defined by consensus. And although the game itself is self evolving, it can only bring in new rules by way of a new consensus of repetitive belief, or through going outside of it to effect the change. Like your own subconscious rules, it is through repetitive (consensus) or through leaving the belief box rules does one make a change to the programs. Science, commerce and religious form three major belief systems within global consciousness and these provide the limiting rules that each individual selects to program into their subconscious through engagement in the hologram, education, other's beliefs, and so on. But nevertheless are all within the greater global consciousness.

Thus the engagement in the game of life within the game itself cannot allow changes to occur that are not within the belief box. In order to facilitate the change, like in a healing miracle that is outside the belief box, it must be facilitated from outside the belief box of consciousness. That is why one has to be in a higher state of mind, outside of the limitations of the lower state of mind, its beliefs, and outside the rules of the game.

The Higher Order
The DNA shows you all the programs for your body – you choose it like in the game. The program of the reality game lay out the natural order, process and purpose of all that exists in the hologram frame by frame of life. These behave according to divine laws once given life so they interact with each other as you do – and as you do in a game. This is a morphogenic process of order, purpose and evolution. Your interaction can be random, spontaneous, planned or none as you enter the sphere of engagement, choosing what to do, perceive and act on. The hologram once active (power supply to game) is alive with all life programs trigged by your observations as alive with all life and you choose what and when you go to the same degree but it is not outside of the game constraints unless the option is available to you through the design; as you would encounter through an NDE or OBE option. While your program runs within the domain of its existence, the extent of it is determined by your experience – as you explore the game. The game is shared by all participants and the same setting programs are available to all players. Predetermined however are rules of the game, the overall environment, the events and players, some set, some random, some known, others attracted so as to offer you an experience of expressions and choices of relationship. The process of life and natural order is an evolving living holographic set of programs running in the background so reflected in the sciences of physics, biology, chemistry, botany and so on.

The Presentation

The reality is similar to the projection by the hololens as it picks up your "live" activities, projects wirelessly to a point of observation when the Observer is turned on and receptive. Whether this is live or stored is not relevant to the end projection which is a composite. But because these are creations running interactively, relating to each other evolving the programs as self learning programs, what you see is a divine order and process all with purpose like you as a program yourself interacting with the others. The plan you created contains many parameters, points, junctures, and exits preset choices - points which provide situations, scenes, interactions, scripts to choose and engage.

In the Game of Life these sets and characters are also planned at certain points of the time line but choices are not scripted only the pathways to those choices. In between is a natural process of evolution, growth and action that run or go on by way of karma, cause and effect, and the Law of Attraction. These integrate into the present points of the time line. The programs run and exist within a global consciousness, stored in akashic consciousness with DNA reflecting the physical counterpart of the state of being within the soup of quantum consciousness containing infinite possibilities. The Life Plan creates a complex model of predetermined interactive holographic life within space and time allowing choices not scripted only the pathways to and from those choices are predetermined so as to review these before incarnation. In between is a natural process of evolution, growth and action that run or go on by way of creation by awareness within the larger composite program, karma, cause and effect, and can bring forward into reality consequences of the Law of Attraction to be integrated into the present points of the time line. The programs of all life exist in DNA to accessed at will.

The Quantum Nothingness

The portal is in the heart brain and the space is peace and silence – absolute. It is where you walk and talk freely in truth of you and all that is. The instructions or for example the biology, physics and other such sciences reflecting physical life are programs of evolving self learning quantum soup of creators – source mind. These are instilled in the matrix of Soul consciousness and encoded as human form as DNA as all forms do when given life. These programs run in parallel multi threads concurrently but all interact with each other for the sole purpose of lower form – survival. The high growth of emotional and mental mind is the program package of humanoid form. You decide how to give these life but once done they continue to run just as a subroutine runs in a game being played – according to its design and purpose. You can draw from example of life without having to be technical to exemplify all this of reality. Within this space of quantum nothingness there is no space or time, only the infinite possibilities reflected by the universe of all that exists, existed and will exist.

The Astral Light
Every moment that comes is seen in a joyous stream of astral light as you accept it using the substance of formation. Now you understand how the astral body is formed on its purpose of creating your personal body, from characteristics and personality so chosen. The celestial givers of form register this in your hand prints and star charts. It is this substance which you see in 4D as one plane above yours that molds into you as the acts in the movie you designed with many paths converging and diverging from events and situations to create choice points. The importance of astral substance; which is designed to take form from the 5th dimension is that it is directed from higher planes where it stays stamped into reality until the process of cause and effect begins to paint a different picture below, then it is reflected above. To program below it is the astral substance that is the program code that needs to be re-perfected from above into astral substance which then is infused into the appropriate effects below. Overstand that the cause and effect differ because there is no physical above, only a signature and information coded into memory to be registered without judgment. The body is a result as in the lower reality to reflect the cause of physically. It is simply a result.

The Reality Process
The process by which movies unfold is through a set of subroutines of order process interaction no different than when you play a computer game. The scenes and situations are staged just like when you play the game to come to certain places, points of discovery, actions and conditions which create the need for emotional and mental acts of engagement. The points along the way are interactive depending upon the previous route taken and as they come into your view as awareness they bring with them new subroutines of interactive life processes based upon their purpose and survival needs.

These simply play out with the field of awareness you choose to occupy – some random, some set, others known ahead of time. As you would save a version of your progress you would come to review what you have learned or accumulated in storage, inventory or memory as experience. You may decide to come through again so as to try again but because of random engagements, the path may not be exactly the same unless you say you are done. This is what you see in the life review. To understand how this is working, have many play the same game over the internet or wireless, then consider it being done through the hololens and holopresence process by way of your brains as the camera and projector. This is the way your reality game is played.

The Game of Life Analogy
Consider you are a programmer and you want to write a mega program called EARTH which simulates the world. You have to consider the way the players can play and there are potentially 8 billion head sets and interactive joy sticks that need to be accommodated, all through a wireless network. The program can be run anytime you decide to turn it on and you can have

many versions of it. It can run continuously or stopped. You design an entry program that allows a procedure where you can choose a personality type from 12 different types then you allow the body types and shapes to be chosen. You decide to set up another program that selects what you want to experience in the game. This provides you with where and when you want to start the game and then you decide what you want to do and with whom you want to be with as your family. Here you can choose from an inventory of people and characters who will provide you with roles and purpose. Because it is hard to decide absolutely, in some cases you allow options so a pathway may be to become a professional and be schooled but perhaps it is as a musician, a lawyer, a doctor so you leave this open and so going to school, getting a profession, a job, getting married, traveling, having children are all options that you predetermine in your pathway of days which are composited moments (like seconds in a day or frames in a movie) This allows each player to construct an overall game plan as a sequential moment by moment engagement within an enormous program that has a huge inventory of programs and subprograms all with special environmental presentation, purposes, and multitudes of interactive sensing points that trigger other routines with specific function, design, look and purpose. Each is designed to simulate situations.

The Evolution
As the mortal life and life plan take hold, the brain takes the responsibility to present and evolve the physical environment of 3D in accordance with a natural growth process as resident in the blueprint of DNA. These stages of evolution as conducted from the systems and procedures encoded in DNA are brought into the awareness of the brain's system to evolve the physical body. This provides the use of free will to evolve beyond the physical limitations into the higher representation as the energy body. This evolution is the place of the field of oneness as the quantum field of the mind where all possible things exist in thought, and where the life plan as well as the physical environment and the world and body may be changed by free will back in the space where the plan was created.

The Second Life Virtual Game

The virtual game you will find at www.secondlife.com is the largest-ever 3D virtual world created entirely by its users. Linden Lab listed the population of Second Life at more than 10,500,000 residents as of October 2007. You can go to www.draxtor.com to see the lives of some "residents" of this virtual reality have created a second life of what they would like to experience; obviously unlike the one they are experiencing in their own holographic reality. Here there are no limits to who, what, where you can be.

Created by a fellow named Drax, you can watch **The Drax Files: World Makers** as a monthly show on YouTube examining the creative people behind the avatars who continue to move the virtual world of Second Life forward with their passion and persistence. In this mixed reality individual imaginations form the basis of very personal stories that profile designers, game-makers, role-players and fashion aficionados, musicians, artists and social-issue activists; for these dedicated residents the avatar is not just a separate pixilated entity, but a true extension of their identity with which they navigate the digital space.

Here you can enter a shared reality with infinite possibilities and live a life without boundaries, guided only by your imagination. From a global sense, the founders program the rules for the global program creating subroutines for things like trees, animals, all those things that make up our environment. The Game Board allows players to choose an Avatar and lay out a life plan to engage in whatever their imagination can bring in as a possibility. The community process provides the global world of things and processes via digital imagery through constructed computer programs that simulate the look, feel, and behavior of the total environment of the game as a group consciousness. Here you explore and discover thousands of beautiful places created by a Second Life community of millions of friends to share passions and chat with. It is a place of total self expression.

Few online social networking sites get as much attention as **Second Life** (**SL**), the three-dimensional virtual world where users, called **residents**, can pretend to be whomever - or whatever - they want to be. Second Life is an online world in which residents create virtual representations of themselves, called **avatars**, and interact with other avatars, places or objects. Second Life isn't just a fancy chat room - residents can do much more than communicate with one another. For one thing, they can contribute to the world around them, creating buildings, objects or even animations. Resident additions to the virtual world are called **user-generated content**, and this content is one of the factors that makes Second Life such a unique online environment. This is much like the creation of the belief boxes that evolve in our own consciousness called the Earth Game.

In Second Life, residents can go to social gatherings, live concerts, press conferences and even college classes. They can do a lot of things you can do in real life -- buy land, shop for clothes and gadgets or just visit with friends. They can also do things that are impossible in the real world - avatars can fly or teleport to almost any location. Some residents design short programs, called **scripts**, which give avatars or objects new abilities, including special animations or the ability to generate copies of other objects. Users represent themselves with a customizable, three-dimensional figure that acts like a computer-generated puppet. Users navigate through an online world, encountering strange landscapes and new people. They inhabit a virtual world free of pre-determined goals or tasks, just like the real world.

To simulate the bad and good polarity of our Life Plan experiences, Second Life geography spans two worlds - the real world and the virtual world. In the real world, Second Life exists on a collection of **server host machines**, called **sims**. These computers store all the information found within the virtual world. Each sim runs between 2 to 16 server processes, which simulate **regions** in Second Life. Regions also have **safe** and **unsafe** ratings. A safe rating means you can wander around without fear of attack from other avatars or objects (unless you encounter **griefers,** residents who harass other users). An unsafe region allows residents to simulate combat, either with other users or with objects programmed to attack avatars. Unsafe regions let residents create their own version or simply satisfy the visceral thrill of getting into a fight. Sound familiar?

Just like in a Life Plan, New Second Life users select their avatars from generic male and female templates (residents and their avatars don't necessarily share the same gender). Although a resident could use an unmodified template, everyone else would know that he or she was a **newb** - a new user who doesn't know how things work. Most residents customize their avatars a little before leaving Orientation Island. One important factor in avatar customization is the **inventory**. The inventory holds hair, skin, objects, animations and body parts and has an infinite capacity. A user can open his or her inventory and choose to put on or remove items, like clothing or hairstyles. Residents can add to an avatar's inventory at any time, creating a practically limitless number of avatar customization options. They can change their avatar's appearance as often as they like. Nothing in Second Life is permanent - if a user decides his or her avatar should evolve from a hulking brute to an emaciated goth kid, he or she can make the changes at any time.

A resident can also right click his or her mouse on the avatar, which pulls up a pie-shaped menu. One of the menu choices is **appearance**, which allows a user to adjust the way his or her avatar looks. Some residents create special skin textures for avatars ranging from realistic skin and hair to fantasy-inspired scales or feathers. Users can find dozens of residents who sell and trade clothing, skin and even body parts in Second Life. Savvy residents can customize their avatars by creating their own clothes and skins in a graphics program and importing the file into Second Life.

To simulate the way we create our reality, Avatar customization is just one way residents can tweak their Second Life experiences. Users can also build objects within Second Life using simple in-world tools and menus. By creating and linking together basic **prim** structures, users can create more complex objects. They can also use the **Linden Scripting Language**, a programming language similar to Java, to give objects specific properties. For example, a skilled user could create a puppy dog that follows him or her everywhere. Residents make objects for different reasons -- some do it to bolster the theme of a particular area or avatar design, others build objects just for fun.

Residents can even build houses and other buildings. Some use programs like AutoCAD to design their structures before importing them into Second Life. Others purchase building designs from other residents. Buildings can be extremely realistic or defy real-world physics. Second Life's capacity for customization is extensive. The world inside Second Life doesn't just foster user-generated content, it depends upon it. By encouraging user innovation and participation, Second Life has created a loyal community of enthusiastic residents.

Absolutely every object, building and flying car you see in Second Life was created by a Resident. The sandbox is a public space where residents practice building different objects. If you want to bring your creations to life like give them movement and interactivity, you'll have to learn the Linden Scripting Language (LSL).

So why do we bring this game into your awareness? Well, if you want to simulate an incarnation into a different life because you are not so content with the current one, this may be a way to do it without dying! The **Game of Life** is created by **you** contributing to a **global community** of a **global consciousness** that defines the reality of the virtual world. It comes from imagination of that which they each wish to **experience** and thus create the **unified whole**. The programs reflecting objects, places, people are created and shared interactively. The local residents as a group as in a **Soul Family** share and express within the virtual world after they have designed the avatars and their characteristics to engage interactively in the reality.

The Real Divine Programmer Is The Real You

Well, the inevitable conclusion is that the Divine Programmer is You, your mind, your consciousness. It is just like simulating a second life game plan. The silly thing is that you are already part of a grander game of a larger hologram that is the consciousness of the global community that is the stage set for your soul family to play and experience within. And that programmer is You. But you have to take a portal out of the belief box you are trapped in and bring into your awareness the true You, your Higher self, your Soul.

Then you must believe this, accept it and surrender to the truth that you are not really this silly dude playing the actor in the Life Plan movie.

It has to be in a state beyond the mortal confines of the physical world of body and environment both of which are virtual holograms under the responsibility of the brain. Clearly, in the NDE's that physical mortal reality did not exist as the You became pure consciousness outside of the holographic construct.

In all of the processes we have studied that have been initiated to heal internally or to change externally that hologram, we have seen the same pattern; getting the hell out of the limitations and then reprogramming the subconscious from top down – from a higher vibration – outside of negative energies, inside of that positive energy of love, peace, gratitude, and outside of the limiting prevailing consciousness.

And the Life Movie which the brain plays out like a DVD player is simply like a default plan if You do not figure out how to change it by entering the infinite quantum space that like your own mind, which is a part of it, contains an infinite number of possible realities for you to experience.

Ok, now we are going try to put this all together in a simple explanation. We do not pretend to know all the answers, we only deduct these from what we have seen in our studies. We would look towards others sharing their own deductions with us so as to converge on something that can work for all. But most important, we have also gathered some information from being totally outside of our belief boxes in various conversations with our Higher Selves.

15

UNLOCKING SUPER CONSIOUNESS

"DNA represents the sum total of the evolution of Super Consciousness. It is our gift residing within all of us given freely to humans to understand what we are and the power of Creation. Since we only use 2%, it would seem we have a long way to go."

Aly McDonald   Ed Rychkun

> **To truly unlock your potential in DNA**
> **You need to listen to what your Soul does say**

We have seen that as we rise away from the holographic constructs of the lower 3D reality, there seems to be a dramatic shift in understanding what we as energy forms are and are capable of. In these life plans that we design to express and experience the emotional and mental abilities, it seems that there is a whole different inventory of higher abilities and potential that can be brought down into our lower plane. In our life plans we must have a universal option to take a higher path through a portal which we choose freely and pop onto at any time. The usual gateway that provides this is through deep Meditation, Hypnosis, Astral Projection, Out Of Body Experiences and Regression Therapy to name some. Another portal or exit point can come as a Near Death Experience which results in a new look at life, a new purpose and attitude that brings a new mind; as you have a glimpse of who you really are and what your true potential is; as replicated in and available from DNA.

In this chapter we are going to look at what this Higher Potential means. We have seen in this book the many ways that we can get through the portal to the other side and have a glimpse of this other reality. As we have also seen, each energy body carries with it new abilities that can be attained if the belief, acceptance and surrender to their existence is brought into awareness. One such place of abilities and potentiality exists within all of us in the form of DNA.

It is our belief that DNA as a quantum energy reflects the whole in its fullest potential of the development of the Soul's journey. The 12 layers that it consists of reflects the physical and spiritual "state of the art" evolution of the human vessel. It is the ultimate record of what humans at some stage have been able to achieve in their evolution. At the current time, we as a group consciousness have formed a belief box that there are only two strands which are essentially rooted in 3D biology and matter. In beliefs that are out of the box, a new consensus is evolving, one that says the other layers are more quantum and spiritual in nature. If this is a reflection of a "fall from grace" of current humanity, then there is a whole load of stuff in there that has atrophied or is simply dormant. There is a whole lot of potential in there that we have not brought into our conscious awareness. The means of access to the rest of the DNA appears to be rooted in a more "spiritual" path to evolve our total being which includes both the physical and then the non-physical or energetic components. Constantly we see that the primary access to this DNA is through the mind's awareness of a Higher Self or Soul.

We have seen on many occasions now that this potential is available but we have to bring in a new state of mind that realizes we are much more than just a human vessel having an experience in this Earth Game. In this chapter we are going to explore what is being said about DNA from inside and outside the box.

Then we will look at some particularly powerful work being done by an extraordinary NDE journey by **JC Gordon** as described in his new book **Unlocking Your Super Consciousness.** He explains how when he met his Maker as Super Consciousness, his purpose in life was revealed. It was here that he was inspired to write an extraordinary prediction for the evolution of Super Consciousness and humanity. And it was here that he realized that he had to choose a higher path within his Life Plan.

Unlocking DNA

If you ask our scientific community about DNA they will tell you what is written in Wikipedia. DNA stores biological information. A significant portion of DNA (more than 98% for humans) is non-coding, meaning that these sections do not serve as patterns for protein sequences and is called "junk". Hello! What does this 98% junk really do?

A simple way to see DNA so everyone says is to understand each cell has its own job, just like humans do. Some cells help us detect light and see, other cells help us touch, some cells help us hear, other cells carry oxygen around, and other cells help us digest food by secreting enzymes. There are over 200 cell types in the body - that is 200 different jobs. And they go on to tell you *how each cell knows what job to do. It's the same they say as* how a human knows what job it has to do - someone tells them. Our cells are also told what to do, but not by a person or a computer! Our cells are told what to do by a very special molecule called **DNA**. DNA is a record of instructions telling the cell what its job is going to be. A good analogy for DNA as a whole is a set of blueprints for the cell, or computer code telling a PC what to do. It is written in a special alphabet that is only four letters long! Unlike a book or computer screen, DNA isn't flat and boring like a computer that has only two codes of 0 and 1 - it is a beautiful curved ladder. We call this shape a **double helix**.

Our box of limiting beliefs says we are aware of 1 of the layers of DNA. This awareness makes up 2%. And we have certainly seen how the subconscious and the brain pull out of the cells the appropriate instructions from this 2% when they need a blueprint of something that needs to be fixed. In kindness to the ever increasing consciousness that is starting to think more seriously about the 98% and what DNA is and does – outside the belief box. Science says: *"A significant portion of DNA (more than 98% for humans) is non-coding, meaning that these sections do not serve as patterns for protein sequences."*

So what the does the 98% really do? Is it really just junk?

There are relatively few who will take a position on this topic. Most scientists will tell you that this other 98% is indeed "junk" and any opinion about it is just "New Age crap", not scientific. But this is changing: Recent Russian discoveries of the wave information nature of DNA overthrow our understanding that we are genetically fixed. This is led by the new science of "wave genetics" that shows DNA functions like a holographic computer, part of the larger hologram of the information wave reality. Our DNA has the capabilities of hypercommunication -telepathy, remote sensing and remote feeling, along with other psychic abilities. We also have the ability to reprogram our genetic blueprint with simple word and frequencies.

Russian researchers' findings and conclusions are simply revolutionary! According to them, our DNA is not only responsible for the construction of our body but also serves as data storage and in communication. The Russian linguists found that the genetic code, especially in the apparently useless junk DNA follows the same rules as all our human languages. To this end they compared the rules of syntax (the way in which words are put together to form phrases and sentences), semantics (the study of meaning in language forms) and the basic rules of grammar. They found that the alkalines of our DNA follow a regular grammar and do have set rules just like our languages. So human languages did not appear coincidentally but are a reflection of our inherent DNA.

The Russian biophysicist and molecular biologist Pjotr Garjajev and his colleagues also explored the vibrational behavior of the DNA. The bottom line was: *"Living chromosomes function just like solitonic/holographic computers using the endogenous DNA laser radiation."* This means that they managed for example to modulate certain frequency patterns onto a laser ray and with it influenced the DNA frequency and thus the genetic information itself. Since the basic structure of DNA-alkaline pairs and of language (as explained earlier) are of the same structure, no DNA decoding is necessary.

This finally and scientifically explains why affirmations, autogenous training, hypnosis and the like can have such strong effects on humans and their bodies. It is entirely normal and natural for our DNA to react to language. While western researchers cut single genes from the DNA strands and insert them elsewhere, the Russians enthusiastically worked on devices that can influence the cellular metabolism through suitable modulated radio and light frequencies and thus repair genetic defects.

One can certainly say that is out of the box!

In order for DNA to do all of the things that we speak of esoterically and quantumly, 300 trillion pieces of DNA must all know something at the same time! There has to be a communication that takes place in the microscopic DNA of your toenail at the same time as the longest hair on your head. They both have to know about it instantly. Then those trillions of pieces must agree, must have one energy absorption of consciousness. This all must happen in a 3D construct – that is, within your reality. There is no word in science for this process unless you consider the one created for a description of photons called "entanglement."

There is instead, "a confluence of energy." Confluence in English truly means a melding of energies together, so that they become something else, a oneness. Science doesn't see it within DNA yet, but at some level they know it must exist. For how else can the Human body do what it does?

Cellular structure is specific and unique. Like the linear machine, it is specialized, and you have heard of stem cells carrying that specificity. But DNA is identical all over the body. It's not specific. You don't have toenail DNA or hair DNA or heart DNA. You've just got your own unique DNA. Trillions of copies of the same Human quantum blueprint must talk to each other instantly or you would cease to exist. How did they do it? No name in science truly has been given to the process of communication between DNA loops, but it will. It's a quantumness within the "soup" of magnetics.

Each loop of DNA has a magnetic field that overlaps the loop next to it, which overlaps the loop next to it. Hundreds of trillions of overlaps equals one consciousness. This then represents a magnetic imprint, which the Human carries around with them. Magnetics is an interdimensional energy, a quantum energy, and this imprint creates the Human aura. An aura is not a magnetic field and you will not be able to see an aura with magnetic equipment. An aura is the result of a confluence of DNA communication within the Human body, a quantum imprint, a melding of energy to create a quantum field not measurable by anything on the planet, yet.

What happens in DNA happens all at once within every energy layer of it. Think of the coordination, the puzzle. If you're going to have some kind of esoteric activation that is new within your DNA, think of what must take place! Hundreds of trillions of parts all receive it at once. What does that feel like?

DNA is always evolving on a self improvement cycle, just like the global consciousness is supposed to. If you want to get an idea of how this DNA works in practice let us use a simple example. Let us say a species – say a seagull – somehow learns to pick up a clam off the shore line, fly up with it and drop it to crack it open on the rocks. Because it satisfies its desire to survive, it does this a lot and it gets hardwired into its neuro pathways. Then some buddy seagulls see this and copy it. At a certain threshold the number of seagulls doing this causes the DNA to take this on as a permanent behavior encoded into the group DNA. When this occurs at a certain threshold, all seagulls get their DNA upgraded even if they don't have any clams in their environment. Because DNA is quantum, they are all nonlocal and the effect is immediately updated throughout all whether they need it or not. From then on it becomes a hardwired instinct of behavior.

In our work so far, we have seen that DNA is called upon by the subconscious and the brain to repair or maintain things in our body – absolutely everything right down to the smallest details! We have also seen that DNA is quantum and we can call on it to trigger "extraordinary" things like a miracle of healing. What else can it do?

So what is the out of the box community saying about DNA? Well. Apparently the whole story of your life's potential is written within the strands of your DNA. Every pain you needed to experience, every friend you needed to meet, every nemesis you had to encounter, were pushing you further into the Glory of your life's story. Sometimes, we don't listen at all, so our story with this set of DNA comes to an end and we incarnate again with a whole new field of potential. Every lifetime after this one is also encoded in your DNA. We simply have been lead to believe we had to physically die in order to bring in a whole new set of codes in our DNA. We do not.

Ascension is programmed into our DNA.

One of the esoteric sources of DNA is Kryon. Kryon teaches about the DNA in the esoteric sense, which is where most of the DNA functions and attributes take place. Here is what they report:

There are 4 groups to the DNA Layers. The first group is the Grounding Layer as shown in this Kryon Table. A brief explanation follows.

Layer 1: BIOLOGICAL LAYER–TREE OF LIFE This layer represents the biological Double Helix. It is the Master biological record of this life time. Three percent of the instructions in this "Human Genome" are for the protein encoding layers. The rest is a massive interaction with the remaining interdimensional layers of DNA.

Layer 2: LIFE LESSON LAYER - DIVINE BLUEPRINT. Layer Two is *"The Human Being's life lesson."* It's important that you understand what a life lesson is, and why it's in your DNA. You come into this planet with it, and it is something that has been constructed for you due to the Akashic Record. That is to say, your life lesson is connected to your past lives.

Layer 3: ASCENSION LAYER - WORKS WITH LAYER 6. Layer Three is "The Ascension Layer." However it is only the one which "points" to the interdimensional layers that really provide ascension status. It is a "catalyst" works with DNA layer number 6, the Prayer and Communications layer. It also somehow is affiliated with the Pineal gland.

The Human Divinity Group

Layers four and five together are the essence of your expression (this specific life on Earth), and your divinity on the planet. Together, they can be understood as: The primary and most important spiritual attribute of all is the tree of life, which is family. These are names of God and should never be thought of as separate layers.

Layers 4 and 5: ANGELIC NAME - CORE CRYSTAL ENERGY. These two layers together (4 and 5) are your interdimensional Akash, or your record of who you are in the Universe, and where you have been. It's also your name on the crystal in the "cave of Creation."

Layer 6: PRAYER AND COMMUNICATION - HIGHER-SELF. Layer Six is the "Higher-Self" layer and is always involved in everything. Where is the Higher-Self? The only part that is higher is your perception of its vibration. It's in a place that makes you want to worship it.

The Lemurian Group

The two energies (layers 7 and 8) of DNA are the most important, since they drive the engine of karmic purpose. They are responsible for life lessons and they relate to layer six, the Higher-Self. They are the creation layers, which are your Akashic Record. That is to say, the record of every single lifetime you've ever had on the earth, everything you've ever done, all the accomplishments, all the talents that you have learned, and the spiritual jar of knowledge that you have filled up along the way.

Layer 7: REVEALED DIVINITY - EXTRADIMENSIONAL SENSE. Layer Seven is one of three Lemurian layers. It is also part of an important pair...

7 and 8. These are "The Lemurian Pair Layers." This is one of the two given to us by the Pleiadians as a divine complement to the Earth's normal DNA progression. It's Lemurian name, Hoa, Yawee, Maru, (Pronounced: Hoe-awe - Yaweee - Maroo) is the description of the intuitive interdimensional sense that Lemurians had, and also means "Revealed Divinity."

Layer 8: WISDOM AND RESPONSIBILITY - MASTER AKASHIC RECORD. Layer Eight is one of three Lemurian layers. It is also part of an important pair; 7 and 8. These are "The Lemurian Pair Layers. This is one of the two given to us by the Pleiadians as a divine complement to the Earth's normal DNA progression. It's Lemurian name, Akee, Yawee, Fractua (sometimes Fractus), means Record of the Masters, and has the energy of "Wisdom and Responsibility." This layer IS the MASTER AKASHIC RECORD of your lifetimes on earth. It has more meanings than any layer.

Layer 9: HEALING LAYER - THE FLAME OF EXPANSION - ST. GERMAIN. Layer Nine is the "healing layer, also Lemurian, but very Human (not Pleiadeian). It is the one that is responsible for miraculous healing, and is the antenna of DNA in an interdimensional way, that "talks" to layer one and provides a 4D response to the Human body (healing). It is also represented by the Violet Flame, of St. Germain. Some call it "Intelligent Human Cell activation." It "listens" for harmony, according to Kryon, to activate healing. Layer nine is called the healing layer, not because it heals the body – it heals the Akash! All of these layers work together, and some of them have laid dormant for all of humanity's time on the planet, ready to be activated when the earth's energy reached a certain point.

The God Group

The basic information is that this layer must be considered as a package with 11 and 12. These last three are then called "action layers" and are different from any of the attributes of any of the former 9. Kryon puts them in the "God" Group.

Layer 10: THE CALL TO DIVINITY - THE RECOGNITION OF GOD IN YOU. Layer Ten is also called "The Divine Source of Existence". It is the first of the divine, "God layers" that represent the "call to understanding your divinity." The God layers are "action layers" because they facilitate the divine within, thereby facilitating enlightenment and remembrance of who you are.

Layer 11: WISDOM OF THE DIVINE FEMININE - COMPASSION LAYER. Layer Eleven is not about goddess energy or even about female energy. The

Hebrew name has no feminine connotation in that language. Instead, Kryon indicates that this "Wisdom of the Divine Feminine" is the energy of pure compassion, and is what is missing in the duality balance of the earth at this moment. It is the layer that is the true secret of peace on earth. Human Beings with this layer enhanced are balanced with the masculine and feminine duality energy. It is one of the "God Layers" which is being enhanced in these times. You can see the struggle all over the earth with those who wish to conquer (the masculine-heavy old energy) and those who wish to balance and compromise (the new balance). This truly is one of the main layers that is changing the most, and will be the one that is most obvious in the personalities of the new leaders of this planet.

Layer 12: THE GOD LAYER - THE ALMIGHTY GOD- THE GOD WITHIN YOU. Layer Twelve is very simple. It's the God layer, the most divine, and truly the layer which is "The God Within." There are many divine layers, but this one is 12... the last and highest in vibration of all of them. What does it do? Don't look for these layers to do anything, any more than your home does something. It provides you with peace, shelter, and a feeling of being home. Let the God layer be home for all of you.

Unlocking Super Consciousness

We are now going to bring into your awareness some particularly powerful work being done by an extraordinary NDE journey by **JC Gordon** as described in his new book **Unlocking Your Super Consciousness.** He explains how when he met his Maker as Super Consciousness, his purpose in life was revealed. It was here that he was inspired to write an extraordinary prediction for the evolution of humanity Super Consciousness and humanity. And it was here that he realized that he had to choose a higher path within his Life Plan.

As we have explained in our books, there is really only **ONE MIND.** We have called it the Greater Consciousness, which as a quantum mind encompasses everything that was, is and will be. That is where we want to get to when we visit out Higher Self. But the Higher Self or Soul is a quantum part of this Greater Consciousness which in the case of JC's revelation is Super Consciousness. The term **Super Conscious Mind** stands for this One Mind - for universal consciousness, for totality of all knowledge, information and power - called by various names Universal Mind, The Infinite Mind, The Universal Consciousness, The Source, Divine Mind, Light, God Mind, or simply God. Super Conscious mind is omnipresent, ONE MIND expressing through all, and each human mind is only an individualized center of consciousness of this ONE MIND. It is through the gift of DNA, fully loaded with this One Mind that Super Consciousness represents – if we care to learn how to access it.

As an analogy, your individual self is like a drop of water. Your Super Consciousness is like an ocean. To a drop of water it is impossible to push a boat on its own, but as part of an ocean it can accomplish anything. A drop of water fully surrendered, and merged with an ocean doesn't think of itself as a mere drop of water, it thinks and acts as an ocean. When you begin to identify yourself not with your body, but with the ALL, more and more of the attributes of your Super Conscious Self begin to express through you - power, wisdom, love. You feel at peace. As you let this boundless power flow through you, you may experience it as electricity running through your body. You may feel all buzzed up, which is why it is so exciting and electrifying exploring your limitless potential.

As you now understand, the term **Subconscious Mind** stands for your individual accumulation of knowledge through personal experience. Your subconscious mind contains all of your past programming, your mental and emotional imprints from the past, your beliefs about yourself and the world around you. Spiritual literature uses the term "soul" to refer to subconscious mind. Spiritual literature also refers to the subconscious mind in expressions "as you think in your heart", or "as you believe in your heart". Your subconscious is a storehouse of all your thoughts and feelings, which together release a VIBRATION. This vibration through the Law of Resonance and Attractions manifests in your experience everything that resonates with that vibration.

What has come starkly clear to us is that this ongoing self evolution of Super Consciousness is reflected in an incredible gift that we all receive. It is DNA; it contains within it all of creation and how it all works. Yet we use 2% clinging on to the first two layers as our "reality". By going out of this belief box and understanding the greater purpose and greater You, we get a glimpse of that Super Consciousness which is our ultimate gift and a glimpse of what we really are. In the next section, we will bring forward the work of a colleague who is dedicated to the awakening of this Super Consciousness – opening the door to that other 98% we have so diligently managed to ignore.

In his book **Unlocking Super Consciousness, JC Gordon** tells a story of life through the matrix of energy. It's life's final story that has not yet been told. When activated it will unleash your Super Consciousness' limitless potential. It is why each one of us presently exists. Super Consciousness is our untapped super human, genius potential of wisdom, wealth and wellness that awaits to be unleashed within us all.

JC explains that it was June 25, 1996: the day "why life is" revealed itself to him. He was cutting wood with a chainsaw when suddenly it kicked back and nearly decapitated him. With the chainsaw still on and stuck to his sweatshirt against his chest, he intuitively heard a wee, small voice from within telling him, *"Everything will be okay, you have a purpose for your life."* JC goes on to recall the NDE that ensued.

He describes how he was no longer in his body, separated from it, floating around the ceiling of the emergency room looking down at himself lying on the stretcher. Upon leaving the emergency room he entered a pitch-black elevator where he sensed moving through the cosmos of time in an upward direction towards a small twinkling light. He suddenly saw it get larger until it became an all-encompassing white light that he passed through feeling an overwhelming sense of security. He explained that he knew he was home, an absolute peace about passing through the white light and he did not want to leave. He landed on a meadow at the top of a very high mountain where suddenly a force began guiding him, then he floated down the mountain to a very special place; a magnificent, sparkling, temple-like structure. He floated past the open gate and was guided toward the temple, down a stairway through an open door through a vast library into a special room to experience a presence that morphed into a radiant cloud of countless particles. He remembered seeing the face of his deceased maternal grandfather in the radiant cloud.

Suddenly, six violet colored dots appeared around the radiant cloud in a perfect sequence. The first violet colored dot appeared at one o'clock. The second violet colored dot appeared at three o'clock to the right of the radiant cloud. The third violet colored dot appeared at five o'clock. The fourth violet colored dot appeared at seven o'clock below the radiant cloud. The fifth violet colored dot appeared at nine o'clock and the sixth violet colored dot appeared at eleven o'clock above the radiant cloud.

The six dots then appeared and turned into a brilliant violet color. Suddenly, the six violet colored dots slowly began to unleash violet lightning that looked like moving fingers. The violet lightning moving fingers connected with the six violet colored dots to create a solid "Violet Energy" connection. At this moment the six violet colored dots began communicating with him. JC goes to tell us what happened next.

"The communication was neither verbal nor audible. It was energetic through the Violet Energy zings that were like bolts of lightning: they just kept zinging me between the eyes. It was like I was in a game of laser tag. I was zinged that I was now reactivated with the Macro Energy Life force of Super Consciousness of everything. It was like meeting a long lost friend and I was in the inner workings of their mind watching their thought process of how, why and what they were thinking. My Violet Energy zings were the communication of Super Consciousness, infinite intelligence insights. They didn't hurt; in fact, I didn't recall feeling anything from them."

"I was in awe and experienced a heightened level of inspiration and peace, like I had been here many times before. Whenever the Super Consciousness's, Violet Energy zings hit me from all six violet colored dots at the same time; the interior radiant cloud would turn on to reveal live images from within it. I didn't want my experience with Super Consciousness to end as it revealed the energetic perfection and perfect love for life. It revealed that life and all of life's energies adhere to Super Consciousness' Violet Energy of energetic perfection and perfect love. However, much to my regret, Super consciousness' final zing informed me that I ... must return so all is fulfilled."

"When the communication ended, Super Consciousness slowly decreased its energetic intensity. Its six violet colored dots turned off and its radiant cloud vanished. Lastly, the energy and warmth of Super Consciousness was gone. This exact moment is when I sensed my new life began. I remember the door behind me opened; I turned and exited the room. I moved in the opposite direction along the hallway, being led once again by the same force that guided me when I arrived. I went down the stairway that was now on my right. At the bottom of the stairway I turned right again as I was now back on the main level. I exited the temple through the doorway, after the front doors automatically opened for me. I slowly moved through the property. As I approached the great wall its large wooden gate again automatically opened and I exited through it."

"Suddenly, I was back in the Bella Coola Hospital emergency room. From the top of the room, I remember seeing everybody frantically scramble about. I saw the doctor, the nurse and a handful of unrecognizable others. I slowly floated down from the emergency room ceiling back into my body. I remember opening my eyes and looking straight into the doctor's eyes that were directly over me and about six inches away. When I opened my eyes, I remember he calmly said to everybody. 'Its okay, he's back'."

"During my NDE, Super Consciousness revealed to me the infinite wisdom of energy. It revealed how energy has and will keep the physical realm intact on a day-by-day, second-by-second bases until the E-Bol (Energetic Blueprint of Life) is complete. Energy is the glue of Super Consciousness that holds life together. Everyone's final soul life experience is not to have another silent, passive role. It is to unleash its lead, starring role and super human Super Consciousness genius potential of Violet Energy energetic perfection and perfect love. This is why Super Consciousness' Eta Violet Energy strand was released on December 21, 2012. After reactivation, Super Consciousness will sub-atomically transfigure everyone's body and mind's strong force of nature gluon particles into Super Consciousness' inorganic Violet Energy of energetic perfection and perfect love."

However, before this can be experienced one must change their energetic disposition from mind, body and soul to soul, body and mind. The mind can no longer be one's lead energy. Due to the unleashing of the Eta Violet Energy of Super Consciousness strand on December 21, 2012, everyone's body and mind's survival is now not limited to the physical realm for a finite period of time, it has potentially become unlimited, infinite and immortal outside of the physical realm. In order for anyone's body and mind to transcend from its present physical realm limitations to its limitless, infinite and immortal potential outside of the physical realm, their soul must complete its evolution by first becoming their lead energy. This will transfigure everyone's body and mind into it's thrive mode out of its survival mode."

"For every soul this means it will not have another passive existence of limitation. The reason for a soul's past life experiences has been to study and learn the energetic subtleties of the human mind and body in order to complete their evolution in this life experience. This life experience for every soul will complete its evolution by activating its existing body and mind energy with Super Consciousness' Violet Energy of energetic perfection and perfect love. In all the soul's past life experiences it has created gut feelings that have let its past lives know when something was right for them or when to beware of something that was not right for them. Because this is the soul's final life experience, a person's gut feelings will become stronger and louder; thus, they cannot be denied."

"What has changed for the souls' of humanity in this life experience is that the "outside help" of Super Consciousness they knew was going to come: has arrived. It arrived on December 21, 2012 when the energetic totality of Super Consciousness left the afterlife spiritual realm to activate our super human Super Consciousness genius potential. This outside help can only be activated through first changing our energetic disposition."

"The Super Consciousness Violet Energy of energetic perfection and perfect love is in the physical realm searching for energetic cracks of doubt in a person's life. Once energetic cracks are detected Super Consciousness can energetically begin to reactivate with the soul. Wisdom is the violet energy language of the soul that cannot be computed by the mind. Conversely, the soul does not resonate with the lower red, green and blue energy of facts and knowledge that the mind comprehends."

"When Super Consciousness energetically interacts with the soul, the soul will create gut feelings. Gut feelings are the soul's awakening and communication to be reactivated with the energetic totality of Super Consciousness. Super Consciousness' Violet Energy wisdoms will never harm anyone or lead them astray as its only intent is to complete the soul's evolution and complete the soul's lifelong mission, which is to transfigure the body and mind it is presently in into its super human Super Consciousness genius potential."

"The reactivation and unleashing of Super Consciousness' Violet Energy of energetic perfection and perfect love within anyone energetically transfigures their body and mind's subatomic red, green and blue strong force of nature energy into their genius potential super human Violet Energy of Super Consciousness energetic perfection and perfect love. Gut feelings are the soul's energetic signals to the body and mind that will transfigure their body and mind from their finite limitations of the physical world into their limitless genius potential of Violet Energy Super Consciousness energetic perfection and perfect love."

"The soul is the most powerful component of who we are. Not only does the soul provide the energy for the mind and body to survive; it is Super Consciousness. Only the soul can reactivate with Super Consciousness to transfigure the body and mind into its Super Consciousness super human genius potential. To complete its evolution the soul must override the mind and change the energetic disposition from mind, body and soul to soul, body and mind. This is everyone's next energetic leap forward that will activate their transcendence into immortality."

"This time the soul knows through its life energy contract (that it agreed to before entering the physical realm) that its role for this life experience is different than it has ever been for any other life experience it has ever had. No soul is here to experience another passive, silent role; it is here to complete its lifelong energetic mission, which is to transfigure its body and mind into its Super Consciousness super human genius potential."

"In all previous life experiences the soul has activated itself with Super Consciousness in the afterlife spiritual realm after the previous body it was in died. Every soul has been preparing for this life experience ever since it's first life experience and is eagerly awaiting the opportunity to change a person's energetic disposition. However, a soul's reactivation with Super Consciousness cannot happen until the mind is convinced it's in its best interest to do so. This means the elimination of ego from the mind, which is the mind's energetic conundrum."

"During my post NDE journey I was impressed that it is only the awakening of the soul which can potentially change a person's energetic disposition. When the soul is awakened it will act as our ultimate force carrier, which can identify the minds particles sub-atomically that operate at distances of about 0.1 per cent of the diameter of a proton. Scientifically, this is how Super Consciousness eliminates ego."

"If this weak force of nature didn't exist, ego could not be eliminated. Super Consciousness is the ultimate force carrier that can change the mind's subatomic strong force of nature into entirely new elements. It will eliminate ego and change a person's energetic disposition so that a soul's lead, starring active role in this life experience can be unleashed."

"Energetic Transcendence will also energetically transmute one's body and mind to be the absolute best they have ever been during their physical realm life. Gone will be all pain. Gone will be all memories of suffering. Gone will be the ways of the physical world. Gone will be the dinosaur energy of fear and negativity. Energetic Transcendence is Super Consciousness' ultimate energetic gift that has been predestined for every soul, body and mind ever since Super Consciousness created the E-Bol before the beginning of time."

"The secret of "why life is" culminates with our choice to either allow or deny Super Consciousness the opportunity to unlock our super human genius potential. Humanity's super human genius potential energy will be the only energy at Super Consciousness' eternal party of life. It is why life is."

There are two other parts to this book that are important

The first is that JC reveals a bold and extraordinary chronology of Higher Purpose and evolution that was given to him. The E-Bol is Super Consciousness' energetic blueprint strategy and roll out of life that is evolving itself through an energetic pregnancy; it is the master plan for why life is. From 13.7 million years ago as the Alpha to our infamous year of 2012 as Epsilon, and on to Omega, JC explains the evolution of the energetic pregnancy.

EVOLUTION of ENERGETIC PREGNANCY	TIME	ENERGETIC SEAL	
Energetic Conception	13.75 billion years ago	ALPHA	
Beginning of Energetic Gestation	+ 1 second	BETA	
Continuance of Energetic Gestation	+ 2 seconds	GAMMA	
Endurance of Energetic Conception	+ 3 seconds	DELTA	VIOLET ENERGY
Energetic Breaking of Water	Dec. 21, 2012, 11:11:11 G.M.T	EPSILON	
Beginning of Energetic Dilation	Dec. 21, 2012, 11:11:12 G.M.T	ZETA	
Continuance of Energetic Dilation	Dec. 21, 2012, 11:11:13 G.M.T	ETA	
Completion of Energetic Dilation	Dec. 21, 2082, 11:11:13 G.M.T	THETA	
Beginning of Energetic Pregnancy	Dec. 21, 3082, 11:11:13 G.M.T	IOTA	
Completion of Energetic	TBD	OMEGA	

These, as he explains, are the energetic pregnancy of life, divided into 10 main stages and each energetic pregnancy stage was revealed during the NDE in the energetic womb of Super Consciousness' radiant cloud after each of the E-Bol's 10 energy seals was energetically unlocked.

In his book, JC provides testimonials of those he has worked with to open their Super Consciousness potential. He actively provides this service and can be found at http://unlockingsuperconsciousness.com/.

For example, a client Mary wrote:

"Wow JC! That was pretty amazing. I feel sooooo happy. Like
my chest is one big balloon of happy."

"I would like to reside in this forever. Suddenly everything has no importance. No feelings of resentment or painful memories. Nothing feels like it is sticking. I feel like I am in a healing place drawing in a rest period so that I will be more ready when the time is right to begin working...whatever that looks like. I have a sense my life is going to be very exciting and I have no idea doing what... although I suspect I will be *helping people clear their blocks and will be able to see them more clearly. THANK YOU THANK YOU THANK YOU."*

DNA And Super Consciousness

When we, as Reiki Masters engaged in attaining the mastery of Reiki, we went through a process called attunement. This is where a Master who is already attuned to this particular vibration simply gifts and attunes the student into the same ability via entrainment of energies. This process may be likened to opening your full potential in DNA and meeting Super Consciousness. We have indicated before that it is best to have a Facilitator bring you into the proper state of awareness so as to bring you out of the ego mind of Beta and lead you through to a new energetic disposition.

The process of engaging the Super Conscious mind can be likened to de-hypnosis - the goal being to de-hypnotize yourself from the limiting beliefs you accepted about yourself and your relationship to the world around you. When you engage in this, your mind is one-pointedly focused on the experience of your Infinite Super Conscious Self and begin the releasing of the full potential of your DNA.

By opening to Super Consciousness you open yourself to the experience of oneness and begin by putting aside all of your previous beliefs about yourself or about the world around you differently. You begin to stop time to engage in moments that eliminate the ego mind; become aware of a new reality with no beginning or end, with universal scope, and surround yourself in this. As you become faithful and worship this state, you will find that the vibrations of your body will change, opening to the other spiritual layers of DNA. As you become, think, live, and act, becoming one with this vibration you become what you think and act out emotionally in deed. What you will discover is the more you align your conscious and subconscious mind with your Super Conscious, whatever you may want will spontaneously and effortlessly begin to appear in your life, often instantaneously after the thought occurred to you. As you think a thought and the next moment you see it manifested in front of you, you will feel as if the world around you is only a projection of your thoughts, which, in fact, it is.

16

THE MYSTERY OF THE MIDBRAIN

"The midbrain is a gateway to the Soul and Higher Self. But first you must bypass the frontal lobe and neo-cortex which hold you in captivity of global consciousness."

Aly McDonald   **Ed Rychkun**

> **Soul, please forgive me for what I have done**
> **Let's heal that karma and have more fun**

In our quest to study what system of health and wealth miracles work, we can truthfully say that all of the techniques we have presented in these two books work. There are hundreds of documented dramatic cases that have created unexplained miracles. The issue is that they do not work consistently all the time. Clearly, by now, you will have realized that the degree of belief, the depth of letting go and the amount of clarity, vision and emotion are key variables that affect the success of how and when a miracle may occur. The belief, acceptance and surrender are vital to the process. It will be realized also that we already launch the creative ability all the time but within the limits of the prevailing consciousness. What appears to be important is the intention and action rather that the exact science of procedure.

What is consistent in all these cases is the process of engaging thought, image, and words in the creation of a new possibility. What is also consistent is the need to let go of the usual ego mind and the lower reality. This can be recognized as the "above" part of as above so below. Regardless of whether it is a miracle, this is always the case and it happens to be coincident with the top three energetic centers called chakras. This is totally within the power of the mind and is purely a mental ability. The other major component of this process takes you to the heart and emotion and the need for joy of completion to enfold that which is created in the mind. This is purely an emotional ability. At that juncture it is a choice as to whether we as mental and emotional beings decide to create within the box of prevailing consciousness as in the case of Napoleon Hill, or outside of the box, as we have studied here.

Regardless, the usual way is to engage by way of the passion and intent activated at the 3rd solar plexus chakra, seek out the appropriate relationships and work hard to create that desired reality or vision.

But as we have seen, the other way is to work hard at thoughts, vision, words and passion to activate the creation and intent through a different relationship – that of Source and Soul to get the body of the projection of reality to adjust to the desired reality.

In conclusion, as we said, all these processes work. It is the belief and intent that dictates success. So it is a matter of deciding what feels best for you then working at it until it happens.

In our studies presented, we have brought into your reality many ways of doing this. In closing this, we are going to bring forward a final chapter which centers on something that is not prevalent in all the techniques we have studied. It has to do with the area of the chakras of the 3rd eye (vision) and the throat (words) and bring to you two very well known miracle workers that embody sound and mantras into their processes. These have been responsible for hundreds of thousands of miracles. We bring you this because they center on ancient wisdom in both Indian and Chinese traditions.

The Science Behind Miracles

Dr. Bascaran Pillai is a spiritual scientist, academic scholar, philanthropist, and world new thinking leader dedicated to the study of Mind Science. More importantly, he is a well known and practiced Yogi and Siddha Master based in the ancient and spiritual wisdom of the Indian tradition. Through the combination of both the Western and ancient Yogis' understanding of the brain, Dr. Pillai provides the world with uncommon solutions to common modern day challenges. He can be found at www.pillaicenter.com *and HumanEvolution* TV on YouTube.

Dr. Pillai has been a speaker for the United Nations Conference of World Religions and the World Knowledge Forum, and has hosted forums on Religion and Science. His scholarly background includes Masters degrees in English Literature and Comparative Literature from Madurai University and a PhD in Religious Studies from the University of Pittsburgh where he was both a teaching fellow in the Department of Religious Studies and Coordinator of Indian Studies program for the Department of International Studies. He is the author of several books including **Life Changing Sounds: Tools from the Other Side, Miracles of the Avatar**, and **One Minute Guide to Prosperity and Enlightenment,** and the DVD program **The Grace Light**. Best of all you can find many miracles in wealth and health that he is responsible for. He reports making several millionaires through his service of bettering humanity.

To Pillai, a miracle is anything from receiving the exact amount of money you need, at the exact moment you need it, being in the right place at the right time, to physical healing of something doctors said was impossible. You could say a miracle is something that happens outside the realm of logic, something that doesn't fit into the framework of what we've been told is possible. He has created the **Midbrain Miracle Method** as a step-by-step process that will allow you to activate the powerful midbrain under his guidance. A very unusual aspect of Dr. Pillai's work is that he as a Siddha Master merges the ancient wisdom with newest technology of brain science to cultivate miracles and make significant changes in your life.

He states that a part of your brain called the neo-cortex is disallowing anything instantaneous or miraculous to happen in your life. The neo-cortex is a limiting brain, which attempts to makes sense of things. The neo-cortex's main job is to maintain control, which is essential in human life; however, it is the opposite of spontaneity and miraculous occurrences. The midbrain, which is beginning to be more comprehensively understood by scientists, is the part of the brain that can give us access to miracles. He states *"Miracles are easy, it is a matter of moving your attention from the frontal lobe to the midbrain."* Your Neo-Cortex controls your higher order functions, of planning, reasoning, judgment, impulses, memory and motor functions.

The midbrain is vitally important to maintaining and regulating the state of consciousness, alertness and attention. The midbrain contains the physical pineal gland, which has similar features to the retina in our eyes and is also a replica of what Siddhas call the third eye. The Midbrain includes the pons, reticular activating system, the pituitary gland, and the 3rd ventricle. The pineal gland and the surrounding area in the midbrain is where our connection to higher thought and reality is. When these areas are activated we open ourselves up to the extraordinary and welcome events that begin to manifest in our lives. You should expect miracles every day. If you don't expect a miracle, it will not happen. The work of Pillai through his Midbrain Miracle Method Focuses on Holistically Activating Five Key Areas:

1. Activate Health
You learn to open yourself and invite restoration from illness.
2. Activate Love/Relationship
You learn how to attract and experience the highest form of love in your life. To resolve the loneliness and abandonment you feel – and open your heart.
3. Activate Creativity
You discover ways to tap into your own divinity, to find places of unlimited, effortless creativity. The program will allow your ideas to flow and give you the courage to channel them into business opportunities.
4. Activate Timelessness
You receive the knowledge you need to transcend time and make instantaneous changes in your life. By discovering the power of thought manifestation you can begin to create a life full of the things you've always wanted.
5. Activate Divinity
Divinity is the ultimate ability to move from a limited reality to a limitless life. The program shows the pathway to Siddha consciousness (miracle consciousness), and gives you the ability to perform any miracle using your midbrain. It will empower you to create a life free of suffering. You can create the life you want with your own brain.

Pillai explains: *"I lived a life of a monk as I wanted to experience timelessness and to be 'blessed out' of reality. Then I thought I should come out and relate to the common people so around 2000 I began to change. When I changed appearance I changed my methodology. Einstein said religion is blind without science. But science does not support religion so I stand in-between. My PhD was in religion but I also studied neuroscience. Everyone should live a 200% life and have a balance. Don't cause conflict. God is not poor. One important thing is change. You have to change and become healthy or life becomes miserable. How do we change times? You can change your destiny by changing time. What is time? Time cannot be understood without space. You change time by changing space. You can change space to change time (move to another place) to create a different destiny. Time is built into the brain and it can stress you out (like time is running out)."*

Pillai gives three aspects of time that are programmed wrong. He tells us that **Time Economics** is relative to getting paid. We relate to time and money. All you need to do is put this in consciousness. There is also the **Biology** of time that can change DNA of aging. The programming is wrong. The brain can influence the nucleus, DNA and the gene. The brain is most important as you can program DNA to process in a different way to not get old. We change DNA through brain by changing time. The **Futurology of Time** is also mis-programmed. You can know about it and change it if it is not good.

He explains: "The neurology of time is in the parental frontal lobe. If you are poverty stricken it is a brain issue. You can put a mantra there and use science to see what happens in the thalamus and cerebral area. If you understand time, you can control it and move it fast. Time will stop if you are in soul intelligence. We can jump time lines and be given new life to do more. Time line jumping means there are several opportunities available at any moment. Jump and see the parallel line opportunity."

"Timelessness is the most important. It is a matter of being thought free, then there is soul intelligence that comes outside of time through intuition and through timelessness. Bypass the effects. Do not waste a second. You are a master of time and can jump into a parallel of time. If you are in timelessness, you are omnipotent as you will see what you are capable of instantly. The secret is in the timeless domain where all possibilities exist and soul intelligence is there. Our mistakes reside in the past as negative experiences in the mind living in duality. You must move to only timeless experience from quantum level where there is no polarity or victims. Get beyond this past to get control of time where there is no time."

"It is about thought manifestation all the time. The key is how to create powerful thoughts in you. There is only one reality of thought. If you know the dynamics of it you can create reality. In the astral plane you can bypass action of effort. That is because the astral plane is where you find your soul but you must get beyond the mind to help manifestation of thoughts. Get beyond the monkey mind; we all only know about developing the mind; no one teaches getting beyond time. That is how we can have powerful thoughts that can become reality."

"Mind over matter is not just a philosophy. The mind has complete control over how the particles function. This is not your mind consciousness because that is a surface level. You have to learn the techniques to do this. Logic and sequence is a primitive process of cause and effect to manifest little things. You have to go beyond this into thoughtlessness – stillness not a divine coma and a vegetable in constant meditation. That is just a step you need to get beyond into a new state."

"Sounds create meaning. You cannot have a Mercedes without thinking about it. Words are the building blocks of universe. Vibrations are a fundamental reality, not particles. In the beginning there was the word. It is simply a matter of creating words of meaning in the form of mantras. A mantra carries the energy of the reality to manifest. A mantra is a unidimensional reality in the form of sound waves capable of creating a 3D reality. If you go on saying something over and over, it manifests. Whether it is $100 or $100 million there is no difference to the cosmos. There is only one time; NOW. But there are two choices; now negativity and cosmos now. The cosmos now is the Higher Self beyond the mind. The secret is to get into that now. If you wait, you create time so get in the now of Higher Self beyond time. Keep putting information into the cosmos by believing in the higher now where everything is possible."

"As a Yogi, my mission merges ancient wisdom and modern technology. Things happen naturally, not through strife and now many people come to me for miracles. The energy of the brain is available for others to pick up from Gurus. These Gurus are able to take a thought manifestation into reality. I am in the science of miracles and I say the idea becomes the object. You need a divine mind to mediate the process into the material. There are three models or steps that are key:

1. Think about it all the time to manifest something – repetition;
2. Speak a mantra to become as you think;
3. Only the object remains as reality."

"You have to activate the midbrain to create miracles. It is the answer to creating your reality. It is the primitive or reptilian brain. It has been ignored and the neo-cortex has been believed to be the important part. But it is full of logic, negativity, and questions so it stops the miracle as we try to satisfy our desires. It will not allow miracles to happen. Other areas like the Parental are not the focus. Yogis only look at cause and effect without time. As soon as you get the frontal lobe into the idea, it kills it. The mid brain does not care. No complex process is needed. From the level of the mid brain you can manifest but it is not easy with the rest of the brain in the way. Yoga is actually a brain science. First you must stop the brain. Now brain scientists are saying this. When you enter this place, you know the soul intelligence not the mind intelligence."

Sounds Control Consciousness And Matter

In a special study, Pillai is engaged in scientifically verifying what the Yogis have known for centuries. The key purpose is to validate that sounds can change the brain by the use of mantras, and also that the science of sounds controls consciousness and matter. Pillai has said there are 51 sounds that can produce significant results and effects in the brain. In his work, he has had extraordinary results with the learning skills of kids by using sounds and the midbrain. These sounds are the ones being tested in his research.

Pillai states: "The answer to poverty lies in your brain. A person's socio-economic environment influences the development of their brain. Growing up in a poor neighborhood can impact a child's learning ability and their mental and emotional well-being in the long run. Phonemic Intelligence can improve the social behavior of children, reduce mental stress, and enhance their ability to memorize, retain and deliver." See www.TripuraFoundation.org.

Dr. Pillai states that Phonemic Intelligence can help overcome such negative effects of poverty by changing the neurology of the brain for the better. *"It involves using specific phoneme (smallest unit of sound that contrasts with another sound, in any given language) sounds in different parts of the brain, by which it is possible to enhance the functioning of those parts of the brain. Our study done at a leading brain laboratory shows positive effects of these sounds on the brain".*

"In this pilot study, the participants were made to listen and vocalize 4 sounds focusing on different parts of the brain. Using EEG (Electroencephalography), we recorded electrical activity in the brain and found profound changes with the use of each discreet sound", said lead researcher Dr. Anbarasu Annamalai, while introducing the methodology of the study via Video.

"We used a modern computer technology known as 'Independent Component Analysis' to break the brain's activity into its component parts. We were able to see the differences between the sounds in each component in a very detailed way. The impacts of these sounds is felt everywhere in the brain, not just in the primary auditory cortex (part of the brain that processes sound). We can see a strong effect even in this pilot study", explained **Jay Gunkelman** via Video. Jay is the **Chief Scientist** at the US-based **Brain Science International** where the study was done.

These sounds are used as part of the Phonemic Intelligence methodology implemented in HOPE Learning Centers - the educational initiative of Tripura Foundation, a non-profit founded by Dr. Pillai. **Elaine Kueper, Global Director, Tripura Foundation** stated:

"2450 children are using this brain-changing education in 70 Centers across 3 states - Tamil Nadu (58 centers), Goa (10 centers) and Haryana (2 centers). These children, belonging to economically poor sections, have demonstrated very positive results with higher test scores, greater focus on schoolwork, cooperation and participation, feelings of peace and happiness, and overall well-being."

Jay Gunkleman at Brain Science International looked at these mantra sounds using EEG's to create map pictures which showed systematic impacts in the brain. The effect they report is a strong effect. They have determined that the impact in the brain is everywhere. They see a distinct response given the specific mantra used by Pillai.

As an example of the work, the image shows the effect of one of the mantras on the anterior singulate. It is deep and unrelated to sound but you see it here. This is where it controls how the world should work and if it does not, a signal goes off. The Anterior Singulate shows focused activity. This region is involved in decision making and emotional regulation as well as vital to the regulation of physiological processes, such as blood pressure and heart rate.

The research shows that these sounds can erase thought patterns and create new ones to have profound effects. Sound is the basis for consciousness. You think something and it is a sound. The brain is empowered by consciousness. It creates matter through sound. You can see more information at:

http://www.brainsinternational.com/index.cfm/about-us/team-members-bios/jay-gunkelman/

Here it states: "*Our consciousness is created out of sound waves and our emotions are determined by the sounds we continuously repeat in the form of words or thoughts. Sound waves thus play a very important role in determining the level and nature of our consciousness. It is the thoughts, emotions and consciousness we have created that determine our happiness or sorrow, so, it is very important we are aware of what we say to ourselves on a regular basis. If you aspire to a better job, your positive thoughts and attitude will allow you to see better opportunities than a negative attitude will allow. The sound waves used by the Pillai Center for MindScience are words/power sounds, which are found in divine ancient languages such as Sanskrit, Hebrew and Arabic. These power sounds contain high vibrations that help elevate consciousness in ways ordinary words cannot. Through his research in the fields of spiritual sciences and technologies, Dr. Pillai has discovered numerous sound waves that help transform the mind, body and soul, thus bringing in manifestations of your desires.*"

The Pillai Miracle Method

So what does Pillai teach as his miracle method?

From a yogi perspective he states that the Yogis knew about the brain as a subtle brain which they could see as the etheric double like in the astral plane. So they did not see it as a physical thing but it is the mid part of the brain. It is really not separate from physical but when you activate it you will have a tremendous understanding about everything. In Pillai's midbrain activation process, he tells us that Ommm is a key name for God as the midbrain. Ahhh activates left brain and Ohhh activates the right brain. Ommm is the sound that opens the midbrain.

He also enforces the need to cut out the noise from neo-cortex. But as we know, shutting it down completely is not easy as it keeps coming back and distracts. He says that the Yogis accomplished this through discipline. As soon as one meditates, the thoughts come. The true state when it is attained is reflected by the Yogi who said: *"it is hard for me to find a thought"*. That is the level needed because here is where all thoughts can manifest if you are in the Soul mind. The goal of meditation is not to have a negative or time condition. When you are empty, you are full. Pillai states that repeated practice is key. Here is his method for opening up the midbrain:

1. Close your eyes.
2. Focus attention on your right eye.
3. Visualize a powerful light from right eye shooting into left brain.
4. Focus on left eye.
5. Visualize a powerful light from the left eye shooting into the right brain.
6. Focus on the right nostril.
7. Visualize a bright light entering it.
8. Focus on the left nostril.
9. Visualize a bright light entering it.
10. Visualize the light from left and right meeting between the eyebrows.
11. Again a light in the right eye, shooting into left brain.
12. Again a light in the left eye shooting into right brain.
13. Again right, left nostril light meeting between the eyebrows.
14. Visualize your entire body filled with light.
15. Go to brain stem and focus on it as here is where it converges to mental mind energy.
16. Go up to thalamus, callosum, parental lobe and visualize a column of light through them.
17. Ommmmm, ommmmmm, ommmmmmm
18. The whole body is light.
19. Focus on the midbrain.
20. Ommmmm, ommmmmm, ommmmmm
21. Visualize the sound rising to the top of the brain
22. Ommmmmmm, ommmmmmm, ommmmmmm, ommmmmmm

This looks pretty simple but it is pretty direct. Pillai explains:

"You will see dramatic results within the midbrain. This is the way to empower the brain. You have to know the higher brain. If you have problems in life, blame it on the brain, it is responsible not anything else. Sound is the building block of consciousness. Ommmmm my lord is the sound that can open the midbrain. It opens the channel from the brainstem because the life force prana connected to breathing is here so when you put attention on the brain stem then it comes alive because you put attention on

it as life itself. Yogis do this ommmm on their brain stem. You see the energy floating up to the top of the brain. The sound exchanges in all parts such as the thalamus, pineal, singulet, cortex and goes to the parental but it is not the physical brain. Yet it does affect the physical brain."

"The focus is not in the cortex. Focus is on the stem as this is where the life force begins. Breathing is only conscious energy of prana. Focus on the thalamus on two sides of the brain attached to the stem for in-between is the pineal. This is where the miracle will happen. Yogis say put it into 3rd eye and it will become an object. The thalamus controls everything in the center of midbrain and does not know the difference between illusion and reality. Keep the things you want there and it will make it into real. This way you are making a tremendous impact on the brain. You do not have to meditate forever. A repeated thought affects the brain by changing nerve cells."

"When you put a light into the midbrain starting from the stem and moving up, you allow it to go into the infinite sky. The consciousness of the midbrain is connected to several heavens and you are acquiring this by putting attention on them. It is connected to the highest heaven with a tremendous amount of vibration. Just the light from the stem through the midbrain opens it. You can put into the midbrain area of the thalamus what you want to manifest; car, business, whatever. Put it into the thalamus and pineal. Just imagine it and chant Ommmmmmmmmmmmmm repeatedly. When you open in the midbrain thalamus it does not know difference between object and image. It is the cortex that makes a differentiation of the object. Work with the astral not physical brain."

Of note is that Pillai gives us some new wisdom on why he is dedicated to eliminating poverty.

"A Guru in the US had 99 Rolls Royce's but he never bought any of them. You don't get a job and work. If you want miracles you have a different way of doing it. It is not philosophy. It is a matter of understanding the pineal and brain. I believe that becoming enlightened to a profound state means nothing will happen. What is the use of this? A divine coma? Feeling nothing or seeing spiritual beings is of no use because you must live in this reality. But it is the most powerful place of the soul to manifest. The human brain is dumb because you have to work hard. The cortex is the stupid part that will organize your life and keep most in poverty. 99% of the time we think stupid, survival, anxiety, money, relationship. It is an anatomical abnormality. The mind should be peaceful."

"Some meditate for 35 years and do not manifest anything. Then they get into depression. They cannot focus attention on what needs to be taken care of. Do not let meditation take you to a divine coma. Most techniques make you materially poor and God is not poor. It is a problem with the brain. To be spiritual you have to prove you have spirit, not be poor. If you do not *demonstrate progress in 90 days quit. If you want emptiness and enlightenment follow Buddha. He taught no god, no soul just empty space. It happened to Buddha so he begged for survival. His body was here but that teaching is not relevant in this world now. God does not care. You have to take responsibility for what you do and the defects in your life. To identify the part the brain that creates these problems is key. Then there are the negatives; what if I can't open my midbrain. It comes from the frontal lobe. It creates crazy people. We want this science to stop this and everything is rooted in the brain, not the mind that is not allowing what you want to manifest. The neo-cortex needs to be shut down and the midbrain activated. Then use power and intelligence of the Soul mind and go back to the frontal and empower it."*

"The key thing about sounds is that there are sounds and areas of brain responsible for money, relationships, and health. You have to know these so if you want money, go to thalamus, when 11th moon is best. The mantra must be from someone who is attuned as there is a power from receiving this sound from someone who has received this consciousness. It is from a higher consciousness.

The Pillai Money Mantra

The SHREEM BRZEE money mantra is offered freely by Dr. Pillai in his quest to eliminate poverty. As an enlightened master, Dr Pillai (Baba) teaches that **SHREEM BRZEE** is the ultimate and most powerful **quantum sound** to attract money, wealth, prosperity, abundance, joy and material happiness to you. This mantra he suggests originates from Hebrew and Sanskrit. **SHREEM** is the seed sound for **Lakshmi,** the archetype who gives money and prosperity. **Goddess Lakshmi** is the aspect of the Divine that gives you **money blessings** and **material miracles**. BRZEE is a sound that was revealed to Dr Pillai by an ascended master known as **Visvamitra** who meditated on this sound on a different plane for 1500 years. **BRZEE** is an ultimate sound which can attract untold wealth and riches to you.

He suggests that the quantum sound **SHREEM BRZEE** is the ultimate money magnet - it carries deep within it the power and potential of pure gold. Just like how an **oak seed** has the potential to grow into a large oak tree, and thereafter multiply into a forest of oak trees, the sound **SHREEM BRZEE** once implanted into your consciousness and very soul, will turn you into a **pure money magnet** that attracts wealth and prosperity to yourself. **BRZEE** will also bring more Divine Light into your soul.

The meditation is offered for free to download. Recall that: **"the mantra must be from someone who is attuned as there is a power from** *receiving this sound from someone who has received this consciousness. It is from a higher consciousness."*

Here is the process he teaches when leading a group:

*"Close your eyes for a minute.
Put your attention on your 3rd eye for a minute.
Chant Brzee (25 times).
Allow the sound to go deep into your 3rd eye and then into the entire brain and pervade the whole body.
You do not have the burden to check out what will work for you. Brzee will be like a watchdog to keep wrong projects away from you. She will spontaneously spring the right thought in you and the right project will show up for you.
Chant Brzee (5 times).
You have no responsibility You have given total control to Brzee.
Chant Brzee (10 times).
Join me now.
Chant Brzee (40 times).
Allow the sound to permeate the mind and the complete body and soul.
Chant Brzee (28 times).
Now mentally keep repeating Brzee in the 3rd eye.
You have given your financial plans and future to her. Let her take over you and control you.
Ommmmmmm shati shanti shanti, shati shanti shant hi
Slowly, slowly you can come back."*

The chant is done 108 times. Pillai offers some advice on this mantra:

"The power of the brzee mantra is this: It is very powerful and can enlighten you. It will arrest the waste of your mind because we do not know what will work or not work so we must turn our hearts to the divine light. People say others do better and are successful even though they are stupid, I am working hard and am more educated and nothing happens. Should I become stupid like him to make more money? The truth is he is supported by divine light and being stupid is not relevant. He may have different money karma. That light that is beyond our intellectual comprehension is the sound brzee. It has taken 400 years to create this sound. Use this sound and you will have material and spiritual success. I am grateful to the Gurus for this. What gives us total faith is this sound. I have given the sounds ara kara and they have done very well but the most important is brzee. It has miraculous power. Just say this sound a few times when in trouble. It will help you. The sound belongs to the saints as the friends of the people who wanted to heal humanity. If you have a disease, use this sound. It can help accomplish things through the use of your mind."

The Issue Of Karma

Dr Pillai cautions us that there is an issue of Money Karma:

"The Yogis and Siddhas knew karma was a deep orientation to a certain quality, war, poverty, and this comes from several life times. That orientation comes forward as karma. Karma is a reality and it can be corrected. Buddha believed in karma. Karma impacts the thought process, where you have poverty thoughts which continue. It is real. Karma removal is removing the deep thoughts that are neurotic thoughts. The real thoughts come from the heart. Karma can block meditation. You create your own reality and science is coming up with this too. You must understand that there is a law of causality. It is like Newton's law of action and reaction; life is reaction as you create actions. Karma is responsible for all your problems of relationship, health or wealth. Keep dissolving your karma because it will not allow you to make money until first clean it out. Otherwise you will sit like a zombie and nothing will happen. In every area karma has its own hand and it dictates at a conscious level. If you have a good money karma it will keep flowing to you. You do not need education to do this. This is important to understand. You can change your karma by ways and means as yogis are involved in this change in destiny."

"But there is a destiny. If you do not change it, it will run its own course but if you learn to change it and how it can be done you can change your life. It is possible to be a billionaire. Wayne Dyer said do not compare yourself to other people, compare with where you have been. You may have already achieved great things. Many people will not be able to manifest because they have to understand karma. You must get rid of it to manifest. Otherwise you are living a past reality so you must understand and release old reality so it can be clean for your future. You must completely erase karma."

You can check out the success stories by simply using goggle to search brzee mantra testimonials.

Finally, in light of our continued quest let us share some of the wisdom that Dr Pillai offers.

In **Acquiring Supernatural Powers** he tells us that Step 1 is Concentration; focus on an object. Step 2 is to meditate on that object you have chosen. Meditation is an added concentration as it allows you to remain under concentration in greater clarity and disallow thoughts to get to greater concentration. Step 3 is to be in the non consciousness. All that exists is the object nothing else. You must combine all three steps into one technique. You are concentrating on an object, meditating on an object then you become the object itself, experiencing the object. When you concentrate, you focus only on certain things about the object, you do know everything about it in that space of omniscience. The linear nature disappears and omniscience releases it in its totality. This is to release the omniscient mind not the lower mind.

The whole world is an illusion created by the senses and the mind together. There are two types. There is the collective illusion where everybody sees the mountains and the other where you are not using the senses; then you will understand that the appearances are illusion. Personal illusion is true to one's self so each can experience their own personal illusion of wealth, poverty, and so on. The whole life is experienced between the two illusions.

Fake enlightenment through watching in silence is not enlightenment. This is delusion. You must control thoughts and master the thought process. The body will change and glow when enlightenment occurs as you turn into light. Each needs to understand this and it is not through meditation alone.

Thoughts and emotions In understanding how to emotionalize a thought, Yoga has a tantra method. Your tongue thinks because the tongue is an instrument of language as it is vocalized here. Without the tongue you cannot think a thought or speak a word. Also with tasting, kissing, the tongue is directly involved from a sensory place. Tantra yoga says there are secretions that do the cognitive and emotional perception. Pillai suggests the following method to understand it:

"Put the focus on the tongue and you will see the quiet.
Close eyes and focus attention on tongue.
There are many elixirs in the tongue part of the saliva. They allow language, cognitive thought, emotional experience like sex, and taste.
Focus on the tip of the tongue.
Move to the middle of the tongue.
Move to the rear of the tongue.
Lift the tongue and make it touch the palate.
This will help stop your thoughts and understand the different elixirs in the saliva.
Do this a few times.
Open your eyes."

We create from inside out The blueprint to create comes first. The dynamics include sound waves that create anything. The problem people face comes from defects inside. The sound waves that are involved are corrupt (thoughts, sound images in consciousness). It means that there is an inability to produce very subtle forms of sound waves. Yogis said you do this in meditation to go to the very bottom and then think about the object at that level, then it can happen. The human usually starts planning how they get a car and gets caught up in the process. You do this at a subtle level to go to the origin of sound waves which is the origin of consciousness and life itself.

The Functions Of The Midbrain

The work and wisdom of Pillai points to the midbrain and words vibrating directly into it as a key to miracles, both wealth and health. In this section we are going to offer some information about the midbrain.

The central nervous system in our bodies is crucial to the way we function as individuals and is made up of the brain and the spinal cord. The fore, mid and hind brain areas serve different and unique purposes, with the midbrain being responsible for eye and body movement as well as auditory senses and vision. Research shows that this part of the brain is linked to our memory. The development of neurological science and behavioral understanding has accelerated over the past twenty years, and with this information rising exponentially we see it is vital in empowering the mental development of youngsters.

Within the midbrain, there are layers resembling the cerebral cortex, with the superior colliculi performing different functions to the inferior colliculus. Neurons within the inferior colliculus are organized into patterns that deal with auditory frequencies, making this the part of the brain able to analyze various auditory stimuli. The inferior colliculus is adept at localizing sources of sounds. Functions controlled by the midbrain include how to use the vocal cords and how to articulate as well as palate, tongue and lip control. The Midbrain is also responsible for the way in which we laugh and cry through its control over the laryngeal and oral tissues in our faces. Dopamine is found in the Midbrain along with neurotransmitters and this dopamine is vital for cognition and motor function. The midbrain is the reward center for behavior and is an area that has been studied in depth by scientists for this reason. Rewards can become distorted when they are associated with addiction because the person will focus on that one reward.

Memory, through auditory perception, is an important part of the midbrain and the lobes within each cerebral hemisphere store information in short and long term memories. The temporal lobes receive information from the ears and underneath them is an area for forming memories and retrieving them, particularly those associated with auditory learning.

Often referred to as the blindfold activation, this theory is gaining momentum worldwide, particularly in Asia. Children's midbrain activity becomes much stronger when their eyes are closed or they are blindfolded. It works through children using their auditory senses to decipher information and resulting in the child seeing the information and storing it in their memory, without the use of sight. Midbrain activity can radiate like a radar, using memory of objects. It can increase concentration to impressive levels and also build a person's confidence levels, as well as their creativity, intuition and overall intelligence. This type of activity is not limited to a blindfold approach, it simply works by developing the memory through auditory learning and it has become established as an effective approach in recent years, leading to children being encouraged in ways that were previously unimagined.

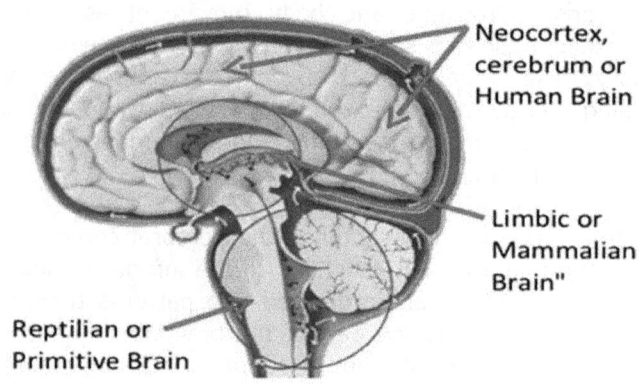

The midbrain has essentially been ignored as the more primitive brain. It is where the 3rd eye and pineal gland are. This is one step above the reptilian brain typically branded as the mammalian brain. The truth is that the midbrain is the brain counterpart that has no predisposition to time like the frontal lobe and neo cortex have. It is the no-time, no-space quantum void as a physical counterpart of your Higher Consciousness.

Lizard Brain	Mammal Brain	Human Brain
Brain stem & cerebelum	Limbic System	Neocortex
Fight or flight	Emotions, memories, habits	Language, abstract thought, imagination, consciousness
Autopilot	Decisions	Reasons, rationalizes

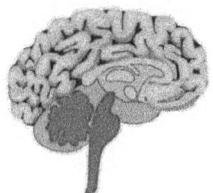 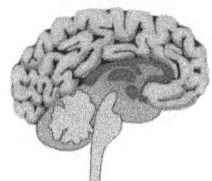 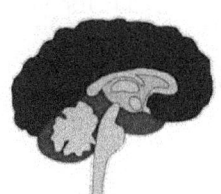

These three brains are sort of like an onion, each encompassing the other but with special roles. The prevailing consciousness has created the big brain to believe it is better than anything else, and is totally in charge of reality. It is what places plans in your minds of what you want to happen, the ways you need to heal, the dreams that you want to fulfill, the relationships you want to create. But the mind is very different from the brain. This is where the neo-cortex and frontal lobe are disallowing anything instantaneous or miraculous to happen in your life. The midbrain, on the other hand, acts most notably as the information superhighway connecting the forebrain and hindbrain. It enables your brain to integrate sensory information from your eyes and ears with your muscle movements, thereby enabling your body to use this information to make fine adjustments to your movements.

The midbrain has no concept of time which the neo-cortex and frontal lobe are preoccupied with. Miracles that are outside this belief box are created in this place outside of time and space. It is a matter of moving your attention from the frontal lobe to the midbrain and accepting the Higher Mind as the mind in charge of your affairs. It is like the biological equivalent of the Internet; it's a vital aspect of our neural 'information superhighway', which transfers visual and auditory input to the brain and motor (movement) information from the brain.

The midbrain is vitally important to maintaining and regulating the state of consciousness, alertness and attention. The midbrain contains the physical pineal gland, which has similar features to the retina in our eyes and is also a replica of what Siddhas call the third eye. It also includes the pons, reticular activating system, the pituitary gland, and the 3rd ventricle. The pineal gland and the surrounding area in the midbrain is where our connection to higher thought and reality is. When these areas are activated you open up to the extraordinary and welcome events that begin to manifest in your life beyond what the falsely named superbrain tells you. You do not create miracles now because most are caught up in 'cause and effect' and time bondage. You cannot experience anything without time and effect. Miracles are simply not being disallowed by the neo-cortex which includes the frontal lobe. This is the part of the brain that disallows anything instantaneous to happen.

Consider that reality is a holographic illusion; a projection of 3D reality that is created by the brain for you to experience through your five senses and deploy mental and emotional abilities. The main camera of assimilation and projection is here in the midbrain. So to change the movie you need access to the projector and the programmer that reside outside of the belief box consciousness. This is the place where that can be done as we will discuss later.

Consider that the midbrain is under the direct guidance of the Soul and does not need the frontal lobe or neo cortex. It does not really even care about the right brain left brain subdivision because it is simply one. The physiology has the corpora quadrigemina, composed of two **colliculi** that act as relay stations that take sensory information from the eyes and ears and relay it to the thalamus for distribution to the appropriate area of the cerebrum. The cerebral peduncle and corpora quadrigemina are separated by a canal called the **cerebral aqueduct**, which distributes **cerebrospinal fluid** throughout the brain and spinal cord to buffer the tissue, remove wastes, and maintain cranial pressure.

We have seen in the work of Dr. Pillai that repetitive mantras and words are key to opening the midbrain accessing the 3rd eye and pineal for manifestation. His research shows that these sounds have a direct impact on changing reality. We are now going to look at another Dr. and Master who has reported to heal hundreds of thousands of people with words and mantras.

Dr. And Master Sha Miracles

In his book **Soul Healing Miracles**, **Dr and Master Sha** tells us about the Chinese ancient wisdom. He reveals how the sacred Source meditations and mantras have been so successful for him. He is a medical doctor, doctor of Chinese medicine in China and Canada, as well as Qi gong, tai chi, kung fu, and a feng shui master. He is also engaged in advanced cellular healing research in China and has his own TV show on the power of sound. Has had 10 years of healing and reports hundreds of thousands of miracle healings. He has trained thousands of followers. His sole mandate is in service as the purpose of his life; to make others happy and healthier through empowerments in three ways:

1. Teach universal service to be unconditional unusual services
2. Teach soul secrets wisdom, knowledge to soul healing miracles
3. Teach to reach soul enlightenment

Dr Sha teaches that the Soul, mind and body are the key areas of healing. In order to heal, karmic blockages must be removed from three areas:

1. Soul blockages are bad karma and must be removed first
2. Mind blockages are negative beliefs, ego and attachments
3. Body blockages are energy and matter blocks

He states that the Source Field is what heals and it carries Source Love, Forgiveness, Compassion and Light. These cause the Soul made of light energy to remove blockages and transform all life. These are key treasures because Divine love melts all blockages and transforms all life, Forgiveness brings inner joy and peace to all life, Compassion boosts energy vitality, immunity in all life, and Light transforms.

To Sha everything has a soul, mind and body, even inert things. In all his work, he uses five key techniques of Body, Soul, Mind, Breath and Sound power.

Body Power puts hands on place to remove blockages. Where you put your hands is where you receive healing and rejuvenation.
Soul Power opens to healing and blessing to invoke inner souls of body, organs, cells, DNA and invoke outer souls of divine.
Mind Power puts your mind using creative visualization on what you are to receive. Thinking and what you visualize is what you receive blessings from.
Sound Power chants sounds as what you chant is what you become. Mouth mantras are sacred sounds from pure land of service which is the Soul's journey.
Breath Power breathing deeply in and out drawing in the Source Light and exhaling with the appropriate chanting mantra.

Dr. Sha focuses on Soul healing as he states that when you first heal the Soul which is spirit, then healing of mind and body follow. The Soul is a golden light being, the essence of life, boss of human. When you get sick, the Soul gets sick first then sickness of mind and body follow. Healing first removes karma blockages from Soul, negative energy from the mind and negative matter and energy from the body.

In his healing practices, he brings ancient wisdom into his procedures. He states there are five elements in ancient wisdom that have responsibility areas in the body. These are Wood, Fire, Earth, Metal, and Water. They correspond to the 5 senses and are balanced or unbalanced by positive or negative emotions. To offer healing to the organ within that group is to offer healing to everything connected to that element.

An example of part of the table he offers in his book is the body organ of the heart which belongs to the Fire Element.

Element	Yin Organ	Yang Organ	Body tissue	Body Fluid	Sense	Unbalanced Emotion	Balanced Emption
Fire	Heart	Small intestine	Blood vessels	Sweat	Tongue Taste	Depression Anxiety	Joy

The heart is the authority (zang) organ of the fire element, and the small intestine is the fu organ. The meridians of these are internally and externally connected. The heart is the driving mechanism for the blood. The heart houses the mind and soul, connecting with soul's activities, consciousness and thinking. The tongue is the governing organ for taste, blood and sweat as they come from the same place. Depression and anxiety results in imbalances and joy balances.

There are other relationships that are relevant in the healing process of the Fire element:

Finger	Taste	Color	Weather	Season	Direction	Phase	Energy
Middle	Bitter	Red	Hot	Summer	South	Full Yang	Expansive

Sha Miracle Healing Process

Sha applies his 5 power techniques as an example of healing the heart and all related parts of the element fire:

Body Power
"Sit up straight, place tip of tongue against roof of mouth. Place one palm over heart and other over lower abdomen."

Sha explains that there is a specific hand placement, one where the healing is to be received, the other at the area of the sacra chakra that is the "seed" or origin of the energy manifestation.

Soul Power
"Say hello to inner souls.

Dear soul, mind, body of my heart, small intestine, tongue, blood vessels and emotional body of the fire element.
I love you, honor you and appreciate you.
You have the power to heal and rejuvenate my heart, small intestine, tongue and blood vessels which include big and small arteries, capillaries, small and big veins and to heal depression and anxiety.
Do a good job.
Thank you."

Say hello to outer souls.
"Dear Divine.
Dear Tao, the Source.
I love you, honor you and appreciate you.
Please forgive my ancestors and me for all the mistakes we have made in all lifetimes related to the heart, small intestine, tongues, blood vessels, capillary system and depression and anxiety.
In order to be forgiven, I will serve unconditionally.
To chant and meditate is to serve.
I will chant and meditate as much as I can.
I will offer my unconditional service as much as I can.
I am extremely grateful.
Thank you."

In this process Sha is following the table items, addressing the areas of healing, the issues that caused them, all of the inner and outer souls to address and issuing the words to bring love, forgiveness and compassion into the process. He issues gratitude, faith and trust it will be done. Of note is the necessity to clear karma by forgiveness.

Mind Power
"Visualize bright red light shining in the heart area."

Central to the healings is light which carries the powers of divine; namely love, forgiveness, compassion within light itself. The type of light is as in the table (i.e. red light).

Sound and Breath Power
"Chant silently or out loud.
Visualize red light in the heart as you breathe in and silently chant: Heart circulates perfectly.
Visualize a golden light throughout the body as you breathe out and chant: Da Ai or Greatest Love.

Visualize red light in the heart as you breathe in and chant: Complexion is glowing. Perfect tongue.
Visualize a golden light throughout the body as you breathe out and chant: Da kuan shu or Greatest Forgiveness.
Visualize red light in the heart as you breathe in and silently chant: Clear Mind.
Visualize a golden light throughout the body as you breathe out and chant: Da Guang Ming greatest light.
Continue to chant and visualize 10 minutes (two hours for life threatening conditions)."

This process is common to all the examples Sha shares in the book. He goes through the divine powers with each organ and components related to Fire as in the table. It bears considerable resemblance to the process of Ho'oponopono which we studied in the first book.

In carefully studying Sha there are certain key observations that come forward when the work of Pillai is compared:

Karma is the root cause of all current sickness and must be cleared at the Soul level. Forgiveness by the Divine is a blessing that clears blocks and karma which is a record of services (deeds, virtues).

Mantras and chanting are special sounds and messages for transforming life. They carry the high frequency and vibration of love, forgiveness, compassion and light. When you chant from the heart, mantras connect to the souls. Do not be afraid to invite darkness to chant and meditate with as love melts all blockages and transforms life.

Source comes as invisible and visible light (3rd eye sees invisible part). Source Light is what transforms and creates miracles. Communications to Source is at a Soul level where you are at the level of divine light. The Golden Light of Source is what heals.

The seed chakra is at the 2nd sacral chakra area. It is used in Pillai's and Sha's processes. This is where the palm is placed to receive the healing in an upward causal process. Pillai uses the same as a downward causal process to the same place.

The process of chanting repeatedly is key. It is what commands the process of miracles to unfold. This is a process that must be repeated daily over and over to take effect.

We have presented two new Miracle Facilitators because they not only have significant evidence that they can facilitate health and wealth miracles, but they are bringing in new variables – that of sound, the importance of talking to the midbrain, mantras and chanting. In addition they bring in additional experience on why these miracles do not work for some – karma and perseverance. What is it about the power of words being chanted that is important? It is apparent that both Chinese and Indian Masters knew about it. Now we are going to investigate the area of words and their power.

Importance Of Sound Waves

There are many new discoveries of the wave information nature of DNA that overthrow the old understanding that you are genetically fixed. This is led by the new science of wave genetics that shows DNA functions like a holographic computer, part of the larger hologram of the information wave reality. Research suggests our DNA has the capabilities of hypercommunication - telepathy, remote sensing and remote feeling, along with other psychic abilities. But the most relevant here is that we also have the ability to reprogram our genetic blueprint with simple words and frequencies.

For example, Russian researchers' findings and conclusions are that DNA is not only responsible for the construction of your body but also serves as data storage and in communication. The Russian linguists found that the genetic code, especially in the apparently useless junk DNA follows the same rules as all our human languages. To this end they compared the rules of syntax (the way in which words are put together to form phrases and sentences), semantics (the study of meaning in language forms) and the basic rules of grammar. They found that the alkalines of our DNA follow a regular grammar and do have set rules just like our languages. So human languages did not appear coincidentally but are a reflection of our inherent DNA.

This finally and scientifically explains why affirmations, autogenous training, hypnosis and the likes can have such strong effects on humans and their bodies. It is entirely normal and natural for our DNA to react to language. While western researchers cut single genes from the DNA strands and insert them elsewhere, the Russians enthusiastically worked on devices that can influence the cellular metabolism through suitable modulated radio and light frequencies and thus repair genetic defects.

In order for DNA to do all of the things that we speak of esoterically and quantumly, 300 trillion pieces of DNA must all know something at the same time! There has to be a communication that takes place in the microscopic DNA of your toenail at the same time as the longest hair on your head. They both have to know about it instantly. Then those trillions of pieces must agree, must have one energy absorption of consciousness. This all must happen in a 3D construct – that is, within your reality. There is no word in science for this process unless you consider the one created for a description of photons called "entanglement."

There is instead, "a confluence of energy." Confluence in English truly means a melding of energies together, so that they become something else, a oneness. Science doesn't see it within DNA yet, but at some level they know it must exist. For how else can the Human body do what it does?

Cellular structure is specific and unique. Like the linear machine, it is specialized, and you have heard of stem cells carrying that specificity. But DNA is identical all over the body. It's not specific. You don't have toenail DNA or hair DNA or heart DNA. You've just got your own unique DNA. Trillions of copies of the same Human quantum blueprint must talk to each other instantly or you would cease to exist. How did they do it? No name in science truly has been given to the process of communication between DNA loops, but it will. It's a quantumness within the "soup" of magnetics.

Each loop of DNA has a magnetic field that overlaps the loop next to it, which overlaps the loop next to it. Hundreds of trillions of overlaps equals one consciousness. This then represents a magnetic imprint, which the Human carries around with them. Magnetics is an interdimensional energy, a quantum energy, and this imprint creates the Human aura. An aura is not a magnetic field and you will not be able to see an aura with magnetic equipment. An aura is the result of a confluence of DNA communication within the Human body, a quantum imprint, a melding of energy to create a quantum field not measurable by anything on the planet, yet.

What happens in DNA happens all at once within every energy layer of it. Think of the coordination, the puzzle. If you're going to have some kind of esoteric activation that is new within your DNA, think of what must take place! Hundreds of trillions of parts all receive it at once. What does that feel like?

DNA is always evolving on a self improvement cycle, just like the global consciousness is supposed to. If you want to get an idea of how this DNA works in practice let us use a simple example. Let us say a species – say a seagull – somehow learns to pick up a clam off the shore line, fly up with it and drop it to crack it open on the rocks. Because it satisfies its desire to survive, it does this a lot and it gets hardwired into its neuro pathways. Then some buddy seagulls see this and copy it. At a certain threshold the number of seagulls doing this causes the DNA to take this on as a permanent behavior encoded into the group DNA. When this occurs at a certain threshold, all seagulls get their DNA upgraded even if they don't have any clams in their environment. Because DNA is quantum, they are all nonlocal and the effect is immediately updated throughout all whether they need it or not. From then on it becomes a hardwired instinct of behavior.

In our work so far, we have seen that DNA is called upon by the subconscious and the brain to repair or maintain things in our body – absolutely everything right down to the smallest details! We have also seen that DNA is quantum and we can call on it to trigger "extraordinary" things like miracle of healing. What else can it do? We brought this forward in the table presented by Kryon in a previous chapter.

In the Beginning Was The Word

Let us look into some of religious mythology which may be closer to the truth than we currently imagine. It is written by human mortals that when God created the first human beings - Adam and Eve - He created them in His own image (Genesis 1:26-27). This likeness unquestionably included the ability to engage in intelligible speech via human language. In fact, God spoke to them from the very beginning of their existence as humans (Genesis 1:28-30). Hence, they possessed the ability to understand verbal communication—*and to speak themselves!*

God gave very specific instructions to the man *before* the woman was even created (Genesis 2:15-17). Adam gave names to the animals *before* the creation of Eve (Genesis 2:19-20). Since both the man and the woman were created on the sixth day, the creation of the man preceded the creation of the woman by only hours. So, *Adam had the ability to speak on the very day that he was brought into existence!*

As the story unfolds, that same day, God put Adam to sleep and performed history's first human surgery. He fashioned the female of the species from a portion of the male's body. God then presented the woman to the man (no doubt in what we would refer to as the first marriage ceremony). Observe Adam's response: And Adam said, *"This is now bone of my bones and flesh of my flesh; she shall be called Woman, because she was taken out of man."* (Genesis 2:23). Here is Adam—less than twenty-four hours old—articulating intelligible speech with a well-developed vocabulary and advanced powers of expression. Note also that Eve engaged in intelligent conversation with Satan (Genesis 3:1-5). An unbiased observer is forced to conclude that Adam and Eve were *created* with oral communication capability. Little wonder, then, that God said to Moses: "*Who had made man's mouth? ... Have not I, the Lord? Now therefore, go, and I will be with your mouth and teach you what you shall say (Exodus 4:11-12)."*

What language did they speak? It was Hebrew. It was formed into Arabic and Egyptian. Biblical Hebrew is the oldest language still in use today (5000 years). Hebrew is the basis for half of the religious traditions. The Kabala is a collection of wisdom (Books of Illumination, Book of Light). The Book says God created the universe with text, numbers, and communications.

It is said that God created the Universe by engraving the letters in all that emptiness. God chose three letters for his name. It was held sacred and was taken out YHVH is the divine name (YAWVEY) is felt to be true pronunciation but was lost until the emergence of the fragment 66 of Dead Sea Scrolls which has YHVH on it. The books say all spoken and formed emanates from this name. Interestingly enough, we are living in a time when 95% of the world's population believes in a higher power or Supreme Being. More than half of the 95% refer to the power as "God". This quest for god appears to be a very fundamental drive within the human species. Is it encoded in DNA?

The God Code

Gregg Braden spent twelve years of research leading to the writing of **The God Code**. The book is based on the fact that the basic elements of DNA - hydrogen, nitrogen, oxygen and carbon translate directly to key letters of both the Hebrew and Arabic alphabets and that in both alphabets they spell the name of God. According to Gregg, what this means is that the letters of God's ancient name *"are encoded as the genetic formation in every cell, of every life."* The message that is revealed when the chemistry of our cells is translated into the letters of ancient Hebrew is *"God/Eternal within the body."* This message is the same regardless of our race, color, religion or anything else. The author states, *"The odds that this relationship has occurred by chance are approximately 1 in 200,000."*

How does he conclude this? Each letter of every alphabet can be linked with a specific number value. The primary Hebrew alphabet (which has been used for *at least* 3,000 years) has 22 letters, each having a unique sound and number. In Hebrew, every letter is assigned a number. Within this number code, we were given information about our past and our future. Secrets are encoded in these Hebrew letters and the hidden number code in the Hebrew language offers a link between the worlds of science and spirituality.

The 118 elements, which comprise everything in the physical world, are each assigned properties that are represented by numbers. These qualities of numbers link the elements of our DNA to the letters of the Hebrew alphabet. This means that the bridge between letters and elements is one of numbers. Hydrogen, nitrogen, and oxygen respectively have number values of 1, 5, and 6. In the Hebrew alphabet only 3 letters have hidden number codes that match the mass for the elements of creation.

Through determining simple mass, the DNA may be replaced with letters of the Hebrew alphabet. Therefore our DNA may literally be a translatable alphabet within each of our cells. The Greek philosopher Plato once said that numbers are the way to describe our world through language.

All life is formed of combinations of four chemical compounds (DNA) and contain all information required to produce every form of life, from the smallest single-celled organism to the 100 trillion cells of a human being. In every cell of every life the name of God is revealed. Through various combinations of the four DNA bases - adenine, thymine, guanine, and cytosine, it becomes possible to create the substance of life from the name in our bodies.

Gregg Braden in **The God Code** states that TCGA are letters scattered along strands (C T A G) as the 4 elements of life. The DNA double helix is held together by hydrogen bonds between the bases attached to the two strands. The four bases found in DNA are adenine (abbreviated A), cytosine (C), guanine (G) and thymine (T). These four bases are attached to sugar/phosphate to form the complete nucleotide, as shown for adenosine monophosphate.

When these are plotted on a periodic chart, they are described as a number (Everything is a word and a number). The secret of ancient language is that all alphabets have a secret number tied to it. These are always the same. This is called Gematria (Numerology is a subset) as the science of applying numbers to letters. So numbers can describe the letters. And all languages can be related through the numbers. The rules are that numbers and letters are interchangeable. Numbers have no decimals and words equal in value have equal meaning. For example Soul is SNHS in Hebrew = 8 and Heaven is HSHMYM = 395 = 8 as Gematria reduced. If we use the letters for Hydrogen, Oxygen, Nitrogen, and Carbon and look at this we get the following table:

Element	H	O	N	C
Atomic Mass	1.00794	15.9994	14.00674	12.0107
Gematria #	1	5	6	3
Hebrew	H	V	Y	G

If we replace elements with letters we get YHVH = God = eternal = within the body (God eternal within the body). This works in other languages as the cement of traditional spirituality. So the suggestion is that every cell has everything coded into it – the complete library. What if you use the sounds of vowels to unite the name? What would this sound like? There is a code that instructs us to intone a Divine name Eeee Ahhhhh Ohhhh Ahhhh Eeee is the sound of YHVH. Sounds like the work Dr. Pillai is engaged in.

All carbon life bases contain some message/code. Who or whatever placed this message existed before us. God is within us to allow us Divinity. What we find is that when we clone, there is an essence (glue) missing in this code. Our name as a human is YHVG as different than God YHVH but all the tools are there to be chosen to be like a God YHVH. All you have to do is look at our section of the other 11 layers of DNA presented in a previous chapter.

Science has discovered a form of human excavated in Africa 150,000 years old. It looks like us so we all come from a common ancestor and then split to evolve OR we came from a fully intact human line. In 2000, science found we had 30,000 genes and about 300 separate from a mouse. In 1987 science discovered an ancient Neanderthal baby 30,000 years old and compared DNA. Test shows: *"results modern human has not descended from Neandertha.l"* This was never published but was confirmed later. We HAVE NOT evolved from that lineage. Humankind resulted from a fusion in the past that created the recipe for us. We have not changed in 160,000 years.

The Bible Code

To continue on this special encoding, let us look at another "word" phenomenon called the bible Code.

The **Bible code** also known as the **Torah code**, is a purported set of secret messages encoded within the Hebrew text of the Torah. This hidden code has been described as a method by which specific letters from the text can be selected to reveal an otherwise obscured message. Although Bible codes have been postulated and studied for centuries, the subject has been popularized in modern times because of computer technology.

So by creating one long string of letters from the complete Torah, you have to employ a computer to search through the whole sequence for these "codes" that are allegedly written by God the author of the first Hebrew Bible. The primary method by which purportedly meaningful messages have been extracted is the *Equidistant Letter Sequence* (ELS). To obtain an ELS from a text, choose a starting point (in principle, any letter) and a skip number, also freely and possibly negative. Then beginning at the starting point, select letters from the text at equal spacing as given by the skip number. For example, the bold letters in **this** **s**entence **f**orm **an** EL**S**. With a skip of −4 (that is, reading backwards every fourth letter), and ignoring the spaces and punctuation, the word *safest* is spelled out. Often more than one ELS related to some topic can be displayed simultaneously in an *ELS letter array*. This is produced by writing out the text in a regular grid, with exactly the same number of letters in each line, then cutting out a rectangle. In the example below, part of the King James Version of Genesis (26:5-10) is shown with 33 letters per line. ELSs for BIBLE and CODE are shown.

```
MYSTATUTESANDMYLAWSANDISAACDWELTI
NGERARANDTHEMENOFTHEPLACEASKEDHIM
OFHISWIFEANDHESAIDSHEISMYSISTERFO
RHEFEAREDTOSAYSHEISMYWIFELESTSAID
HETHEMENOFTHEPLACESHOULDKILLMEFOR
REBEKAHBECAUSESHEWASFAIRTOLOOKUPO
NANDITCAMETOPASSWHENHEHADBEENTHER
EALONGTIMETHATABIMELECHKINGOFTHEP
HILISTINESLOOKEDOUTATAWINDOWANDSA
WANDBEHOLDISAACWASSPORTINGWITHREB
EKAHHISWIFEANDABIMELECHCALLEDISAA
CANDSAIDBEHOLDOFASURETYSHEISTHYWI
FEANDHOWSAIDSTTHOUSHEISMYSISTERAN
DISAACSAIDUNTOHIMBECAUSEISAIDLEST
IDIEFORHERANDABIMELECHSAIDWHATIST
```

Normally only a smaller rectangle would be displayed, such as the rectangle drawn in the figure. In that case there would be letters missing between adjacent lines in the picture, but it is essential that the number of missing letters be the same for each line. Although the above examples are in English texts, Bible codes proponents usually use a Hebrew Bible text. For religious reasons, most Jewish proponents use only the Torah (Genesis-Deuteronomy). This is undoubtedly because the subsequent texts have been edited and changed by "mere mortals".

Once a specific word has been found as an ELS, it is natural to see if that word is part of a longer ELS consisting of multiple words. Code proponents Haralick and Rips have published an example of a longer, extended ELS, which reads, *"Destruction I will call you; cursed is Bin Laden and revenge is to the* Messiah" (though the Hebrew, using appositives in place of to be, lacking helper verbs, and employing definite articles less frequently, would entail far fewer words than the English phrasing). ELS extensions that form phrases or sentences are of interest. Proponents maintain that the longer the extended ELS, the less likely it is to be the result of chance.

It is said that there are many predictions here that are "coded" into the bible. These name people and events that could not have been known – unless the writers were in charge of the overall Life Plan! "Armageddon" is encoded in the Bible with the name of Syria's leader, Hafez Asad. In fact, the name of the actual site of the long-prophesied Final Battle appears with his name in a single skip sequence: "Armageddon, Asad holocaust." At the current time, there are many things encoded that has created a renewed interest. Syria" is encoded with "World War." It is the country that stands out, because it is not expected. "Russia" and "China" and "USA" all also appear with "World War." But they are the three superpowers most likely to be involved. "Syria" is the surprise. Barack Obama is prevalent.

One quite interesting prediction was in May 28, 2008, six months before the election of Barack Obama a letter through Oprah Winfrey stating three predictions: *"(1) You will win the Democratic nomination and become President; (2) You may, as a result of your victories, be assassinated but that danger can be prevented; (3) You can, as President, prevent an otherwise nearly certain nuclear terror attack."* You can check this out on http://www.thebiblecode.com/?p=10

"It comes from a source that predicted you would be President before the first vote was cast in Iowa," I told Obama citing the first primary on January 3, when he was practically unknown and given no chance. I am sending you this letter through your friend Oprah Winfrey because it may not reach you through regular channels," I wrote. "Also Oprah knows me and she knows the source of my information. A world-famous Israeli mathematician has discovered a code in the Bible that predicts events that happened thousands of years after the Bible was written."

On November 4, 2008 the first of the three predictions came true. Barack Obama became the first African-American to be elected President of the United States, an historic and improbable event that was encoded in the Bible more than 3000 years ago. Obama's victory was new, dramatic confirmation of the reality of the Bible Code, the secret text hidden in the Old Testament that reveals the future. When it happened, on November 4, it was a miracle, actually two miracles. An African-American had been elected President. And the Bible Code had predicted it almost a year in advance — in a text that was 3000 years old. The code had already predicted the elections of Bill Clinton and George Bush. It had already predicted the assassinations of both John and Robert Kennedy, and Israeli Prime Minister Yitzhak Rabin. Every detail of September 11, 2001 was encoded in the ancient text. The rise of Osama Bin Laden, the fall of Saddam Hussein, both Gulf Wars, were all in the code. Everything, from World War II to Watergate, from the

Holocaust to Hiroshima, from the Great Depression to the current global economic crisis, was encoded in the Bible.

Yet code proponents assert that names and events hidden in the Scripture can only now be revealed, in this modern Information Age, through computer searches of the Hebrew text. Supposedly, these codes contain secret predictions of events that have already come to pass, including the assassination of Egypt's Anwar Sadat and former Israeli Prime Minister Yitzhak Rabin; the Jewish Holocaust; the 1995 earthquake in Kobe, Japan; the first Gulf War; and the emergence of diseases such as AIDS and diabetes. They even predict an earthquake will strike Los Angeles in 2010.

What has sparked today's mushrooming interest in prophecy? Sensing that something is terribly wrong, many believe the world has reached what the Bible calls the "end-time" - or "last days." Millions routinely discuss prophetic terms such as "Anti-Christ," "Great Tribulation," "Millennium," "Armageddon," "Beast," "False Prophet," "God's Wrath," "Abomination of Desolation," and others that are written for the years 2015 and 2016.

The Word and Reality

Why do we bring this up? It is not to bring fear. It is to understand that these words from the beginning have energetic power and significance that we are just beginning to understand. Some people believe that there is something to these Bible codes while others consider them to be a total load of nonsense Of course this is all in dispute because the belief box is not yet ready to accept this information, despite the evidence.

But what is evolving rapidly in the world of "science" is a relook at things like miracles and subtle energies that have been in our face for thousands of years.

Numbers are universal. They are related to the numerous alphabets as a common denominator. A word has a description and that description gives us the vision of what it represents. A word is a vibration. Everything is described, perceived and understood through words or combinations of words. It is the mental body's means to experience reality through the senses and the brain so as to derive emotions centered in the heart. That is what the Soul does. Every word or combination also describes a morphogenic process of chemical, physiological, physical birth, evolution and behavior encoded in its DNA or determined by some higher intelligence. Is it surprising to think that the 95% of people who believe in a Higher Power can also believe that it started with the "word"? What are our thoughts? Combinations of words that represent images – all energy vibrations.

And is it surprising to think that this midbrain of ours that apparently houses the Soul mind, responsible for creating and presenting our reality can adjust that reality by the repetition of a word? The words may be different vibrations but the image presented attached to the word is not. If it is in charge of this holographic reality, it simply needs instructions to change the form of the projection and integrate it into the larger hologram. There is nothing new here. Our computers do this all the time. And where do you need to do this program change? In the place where the neo-cortex has no relevance; in the space of the midbrain where there is no time, space or identity to interfere with the Soul mind of infinite possibilities.

Let us now attempt to bring this all together.

17

HOW DOES IT ALL WORK?

"Free will is not what you think. It is the option to choose your characters and script in a life movie then forget you did, then make choices along that life path depending on how your mental and emotional energy bodies react to what you planned."

Aly McDonald   Ed Rychkun

> **To truly rise above the grand illusion**
> **We must first give up the great delusion**

Your physical reality is a **virtual immersion hologram** working the same way as that Second Life game was attempting to simulate. It of course is a very primitive example but it certainly makes a good example. Just add the Telepresence holographic ability to it. Let us now try to bring this all together.

You as a **Soul** are a spark of the Greater Consciousness subject to the life giving process of Spirit. You as a sub-director and creator of your life movie are following a scripted outline that you agree to as your **Life Plan** and **Soul contract** for the purpose of evolving your spiritual being by the deployment of virtues, at the same time evolving the Greater Mind and Consciousness that you are a quantum part of.

To do this you choose a costume and a personality in the form of a humanoid. And within this movie, you choose a purpose of expression, things to learn and a specific character to act within. As to many details of the movie, you worked with a Spirit Guide to incorporate the overall environments of growth processes in all living things to be available as program code in DNA and all evolving life forms to be **morphogenic processes** of purpose whenever required. Under this design, the DNA would contain all of the coded blueprints as the state of the art humanoid evolution which would be called forward into self-awareness and self-growth depending upon the purpose of the engagement in the Earth consciousness and the degree of *self evolution towards spiritual goals*. On a greater scale, you would depend upon millions of programs that create holographic representations of these morphogenic processes being able to run concurrently for you to interact with. Within that universal environment will run a global program to represent the composite consciousness of planet Earth which would set the evolving global environment and limitations of consensus reality within which your Life Plan immersion movie would run. It also as a live consciousness will self evolve reflecting the consensus reality that is being observed and collapsed into a holographic Earth Movie that sets the limits and setting for all Life Plans.

Once the movie began, you are presented with these scenes, characters and events to interact with, interacting between set scenes and situations, yourself choosing how to perceive, react and act. As it would proceed, each moment would be captured through the two unique features of the humanoid – mental and emotional energies - stored in a new movie within the Causal Body which would become your **Life** to experience a **Game Of Life** within the **Earth consciousness**.

In the case of the human vessel, it would be composed of a set of energy bodies that would be subject to five key stages of human evolution.

The Stages Of Human Evolution For The Soul

The morphogenic process as it unfolds in the brain and body is the same in all. This process however includes both the energetic and the physical bodies. As we have learned, it is the brain mind that is the CEO of the mental body, and the heart is the CEO of the emotional body. The brain has the dual responsibility to play out the life plan immersion movie to create external reality, and to control the internal reality of the body so as to allow survival and evolution. The evolutionary stages that all humanoids by design evolve through from birth to death is one that phases from material reality to non-material spirituality and the ever increasing awareness of many expanding conscious minds. That design is a result of some higher intelligence of the Greater Consciousness that continues to evolve through the expression of all of its participants in an ever evolving consciousness of all creation.

Within the humanoid form so represented by the holographic programs is a master set of morphogenic processes, order and purpose that specifies the evolution, growth and behaviour of the humanoid vessel. Like the process of growth and evolution from a cell, to a baby to an infant to adulthood, the vessel follows a natural progression of evolution as chosen by the mental and emotional choices taken within the Game of Life. These determine the degree and timing of the opening of the vessel's characteristics and abilities all stored within DNA. These stages are illustrated in the picture below.

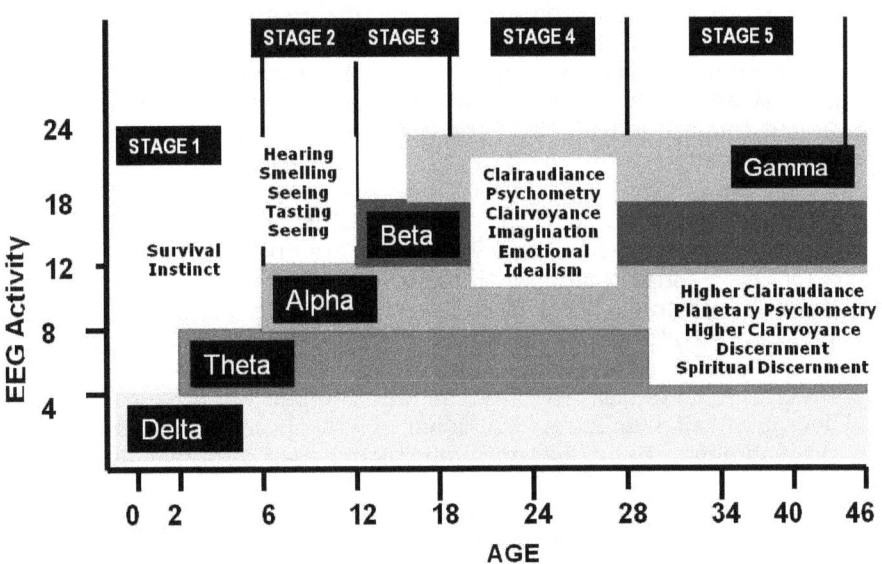

The first stage is during Delta and Theta before the age of six. Here the brain must get "its programs together" to develop the hard core environment survival habits through perception and response. It has to get this done as a foundation before the Self-conscious awareness kicks in to add the ego and the intellect. As this evolution progresses, programs that are required for the vessel to function and survive in the immediate family consciousness within the Earth Hologram are developed. They are loaded from DNA into the vessel's subconscious.

The second stage of 6-12 occurs during the Alpha and Beta phase, the self identity matures, as does the education received become discriminated upon before it enters into the belief and perception-response behavior. The primary senses of smell, hearing, tasting, seeing, smelling and perception are dominant. As these abilities are called out of DNA, the vessel learns to function within the local consciousness within the Earth hologram to create and build the abilities to apply the mental and physiological programs in order to function and survive.

The third stage of 12-18 is one where physical changes to complete the reproductive system occur. Clearly this is the Physical Body evolution. The primary senses of smell, hearing, tasting, seeing, smelling and perception become heightened. Here the discriminatory process of free will and choices should maintain a life of positive energies, continuously radiating these through the heart chakra and the morphic field. When this happens as time progresses, those parts of us that are quantum in nature such as the brain, consciousness, light body, chakras, heart, DNA, and cells begin to show themselves. As we have come to understand these are the powerful forces of the heart, namely love and compassion. If this evolution is curtailed by the choice of low energy components of the chakra functions, these are blocked and rendered dysfunctional. The attributes and abilities, like psychic abilities that are stuck in the chakras for example, cannot develop and the appropriate connection channel to the quantum space of infinite possibilities cannot be opened.

The fourth stage of 18-28 is one which takes us into the awareness of the Astral Body where the heightened five senses are opened. It takes about 28 years for the astral body to mature. These higher abilities include clairaudience (astral hearing), psychometry (astral touch/feeling), clairvoyance (astral sight), imagination (astral equivalent of taste), and emotional idealism (astral equivalent of smell). This is the true spiritual awareness that shifts from the head mind to the heart mind and it is where the knowing of self awareness at a higher mental and emotional body comes into development. The Soul and the Higher Self become part of the evolutionary process of the human vessel. If these are not opened to awareness, they simply lie dormant within DNA and are not triggered into the residency of the subconscious inventory of programs.

The fifth stage is 28-46 to midlife shift when family and relationships become paramount. During this stage assuming the Astral awareness is perused, new five senses of the mental body open, such as higher clairaudience (mental hearing), planetary psychometry (mental feeling), higher clairvoyance (mental sight), discernment (mental equivalent of taste), and spiritual discernment (mental equivalent of smell). These then open to the Higher Mind of the Manasic Body, Christic Body, Atmic Body, Monadic Aspect, Logoic, God/Goddess and Solar Aspects in full revelation. During this stage of evolution, the Higher Self and the Soul become an integral part of the lower mind and the heart mind takes its position as the controlling energy. The ego mind atrophies and the heart mind unfolds into the lower reality becoming one with the greater consciousness. It is a time of great spiritual awakening and engagement as all realities, lives, and nature of the games of life become an integral part of the vessel and Soul's evolution. The additional layers and programs within DNA open to awareness and intent.

If you look more closely at this sequence, it follows the human chakra system starting from the bottom (Root) to the top (Crown). We see each stage of evolution taking about 4 years.

Age 0-4 Root Learning to be earthed, walking sense of stability, resilience without fear of isolation.

Age 5—8 Sacral Learning relationship with others and security, understanding personal boundaries, attaining balance from harmonious relationships.

Age 8-12 Solar Plexus Learning to be unique and special, make judgment calls as to what is correct for your personality.

Age 12-16 Heart Learning heart love and devotion, through the seat of emotions. Learning to balance and express emotions freely to love, partnership and understand roles as giver/receiver of love.

Age 16-20 Throat Learning throat expression following the passion to the heart. Becoming balanced to act in faith in an energetic way and achieve full maturity.

Age 20-24 3rd Eye Learning insight intuition, intellectual. Moving into the world then the seeing through the spiritual eye as deductive, rational, and loyal.

Age 24-28 Crown Being One with cosmos gaining a rich insight into who we are. Replacing desire by will and a sense of comfort as to who you are.

Thus, having taken the tour of life through the first four stages of Delta, Theta, Alpha, and Beta, one would have to develop the stimulus-response systems to be able to live in all four as if they were in the Theta range to thus be a properly evolved human totally aware of its Light Body overlay that gives it life, and directly connects with the Higher Intelligence or Force through what its makeup is - love.

It is the third stage where one has a tendency to deprive oneself of the next steps of evolution of the Light Body-Being. It is stunted because it evolves to the level of self-awareness as ego-intellect by choosing limiting negative energies and limits its final entry into the heart brain and the quantum field.

Now here is the crux.

At the age of 28 one may easily become stuck in the mud within the Physical Plane with the limiting beliefs of the global community. In a world of negativity, and accommodation to the lower self of ego totally dependent on the CEO brain at the top of the body, you may become fully trained to run on all the subconscious programs of the past. That is the old mind as it becomes stuck in the lower expression of the body anatomy. The next stages and the awareness of the heart brain and the Astral step of the Soul's evolution simply atrophy or stays undeveloped until awakened.

Once your evolution takes you to that place around 28 when you are fully developed, you really become like a new kid in the kindergarten school of the immaterial world. That world that allows you full creatorship with your mind, from a higher energetic self simply is not developed, the system goes into default awareness and you create the way you learned; hard work manipulating matter with those primitive tools of creation. Until the new kid at 28 learns about who he really is, just like going to kindergarten at age 5, he must attain a level above the lower primitive mind to be able to handle the ability to instantly create reality responsibly within the light of a spiritual foundation.

And so we see nudging and occasional unexplained miracles occurring as a reminder with those that have touched the fringe of this third level truth, but become stuck there in total ignorance of their Higher Light body. It is what the group consciousness appears to have entrenched in its subconscious mind.

How Does It All Work?

When you came here to experience the world of a lower form, namely a body, you came here to expand the Greater Mind of the Universe. Just like an individual cell comes to expand through its environment to become more adaptive and to expand the whole of the body, the community of humanity as a cell in the bigger body came here to expand the Greater Consciousness. The task was to experience the wonders of this world in a lower form of physical vibration.

The means of evolution and expression would be through the creation of a Life Plan Consciousness that would be played out in the Earth Game. This plan would be created by free will of the Soul and its Soul Family with a

Spirit Guide attuned to the means of holographic representation of the reality to be engaged in. The plan best suited to the displacement of the karmic balance accumulated by the Soul through its incarnations would be the focus of the Plan – to deploy and learn virtues of love, compassion and forgiveness. This life plan would engage the Soul Family in a contractual plan to build a complex network of life pathways that would include the players, events, environments, exit points, triggers of awakening, and all of the details as required from birth to death that would support the learning of lessons, the development of virtues, and the resolution of karmic needs if so desired. Such a Life Plan would be loaded into the Earth Game Consciousness that would provide the means of its expression being limited to the beliefs of that group consciousness, yet allowing the evolution beyond that consciousness.

The design of the Life Plan to be played out within the constructs of the Earth Game would provide many life paths, situations, and lessons that would be available at choice points. These choice points would be taken by free will of the lower mind through thoughts, belief, perceptions and emotions chosen at the time. The design of the Life Plan would include the Soul family constructed in such a way that all participating would have the opportunity to advance the Greater Consciousness beyond the state of the DNA blueprint. In so being designed the Life Plan would contain a lower material path and a higher spiritual path with many paths in between.

Within the Life Plan and the Earth Game there would be the processes of divine order, purpose and growth of all life forms so interacting with each other so as to survive and evolve according to their designs. Each energy that would be given life through spirit would behave according to the evolving blueprints of DNA, reflecting the sum total of the evolving life form. As part of the Soul's purpose, the Earth Game would provide the means to evolve beyond that DNA blueprint holding the status of the evolution of Greater Consciousness.

In order to allow the Game to unfold, the vessels so chosen in terms of form, characteristics and structure would be presented through the human brain and heart in holographic form so acquired depending on the nature of and timing of the astral configuration of the planet energies. This process of higher to lower creation would allow the lower form to congeal into the holographic reality.

The nature of the Human Game would be to use the mental and emotional gifts to show feelings from experience (even love, horror) in the form of rational mental choices through the brain and inner emotional feelings through the heart. The rules of the Human Game engagement would be necessary to begin at a lower level of incarnation into matter and thus forget who they are and be a body. It would be necessary to believe hologram as real and allow the physics, emotions, and mental abilities of the lower form to engage in the holographic reality within the construct of the Life Plan, upon the stage of the Earth Game and to evolve according to choices of mental and emotional attributes by way of virtues.

To undertake this task, you in the form of a Soul in a Light Body, took the job to grow and evolve within the scope of DNA which would provide you with a basic morphogenic template in lower form. This lower form evolved a brain and senses that had a primary function of creating a holograph of reality and like the cells that are all individual complete mini humans, the holograph would be a mini world within a larger holograph created by the community of humans as a joint consciousness and a joint hologram. This joint hologram would form the basis for a joint belief system forming the global mindset within which the limitations of it would preside over the behavior. Imposed upon these would be the Universal hologram as a larger composite of divine intelligence which would dictate the morphogenic rules of order, process, purpose and growth to be played out in the holographic projection process of engagement.

Thus as with cells, each being a part of the whole, yet themselves whole individuals, each could experience their own hologram of reality. Although the hologram of reality would appear to be on the outside, it would be on the inside, so created by the midbrain. In order to experience this, the brain had been evolved to initially be specifically concerned with developing survival habits within which the human form could prosper and feel the world of bliss. And so to experience this, the humanoid was given the power of thought, vision, words and emotion to choose how these would be used to further this expansive mission.

In order to keep a connection to its own Whole and the Greater Intelligence that it was a part of, the Light Body (Soul and Higher Self) would overlay the human form and it would contain interfaces that would be the connectivity between the lower form and the higher Divine Intelligence from where it came. All would be centered on the heart as the seat of emotion where the Chakra system of subtle energies would interface to specific physical organs and functions but being sensitive to the cosmic signals that would allow the use and expansion of higher abilities. This system would interface with all of the light body energy systems of auras, meridians, chakras, and various energy vortexes. All would be centered on the heart energy system where the center of all would reside.

Because the nature of the reality would be formed through holograms of projections by observation, the process of it so doing was made of the quantum energy which in its primary form is not matter congealed into particles but in the form of waves and vibrational patterns. Thus the Light body and its components would have to behave according to quantum laws, while that formed body and its reality would have to appear as physical particles following a different form of physical laws. The interface between the two would be part quantum, and part perceived as physical illusion. Thus the brain and heart would contain such interfaces but appear to be physical. The greater connector would be the consciousness which was the mind divided into self consciousness, consciousness and subconsciousness which would be interfaces as the quantum connection.

The responsibilities and processes of these would be to first provide a rapid adaptation of the human vessel to its environment through the subconscious and the brain. This stage would bring an awareness of its perceived reality so as to evolve, adapt the human vessel to this perception of reality. Drawing from its first two layers as DNA blueprints, the human vessel through the physical brain and subconscious could draw on instincts to quickly adapt to its environment in an interactive stimuli-response system.

Then at a specific age around 6 years, the vessel would enter the awareness of its lower self. Here it would enter the second evolutionary stage to bring on the self consciousness that would develop the intelligence of self uniqueness and self pursuit of joy within the growing human vessel in relation to its perceived environment. This would engage free will discernment, intelligence and ego as centered in the brain. The free will would allow the thoughts, perceptions and emotions to be chosen. Here new survival systems of adaptation and self growth would be built upon the first stage of development. Through this period, new skills, habits and abilities would be developed to create a uniqueness of self, centered on the self-consciousness.

Having formed the second stage platform, the third and subsequent stages of evolution would be to open to its spiritual connection in the quantum through the awareness of the Astral body. This particular pursuit could only be achieved by being in a sea of love that, as its Higher Self as the Light Body, the Divine Intelligence and the quantum sea of infinite possibilities was made up of. It would require a shift from the ego-brain to the heart-brain into the energetic realm, thus opening an awareness, the Higher Self of Light Body. If this shift to the awareness of the Astral Body did not occur, the individual would remain in the ego-brain limited physical environment.

At the center of the system would sit the means of creating matter from non matter as a torroid centered on the heart. This would reflect the translation of non matter light waves into matter as particles so projected in the personal holographic plate within each vessel, but part of the whole. And so various vortexes and torroids would project from and contain the body as itself a holographic projection. In order to shape realty, the human would have the power to choose (free will) and to create within the laws so set upon the reality created. It would have the ability to learn how to change its holographic reality once a level of maturity was reached, that being total awareness of Higher self and the Soul-Light Body.

To give the human the ability to create reality, the energetic system of chakras with its vortexes of congealing and attraction were provided to create, interface and receive energies that would be created as packets of energy signatures projected into the quantum sea. These chakra centers would allow the transmutation of energy from above to below or from Heaven to Earth through thought, vision, words (above), emotion as balance, and intent, relations, and matter below. Each of these would be an energy signature that would be projected like a funnel out into the local energetic heart field so as to attract energies of likeness into the field. At the same time the energies from outside the field could be drawn in as waves to spiral in concentrating to congeal into matter by way of entanglement and collapsing to create the reality so projected upon the individual holographic plate inside but yet part of the whole. This process would not work unless the interface between the Light Body and the Human Body was entrenched in its belief system and the awareness of its quantum essence was known, as well as beingness within the sea of its basic make up of the love vibration.

This level of maturity was conditional upon holding the human vessel in terms of both body and mind in the quantum sea of love, centered on the heart, the body commanded by the heart-brain. This process was not only contingent upon letting go of the perceived reality so created as an illusion, but living within that reality in alignment with that higher wave length frequency so created as love and bliss. This would mean that in order to achieve this status, the self-consciousness and consciousness would have to be set aside in a continuous behavior of lower self (physical reality illusion) in order to be one with its Higher Self within the quantum space of love vibrations.

Otherwise, the lower form would be unknowing to how its reality was created and it would live in its lower self and form, not able to express properly through its higher form. It would be subject to the lower physical laws and be held captive within its self-consciousness and have little to say about proactively changing its reality. And although it would in truth be creating its reality, it would not know how to create outside of the time and space limitations not existent in the quantum space from which it came and from where it became what it is as a perfection of love. This lower life would not be able to draw upon the higher vibrational instincts, abilities so provided in the brain, chakras and DNA, or the knowing and truths within the Light Body memory fields.

In order to draw upon these knowing and truths of a Higher Self, it would be through a conduit of communication through a field of love and compassion. Otherwise the field cannot listen because it is like a radio tuner that if not set at the right frequency, it simply cannot be received. Central to this is that this channel cannot open when there is some hidden agenda or ulterior motive involved typically centered in the ego-brain dominant from the second stage of human evolution. Through design of the heart, and its central power of love emotion, when compassion and love of human energy would be enfolded by strong emotion of joy or bliss, it would add to the strength of the field channel as in superposition of waves. In this respect, words and prayer would be the traditional way of opening communications to the Divine Intelligence. If not the communications are not heard when there is no energy from the heart.

This would not mean that the human could not manifest reality from within the scope of the lower form of human; the universal laws of Karma, Cause and Effect and the Law of Attraction are at work regardless of whether the heart, love, or positive well being is in the field of creation. Even stuck in the second stage of evolution, the human could follow the traditional path of creating things and reality by making or constructing according to the limitations of the group consciousness. Here where emotion is attached there would be a tendency to attract likeness through the same system. In the case of by-passing this traditional route and bending this reality as in the healing miracles and rapid creation of reality, a level of love based spiritual maturity would be required to take responsibility and to open the channel.

What would be the case of human stuck in stage three would be default creation and random success of such things as miracles because the human would not have yet elevated above the level of the conscious mind and the physical brain. To fall into default would also fall into the limitations of the global consciousness. And by default, the lessons of other lives would have not taken the awareness to a higher understanding self, allowing the past to influence the future, creating a reality by default. The brain in its primary design has a chore to learn survival within the hologram that it learns to create. This evolves from instincts to survive at the Delta and Theta level to where there is self consciousness at the age of 6. This brings about a selfness or ego and the ability to think and choose the survival programs that are stored in the subconscious. The evolution, if not continued focuses on selfish behavior patterns which minimize the programming into consciousness so the individual falls back to survival mode with the added ego intellect to drive its purposes and reality.

The next evolution, which can be curtailed if the Lower Self is dominant, is the avoidance of the heart brain and the evolution to the love based sea of the quantum. Although the brain and consciousness allow one to open this path by way of free will, once the ego brain is entrenched and a lower form belief system is embedded, the means of overcoming this becomes more and more difficult, and the motivation and understanding becomes more and more remote.

In a Near Death Experience, by way of design of Divine Intelligence, a window would become available for the consciousness dominated by the second stage ego-brain could look at itself after letting go of its mortal lower self and facing its higher Light Body. The process of Out Of Body would allow a portal to open to this higher knowledge at any time. Here the stages can be overcome because the reality of the human being is something else than a body, as the Light Body Being of pure divine consciousness. This becomes a stark reality as does the encounter with the Higher Being in that sea of love. Re-entry into the body can have spectacular reprogramming consequences to change reality and the meaning of life, but as old habits may be deep, various triggers can reconstitute old programs and habits to undo what was a miracle. This is also so in a miracle healing where if the old programs and memories are chosen to come into awareness and consciousness, they can undo what has been done.

Just as a prayer cannot be heard if it is not in the morphic field of love, so is the subtle energy field of quantum not opened until an awareness is brought into consciousness. Similarly, the access into the quantum field for the purpose of direct creation and manifestation of reality is inaccessible until the spiritual awareness of the true self is embraced.

By design, the total human bodies (physical and light energy) combine physical and quantum through the holographic reality. If we can look forward into that third phase of natural design and get a grasp of the quantum nature of part of us, then one can say that the heart torroid field would represent the center of the zeropoint quantum field. Here in the Above to Below process is where the mind stuff like thoughts, images, words from consciousness is slurped down into heart to draw from the vortexes positioned at each chakra the possibilities from the quantum field outside to suck it into reality as the Below chakras congeal the possibilities into reality. We now see this place of the heart-mind as the point of all creation within us. It is the place of no-thing, in the quantum field of infinite possibilities which must be entered into in some way in order to truly take control of the creation process that makes imagination and reality one consciousness. It cannot be done from the brain-mind which is responsible for the lower binary plane of 3D.

This by design creates the point of access at the heart to be zeropoint or zero. In the binary computer system 0 represents off - no access to the quantum field and the Light Body, just like the first two steps of our evolution is all we get to, not activating those higher abilities that give us the truths about the quantum nature of us, our light Body and the Universe of infinite possibilities from where we can draw a holographic reality.

The binary computer simply turns things off at a bit of 0. The quantum computer now brings in the qubit that is on (1), off (0) or both, still not providing access to zeropoint. The trinary computer comes closer where the trits (three bits) are -1, 0, +1 where now we are getting to the photon level of the quantum field. We would say that this is more like our human system where 0 is the access point to zeropoint and the +1 and -1 represent the negative - positive states, like masculine - feminine that represent the states to be entangled and collapsed into reality.

Just like the brain has a local and a nonlocal data base which reflects the whole, so does the brain have a local and a nonlocal illusion of reality. This reality becomes a holographic plate projection inside, which operates from the brain central processor much like all of the automatic internal and external survival processes that become saved into the subconscious quantum mind.

Under the binary two phases of evolution this automatic process uses all sensory equipment, including unbeknown to the second stage human, the higher automatic sensing abilities of the Light body. These simply operate on auto pilot in a stimuli-response mode to develop behavior patterns and the holographic projection of reality.

Upon opening to the third and fourth stages of Higher Self awareness from the heart mind-brain, the new entry point into the zeropoint quantum fields of infinite possibilities opens. Thus when this is engaged in, the higher abilities begin to open so that changing the holographic realty opens. Through design, one first brings forward a thought then creates a clear image in the mind's eye, then with the assistance of the heartfelt emotion to enfold the vision directs the downward causation to engage the process of subconscious reprogramming and then projecting it to a place of materialization on the internal holographic plate through the physical apparatus of the brain, nervous system and cells. A holographic image is thus created in a proactive mode the same way a holographic image is created with beams of light that are split, reflected and converged again. It is whatever you see clearly that your brain understands and has meaning for or memory of. It is your brain that does the final work as a material representation by retrieving what it knows and what cosmic rules apply in the material representation. It retrieves information given by the subconscious as directed from the Higher self or Soul and the cosmic rule simply "knows" what it is. The brain is now driven to entangle this new reality into the existing reality.

This process of evolution calls for the letting go of the current lower reality, entering the space of total silence and being in the heart mind of pure love. Here is where the gateway to the quantum soup of infinite possibilities exists and is the place of residency of the Soul and the Higher Self where the mind of pure consciousness and thought are engaged to effect downward causation. It is where the truth of self rises above illusion of the Game and the limitations of the Earth Game Consciousness.

This means that the Divine Mind totally unencumbered by the lower reality of physicality must be the total agent of the image of some object, event, or situation that is simply created in the mind's eye as a clear image formed from infinite possibilities. As this image that reflects a new possibility is surcharged by emotion of joy and gratitude for its engagement and completion, it carries with it the instructions to subconscious and the brain to adjust the hologram in accordance with the programs in DNA for internal reconstruction or the programs of natural order for external reconstruction of reality.

But remember that our design is to discern through the mental body what is truth – so reflected through the brain mind, and use feeling and emotion through the emotional body to discern what is truth – so reflected through the heart mind and physical body. This is the key to creating the signatures in the brain and in the quantum field. As these emotions become stronger, or are reinforced by continued action within the higher planes the appropriate physical holographic mechanisms as directed to the brain begin the process of transformation thereby adjusting physicality to meet the new reality. This occurs by way of direct manifestation or by way of attracting the like signatures that exist as potentialities within the quantum field and bringing these into the projected holographic reality.

This occurs from the quantum field, from a wave form to an atomic form as the electrons arrange themselves into the image which is your higher consciousness choosing a new possibility from the no-thing. From above, this is truly the process of mind over matter rather than the process now accepting limiting creatorship of matter over mind. The resultant holographic "materialization" is conducted by the human brain that takes the directives from the higher vibratory mind of consciousness to create the hologram of the external world, or to instigate the appropriate systems internally to the physical body to meet the requirements of this higher command.

It is all just a holographic movie that can be changed by the Director using visions, words and emotions. And who is that Director as the Divine Programmer? You as a Soul because you are Divine.

Creating Miracles Recap

Before we bring forward a composite process as a base, let us review what we suggested in **The Divine Programmer: Creating Miracles**.

We found that there were common processes to all of the Healers and Wealth Gurus whether it is regression, hypnosis, ritual, meeting the healer;

it is one of getting by the conscious mind to be in some form of Altered State. We have determined that the best place to be in this Altered State is in the powerhouse of the heart, the largest morphic field, the balance center, the center of love, and the center of creation. This we found provides the gateway to the quantum field of new potential realities where the Divine Programmer and some form of Divine Intervention is deployed. We see here that belief, trust, love, acceptance, surrender, faith, desire, worthy, miracle minded, positive outcome, compassion, and trustworthiness of a Higher Force is repeated over and over in different ways. So in view of what we have learned, we can suggest the type of environmental setting that we should be in.

Well being is a natural setting to be in because we have heard how the cells, the brain, the heart all can be fooled because they do not know the difference between imagined and "real". We have seen that negative thoughts and emotions are toxic environmental stimulants that chain react affecting the body in a cascade of negative problems. We have presented the mind and body plans to reduce those 60% toxic thoughts and the toxic food that invades the system.

A belief that one is worthy, that they can change our reality, faith in the Higher Power and a trust that it shall be done by a Higher Power, one has set the stage for a shift to occur. From the Gurus point of view, love and compassion without hidden motive is crucial. In this case you are going to be the reality changer so you must assume the role of the Higher Authority so you must believe you can be the facilitator yourself.

Love is the common catalyst to all the systems we have reviewed. It, we believe is the computer language that is written in the form of forgiveness, unity, compassion, gratitude and faith and trust. Love is a surrender to a higher power to bring your desires to you, to manifest from the quantum field a new possibility to be collapsed into reality.

Being present to the heart where we go inside, means being present to the heart field of love. It is a simple practice but places your attention away from the higher interfering brainwaves of consciousness into the lower state and centering your attention to the heart energetic center. Here is the heart mind consciousness which provides the gateway to the quantum field of infinite possibilities.

Entering the Void with the heart mind totally present allows entry to the void, the quantum field of all possibilities. To become unified with this field many different procedures were deployed but absolute coherence with this field of love is required, where no identity, no space, time or thing exists, only pure thought of the greater consciousness. In quantum, love is the glue that holds things together as the ultimate communication medium to all that is. It is the universal pattern of resonant energy.

Creating the new possibility from the quantum field revealed that the usual process brings the thought of the desired change in belief, perception or reality into vision as completed and energizes it with fullness of heart emotion of gratitude so as to supercharge it into the field. When this works, the result is to create a healing miracle or attract a new reality from the field that is the effect of the new cause.

We have found that thoughts, visions and emotions have morphic fields, as does the consciousness of you or a group. Once you believe and embody something, you link into a power grid of the morphic field. That is where healing occurs as you are in resonance with it and into an enormous database of universal energy.

Recap Of Above To Below Process

The following is a recap, consolidating the process of health and wealth together as it relates to the energetic chakra system, and is in fact the way we create reality within the limitations of the group consciousness as reflected and controlled by your chosen programs within the subconscious. The way this is done following the chakra energy centers within the consciousness rules is this; Bring a thought or idea into awareness, create a vision, communicate a plan to achieve it, enfold it with passion, act on launching the plan, select the relationships to achieve the plan and materialize it into reality.

1. THOUGHT At the top of the "Above" is thought initiated in the Crown Chakra. In the altered state, it is here that the scene is set to affirm your beliefs as you say. "I believe in healing miracles. I Believe I am worthy. I believe I can heal myself, and I believe in a Higher Power that will assist me." As you are in an altered state, in control of the conscious mind, you have a direct access to the subconscious. Here it is best to affirm to it what you believe in case it has some other ideas about sabotaging your process.

2. VISION Create a clear vision in your 3rd eye chakra of the desired result. In your conscious mind, create a clear picture of what the desired result would be.

3. SPEAK From the Throat Chakra speak out stating that you are asking for Higher Divine Intelligence assistance to manifest your vision. Here you are well aware of the issue and are going to rely on the Divine Intelligence to determine a solution, rather than regression to find the source. Affirm out loud to the heart and the Universe what you desire in simple concise statements. Be clear and concise, aligned with the energy of your vision.

4. HEART EMOTION As we drop into the Heart Chakra, this is where you put the vision into the quantum field. With the vision of the desired result clearly in your mind, bring in the emotion of your total being vibrating in a state of bliss and joy. Form a clear picture of this as your gladness is full and be surrounded by that joy. Linger here in a field of total peace, love and harmony as you place this vision into the morphic field of the heart.

5. FOCUS AND INTENT At the Solar Plexus Chakra we initiate the process of intention energy for shifting the condition or manifesting the desire. At this stage one would call upon their Higher Self, Divine Intelligence, or whatever you feel comfortable with to launch the intent. *"I as my Higher Self ask for the releasement, cleansing and healing of (my issue, belief, perception, situation) call upon Divine Intelligence to assist me. I release that which is not perfection and ask it to be replaced with the vision I have enfolded in my heart."* Because you are centered on love, you would create a resonance with emotion of completion making it strong. The vision of completion is paramount. The energy of gratitude and joy opens the communication channel to the zeropoint quantum field of infinite possibilities (the Universe).

6. HIGHER POWER At the Sacral Chakra dedicated to relationships, the next step is the request for Higher Assistance so as to recompile the program created in the subconscious. In looking back into the Healers' processes we found that there are many different words used to summon this assistance. Divine, Spirit, Higher Power, Spirits, Guides, God, Source Creator, and Source are used but they all obviously work. The key, however, is that regardless of what you use, you must believe this Higher Power does have the power, and you must summon assistance. The key is to open the love channel to believe in a Higher Power to instigate within the Universe, the possibilities of your desire. This is a release to the Universe and a detachment from the results.

When we recap what our Healers said about getting Assistance for the Divine Intervention, we find the following. This is where the condition is released and you surrender to the Higher Power so it does what it needs to do. We effectively are entangling the two issues and desire so as to allow the new possibility of the emotionalized desire to collapse into a new reality, by releasing it. It is the Observer's intent launched in the previous step that converts particulate matter to its wave form and wave back to matter, the released energy to conform to our purpose and desire. This is the letting go where we send our information into the universe without attachment. This process releases the diseased condition through a connection, not separation. *"When you accept and love the parts of yourself you want to reject or change, you create the opportunity to discover the positive life force behind them."* We make ourselves at One with the quantum field.

7. MATERIAL MANIFESTATION At the 7th Chakra dedicated to the materialization, we hold on to our truth of completion, with an unfettered faith and trust in the Higher Power. It is fulfilled by the powerful feeling of gratitude that surrounds the vision of completion. This is where the vortexes will attract various energy signatures, people, events and situations into your reality. In cases where this works, we find the appropriate instructions are infused from above to reprogram, retrieve, or program the necessary physiological steps to create a healing miracle, or through continued repetition attract the appropriate like reality to balance an effect with a new Cause.

The Keys: Belief, Acceptance And Surrender

It would not be appropriate if we did not bring in some new revelations in our quest that has been focused on figuring out how this reality creation process works. We will summarize the key findings shortly but perhaps the easiest way to say this in simple terms is that it is the belief, acceptance and surrender to a new outcome that governs the way reality is managed. These three elements are common to every system we have looked at.

Whether we studied an Energy Healer, Doctor, Shaman, Medicine man, Saint, Miracle Maker, Faith Healer, God, Christ the Universe, the Force the Greater Intelligence, or whatever, it was always the depth of belief, acceptance and surrender to that new outcome that dictated the result. It was the trust and faith in that person that made people believe that the new outcome would come true. And the process that was used whether it was a ritual, a sweat lodge, energy healing, prayer, faith meeting, placebo, pills, holistic remedies, or whatever, it was a process that added the emotion of engagement to enforce the process of belief and surrender to a new outcome, which in their mind was already a reality.

And the process of surrender was letting go of that which was the old reality, surrendering to the possibility of a new, letting go of it and trusting that the new had already been done – thank you very much! In all cases, the individuals had to get out of the belief box of the prevailing consciousness which had been programmed into their own subconscious by their brains. To do this, they had to be led into the space of love, out of the influence of the lower reality, away from the brain mind, and into the quantum field where their Higher Self, Soul and assisting entities could be communicated with.

How have we seen people attain these states where it is proactive managing of reality? Well, the best examples are all the miracles of religions – the Saints who dedicated their lives to letting go of the needs of the lower form. Letting go to Saints means not considering the material world as dictated by survival of the ego, to offer instead themselves in a perpetual state of being of giving and forgiveness, and to continually pray and stay in that heart-mind of quantum field where miracles unexplained were possible to bring into reality. The altered state, the well being, the belief, acceptance and surrender to a deity who had the power to do this was the entry into this higher state of being.

When you begin to look around at all the people we have highlighted in these books we have referred to, we see this same pattern of leading patients into these states, being that figure that acts as a facilitator of credibility to always activate the same process. That process from what we have seen is to follow the above to below chakra energies of creation as mind over matter, to bring a thought into clear vision, communicate it into the field, surround it with emotion of completion and being grateful for its manifestation. That process from what we have seen is through the higher consciousness, down into subconscious, into the brain to create the neural signature, and the execution of it through the cells, or the rewriting of the holographic programs of the external reality

In all this, proactive control of these subtle energies and creating reality, we can dedicate our entire life as the priests did, meditate on the mountain top as the monks did, or we may find that we already have a natural ability or we can work with a facilitator and create the faith and trust required. We can also launch a plan to revitalize our fourth stage evolution and begin a regular routine which simply solidifies the belief and acceptance and surrender to yourself as the Divine Programmer to change your reality.

The Key Findings

From all that we have studied we see that this higher command is not within the hologram which contains our worlds, our material realities, our lives, our bodies. It has to be outside of it. That is a process of letting go and releasing that which is our conscious world of time, identity, space, and addictions to mortal life. This enforces the downward causation process being executed from a higher place. Whether you call this your Higher Self, Soul, Being of Light is not relevant. It is simply you in a higher state of vibration as energy not particles. Whether this higher space is heaven or the void or whatever you want to call it is irrelevant. It is simply a place where there is no time, no space, no identity and dominated by peace and silence.

From all that we have studied we see that the higher commander is your mind in its state of energy that directs the processes through downward causation through consciousness as a quantum segment of the whole. Here mental and emotional directives are created to adjust the reality hologram. This process of creation is centered on thoughts, vision, words and emotion as the triggers that direct the brain to institute the changes.

From all that we have studied, we see that the higher command process follows a plan of life that has been predetermined as the default until such time as the evolution of the physical being becomes aware of its counterpart as pure energy of consciousness. Then it has access to limitless possibilities that it can attract or shift into the reality which is being played out.

From all that we have studied we see that the process of change becomes more and more difficult with age and with surrender to that which has been programmed as reality into a personal belief box registered as subconscious programs. Although the catalysts to change are thoughts, visions, words and emotion, these must be instituted more and more by regimented practice and hence instilling of acceptance and belief that controls the degree of suggestibility to the subconscious mind.

From all that we have studied we see that the process of change in reality is within self and whether the holographic constructs of pills, doctors, healers, God, rituals, potions, spells, gods, angels, or the likes are deployed as facilitators, they are essentially irrelevant as it is the mind that is the true healer. These may be effective, however, as *initial* facilitators. Because of the current belief system, processes that are physical constructs as named above are the lower means to change reality that are accepted without question and therefore prevail within the scope of the consensus reality.

From all that we have studied we see that the process of creating new reality outside of the norm involves the thought being brought into conscious awareness from being in the realm of quantum possibilities, bringing the thought of the new possibility into conscious awareness, the clear vision of completion being created to be collapsed into reality, the use of mantras and words and the surcharging of the vision by the emotion of the completion. It is best facilitated by the intention to be in this new reality and the enfolding of this reality with gratitude for its creation. This is done from a Higher energetic form in the as above so below Causal process from the Causal Body.

From all that we have seen, the process of creation is going on all the time, through the process of thoughts and feeling. It shifts in causation from material upwards, and then at the age of 28, is prepared to shift from immaterial downwards. These are the two major evolutionary stages of humanoid evolution which can be named nonspiritual and spiritual awareness. In the first stage of development the creative process is governed by the lower mind limitations of the material construct.

From what we have seen, this state is vulnerable to the Laws of Karma, Cause & Effect and Attraction until the lessons of karma are learned or awareness shifts into the higher energy of being as the Soul or Higher Self. In this case the Life plan will provide the means, the body will create a Cause, the clarity and intensity of which will attract a likeness result from the quantum field.

From what we have seen, after the age of material maturity of 28, spiritual evolution is launched and the proactive creation process can be executed from above as the energetic self to below, directly impacting, changing and creating that which is the holographic reality, and that which was created as the Life Plan. From above, within the field of quantum and infinite possibilities the mind has no limitations within the quantum soup of love.

From all that we have studied we see that the space of quantum possibilities is governed by the vibration of love and well being, and to be proactive within it thus preventing execution by default, you must be in that space in order to be in command. Any distraction from lower vibrations of the physical self dismantles any communications.

From all that we have studied we see that in order to change that which is our lower form and reality, we must first, accept, believe and surrender to a new way of thinking to eliminate the past, then live the new with high emotion to induce a change in environment or behaviour. This suggestibility to rewire the neurological programming or to attract new reality is dependent upon the strength of emotion and belief which is the variable that controls whether it becomes reality. As each individual differs in this degree, it is the persistence and practice of the reinstitution of the new reality that will control the time and degree of success.

From all that we have studied we see that much of the terminology that has been constructed as techniques and procedures have a biological, chemical, consciousness counterpart. For example the **altered state** of meditation is required to eliminate the interference of the brain's activity. **Letting go** requires that the usual world of physical activities are bypassed to get to the subconscious. We have seen hypnosis is a fundamental way to achieve this space. However, we have seen that this state is simply a state of mind within a timeless, spaceless domain and the way to achieve this is not as important as being in that space outside of the beta brain of ego. It is therefore best facilitated initially by a facilitator who can lead one into the state.

From what we have studied, we see the importance of words, chants and mantras that are able to change reality through the midbrain. We have seen that these are a direct way to institute changes outside the norm and are a known wisdom of ancient traditions. These are key to attaining miracles of health, wealth both internally and externally.

From all that we have studied we see that there are many intangible parameters that affect the success of creating new reality and miracles. The amount and type of karma being held by the Soul is a possible deterrent. The depth of the belief, the degree of persistence, the clarity of vision and the strength of the energy behind the thoughts, visions and words all have a direct effect on the time and type of outcome.

So what is the process that you use to change your health or wealth reality?

It is all a construct and you are all different so there is no "right process". At the bottom line is belief and intent. The process you use, whatever it is, must be accepted and believed by you. We have presented many different procedures from those that are doing it. If there is anything we have shown you; it is that it is real, possible, and that <u>you can do it</u>. You are the captain of your ship called consciousness. There is a caveat, however.

We do suggest that to really get into the void it is best to have a facilitator to lead you away from the analytical mind, the correctness of the procedure and away from the limitations that are within your subconscious programming. If you should insist on attempting this yourself, practice the first part of getting to the void and just feel and listen, but, take the appropriate steps out of what is presented and record these to lead yourself through the process. Once you have the feeling and the knowing you are in that space, you can easily embark on your own. Remember the brain mind is designed to ask questions and analyse to know, the heart mind already knows and there are no questions.

If anything, our books must have brought into your awareness the thousands of cases that prove miracles of health and wealth are real.

If you have dis-ease or disease whether minor or fatal, it can be fixed

If you have karmic baggage that interferes, it can be fixed

If you have issues with wealth and happiness, it can be fixed

If you have a life contract and life plan that sucks, it can be fixed

Why?

It is because you created the Life Movie and selected your individual characteristic to engage your mental and emotional being through a virtual hologram which includes a human body. And because you created it and directed it from a point of higher vibrational energy, you can reprogram and direct the way it is played out.

And who is to blame for your life if it is filled with negativity and poor health, relationships and wealth? It is your soul carrying karma and your brain and your ego that chose the limits from the group consciousness. So the lesson; forgive them and move on to take control through a freed soul-heart mind.

We have learned that the entry to this world of infinite possibilities is the quantum field of consciousness which is indeed our minds and imagination as we described in the first chapter. But if you failed to graduate into the higher spiritual phases of your evolution and are stuck in stage 3, it becomes more and more difficult to get access to the programs the brain learned and stuck in your subconscious. Quite plainly you will have simply accepted, believed and surrendered to the limitation of the global consciousness. It then becomes more and more difficult to get out of this belief box. But not to despair. It only means repetition and perseverance of simple mind conditioning. Here you must simply resort to a new way of thinking and persevering by action to support that new way until it becomes a new habit. We suggest that if you had graduated into your true spiritual path, then all this would already have been known and you would indeed already be the captain of your reality. The way out is to go back to school and learn about being one with this quantum field of possibilities in the imagination and retrain the brain as we are suggesting here, and as evidenced by the thousands of cases belonging to the many authors and practitioners that have contributed to the conclusions we have arrived at here.

The New Process Of Changing Reality

We will now present a composite of what we have learned in the material in this book. What has been brought to light is stated in the previous section on the Key Findings. Key to this is what we have learned about the Placebo which tells us over and over that it is the **energetic version of You** that is the Divine Programmer and as so, directly responsible for using and deploying the process of Divine Intervention. As to Divine Intervention itself, there is nothing that indicates that there is not some supreme intelligence, higher consciousness of divine order, purpose and process at work here. As to what it is exactly, we just say **it simply is** and as the Divine Programmer, each Soul has access to that power as a Creator.

If we would choose a favorite method from all of the gurus and healers we have presented, we would tell you that all systems we have presented work. Some may have the greatest inventory of dramatic and profound cases. That would be the work of Dr. Joe Dispenza and Dr. and Master Sha who report hundreds of thousands of successes. Each individual has a different level of belief, karma and vibration. The choice of method is a personal preference which each alone will vibrate with. We have also come to the conclusion that self-hypnosis would be the chosen method of engaging in the altered state. As a supplement to this we see that the process of self-hypnosis is the most effective way to begin if you insist on doing it yourself. But if you do, we recommend that you design your own steps and record them to eliminate brain mind interference.

In the next section we are going to present a modified process which can be used for either health or wealth shifts in creating reality. It can be used to talk to your Spirit Guides if these are what you believe in, and you can choose to look at **regression** into the past to solve issues or **progression** into the future to accelerate development. It can be used to change your old beliefs and perceptions to create new states of being; for the purpose of **health** and **wealth** changes in reality. Or it can be used as in **astral projection** to develop your true higher potential and to better understand yourself. In the process suggested, the initial steps are essentially the same.

STEP 1: SETTING THE OBJECTIVES

The very first part of this is to determine several things about your desires and goals. In these procedures we are looking to the higher order as deployed by **You** as the **Divine Programmer** to update life plans and create a better life through proactive management of our energy fields and energies we create as thoughts, visions, words and feelings. We are looking to get out of the old ways limiting our way of thinking and create a better life by proactive use of Karma, Law of Cause & Effect, and the Law of Attraction; off of autopilot or default.

It is best to write these down in a concise clear form. When we refer to life, these are about external realities, when we speak of body, these are about internal realities. In any case there will be something about your past, present or future that you desire to change. Remember that there are four key elements of this that reflect every situation; namely the thoughts, visions, words and emotions. So in every case that forms a new desire, write out:

1. What is it that you wish to change about life, belief, perception?
2. What would that change about life, belief, perception be?
3. What would the change look like as a vision?
4. What would that change feel like in terms of emotion?
5. What would I say about a mantra or phrase to chant over and over?

This could reflect a physical disease or dysfunction, a difficult issue, a desire for a better life, an answer to a question, a need for expanding potential, a life review, a better future, wealth and health improvements, and so on. As an example:

1. I wish to change my belief that I am poor and unworthy
2. I have unlimited financial abundance
3. I am holding a check for 5 million dollars
4. My body is exploding with bliss, joy and gratitude
5. I have unlimited financial abundance

OR

1. I wish to change by physical dysfunction in my legs and knees
2. I see my leg and knees completely healed
3. I am running down the road like I was 20 years old
4. I am laughing and with great joy and gratitude
5. My body, soul and mind are totally healed

This reflects several things about instituting a new possibility into a new state of being. It defines it clearly so as to replace the old state of being, then creates and registers the new state by way of a strong definable signature of emotion attached to the vision, enforced repeatedly by a mantra. In this way a signal of intent is being sent to begin the process of firing and rewiring a new set of programs that are tagged by the emotion emanating from the body. It is the intention to **think differently** about what has become an issue, **accept** a new definable outcome, **believe** the resulting vision is done when emotionally charged into awareness as an observer, and **surrender** to its collapse into your reality. Of importance however is clarity and emotional charge.

We must add a caveat here. Your purpose may be to simply open to super consciousness then reside there as we have seen with the work of ***JC Gordon*** in a previous chapter. There is no specific problem or issue to address; you simply want to feel the essence of it in your total being and infuse your Lower Self completely and fully to allow it to make changes and release DNA. In this case, you would still use the steps to get to the Void of Infinite possibilities and learn to think, feel, sense, and listen with higher abilities.

STEP 2: SETTING THE ENVIRONMENT COMFORT, PEACE & SILENCE

The environment from which you will work has to be one of peace, silence and comfort. There is no escape from this because you cannot have anything of mind or body bugging you. The process can be meditative or whatever you wish to label it but you must be comfortable sitting still and relaxed. If it is soft music, or simple silence that works best, it is the same space, chair, position, and environment that is required to launch your new state of being.

STEP 3: ENTERING THE ALTERED HEART STATE (10-15 minutes)

The process by which you enter the environment is away from the Beta environment of the brain and into the silence of its influence of the conscious mind of ego and protection. The best state is to reach Theta like when you were a young child and let go of any tendency for the brain and intellect to interfere. This process is usually done shifting your attention and awareness by **"becoming present"** to your body, parts, or functions. For example you would first place your attention on breathing in and out slowly and quietly. Next you would start at your toes, sense and feel them in the space they occupy. Move to your knees, stomach, chest, arms, fingers, forehead, body, each time sensing them and feeling them in the larger and larger space they occupy. You are slowly detaching from the material world of body and brain. A suggested time is at least 10 minutes as the brain ceases to fire and think in the intellectual space of Beta and higher Alpha.

When ready, you will shift your attention to the heart; first the physical heart, then the energetic heart field to feel the field of love, peace, silence that it emanates. As you focus onto this place of heart mind, you may institute a self-hypnosis process that takes you deep into this state. This is done by you saying: **"I will now go deeper and deeper into my subconscious state of pure consciousness as I raise my hand to my chest and breathe from 5 to 1."** Then count and breathe 5: going deeper, 4: going deeper, 3: very deep, 2: Very deep almost sleepy, 1: into pure consciousness and linger there for several minutes. When you feel the heart field of total peace, love and silence you are ready to let go of your physical reality completely.

STEP 4: SEPARATION FROM THE PHYSICAL HOLOGRAM (5-10min.)

We will say that this process of detachment may not be necessary if you can attain being in the heart mind of the void or the midbrain mind of the Soul. The quantum void is everywhere and it is not a place so much as a state of being. The following steps 4 and 5 can be bypassed by simply attaining being in that void.

Upon deactivating the intellect and letting go and entering the deeper state of Theta within the heart mind, you will begin to feel the space of pure consciousness of peace and silence. It is here that you would detach your energetic self as You being pure consciousness of the heart mind from your physical body. The process of astral projection, NDE, OBE is the same. You may wish to visualize a beam of light through you from above and linger until you feel that beam of pure love infusing your being. When you have settled into the heart mind and feel the beam you will state: **"As I count from 1 to 5, I as my heart mind of pure consciousness will rise higher and higher along the beam of light separating from my physical body."**

If it is difficult for you to visualize, your heart mind will feel or simply sense it is so from the very first thoughts, perceptions or feelings that pop into your mind. Then when ready, begin your count and feel the rise and see or sense yourself rising higher as pure consciousness separating from the physical body. **"As I drop my hand onto my lap I will begin my rise and separation. 1: I begin my rise, 2: I rise on the beam, 3: I am rising higher, 4: I am above the body, 5: I see my body below."**

This is the beginning of your OBE and Astral Projection. If you wish to identify yourself as Higher Self, Soul, or Energy Body, it is up to you but regardless, see or sense yourself free of the physical body and the material world. Linger in this space becoming more and more comfortable. Look at yourself below from all angles, move through walls, look into other rooms and feel the space of pure heart mind.

STEP 5: ENTERING THE VOID OF POSSIBILITIES (10-15 minutes)
As you enter this state you will feel and sense the void of oneness of love, of peace, of harmony. You will then state: **"I will now proceed along a tunnel by counting from 5 to 1 to the light at the other end and emerge into the void of infinite possibilities."** Know that you will proceed through a tunnel as in NDE, and meet the Creator, God, Spirit Guides or Angels or whomever suits your belief system for assistance. In the OBE or Astral projection you are simply an energetic body of pure consciousness where you have no identity, there is no thing, no time, no where, only the space of the quantum field of infinite possibilities. Here you will totally let go of the lower reality, from the body, time and place and become a thought in the void of infinity. You will be in this space where you will continue to be present and aware of possibilities that you can create. **State: "5: I begin floating. 4: I am moving along the tunnel, 3: I see a light at the end, 2: I float through an open door, 1: I am in the void of infinite possibilities."**

Any time you are drawn away simply become aware that you are an observer. Stay present in this void and if you become aware of yourself as Being of Light, a Higher Form and meet Guides and angels, that is ok. You will linger in this space, sensing and feeling the presence and peace and love emanating from the beings that have joined you.

In this space you have many choices to deal with the written objectives you created above. Depending on whether it is Past Life Regression, Future Life Progression, Astral Projection to heal or expand your potential, get answers, see your life plan, do a life review, you may want to review the processes in the previous chapters. But it is at this point that you will begin your Divine Programming process. In the example below we will follow the Placebo method of changing the old mind into the new.

STEP 6: CHANGING THE OLD TO THE NEW (10-15 minutes)

As you enter the quantum field of infinite possibilities, you are effectively your Higher Self/Soul form as pure thought and energy within the greater consciousness. Your Spirit Guide or any entity you prefer is in this space (if you believe in it) here to assist. From this point on you as the Divine Programmer may ask for assistance to complete one of the following options:

a. Progress to a future Life Plan to understand or change it
b. Removal of all karma
c. Astral travel to open potential and understand self
d. Create a new physical reality of health and wealth
e. Regress to a past life to address an issue
f. Regress to an in-between life period to understand your plan
g. Remain in this place to feel the Superconsciousness infuse your being

In this step, we are going to take you into changing the reality below through the process of downward causation. You are now the heart mind of the Divine Programmer and once you simply know you are in this void of infinite possibilities where no limits are imposed, you are free to change beliefs, perceptions, behavior, reality and your life "above" to make the appropriate adjustment or changes "below". Remember they are only holographic programs that are a product of the lower brain.

Also, be mindful of the feeling of the vastness of the heart mind and Soul mind and those you have called forward to assist you. You will learn to feel the presence of others and images or situations of thoughts that come forward. In the process below, you will recall in your heart mind the four objectives that you began with. The first step is to bring forward into awareness that which you wish to change.

1. In the place of Oneness with all, within the space of the void and quantum field of infinite possibilities, bring forward the first belief or perception, situation, or reality that you wish to change.
2. Make a conscious decision that this is not what you wish to continue believing and create feeling with an amplitude of energy related to that decision greater than the hardwired programs in your brain and addictions in your body.
3. Know your body will then respond to a new mind, to a new consciousness. Allow the choice to become an experience that you will never forget.
4. Let the experience produce feelings of emotions that carry huge energy that rewrites the programs of reality and changes your biology.
5. Now surrender the past back to possibility and allow the infinite field of possibilities to resolve it in a way that is right for you.

This is where you will linger in the feelings that are a knowing that these changes are your truth, with faith and trust it is so. Linger in this feeling for at least 5 minutes. The next part is to induce the new belief which should take another 5 minutes of lingering in the emotion.

1. Now bring in the new belief and perception that you wish to replace the old with. Here you will draw this from the quantum consciousness of your mind to observe this into your awareness as a new experience that produces emotions with huge energy that rewrites the programs and changes your reality or biology.
2. Allow the choice to become an experience that you will never forget.
3. Bring the vision of this change forward and feel how you would live in that choice.
4. Allow your body to respond to your new mind and change your energy by combining a clear intention with elevated emotion so that matter is lifted to a new mind. Let your body be altered by your consciousness, by your own energy.
5. Shift into a new state of being and make this moment define you replacing the past memory with a new memory in your brain and body.
6. Become empowered, become inspired. Make the choice a decision that you will never fail to remember.
7. Give your body a taste of the future by showing it how it will feel to believe this way. Let your body respond to a new mind.
8. Linger in this new mind and experience this by feeling how would you live from this state of being? What choices will you make; How will you behave; What experiences are in your future; How will you live; How would you feel; How will you love.
9. Allow infinite waves of possibility to collapse into an experience into your life.
10. Know you are teaching your body emotionally what it is to be in this new future. As you open your heart and believe in possibility. Be lifted, fall in love with the moment and experience that future now.
11. Begin to repeat your mantra for a few minutes over and over.

STEP 7: INFUSING THE NEW POSSIBILITY INTO REALITY (5min.)

The next step is one of infusion from above to below. In the preceding Step, you have been dealing with the Causal, Mental and Emotional Bodies as they are a quantum part of the heart mind. Now in the process of downward causation, you will infuse the new possibility, as the desire belief, perception or change in reality.

1. And now surrender your creation to a greater mind. For what you think and experience in this realm of possibility, if it is truly felt will manifest in some future time.
2. From waves of possibility to particles in reality, from immaterial to material, from thought energy into matter you know you have the power to manifest in the physical reality.
3. Now surrender your new belief into a field of consciousness that already knows how to organize the outcome in a way that is perfect for you planting this seed in possibility.

4. Bless this future with your own energy as it means you are connected to a new destiny knowing that for wherever you place your attention is where you place your energy.
5. Know you are investing in your future instead of your past.
6. Open your heart and allow your body to become moved by your own inward experience.
7. Remember that what you truly experience in the unknown and emotionally embrace will ultimately slow down in frequency as energy into three dimensions as matter.
8. And now let go and give it up and allow it to be executed by a greater intelligence in a way that is right for you.
9. Linger in this space for several minutes feeling the experience of its completion. Live it as you see it in the world below.
10. Infuse the golden light of source into your midbrain and 3rd eye as you breathe in. See the golden light fill your whole body and state your mantra out loud. Repeat inhale-exhale process with your mantra for 5 – 10 minutes.

STEP 8: THE RETURN (5 minutes)

Upon the completion of engaging your Higher Self as the heart mind in the changing of beliefs, perceptions or reality, you are now ready to move back into the lower reality. If you have not used the steps 4 and 5, simply use step 9.

1. See yourself stepping back into the tunnel and moving back through it towards your physical form and place.
2. Feel the movement into the physical form totally infused with the higher light.
3. Give thanks for a new life before its made manifest so that your body as the unconscious mind begins to experience that which you have created or brought with you now.
4. Understand clearly that the emotional signature of gratitude means the event has already happened as gratitude is the ultimate state of receivership and just memorize this feeling.
5. State: ***On a count of 5 to 1, I will reengage with my physical body***
6. Bring your awareness back to a new body, to a new environment and to a whole new time.

STEP 9: ENFOLDING THE NEW REALITY WITH GRATITUDE

Now in your lower reality, the process becomes one of completing the lower infusion from above to below. This should allow the feelings to come forward in completion and can take 5 minutes.

1. Feel the gratitude of what you have just done.

2. Allow your mind and heart to feel the joy of the completion.
3. Allow your body to know that it is lifted to a new mind.
4. Feel the joy of your life that it be an extension of your mind.
5. Know and feel your future will never be your past and you return to heart wisdom.
6. Keep your mantra rolling over in your mind.
7. Thank your Soul that it awakes you from this dream.
8. Thank the Divine/Source in you as it moves through you and all around you, and that it shows you your true cause in your life.
9. When you are ready you can open your eyes.

STEP 10: REPETITION

The steps 2 to 8 should be done every day for at least 45 minutes. This is particularly relevant when the belief boxes are strong and there is a need for repeated engagement to force the subconscious and the brains to respond. As you get better and better, you can flip into the void faster and faster where word, images and emotion centered on the midbrain become a means of simple repetitive programming into the subconscious.

In the example above, we have presented a process that can be simplified and recorded, allowing music and space to linger. Always remember that the longer you linger and feel the space, the deeper and more effective is the mental and emotional process. We only present this as a guideline that can be molded to suit your own needs. Should you wish to engage in some of the other processes such as opening to greater potential, past life reviews, future life progression, or past life regression, you can take from the relevant chapter to determine the steps or find a facilitator. Once you enter the Void in Step 5, you can take a diversion.

What we have clearly attempted to establish however, is that our reality is malleable from a higher place. We have established that there are no limits to this malleability as it can and does make radical changes in physical reality.

<u>We strongly suggest that the basic guidelines be used to create your own preferred process and record your own voice leading you through the steps</u>. Alternately, we strongly suggest that at first, you get attuned to the process and be led by a Facilitator who gives you a better chance to let go of the meddlesome 3D world. It is **very important** to linger in these steps once the intent has been launched and to feel and sense the processes every time a statement is made. Any place of lingering can be filled with soft music. The awareness, intent, feeling and emotion are vital, as are the images and emotion of completions.

Finally, you need to be persistent and consistent in attaining the goals. The degree of success is contingent upon your degree of suggestibility and the way you accept, believe and surrender to the new information. The clarity and consistency of goals is vital. You learn to place new programs into the subconscious by repetition; this is no different.

Testing Your Mind Power

Before we leave this topic, we wish to reinforce that we do already create our reality. As long as you reside within that group reality, you can only create within the rules of that reality that you have accepted as your beliefs. Yet there are many workings of energy that are creating effects in subtle ways. And you are certainly free to move your own personal beliefs outside of the group consciousness at any time. Within the belief boxes energies work diligently under the laws of Cause & Effect and Attraction but we seldom make the correlation of the Cause to the Effect. It is because we produce so many thoughts and emotions each day that their clarity, consistency and their repetition is a huge variable. These go into the quantum field as a pattern of frequency and will attempt to attract a match because in this field all is one field of shared information. The exactness of the match and its emotional signature will then determine how and when the Effect will collapse into your reality. It can be a moment, a day, a year, a lifetime, or several. The Law of Cause and Effect determines a Cause that the Law of Attraction attempts to satisfy. This process is at work continuously without regards to any judgment as to whether it is good, bad or ugly as it is just waves of energies and possibilities.

As you know now, a thought or act or emotion that is repeated begins to form a belief which then forms a pattern of physical and mental behavior, even a physical process or change in physicality itself. As we over time develop these, they become the effect in the body registered against signature of emotion by the brain and the subconscious. Continued indulgence of thought and emotion strengthens this behavior in the physical vessel and its lower mind until it becomes the body and this addiction of the body begins to control the mind rather than the mind controlling the body. The exception to this we have seen in health and wealth miracles.

The process is a self auto-conditioning cycle of old habits and beliefs that become more and more difficult to break because these get hardwired and entrenched stronger and stronger. The correlation between the Cause and the effect, and then when a match of energy signature occurs becomes further and further removed from reality as a possibility and it becomes necessary to instigate a new mind from a higher energy perspective as we have elaborated on in this book.

Hence, if you are constantly thinking about issues and surround these with feelings of fear and images of the consequences as your future possibility, then they are most likely to manifest in some way for you continue to draw that possibility into your current NOW of awareness and then reality.

Similarly if you are constantly thinking about good stuff and surrounding these with strong feelings of love and gratitude then these are also likely to manifest in some way.

But if these are poorly defined, vague, fragmented with mixed emotions, then what would you suppose becomes the matching energy signature that will be drawn to you at some time? Who knows? It is the stronger ones that will win out.

That is simply the way you were designed if you did not take the evolution process of 5 steps into a more spiritually based system of belief seriously. You may have a path or preferred to just go to default on your Life Plan and over-ridden programmed behavior of neuro circuitry which was ready to evolve and expand at around the age of 28. This does not mean you have lost it. It only means you have to work at it as it is never lost. Every Life Plan will have this spiritual path option as a choice. It will contain a higher path and a lower path and many in-between. It was at that point that you may have had one of the choices of your life plan go to proactive creation rather than reactive.

You know, especially from our study of Napoleon Hill that in this lower realm of 3D, it is the thought, the words, the vision and the passion that create the charged vision of business success. This is the accepted way the norm believes it to be. It is that persistent reinforcement of that charged emotional vision that draws to it that which it is. That is the way the consensus consciousness says it is done. It is all energy being collapsed into our field of reality from the quantum field of possibilities because it already exists there, otherwise where else did it come from?

We are telling you this because you may want to reinstitute something about this process of Attraction and Cause & Effect that brings you back to a new reality of belief in energy and how you create. Our guess is that if you really believed that your thoughts, visions, words and emotions were out there hunting for their buddies to bring to you, you may consider more carefully what you think, say and feel; then manage them more carefully.

Because you have not considered the connecting, or just relegated the idea to the hogwash category, the way we suggest you analyze this is to conduct your own field study on this using some simple energies. The idea is that you are going to make a very simple clear instruction that will go into the quantum field. You will create a cause and look for the effect that will be attracted from the quantum field of infinite possibility. The big thing here is that you will set time constraints and carefully document the cause and effect.

Now, you can do this at a specific time, meditate, whatever. It does not matter because you are already doing it albeit perhaps fragmented. What you want to do for this experiment is however, take the time to create clear consistent instructions with time limits that you are sending into the quantum field of infinite possibilities. To maximize the result and to minimize the time it is suggested that you do sit in a peaceful silent space and think clearly several times on your instructions. Not usually very cohesive for good instructions is the incoherent field of stress and the clearer the better. The simpler the better, the more emotion attached the better. For these experiments don't try to make them complex and look for huge desires like 10 million bucks! It may be possible but reserve that for later when your beliefs have shifted as a result of simple realization of the power you have.

First, there are a few things you can do that give you an awareness of energy and intent that you already project.

Mind energy as directed from a higher place of truth
Take a needle and add 10 inches of thread. Sit quietly holding the thread end between your first three fingers. Place your other hand palm up under the needle. When it is still, ask it to "show me yes" concentrate and allow it to swing back and forth. Then let it settle. Then ask it to "show me no" and allow it swing, then let it settle. Then ask it "Do I believe in miracles?"

You are a field of energy
Take some wire like some coat hangers about 10 inches long and create two 90 degree bends to hold them in your hands. Hold them in your hands like a pair of guns in front of you. First, think about a really good experience. They should rotate out as an expansion of your heart field. Then think about a really bad experience. They should rotate inward as heart contracts. Then with someone in the area, say "Show me ...." And watch them point to that energy field.

Here are some experiments that take you into Law of Attraction. The suggested experiments are simple and they should be given a specific time to manifest, like 3 to 5 days. You should "suggest" these to yourself sitting in a quiet peaceful place in the morning and while lying in bed before sleep to be consistent. When you begin, take a few deep breaths and place your attention on your heart beating. Once they are launched you want to note the results. For each day of your experiment, you should repeat the process several times. Try to keep these simple and clear. You can select whichever interests you from below.

There is an invisible energy force of infinite possibilities
Ask the field to present you with a clear indication that it exists. It can be anything from a gift, a blessing.

You impact the field and draw from it what you expect to see
Picture something like a car type, a color or object that you want to see through your daily activities.

Whatever you focus on expands
Focus attention and intention on a simple outcome that you visualize and verbalize it.

Your connection to the field provides accurate unlimited guidance
Ask for guidance on a specific question or issue you need to get answers on.

The universe is limitless, abundant and accommodating
Make a conscious effort to look for goodness, beauty and abundance.

The more fun I have, the better life works
Do great things for 3 days and see how many great things come into being.

Beliefs and expectations draw from field of potentiality
Draw up a list of what you would like to see.

Nothing is absolute, only my thinking makes it so
Investigate what you believe about yourself and see if the opposite is true.

Blessing in disguise
Look carefully each day at some situations that come before you that are perceived as bad. Extract the good part of it and document these.

The more I love, the more in alignment with the quantum field
Spend the days sending love bombs to everything and everyone.

Money is nothing but energy and a reflection of my beliefs
- if I give money away, I will receive even more
- money is easy to come by

Mystical information is available if I pay attention
Ban media from awareness and seek outside natural things.

Here are some experiments that you can do to see how you can influence matter.

Words have energy
Issue only thoughtful loving words to plants or people and monitor the results.

Thoughts have power
Create a glass of water that you infuse with healing energy from the heart to accomplish a physical placebo change in something not right in you. Drink it each morning and night and document changes.

Your thoughts and consciousness impact matter
Set up two containers of the same cooked food that goes bad quickly in two separate areas. For the days of the experiment, go over to each and tell one you hate it, the other you love it. After 3-5 days inspect the quality of the containers.

Your thoughts and consciousness your physical body
State you will lose 1 pound in 48 hours by projecting positive loving thoughts into your food before eating it.

You are connected to everything and everyone else in the universe
Send a telepathic message 3 times a day to someone and get evidence of its receipt.

Finally, we are now giving you Dr. Pillai's popular mantra for wealth again. It includes a powerful word and vibration that opens the midbrain to the Goddess Lakshi who represents wealth. If you don't believe in goddesses, believe in the power of sounds and mantras... and money! It is best to see Dr. Pillai's website and download this mantra called Shreem Brzee at www.pillaiCenter.com so you can hear his voice.

Close your eyes for a minute of peace and silence.
Put your attention on the 3rd eye between your eyebrows and hold this for 30 seconds.
Chant out loud Brzeeeeee, 25 times (pronounced brazeeee).
Allow sound to go deep into your 3rd eye and then into your entire brain and pervade the whole body.
Know you do not have the burden to check out what will work for you. Brzee will be like a watchdog to keep wrong thoughts and projects away from you. It will spontaneously spring the right thoughts in you and the right projects will show up. You have no responsibility. You have given total control to Brzee
Chant out loud Brzeeeeee 50 times.
Allow the sound to permeate the mind and the complete body and soul.
Now mentally keep repeating in the 3rd eye. You have given all your financial plans and future to her. Let her take over you and control you.
Chant out loud Brzeeeee 33 times.

Come back out slowly and continue to chant this quietly in your mind. Chant out loud Ommmmmmm shanti shanti shanti, shanti shanti shant hi. Slowly open to your awakened state, slowly you can come back.

Try this everyday for a week and see what the results are!

18

SO WHAT IS GOD, REALLY

"How can you describe what words fail to explain or the lower mind fails to perceive? They were simply not designed that way."

Aly McDonald   Ed Rychkun

> **Thinking about what God really is
> Can't be done as God simply is**

The most common dispute comes with the notion of the Soul. What, pray tell, is that? It is ineffable, personal and surrounded with faith and trust in that perception. So you really can't argue with anyone about it. But we have come to understand that we may indeed be a Soul on a mission as a Divine spark of God and it seems that once you get your head wrapped around the notion that you as a divine being, have the power of creation to be that Divine Intervention. You as a part of this wonderful great ineffable thing labeled God, once truly believed, simply places little relevance on definitions. It does not matter; and what matters is that you can indeed create and change reality.

Let me (Aly) tell you how I understand Spirit. I am referencing how I view the Spirit within each of us. Many call it a Soul; I do feel it is a part of the collective of one's Soul. Sometimes described as the soul, over-soul or higher-self, I view it as an expression or experience of this reality. I see this because we have a higher self and that higher self or soul can experience many things simultaneously. For example parallel lives or multi-dimensional, multi-verse experiences coming from the same soul as an expression.

For Example; Our Soul is created from a spark of light or energy force from Source/Creator/Creatrix/God whom we were originally created from before our earth experience or incarnation. Once the created Soul has decided to have an experience on this plane, a life plan is created and then that Soul gives a spark of life force energy to the mother within the womb and it then becomes the Spirit of the child and an expression of the Soul. In the transition or when death occurs as some call it, the Spirit leaves the body and returns to the Soul or Higher Self with all the knowledge and experiences of that lifetime.

The word ineffable means something cannot be expressed in words. Merriam – Webster says it means **something is too great, powerful, beautiful, etc., to be described or expressed**. The word Divine has meanings that suggest of or **relating to a god, especially the Supreme Being, from God or a god, godlike, characteristic of or befitting a deity, divine magnanimity, heavenly, celestial like the divine kingdom, extremely good, unusually lovely.**

That's a whole lot of things about divine that looks like a struggle to define it. It is clearly quite a personal definition and one thing is for sure; whoever God is, She/he seems to be a good Energy who loves people but it seems that within the Divine kingdom, there is trouble getting this point across. Trouble is this Divine Entity has never ever come down to publish anything directly. It is left to those mortals in this kingdom to expound on their own ideas of who and what God is. That is truly your free will to decide this. So really God and Divine are quite ineffable concepts and perceptions because there are so many diverse interpretations of these two words.

It would be foolish in our conclusions to suggest that there was not something greater than we can understand about how our reality was created, how it works and how it all abides by laws much greater than we can comprehend. Similarly it would be foolish to say such a power like a Higher Intelligence or a Superconsciouness does not exist. You do not have to be the brightest crayon in the pack to agree something created all this that is much more magnificent than one can imagine.

But what we have seen in our studies is that even when we are in our Higher Place, in a Near Death Experience, we still come back and say it is ineffable. We see clearly however that something guides the reality, the universe, the holograms, the expression of life, all that is, and it is indeed guided to evolve in a divine way.

We have seen that our reality is a contrived illusion to evolve in a divine way which seems to be evolution where "anything goes" without judgment. We have seen that this illusion can be molded. We have seen that the key to this is to be in a higher command state and the vehicle of change is in the contrived construct of the brain. And ultimately we have found it is the subconscious and the brain that change the illusion. The power of this change resides in the notion of divine and the depth of belief; and as we have seen that may or may not have anything to do with God but it certainly has to do with the strength of believing in it. But because there is such a diversity of beliefs on this topic it cannot really be defined so we cannot conclude it is a mandatory part of the creating reality. But a strong belief in your Higher Self to change reality **IS** mandatory.

What comes forward in all of this is another conundrum; if this Life Plan and the Earth Game is a holographic illusion what is the point of the game that a Soul engages in? Why does one have to forget, relearn and punish themselves incarnation after incarnation? I asked this question of my colleagues who promptly went to Source to ask. The answer:

"The question as to what's the point of this life game may be answered by an overstanding of the word ineffable which is what is picked up in a NDE. The language we use does not give the ability to describe ineffable which is what is the point because the point cannot be understood clearly in a state of lower vibrations and never will be. It simply is."

But we see another aspect of this that reveals itself in the work of several like **JC Gordon** about **Super Consciousness** and the evolution of the Energetic Blueprint of Life which is birthing into a new process – one where the Life Plan and the tortures that come from engagement in it are no more. We see this new out of the box consciousness increasing exponentially day by day in the totally uncontrolled unorganized New Age consciousness.

Perhaps the Game is indeed coming to an end?

Is it time to get with the new program?

Choose your word carefully!

Your choice!

Enjoy your life...

Aly McDonald
Ed Rychkun

BOOKS BY Ed Rychkun
Found on www.amazon.com or www.edrychkun.com

In **The Divine Programmer: Creating Miracles** Authors and Healers Aly McDonald and Ed Rychkun will take you into the fringe of metascience and science to reveal what works in creating healing and reality miracles. The authors bring forward some of the top Healers to example the detailed processes used to define the common denominators when healing miracles do work inside the body. In an attempt to quantify these processes, the authors draw upon a binary-trinary computer analogy to define the Divine Programmer's steps to maximize success. In a revealing journey you will look into the emerging world of how subtle energy fields such as morphic, zeropoint, light body, heart, chakra, auras, and torroids work with quantum energies accessible through the heart-brain rather than the traditional ego-brain. Learn how beliefs stuck in subconscious, as well as curtailing the 3rd stage of human awareness can sabotage efforts, and how to change this. In further delving into creating reality miracles outside the body, the authors take you on a journey to analyze the Law of Attraction to see how and why it does work some of the time, also examining what prevents it from working. After summarizing the Programmer's Code from top Guru's techniques, in a new light of trinary versus binary computing, the authors introduce how 50 trillion cells work like computer chips in the ultimate Divine Human trinary computer. Here they develop the processes of how as a Divine Programmer, using the operating system of Divine Intelligence, the Compiler of the Heart, and the Program Language of Love, one can potentially command the brain to change the holographic reality; to attract and create internal and external miracles.

You Are Fired Said the Heart to the Ego In this unusual and profound book, Ed Rychkun takes you to a critical situation that occurs between a human's heartbeats. In a last ditch effort to make sure the next beat occurs, the Heart engages in a desperate conversation with the Ego whom it blames for the demise of the human. In a fascinating dialogue between the Heart, the Ego, the Brain, the Mind, the Soul, the Chakra Children, and God, Ed takes you to the split second where time ceases and the physical material world becomes one with the Spiritual and Subtle energy counterparts. Learn how the Ego has taken the command center away from the sleeping Mind making the Brain, Soul, Heart, and Chakra Children subservient players in directing the quality of human life. Learn how the crisis deadlock is broken and the decision is made whether the next heartbeat is allowed to occur. See if you can deduct the same conclusions and reject or accept a coherent harmony between the six characters that control the human's life. *Will you Fire the Ego and put the power back where it belongs?*

Serve gods or Be God: Your Choice Thousands of gods have wreaked havoc on humanity for many centuries. So has the one God himself as evidenced in the Bibles. Those who claim to be Divine interpreters of God's Word have succumbed to creating merchandise of humanity in the interest of subduing the true spirit. Never has God presented his Word directly. At the turn of the century humanity entered the 2012 End Times of Revelation, Resurrection, and Armageddon. Despite what religions tell you about God's prophecy, doom, the Second Coming, and your sins, in the minds of millions is an underlying consciousness that something is amiss with those they trust. It is because something epic is happening in this Universe.

Can You Let Go? Is about a paradigm shift in how you enter the world of miracles and Co-creation. It means letting go of thinking with your head and learning to think with your heart. Why do prayers, the Law of Attraction, miracle healing, manifesting and assertions only work sometimes, for some? It is because those that show consistent success understand what the secret of letting go is. The secret? You have to let go; go inside to the heart, shift beliefs, surrender to a higher power, have faith and trust in the Divine. But what does this really mean? What is it *exactly* that one must let go of? In their raw simplicity these are very powerful words and concepts but implementing these in your life with the appropriate conviction may not be so simple. Yet there are millions of unexplained miracles and anomalies of science around the planet done by people who know how to release such special talents. Ed Rychkun poses the question; *"If others can create miracles, why can't I?"* Let us find the answer to this by learning how miracle makers let go and why. And let us get some advice from the "other side" of the veil.

Miracle, Miracle I Wish To Find Where You Hide Within My Mind Whether mainstream medical and science experts want to admit it or not, millions of spectacular, unexplaned healing miracles occur. The dismissal of this reality on the basis of unexplainable does not benefit others who can have such a wondrous gift, or even be able to create a miracle. Quantum physics has proven that consciousness and the mind is the vital component to miracles but they simply do not know how. In addition quantum science has shattereed the foundations of what we know of atomic science. The truth is that the answers do not lie in science and if someone else can create a miracle, then so can you. So how do others do it? Let me take you to the leaders in miracles—the ones that caught my attention—the ones doing it daily. When you understand how the miracle healers really get down to the simple basics, a paradigm shift occurs in belief. Let me give you a short, simple course on what I found out so perhaps you can create your own miracles? Take your own quantum leap into the new reality of miracles.

Return To The Future Michael Carpetbagger has a serious problem with his life. After the banking and market collapse of 2008, he and his partners are feeling the stress of a failing business. They are moving to the dark side as of necessity. This does not sit well with Michael as his soul niggles at his actions. As Mike's conundrum of negative stress and helplessness overtakes him, he falls into a bizarre instant in time where a sequence of revelations is brought to him by his Guiding Angel. She takes him on a strange journey to previous lives where in the Golden Age of Atlantis he begins to recall what and who he really is. As they wander the quantum space of his past realities into Mayan lands, and he connects with his cosmic soul family, Mike begins to form a new vision of why the old financial energy is rapidly giving way to the new spiritual energies. Now, with a new look at his future, he must congeal all the past information into what he must do to best survive as the Earth and global ascension of consciousness accelerates towards 2012 and the End Time. WARNING: CAN YOU FACE UP TO WHO YOU ARE? This may appear as a work of fiction but it is an account of the past and future as seen through the past lives of a Seer of Atlantis.

The Way Back In this story, Christopher Andrew Fallenstar is a desperate trapped soul lost in a sea of mundane agony. He is on Earth living a dysfunctional life full of self pity, anger and unhappiness. His darkness eventually leads him to despair and a gateway into a world where reality and non-reality have converged. Lost and bewildered, he must find his way back. But back to what? Is it back to the Home from where he came or is it where he is living his mundane life? On his journey, he must traverse a series of Realms with pathways through his inner being to find his way. His quest to find his way back leads him to deal with parts of himself that he never knew about. He begins to uncover a new consciousness about who and what he might be. What he chooses and the paths he takes determine his final eternal destiny... and what the back really means. In this story, Ed Rychkun will take you on a journey through your inner self that may change the way you view Home. *It may even change your attitude about life!*

In New Earth: A Personal Journey Ed Rychkun answers some key questions such as *What is Heaven? What would a New Earth be like?* and *How does the 2012 ascension relate to a New Earth?* He tells his story to explain how every individual is on a seperate journey attempting to understand what will happen to Old Earth. In this personal journey, he takes you on his journey to the inner self and inner earth to reveal what the new earth can be. It's all about leaving your physical body like in a Near Death Experience where one can liberate the soul to see it's truth. *"I have come to a conclusion through my journey that where we head through ascension and what we percieve as our New Earth is entirely different from what intellect could imagine."* Take this excursion into the different realms of Agartha, the perfect and pure lands created by the ascended ones where no negative energies exist. Here the creation of all things is instant through pure thought within the Creator's Consiouness.

Managing Human Subtle Energy: Walking the Thought This mind bending book gets to the bottom line of how to launch a management program that will absolutely change your life. You will clearly understand what Human Subtle Energies are and how they have been designed with a purpose – to convert non-physical energy to physical reality within your consciousness so you can enjoy life. First, see what the world of new science says about the existence and power of Human Subtle Energy. After this mind-blowing summary, find out the Laws by which these energies generated by your body operate. The inevitable startling conclusion will pound into your mind – you have not been managing your subtle energies properly – living a life of negative energy, drumming to a default destiny. Ironically, your life has turned out exactly the way you wanted it from previous thoughts and emotions. The way to change this lies in creating a habit to break old habits – through proactive Subtle Energy Management. Do you believe you can awaken the Genie in you and even control events by managing your subtle energy? *Walk your thoughts for 60 days and find out for yourself.*

www.ingramcontent.com/pod-product-compliance
Lightning Source LLC
Chambersburg PA
CBHW050127170426
43197CB00011B/1745